Credibility

Theory and Applications

Academic Press Rapid Manuscript Reproduction

Proceedings of the
Berkeley Actuarial Research Conference
on Credibility
September 19-21, 1974
The University of California, Berkley

Credibility
Theory and Applications

Edited by

P. M. Kahn

ACADEMIC PRESS, INC. *New York San Francisco London 1975*
A Subsidiary of Harcourt Brace Jovanovich, Publishers

ACADEMIC PRESS, INC.
111 Fifth Avenue, New York, New York 10003

United Kingdom Edition published by
ACADEMIC PRESS, INC. (LONDON) LTD.
24/28 Oval Road, London NW1

Library of Congress Cataloging in Publication Data

Berkeley Actuarial Research Conference on Credibility, University of California, 1974.
Credibility.

Bibliography: p.

1. Insurance, Life–Mathematics–Congresses.
2. Insurance–Mathematics–Congresses. I. Kahn, P. M. II. Title.
HG8781.B44 1974 368.3'2'011 75-33406
ISBN 0-12-394650-6

PRINTED IN THE UNITED STATES OF AMERICA

This volume is dedicated
with respect and affection to

EDWARD A. LEW

who proposed and nurtured the annual
Actuarial Research Conferences
as Chairman of the
Society of Actuaries' Committee on Research

Contents

Contributors

Craig Ansley, The University of Michigan, Ann Arbor, Michigan

Clarence R. Atwood, California Department of Insurance, Los Angeles, California

Howard Bolnick, Continental Assurance Company, Chicago, Illinois 60685

Hans Bühlmann, Federal Institute of Technology, Switzerland

Russell M. Collins, J.C. Penney Company, Inc., New York, New York

William H. DuMouchel, University of Michigan, Ann Arbor, Michigan 48104

William J. Falk, Continental Assurance Company, Chicago, Illinois

Leonard R. Freifelder, University of Pennsylvania, Philadelphia, Pennsylvania

Hans-Ulrich Gerber, The University of Michigan, Ann Arbor, Michigan

David J. Grady, The Travelers Insurance Company, Hartford, Connecticut

Charles A. Hachemeister, Prudential Reinsurance Company, Newark, New Jersey

Charles C. Hewitt, Jr., Metropolitan Property and Liability Insurance Company, Providence, Rhode Island

James C. Hickman, The University of Wisconsin–Madison, Madison, Wisconsin

Paul Jackson, Wyatt Company, Washington, D.C. 20006

William S. Jewell, The University of California, Berkeley, California

Vernon Johns, Stanford University, Stanford, California

Donald A. Jones, The University of Michigan, Ann Arbor, Michigan

Paul Markham Kahn*, Beneficial Standard Life Insurance Company, Los Angeles, California

Dale Lamps, Independent Liberty Life Insurance Company, Grand Rapids, Michigan

Kenneth M. Levine, Insurance Company of North America, Philadelphia, Pennsylvania

*Present Address: American Express Life Insurance Company P.O. CS-3970 San Rafael, California 94902

Myron H. Margolin, Prudential Insurance Company of America, Wayne, New Jersey

Robert B. Miller, University of Wisconsin–Madison, Madison, Wisconsin 53706

John O. Montgomery, California Department of Insurance, Los Angeles, California

Richard Olshen, Stanford University, Stanford, California

Al J. Quirin, The Hartford Insurance Group, Hartford, Connecticut

Richard S. Robertson, Lincoln National Life Insurance Company, Fort Wayne, Indiana

David Skurnick, California Inspection Bureau, San Francisco, California

Erwin Straub, Swiss Reinsurance Company, Zurich, Switzerland

G.C. Taylor, Macquarie University, New South Wales, Australia

Oakley (Lee) Van Slyke, Booz, Allen - Consulting Actuaries, Newport Beach, California

John C. Wooddy, North American Reassurance Company, New York, New York

Preface

This volume consists of a collection of papers and the discussion of these papers presented at the Actuarial Research Conference on Credibility held at The University of California, Berkeley, September 19-21, 1974. The Conference was jointly sponsored by the Committee on Research of the Society of Actuaries, the Casualty Actuarial Society, the ASTIN section of the International Actuarial Association, and the Department of Industrial Engineering and Operations Research and the Graduate School of Business Administration, both of The University of California, Berkeley. The Cochairmen of the Conference were Charles A. Hachemeister, William S. Jewell, and Paul M. Kahn.

The principle objective of the conference was to exchange ideas on the foundations of credibility and its applications to experience rating in life and casualty insurance. The conference also considered the application of credibility theory to group life insurance, reinsurance, and such casualty problems as the determination of reserves for claims incurred but not reported (IBNR).

For a brief introduction to the theory of credibility, the reader is referred to the paper, *Introduction and Historical Overview of Credibility*, by James C. Hickman.

The bibliographies originally contained in each paper have been assembled into a single bibliography to be found at the end of the volume.

We wish particularly to express our gratitude to The University of California, Berkeley, for the generous hospitality in allowing the use of their very fine facilities at Evans Hall, and in particular to Dean Robert H. Goshay, Professor William S. Jewell and his excellent staff for their superb handling of the arrangements. We wish to thank Dr. George J. Maslach, Provost of the Professional Schools of The University of California, Berkeley, for his gracious welcome. The editor wishes particularly to record his thanks to Mrs. Laurie Beerman, who typed the entire manuscript for publication.

The Conference Committee express their appreciation to the *Scandinavian Actuarial Journal* for permission to reprint Professor Bühlmann's paper, to the Society of Actuaries for permission to reprint the paper by Professor Jones and Professor Gerber, and to the American Statistical Association for permission to reprint the paper by Professor Miller and Professor Hickman.

Credibility

Theory and Applications

Minimax Credibility

Hans Bühlmann
Federal Institute of Technology, Zurich

I am reporting on some ideas originating in discussions which I had with one of my doctoral students, Alfio Marazzi. The paper presented today describes the set-up of the problem and its analytic treatment. The forthcoming thesis of Marazzi is mainly devoted to the numerical methods derived from the problem.

1. The Problem

For a more detailed discussion of the problem see Bühlmann and Straub (1970). Consider the following rectangular array of random variables

$$\begin{matrix} X_{11} & X_{12} & \cdots & X_{1N} \\ X_{21} & X_{22} & \cdots & X_{2N} \\ \vdots & & & \\ X_{n1} & X_{n2} & \cdots & X_{nN} \end{matrix}$$

with the following interpretation

- X_{ij} stands for the risk performance of risk j in the year i
- The array represents the risk performances of N risks during n years
- Columns represent random variables belonging to the same risk
- Rows represent random variables belonging to the same year
- The distribution function belonging to the random variable

X_{ij} is not determinate but depends on an unknown parameter θ_{ij} and we use the abbreviation $F_{X_{ij}}(x/\theta_{ij} = \theta) = F_\theta(x)$ as well as

$$\mu(\theta) = \int x dF_\theta(x) \qquad \sigma^2(\theta) = \int x^2 dF_\theta(x) - \mu^2(\theta)$$

We make the following <u>hypotheses</u>:

1) Homogeneity in time: $\theta_{ij} = \theta_j$ independent of i (all random variables in the same column have the same distribution)
2) The parameters θ_j themselves are random variables independent and with common distribution function $U(\theta)$. So far we assume $U(\theta)$ to be known.
3) Independence of risks: The columns are independent
4) Conditional independence in time: Given the value θ of the parameter θ_j the random variables within column j are independent.

The <u>problem</u> is to estimate the expected risk performance $\mu(\theta_k)$ for the risk k by a linear estimator

$$\gamma \frac{\sum_{i=1}^{n} X_{ik}}{n} + \delta.$$

The <u>solution</u> to the problem (see e.g. Bühlmann, 1967) is

$$\gamma = \frac{n}{n + \beta} \quad \text{with} \quad \beta = \frac{E[\sigma^2(\theta)]}{Var[\mu(\theta)]}$$

$$\delta = \frac{\beta}{n + \beta} E[\mu(\theta)]$$

This solution minimizes the expected square deviation from the expected risk performance.

2. The reduced problem

Let $Y_k = \frac{1}{n} \sum_{i=1}^{n} X_{ik}$ and consider now instead of the rectangular array of X's the single row of Y's

$$Y_1, Y_2, \ldots, Y_N$$

with distribution functions

$$G_{Y_j}(x/\theta_j = \theta) = G_\theta(x) \quad \text{and} \quad \bar{\mu}(\theta) = \int x dG_\theta(x)$$

$$\bar{\sigma}^2(\theta) = \int x^2 dG_\theta(x) - \bar{\mu}^2(\theta)$$

Obviously from assumptions 1) and 4) in section 1 we have

$$\bar{\mu}(\theta) = \mu(\theta)$$

$$\bar{\sigma}^2(\theta) = \frac{\sigma^2(\theta)}{n}$$

<u>Hypotheses</u>:

1) no more needed
2) θ_j are random variables independent and with common distribution function $U(\theta)$ (known)
3) $(Y_j)_{j\in\{1,\ldots,N\}}$ are independent
4) no more needed

<u>Problem</u>: Estimate $\mu(\theta_k)$ by $\gamma Y_k + \delta$

<u>Solution</u>: $\gamma = \dfrac{1}{1+\bar{\beta}}$ where $\bar{\beta} = \dfrac{E[\bar{\sigma}^2(\theta)]}{Var[\bar{\mu}(\theta)]} = \dfrac{1}{n}\beta$ (hence we have as in section 1 $\gamma = \dfrac{1}{1+\bar{\beta}} = \dfrac{1}{1+\frac{\beta}{n}} = \dfrac{n}{n+\beta}$)

$$\delta = (1-\gamma)E[\bar{\mu}(\theta)] = (1-\gamma)E[\mu(\theta)]$$

We see from this reduction that our estimation problem allows us to <u>eliminate time</u> by switching over to the reduced problem. In order to have a most concise terminology we are therefore working from now on with the reduced problem only. We shall also omit all bars (hence writing e.g. $\sigma^2(\theta)$ for $\bar{\sigma}^2(\theta)$) in our formulae.

3. The game of the actuary against (malevolent) nature

Until now we have assumed that both

a) the parametric family $\{G_\theta(x)\}$

b) the structure function $U(\theta)$

were known. In reality this is mostly not the case. Hence we can define a game of the actuary against nature

Actuary: chooses an estimator $\gamma Y + \delta$
or equivalently a real pair $(\gamma, \delta) = A$

Nature: chooses a) a parametric family of distribution functions $\{G_\theta(x)\}$
b) a structure function $U(\theta)$ which we denote symbolically by $(G, U) = P$

Loss function: (quadratic loss)

$$r(P,A) = \int [\gamma Y + \delta - \mu(\theta)]^2 \underbrace{dP[Y/\theta]dU(\theta)}_{dP[Y,\theta]}$$

$$= \gamma^2 v + (1-\gamma)^2 w + [(1-\gamma)m - \delta]^2$$

where $v = \int \sigma^2(\theta)dU(\theta) = E[\sigma^2(\theta)]$

$w = \int \mu^2(\theta)dU(\theta) - \left(\int \mu(\theta)dU(\theta)\right)^2 = \text{Var}[\mu(\theta)]$

$m = \int \mu(\theta)dU(\theta) = E[\mu(\theta)]$

Definition: If the parametric family $\{G_\theta(x)\}$ is given and nature is only allowed to choose the structure function $U(\theta)$ we call the game parametric. If the parametric family $\{G_\theta(x)\}$ is not fixed in advance we call the game nonparametric.

4. Redefinition of the strategies of nature

As far as our game is concerned the strategies of nature enter into the loss function only by means of the three real quantities v, w, m.

We therefore can considerably simplify our description of the game if we directly use the real triples (v,w,m) as strategies of nature. Hence we redefine

Nature: chooses $P = (v,w,m)$.

In this terminology the distinction between a parametric and a nonparametric game can be stated as follows:

Parametric game: The admissible triples P underly certain restrictions. For example in the Poisson case we have $\mu(\theta) = \sigma^2(\theta)$, hence $m = v$ which means that only such $P = (v,w,m)$ are admissible where the first and third component are equal.

Nonparametric game: no restrictions on the admissible P's.

Thus we finally arrive at the following description of the game of the actuary against nature

Strategies of Actuary: $A = (\gamma,\delta) \in R^2$

Strategies of Nature: $P = (v,w,m) \in \Gamma \subset R^3$

Loss function: $r(P,A) = \gamma^2 v + (1 - \gamma)^2 w + [(1 - \gamma)m - \delta]^2$

In the case of a parametric game Γ may only attain such triples P which satisfy the restrictions imposed by the parametric family.

It is remarkable that this game is usually easier to handle in the nonparametric than in the parametric case, the latter meaning that one has to observe additional side conditions.

5. A nonparametric example

Let

$$\Gamma = [v_{min}, v_{max}] \times [w_{min}, w_{max}] \times [m_{min}, m_{max}]$$

This means that we allow nature to choose its strategies in a threedimensional closed rectangle with no other restrictions, a situation which may arise in practice when estimating the quantities v, w, m from collective data. All research in credibility has so far concentrated on finding point estimates for v, w, m and then by proceeding with these estimates. We can now discuss how to proceed after obtaining <u>interval estimates</u>. The problem of how to find these interval estimates is however in general not yet solved. In practice we may of course be prepared to agree on such a region Γ by a combination of data analysis and judgement. What does now happen if both the actuary and nature are using <u>pure strategies</u>?

a) <u>lower pure value L</u>

$$\inf_A r(P,A) = \gamma^2 v + (1-\gamma)^2 w \quad \text{with} \quad \gamma = \frac{w}{v+w}$$

$$= \frac{vw}{v+w} \quad \text{(increasing function both in } v \text{ and } w\text{)}$$

$$L = \sup_P \inf_A r(P,A) = \frac{v_{max} \cdot w_{max}}{v_{max} + w_{max}}$$

b) <u>upper pure value U</u>

$$\sup_P r(P,A) = \gamma^2 v_{max} + (1-\gamma)^2 w_{max} + \max\{[(1-\gamma)m_{max} - \delta]^2, [(1-\gamma)m_{min} - \delta]^2\}$$

$$U = \inf_A \sup_P r(P,A) = \tilde{\gamma}^2 v_{max} + (1-\tilde{\gamma})^2 \cdot \underbrace{\left[w_{max} + \left(\frac{m_{max} - m_{min}}{2}\right)^2\right]}_{\tilde{w}}$$

with

$$\tilde{\gamma} = \frac{\tilde{w}}{v_{max} + \tilde{w}}$$

$$\tilde{\delta} = (1-\tilde{\gamma}) \frac{m_{max} + m_{min}}{2} .$$

Hence

$$U = \inf_A \sup_P r(P,A) = \frac{v_{max}\tilde{w}}{v_{max} + \tilde{w}}$$

c) the minimax pair

Since $U > L$ the game does not have a pure value. The calculations have nevertheless been helpful inasmuch as they suggest the following pair of minimax strategies:

for nature: $\tilde{P}^*$ (the star shall indicate that the strategy is randomized)

$$\tilde{P}^* = \begin{cases} (v_{max}, w_{max}, m_{min}) & \text{with probability } 1/2 \\ (v_{max}, w_{max}, m_{max}) & \text{with probability } 1/2 \end{cases}$$

for the actuary: $\tilde{A}$ (a non-randomized strategy)

$$\tilde{A} = (\tilde{\gamma}, \tilde{\delta}) \quad \text{where} \quad \tilde{\gamma} = \frac{\tilde{w}}{v_{max} + \tilde{w}} \quad \text{(as under b))}$$

$$\tilde{\delta} = (1 - \tilde{\gamma}) \frac{m_{max} + m_{min}}{2} \quad \text{(as under b))}$$

Proof that $(\tilde{P}^*, \tilde{A})$ is a pair of minimax strategies

It suffices to show that

i) $\inf_A r(\tilde{P}^*, A) = U$

ii) the inf under i) is reached for $A = \tilde{A}$

This is easily verified from

$$r(\tilde{P}^*, A) = \gamma^2 v_{max} + (1 - \gamma)^2 w_{max} + 1/2[(1 - \gamma) m_{min} - \delta]^2 + 1/2[(1 - \gamma) m_{max} - \delta]^2$$

Remark: It is worthwhile to observe that in the special case treated we have found the following results

1) There exist minimax strategies for both players
   - the minimax strategy for nature is mixed
   - the minimax strategy for the actuary is pure (this will certainly be appreciated by all practical actuaries)

2) In our example both minimax strategies for nature and the actuary are unique.

6. The general result

Most results found in the preceding example carry over to the general case. This is summarized in the following theorem.

Theorem: Let $(\Gamma, R^2, r(P,A))$ be a game as defined at the end of section 4.

If Γ is compact then

1) There exist minimax strategies for both players
2) The minimax strategy for the actuary is always pure
   The minimax strategy for nature is generally mixed
3) The minimax strategy of the actuary is unique (but that of nature not necessarily).

Proof: (for readers who like proofs, otherwise you may go on to the next example in section 7).

For 1: We have to show that the actuary can restrict his strategies to a compact subject $\Delta \subset R^2$. Then 1) follows from a general theorem in game theory (see e.g. Blackwell and Girshick (1954), page 46).

Let $M = \sup_{P \in \Gamma} m_p$ which is finite because of compactness of Γ and define Δ as sketched below

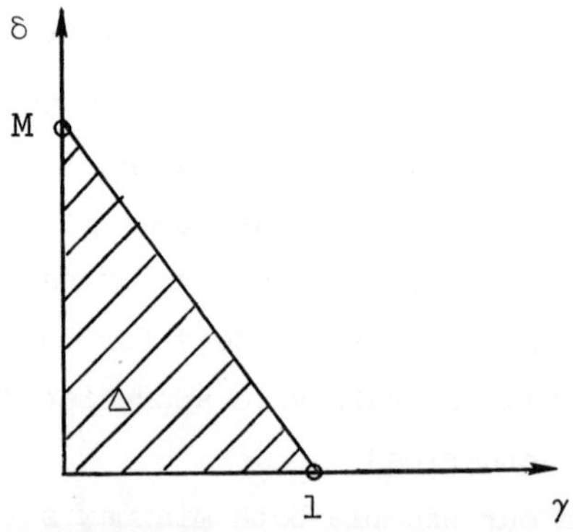

$$\Delta = \{(\gamma,\delta)/0 \leq \gamma \leq 1;\ 0 \leq \delta \leq (1 - \gamma)M\}$$

We prove the following lemma, which allows the actuary to restrict his strategies to Δ.

<u>Lemma</u>: To every $A = (\gamma,\delta) \in R^2$ there exists $\hat{A} = (\hat{\gamma},\hat{\delta}) \in \Delta$ such that

*) $r(P,\hat{A}) \leq r(P,A)$ for all $P \in \Gamma$

<u>Remark</u>: If $A \notin \Delta$ then we have even the strict inequality.

<u>Proof for the lemma</u>: We show that *) is correct for the following choice of $\hat{A} = (\hat{\gamma},\hat{\delta})$

$$\hat{\gamma} = \begin{cases} 0 & \text{if } \gamma < 0 \\ \gamma & 0 \leq \gamma \leq 1 \\ 1 & \gamma > 1 \end{cases}$$

$$\hat{\delta} = \begin{cases} 0 & \text{if } \dfrac{\delta}{1-\gamma} < 0 \\ \dfrac{1-\hat{\gamma}}{1-\gamma}\delta & 0 \leq \dfrac{\delta}{1-\gamma} \leq M \\ (1-\hat{\gamma})M & \dfrac{\delta}{1-\gamma} > M \end{cases}$$

(if $\gamma = 1$ put $\hat{\delta} = 0$)

The following drawing may illustrate the construction of $\hat{A}$, the arrows all pointing from A to $\hat{A}$

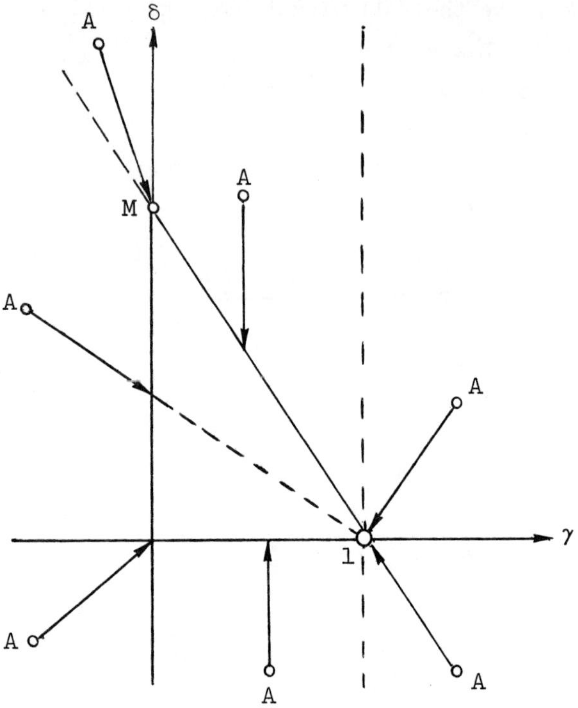

$$r(P,A) = \gamma^2 v + (1-\gamma)^2 w + [(1-\gamma)m - \delta]^2$$

<u>1st case</u>: $\gamma \geq 1 \rightarrow \hat{\gamma} = 1$

$$r(P,A) \geq \gamma^2 v \geq \hat{\gamma}^2 v + (1-\hat{\gamma})^2 w + [(1-\hat{\gamma})m - \hat{\delta}]^2$$

$$= r(P,\hat{A}) \quad \text{for all} \quad P$$

(equality only holds for $(\gamma,\delta) = (1,0)$ i.e. for $A \in \Delta$)

<u>2nd case</u>: $0 \leq \gamma < 1$

$$r(P,A) = \gamma^2 v + (1-\gamma)^2 w + (1-\gamma)^2 \left[m - \frac{\delta}{1-\gamma}\right]^2$$

$$\leq \gamma^2 v + (1-\gamma)^2 w + (1-\gamma)^2 \left[m - \frac{\hat{\delta}}{1-\gamma}\right]^2$$

$$= r(P,\hat{A}) \quad \text{for all} \quad P \in \Gamma$$

(equality only holds for $\delta = \hat{\delta}$, i.e. for $A \in \Delta$).

3rd case: $\gamma < 0 \rightarrow \hat{\gamma} = 0$

$$r(P,A) = \gamma^2 v + (1-\gamma)^2 w + (1-\gamma)^2 \left[m - \frac{\delta}{1-\gamma}\right]^2$$

$$< w + \left[m - \frac{\delta}{1-\gamma}\right]^2 \leq w + [m - \hat{\delta}]^2$$

$$= \hat{\gamma}^2 v + (1-\hat{\gamma})^2 w + [(1-\hat{\gamma})m - \hat{\delta}]^2$$

$$= r(P,\hat{A}) \quad \text{for all} \quad P \in \Gamma$$

which completes the proof of the lemma.

For 2: Let $P^*(v,w,m)$

$$A^*(\gamma,\delta)$$

be a pair of mixed minimax strategies.

Then the value V of the game can be written

$$V = \iint \{\gamma^2 v + (1-\gamma)^2 w + [(1-\gamma)m - \delta]^2\} dP^*(v,w,m) dA^*(\gamma,\delta)$$

$$\geq \int \{[E^*(\gamma)]^2 v + [1 - E^*(\gamma)]^2 w + [(1 - E^*(\gamma))m - E^*(\delta)]^2\} \cdot dP^*(v,w,m)$$

where equality only holds if

$$Var^*(\gamma) = 0$$
$$Var^*(\delta) = 0$$

Hence the minimax strategy of the actuary must be pure.

For 3: Any minimax strategy $A = (\gamma,\delta)$ of the actuary must satisfy the equation

$$\gamma^2 E^*[v] + (1-\gamma)^2 E^*[w] + E^*[(1-\gamma)m - \delta]^2 = \text{minimum}$$

where E^* is the expectation with respect to any mixed minimax strategy $P^*(v,w,m)$ of nature.

But this equation has the unique solution (except for the degenerate case $E^*[v] + E^*[w] + Var^*[m] = 0$)

$$\delta = (1-\gamma)E^*[m]$$

$$\gamma = \frac{E^*[w] + Var^*[m]}{E^*[v] + E^*[w] + Var^*[m]}$$

Remark:

1) There may be several minimax $P^*(v,w,m)$ for nature but for all of them we must have

$$\frac{(E^*[w] + Var^*[m]) \cdot E^*[v]}{E^*[v] + E^*[w] + Var^*[m]} = \max$$

2) Marazzi shows in his thesis how from this last equation one may numerically obtain a minimax strategy of nature.

7. A parametric example

In section 4 we have seen that the Poisson case is characterized by the restriction $m = v$. This includes also the compound Poisson case when the distribution of the claims' amount does not depend on the unknown parameter θ. This is seen as follows:

Let

$$Y = \sum_{j=0}^{N} Z_j$$

where $\{Z_j\}$ independent with identical distribution $G(z)$

N Poisson with parameter θ.

We then have

$$\mu(\theta) = E[Y(\theta)] = \theta \cdot E[Z_j]$$

$$\sigma^2(\theta) = Var[Y(\theta)] = \theta \cdot E[Z_j^2]$$

Hence

$$m = v \cdot \frac{E[Z_j]}{E[Z_j^2]}$$

but by choosing a suitable scale for money, the factor $\frac{E[Z_j]}{E[Z_j^2]}$ may always be made equal to 1.

Let us then consider the following game:

Strategies of nature: $P = (v,w,m)$ with

$$(v,w) \in \Gamma = [v_{min}, v_{max}] \times [w_{min}, w_{max}] \quad \text{and} \quad m = v$$

Strategies of the actuary: $A = (\gamma,\delta)$ $A \in R^2$

Loss function: $r(P,A) = \gamma^2 v + (1 - \gamma)^2 w + [(1 - \gamma)v - \delta]^2$

Because of our general theorem in section 6 the pure upper value is equal to the value V of the game. We therefore have

$$V = \inf_{A} \sup_{P\in\Gamma} r(P,A)$$

The pure strategy $\tilde{A}$ which achieves the infimum is then the <u>unique minimax strategy of the actuary</u> which we want to determine.

We start from

$$\sup_{P} r(P,A) = (1-\gamma)^2 w_{max} + \max[\{[(1-\gamma)v_{max} - \delta]^2 + \gamma^2 v_{max}\},\{[(1-\gamma)v_{min} - \delta]^2 + \gamma^2 v_{min}\}]$$

and first want to find δ which minimizes the right side for fixed γ.

We must distinguish two cases according to the relative position of the two parabolae in the (x,y)-plane

$$Y = \gamma^2 v_{max} + [(1-\gamma)v_{max} - X]^2 \quad \text{maximum-parabola}$$

$$Y = \gamma^2 v_{min} + [(1-\gamma)v_{min} - X]^2 \quad \text{minimum-parabola}$$

<u>Case A</u>: Vertex of maximum parabola outside minimum parabola

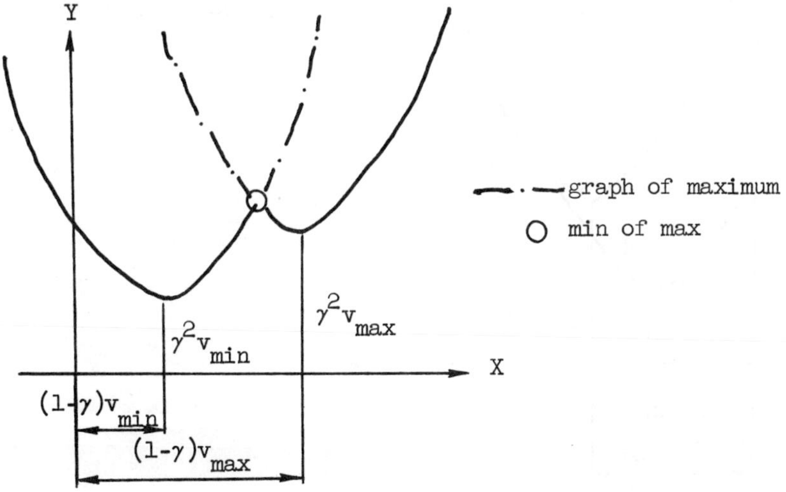

condition A: $[(1-\gamma)v_{min} - (1-\gamma)v_{max}]^2 + \gamma^2 v_{min} \geq \gamma^2 v_{max}$

from which

$$A: \quad (1-\gamma)^2 \Delta v \geq \gamma^2 \qquad (\Delta v = v_{max} - v_{min})$$

or

$$A: \quad \Delta v \geq \left(\frac{\gamma}{1-\gamma}\right)^2 \leftrightarrow \gamma \leq \frac{\sqrt{\Delta v}}{1+\sqrt{\Delta v}}$$

Under condition A, $\inf_{\delta} \sup_{P}$ is attained for $\delta(\gamma)$ with

$$\gamma^2 v_{max} + [(1-\gamma)v_{max} - \delta(\gamma)]^2 = \gamma^2 v_{min} + [(1-\gamma)v_{min} - \delta(\gamma)]^2$$

which leads to the equation

$$\gamma^2 \Delta v + (1-\gamma)^2 [m^2_{max} - m^2_{min}] = 2\delta(\gamma) \cdot (1-\gamma)\Delta v$$

and hence

$$\delta(\gamma) = (1-\gamma)\left[\frac{v_{max} + v_{min}}{2} + \frac{\gamma^2}{2(1-\gamma)^2}\right]$$

We therefore have

$$\inf_{\delta} \sup_{P} r(P,A) = f_1(\gamma) = (1-\gamma)^2 w_{max} + \gamma^2 v_{max} + (1-\gamma)^2 \left[\frac{\Delta v}{2} - \frac{\gamma^2}{2(1-\gamma)^2}\right]^2$$

<u>Case B</u>: Vertex of maximum parabola inside minimum parabola

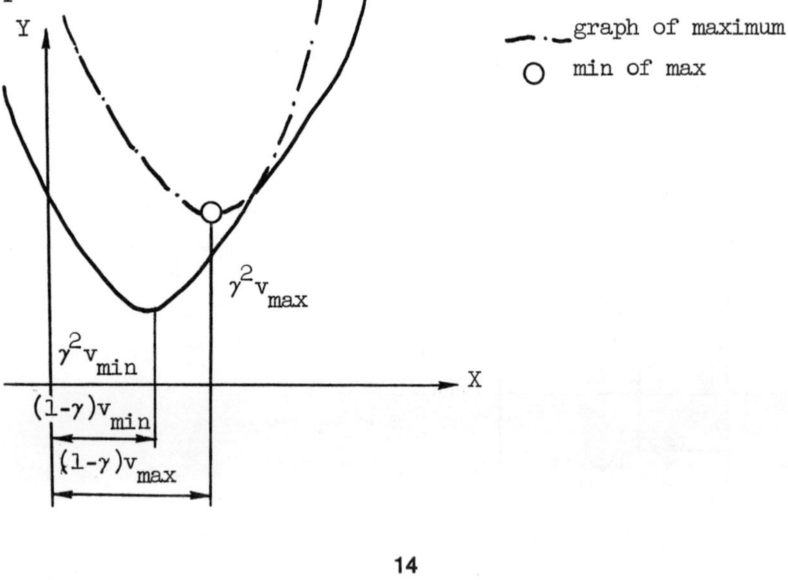

$$B: \quad \Delta v \leq \frac{\gamma^2}{(1-\gamma)^2} \longleftrightarrow \gamma \geq \frac{\sqrt{\Delta v}}{1+\sqrt{\Delta v}}$$

Under condition B we have

$$\delta(\gamma) = (1-\gamma)v_{max}$$

and therefore

$$\inf_{\delta} \sup_{P} r(P,A) = f_2(\gamma) = (1-\gamma)^2 w_{max} + \gamma^2 v_{max}$$

It remains to minimize the function $f(\gamma)$ on $[0,1]$ where

$$f(\gamma) = f_1(\gamma) \quad \text{for} \quad \gamma \leq \frac{\sqrt{\Delta v}}{1+\sqrt{\Delta v}} = \gamma_0$$

$$= f_2(\gamma) \quad \text{for} \quad \gamma \geq \frac{\sqrt{\Delta v}}{1+\sqrt{\Delta v}} = \gamma_0$$

Define γ_1 as value which minimizes $f_1(\gamma)$ on $[0,1]$

γ_2 $f_2(\gamma)$ on $[0,1]$

γ^* $f(\gamma)$ on $[0,1]$

and observe that

$$f_1(\gamma) \geq f_2(\gamma) \quad \text{on} \quad [0,1]$$

and $f_1(\gamma_0) = f_2(\gamma_0)$ (otherwise the inequality sign holds in the relation above)

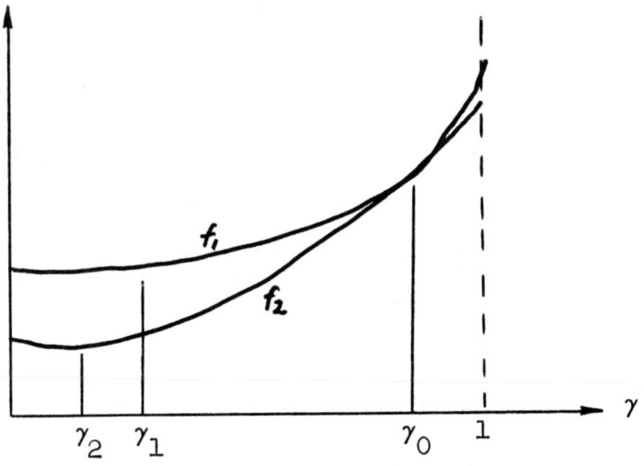

We claim

a) If $\gamma_2 \leq \gamma_0$ then $\gamma^* = \gamma_1$

b) If $\gamma_2 \geq \gamma_0$ then $\gamma^* = \gamma_2$

Proof:

for a): If $\gamma_2 \leq \gamma_0$ consider $\gamma > \gamma_0$ then

$$f_1(\gamma) > f_2(\gamma) > f_2(\gamma_0) = f_1(\gamma_0) \rightarrow \gamma_1 \leq \gamma_0$$

$$\rightarrow \gamma^* = \gamma_1$$

f_2 increases on the right of γ_2

for b): If $\gamma_2 \geq \gamma_0$ then obviously $\gamma^* = \gamma_2$

Numerical calculations of γ_1 and γ_2

Obviously

$$\gamma_2 = \frac{w_{max}}{v_{max} + w_{max}}$$

γ_1 is minimizing $f_1(\gamma)$

$$f_1(\gamma) = \gamma^2 v_{max} + (1-\gamma)^2 w_{max} + (1-\gamma)^2 \left(\frac{\Delta v}{2}\right)^2 - \frac{\gamma^2}{2}\Delta v + \frac{\gamma^4}{4(1-\gamma)^2}$$

$$f_1'(\gamma) = 2\gamma v_{max} - 2(1-\gamma)\left[w_{max} + \left(\frac{\Delta v}{2}\right)^2\right] - 2\gamma\frac{\Delta v}{2} + \frac{16(1-\gamma)^2\gamma^3 + 8\gamma^4(1-\gamma)}{16(1-\gamma)^4}$$

Hence to find γ_1 we have to solve the equation

$$\gamma\,\frac{v_{max} + v_{min}}{2} - (1-\gamma)\left[w_{max} + \left(\frac{\Delta v}{2}\right)^2\right] + \frac{\gamma^3}{2(1-\gamma)^2} + \frac{\gamma^4}{4(1-\gamma)^3} = 0$$

or

$$\frac{\gamma}{1-\gamma}\,\frac{v_{max} + v_{min}}{2} - \left[w_{max} + \left(\frac{\Delta v}{2}\right)^2\right] + \frac{1}{2}\left(\frac{\gamma}{1-\gamma}\right)^3 + \frac{1}{4}\left(\frac{\gamma}{1-\gamma}\right)^4 = 0$$

Let

$$A = \frac{v_{max} + v_{min}}{2} \quad \text{and} \quad B = w_{max} + \left(\frac{\Delta v}{2}\right)^2 .$$

This leads us to the equation

$$4Ax - 4B + 2x^3 + x^4 = 0$$

with

$$A = \frac{v_{max} + v_{min}}{2}$$

$$B = w_{max} + \left(\frac{\Delta v}{2}\right)^2$$

$$x = \frac{\gamma}{1 - \gamma}$$

Numerical examples

I: $m_{max} = v_{max} = 2 \qquad w_{max} = 3/4$

$\Delta v \qquad = 2 \qquad w_{min} = 1/4$

We find

$$\gamma_0 = \frac{\sqrt{2}}{1 + \sqrt{2}} = 0.59$$

$$\gamma_2 = \frac{3/4}{2 + 3/4} = 0.273 \rightarrow \gamma^* = \gamma_1$$

For the equation of 4th degree we have $A = 1$, $B = 3/4 + 1 = 7/4$ hence

$$4x - 7 + 2x^3 + x^4 = 0 \rightarrow x = 1 \rightarrow \gamma^* = \gamma_1 = 0.5$$

$$\delta = 0.5[1 + 1/2] = 0.75$$

II same as I but $\Delta v = 1$. We find

$$\gamma_0 = 0.5$$

$$\gamma_2 = 0.273 \rightarrow \gamma^* = \gamma_1$$

We then have $A = 1.5$, $B = 3/4 + 1/4 = 1$ and must solve

$$6x-4+2x^3+x^4 = 0 \rightarrow x = 0.582 \rightarrow \gamma^* = 0.368$$

$$\delta = 0.632\left[\frac{(0.582)^2}{2} + \frac{3}{2}\right] = 1.055$$

III same as I but $\Delta v = 0$. We find $\gamma_0 = 0$ and hence

$$\gamma^* = \gamma_2 = 0.273$$

$$\delta = 0.727 \cdot 2 = 1.454$$

The following estimation formulae are the minimax strategies for the actuary

$\Delta m = \Delta v$	formula
2	$0.5Y + 0.75$
1	$0.368Y + 1.055$
0	$0.273Y + 1.454$

Discussion By M. Vernon Johns of Minimax Credibility

It is a previlege to have the opportunity to comment on Professor Bühlmann's very interesting and stimulating paper. The most striking feature of this paper is the incorporation of the minimax concept into the area of credibility estimation procedures. This concept, which originated in game theory in the work of Borel and others in the early part of this century, was introduced into the formulation of statistical decision theory by Abraham Wald in the late 1940's and played a major role in the subsequent development of this subject by Blackwell, Girshick, Wolfowitz and others.

The minimax principle as applied in traditional statistical decision-making has incurred some criticism over the years on the grounds that it tends to be conservative to the point of unreasonable pessimism in that the actions required by the principle are those most effective against the worst possible real-world situation. That is, "nature" is assumed to be a malign antagonist rather than a neutral process. It seems to me that Professor Bühlmann's minimax credibility estimator gets around this difficulty rather neatly by limiting the range of "nature's" choices to a relatively small region determined by prior or collateral information. This keeps the inherent conservatism of the minimax idea from impairing the efficiency of his estimator.

It is probably worth noting that Bühlmann's procedure is not really "Bayesian" in conception, although the existence of a prior "structure" distribution $U(\theta)$ is assumed. The spirit here is more consistent with that of "empirical Bayes" procedures where information about $U(\theta)$ is based on actual collateral data. Thus the limits on $U(\theta)$ are imposed on the basis of objective data and it otherwise plays a role only as a technical device in the development of the restricted minimax solution.

I would like to take this opportunity to interject a parenthetical remark to the effect that insurance rate making provides one of the best examples I know where the pure Bayesian approach based on subjective prior probabilities is not appropriate. The point here is that the actuary's subjective prior may well be substantially different from those of the insurance commissioner or the client even if they have access to similar collateral information, since their interests do not coincide. The Bayesian philosophy does not really provide for the negotiation of such differences.

It may be that a little further manipulation with one of the numerical examples given in the paper will serve to illustrate some of my comments. Consider example 1. For this case, nature's choices of v $(= m)$ and w are constrained to lie in the rectangular region shown below:

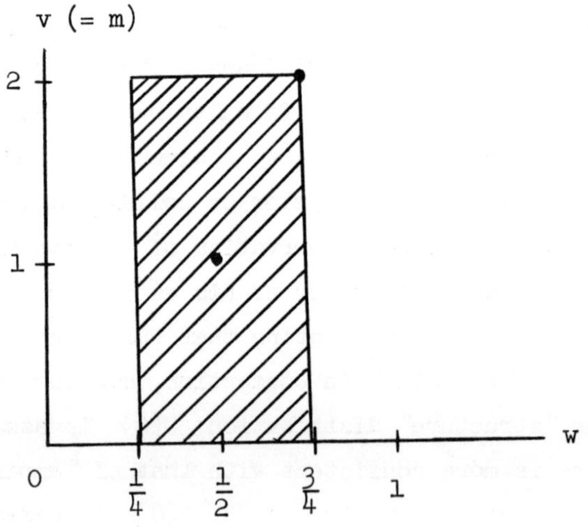

Bühlmann's minimax estimator for this case which I shall call T^* is

$$T^* = .5Y + .75 .$$

If in fact nature had not chosen the "least favorable" strategy but had instead chosen the center point of the permitted region (i.e., $v = 1$, $w = 1/2$) then the value of the expected loss or risk if T^* is used, which I shall call $r(T^*)$, may be computed from the appropriate formula as follows:

$$r(T^*) = \gamma^2 r + (1 - \gamma)^2 w + [(1 - \gamma)r - \delta]^2$$

$$= (.5)^2(1.0) + (.5)^2(.5) + [(.5)(1.0) - .75]^2 = .4375.$$

This value will, of course, be smaller than the risk for nature's worst strategy. If, however, the actuary were to correctly guess that nature would choose the center point, he would be led to use the Bayes optimal solution for this choice (which I shall call T_{opt}), which is

$$T_{opt} = \left(\frac{1}{3}\right)Y + \frac{2}{3} .$$

The risk for the Bayes optimal solution for this case is given by

$$r(T_{opt}) = \frac{wv}{v + w} = \frac{(.5)(1.0)}{.5 + 1.0} = .3333 ,$$

which is about 76% of the risk when T^* is used. Thus one gains about 24% by being a Bayesian and guessing right. On the other hand, if the actuary uses the estimator which is optimal for the center point when in fact nature has chosen the upper right hand corner point ($r = 2$, $w = 3/4$), one may easily compute the risk using T_{opt} to be

$$r(T_{opt}) = \left(\frac{1}{3}\right)^2(2) + \left(\frac{2}{3}\right)^2\left(\frac{3}{4}\right) + \left[\left(\frac{2}{3}\right)(2) - \left(\frac{2}{3}\right)\right]^2 = 1.00,$$

which is three times as large as the Bayes optimal risk. Thus the penalty for an incorrect Bayesian approach may be severe.

This should be contrasted with the result for the risk of Bühlmann's minimax estimator for this case, which is easily seen to be

$$r(T^*) = \left(\frac{1}{2}\right)^2(2) + \left(\frac{1}{2}\right)^2\left(\frac{3}{4}\right) + \left[\left(\frac{1}{2}\right)(2) - \frac{3}{4}\right]^2 = .75 ,$$

which is considerably better than the risk for the incorrect Bayesian estimator. Thus, Bühlmann's restricted minimax procedure provides protection against gross errors without much loss of efficiency compared to procedures which are "best" given a degree of prior information not usually available.

The possible ways of obtaining the region to which "nature's" strategies are restricted have not been pursued at length in this paper, but it seems clear that collateral information not strictly pertinent to the estimation problem at hand could be used for this purpose. For instance, past observations could be taken into account even if the situation were not strictly time homogeneous.

In conclusion I would like to suggest that the central idea of this paper, the use of restricted minimax linear estimators, may well have useful applications in a variety of other non-actuarial areas of statistical inference.

On the Distributions of Claims Costs

William H. DuMouchel
The University of Michigan and University College, London

and

Richard A. Olshen
The University of Michigan and Stanford University

1. Introduction

This paper is concerned with the distributions of total case costs in workmen's compensation insurance, and also with the computation of "fair experience premiums." Section 2 is a description of our data, and in Section 3 we compare various models which fit them. Stimulated by Mandelbrot we first fit stable distributions to part of the data, only to abandon that project in view of two consequences of the best fitting stable model.

In an attempt to "let the tails of the data speak for themselves" we fit Pareto distributions to the tails of the distributions of total costs, and compare the Pareto models with approximate log-normal models.

Section 4 contains a study of the relationship of case costs and case duration. The logarithm of total costs is fit by an affine function of the fractile of case duration. We discuss implications of the discovered relationship for the reserving process.

Section 5 is concerned with the computation of fair experience premiums. We review Ericson's result on posterior expectations in the exponential family, and explore its applicability in view of our data to an exponential--gamma model. Next we discuss statistical and probabilistic problems of the reinsurer from the point of view of the previous models and data, and find in particular that the distribution of total costs can bear too strong a resemblance to a distribution which arises in the St. Petersburg paradox.

Three appendices contain technical details which are pertinent to the techniques and arguments of Sections 1 through 5.

We thank Insurance Technology Company of Berkeley for the use of their data, and A. C. Olshen for helping us to see the implications of those data and our models for reinsurance. Also, Bruce Hill and Michael Woodroofe helped with discussions of the test described in Table 3 and in Appendix II.

2. The data

The next two sections consist of analyses of two sets of data from each of two offices -- call them office A and office B -- of a leading carrier of workmen's compensation insurance. The data of primary interest are total case costs in dollars: payments for temporary and permanent disability, medical costs, and (the minimal) allocated loss adjustment expenses. The data from each office fall into two groups, cases opened in the same two successive months in each of two successive years -- call them year I and year II. In each group of each office, costs were available for the first 90% of cases to close. Of course substantial costs can be expected from the remaining 10% of cases in each of the groups, but our purpose here is to ascertain which models fit the data we have. Our conclusions, as the reader will see, are that very heavy tailed distributions indeed fit best. The implied warning to users of traditional credibility formulas, especially in reinsurance, is all the more pertinent for the full set of data. The cases from office B are rather well matched by year as to nature and sight of injury; those from office A are not. This lack of homogeneity is not crucial to the essentially consistent qualitative nature of our conclusions. Very heavy tailed distributions of workmen's compensation claims costs have been noted by previous authors; for references, see the book by Seal (1968, page 30).

3. The distributions of total costs

A first step in our analysis is the examination of distributions which fit the empirical costs. The summary statistics of Table 1 indicate that the data have very heavy tails.

Table 1

Descriptive Statistics of Raw Total Costs (in Dollars)

Office	Year	Sample Size	Sample Mean	Sample Standard Deviation	Maximum
A	I	182	825	1509	12,514
A	II	203	1093	2053	16,355
B	I	191	929	1566	11,313
B	II	175	509	641	4,982

Data with heavy tails often are studied by means of their logarithms, and the reader will see that shortly we do so for our data. We are thus led in some studies to combine both years' office A data. For if the data from year I are multiplied by 1.27 the mean logarithms for office A, year I and year II, coincide. Rough histograms indicate that the transformed year I and raw year II data may be combined with impunity. In view of their notorious sensitivity to non-normality, no tests of the equality of variances of the logarithms were carried out (see Box, 1953).

Mandelbrot's insistence on stable models for economic data provoked us to think first of fitting stable distributions to our data (see Appendix I). Because costs are always non-negative, we set the skewness parameter β of the fitted stable laws equal to 1 automatically, thereby rendering the left tail of the fitted distributions as light as possible. Maximum likelihood estimation was carried out for the combined office A data. The maximum likelihood estimate of α, call it $\hat{\alpha}$, is 1.22 with a standard error based on the curvature of the likelihood function of .04 (see DuMouchel, 1974b). Therefore, were the stable model correct, the probability a random case from office A has total costs exceeding x is approximately proportional to $x^{-1.22}$ for large x (see (A1) of Appendix I). Values of α larger than 1.4 are ruled out by the data, and thus ((A1)) the putative stable model firmly rejects the notion that the distribution governing office A claims costs has a variance.

In fact, we reject the stable model altogether, and for two reasons. First, the maximum likelihood estimate that a random office A total cost is less than 0 is approximately .08, and of course the true probability is 0. More importantly, the stable laws are chosen for study in large part because their tails appear to fit well the tails of our data. Therefore, it is logical that the information about α in the data should come primarily from the tails of the data. Yet when $\beta = 1$, and $1.1 < \alpha < 1.3$, nearly all the information in the data about α comes from the central or left part of the data in the following sense (DuMouchel, 1974a, Table 2). If only the data up to the 75th percentile, the 75th percentile, and the 95th percentile are recorded, then α can be estimated by the method of maximum likelihood with approximately 99% asymptotic efficiency. Thus, when $\beta = 1$ as opposed to when $\beta = 0$ (symmetric case), the maximum likelihood estimate of α makes little use of that information with which we are here most concerned. The technique of fitting stable laws to our data did not seem more promising for the office B data than it proved to be for those of office A.

In order to "let the tails speak for themselves" we postulated next the following Pareto model for the tails of the distribution of a random total cost Y (see Hill, 1974):

$$P(Y \leq y | Y > K) = 1 - (y/K)^{-\alpha} \quad \text{for some fixed } K \text{ and all } y > K. \tag{1}$$

If (1) holds, then $Z \overset{\text{def.}}{=} \log(Y/K)$ has an exponential distribution for which $P(Z \leq y) = 1 - e^{-\alpha y}$. (The reuse of α as a measure of the heaviness of the tails of Z is deliberate and is intended to parallel the parameter α of stable laws.) If costs $Y_1, \ldots, Y_m$ exceed K then the maximum likelihood estimate of α (call it $\hat{\alpha}$) is $1/\bar{Z}$, where $\bar{Z}$ is the mean of the Z's. (If the distribution of Y is a simple mixture of the conditional distributions of Y given that Y is (respectively) $\leq K$ or $> K$, then the maximum likelihood estimate of α depends only on those observations which exceed K.) Furthermore, αZ has a standard exponential distribution, and it is easy to obtain approximate confidence intervals for α by means of the t-distribution. Our findings are summarized in Table 2. If (1) is correct for office A, and $K \leq 1000$, then the values of $\hat{\alpha}$ in the first two rows of Table 2 estimate the same constant. Our data are inconclusive on this point.

In the past the log-normal distribution has been used to fit total costs in workmen's compensation -- for references see Seal (1969, page 30). The log-normal has much lighter tails than does the Pareto. In fact, all positive moments of the log-normal distribution are finite, though interestingly they do not characterize the distribution (Heyde, 1963).

Table 2

Fitted Parameters for the Exponential Tail Model:
$P(\text{COST} \leq y | \text{COST} > K) = 1 - (y/K)^{-\alpha}$

Data	K	Costs Exceeding K	$\hat{\alpha}$	Approximate 95% Confidence Intervals for α
Office A, Combined	1000	92	1.20	(1.02, 1.41)
Office A, Combined	2000	43	1.44	(1.20, 1.90)
Office B, Year I	1000	50	1.24	(1.02, 1.57)
Office B, Year II	1000	25	2.02	(1.54, 2.92)

We compared our Pareto model (1) with a competitive approximate log-normal model for the tails of Y. More precisely, we assume Z has distribution function

$$P(Z \leq z | \alpha, \tau) = 1 - e^{-\alpha z - \tau z^2} \qquad (z > 0) . \qquad (2)$$

(The slight departure from strict log-normality is made for mathematical tractability in Appendix II.) In the model (2) we test $H_0 : \tau = 0$, that is, (1) holds, versus $H_1 : \tau > 0$. If $\tau = 0$, then the expectation and standard deviation of Z coincide, and in fact a good test of H_0 against H_1 depends on the ratio of the sample standard deviation to the sample mean. Appendix II contains a discussion of Neyman's theory of $C(\alpha)$ tests (1959) and a derivation by means of the theory of an asymptotically locally most powerful test of H_0 against H_1. The test rejects H_0 for large values of

$$\sqrt{\frac{m}{8}} \left(1 - \frac{S^2}{(\overline{Z})^2}\right) , \qquad (3)$$

where, as before, $\overline{Z}$ is the sample mean of (a random sample of) m Z's, and S^2 is the corresponding sample variance (cf. Hill, 1974). The results of the test are summarized in Table 3.

The data do not discredit H_o. To the reader who is puzzled at our discovery that so heavy-tailed a distribution is consistent with our data, we offer two remarks. First, were it so that the total costs per case from each firm which purchased insurance from the insurance carrier had an exponential distribution with fixed parameter, those parameters having a gamma distribution across firms, then it is easily demonstrated that the costs which accrue to the carrier have unconditionally a shifted Pareto distribution (Seal, 1969, page 40). Second, the salient feature of the models implied by Tables 2 and 3 is not that the first three distributions seem not to have variances, but rather that their sample means are dispersed more or less as individual observations. The late Leonard J. Savage offered the following example in a different context.

Suppose a town contains one multi-millionaire, and the remainder of the town consists of homogeneous middle class people. Assume I wish to measure "mean household income." If I sample 50 households, of say 20,000, I am not likely to get the home of the multi-millionaire, and my data are likely to be clustered about the average of the other households. If I sample 50 groups of 50 households, on the other hand, I have a 1/8 chance of obtaining the multi-millionaire's household, and the distribution of the 50 averages may well have a larger sample variance than did my original data. In short, "mean household income" tends to be a silly statistic.

4. The relationship of total cost and case duration

We mentioned earlier the widely known fact that total costs tend to be increasing functions of case duration. In

Table 3

Tests of the Hypothesis $\tau = 0$ in the Model (2):

$$P(Z \leq z | \alpha, \tau) = 1 - e^{-\alpha z - \tau z^2} \qquad (z > 0)$$

Data	K	Costs Exceeding K	(Sample mean, Sample standard deviation)	Approximate attained Significance level
Office A, Combined	1000	92	(.845, .646)	.079
Office A, Combined	2000	43	(.691, .555)	.205
Office B, Year I	1000	50	(.806, .601)	.134
Office B, Year II	1000	25	(.496, .370)	.217

an attempt to assess the phenomenon for our data we studied the (natural) logarithms of total costs by year as affine functions of duration. The scatter about each fitted regression was approximately constant if case duration was plotted by fractiles. Thus, we arrived at the analysis of covariance model

$$\text{Log(Total cost)} = a_{\text{year}} + (b_{\text{year}})(\text{Fractile of duration}) + \text{Error} . \qquad (4)$$

The office A data were not pooled for the present investigation. The model (4) fits better for year II than for year I for each of the two offices. Multiple correlations are, by year, .369 and .444 for office A, and .217 and .372 for office B.

The attained significance levels of our tests are based on the normality of the distributions of errors and on their independence. Results of the last sub-section indicate that while the logarithms of total costs are more nearly normal than are the raw total costs, the logarithms are also not normally distributed. Therefore, any assumed normality for the distributions of errors in (4) is suspect. Fortunately the fixed effects analysis of variance theory used here is quite robust against this departure from standard conditions (Scheffé, 1959, Chapter 10 -- especially page 337).

We studied (4) by office with a view towards simplification. The analyses of variance are summarized in Table 4. For each office the first attained significance level pertains to the null hypothesis $b_I = b_{II}$; the second pertains to the null hypothesis $b_I = b_{II}$ and $a_I = a_{II}$. Notice that for each office we may fit a common b but not a common a. None of the regressions is 0. In view of Table 4, the model (4) simplifies to

Table 4

Analyses of Variance for Equality of Slopes and Intercepts in the Models (4)

Office A

Source	Degrees of Freedom	Mean Square	F-ratio	Approximate Attained Significance Level
Equality of slopes	1	.051	.053	.82
Equality of regressions	2	79.176	82.820	.00
Error	381	.956		

Office B

Source	Degrees of Freedom	Mean Square	F-ratio	Approximate Attained Significance Level
Equality of slopes	1	.469	.449	.50
Equality of regressions	2	4.632	4.436	.01
Error	362	1.044		

$$\text{Log(Total cost)} = a_{\text{year}} + (b)(\text{Fractile of duration}) + \text{Error} \; . \qquad (5)$$

Our least squares estimates of parameters are summarized in Table 5, which the reader may prefer to exponentiate.

Notice that the two slopes are unequal. The data and fitted line for office B, year II are displayed in Figure 1, which qualitatively resembles its three companion plots.

Recall that our data actually arise from only the first 90% of cases to close, so extrapolation of the regressions to Fractile(duration) = 100(10/9) is of interest here.

We feel that the model (5) may have serious implications for the reserving process. For example, suppose a large number of cases opened approximately simultaneously, and that $\upsilon\%$ of them have closed already. If (5) holds, and errors are identically distributed, then the expected amount to be paid on the remaining $(100 - \upsilon)\%$ of cases is

$$E(e^{\text{Error}})e^{a} \sum_{j=N_\upsilon+1}^{N} e^{bj/N} \, , \qquad (6)$$

where $N_\upsilon = \upsilon N/100$. Now rewrite (6) as

$$NE(e^{\text{Error}})e^{a} \sum_{j=N_\upsilon+1}^{N} \{e^{bj/N} \cdot \tfrac{1}{N}\} \, , \qquad (7)$$

and recognize the sum in (7) as a Riemann approximation to

$$\int_{\upsilon/100}^{1} e^{bx}dx = b^{-1}\{e^{b} - e^{b\upsilon/100}\} \; .$$

Thus the expected amount to be paid on the remaining $(100 - \upsilon)\%$ of cases is approximately

$$NE(e^{\text{Error}})e^{a}b^{-1}\{e^{b} - e^{\upsilon/100}\} > \qquad (8)$$

$$Ne^{a}b^{-1}\{e^{b} - e^{b\upsilon/100}\} \qquad (9)$$

according to Jensen's inequality provided E(Error) = 0. Notice that the expectation in (8) is the value at 1 of

Table 5

Predictive Models for Log(Total Costs): (5)

<u>Office A</u>

$$\text{Log(Total cost)} = \left.\begin{array}{ll}\text{(Year I)} & 4.557 \\ \text{(Year II)} & 2.000\end{array}\right\} + (.0145)(\text{Fractile of duration})$$

Multiple correlation coefficient: .415

Standard error of $\hat{\beta}$: .0009

<u>Office B</u>

$$\text{Log(Total cost)} = \left.\begin{array}{ll}\text{(Year I)} & 4.886 \\ \text{(Year II)} & 4.576\end{array}\right\} + (.0218)(\text{Fractile of duration})$$

Multiple correlation coefficient: .291

Standard error of $\hat{\beta}$: .0018

the moment generating function of the distribution of errors in (5).

The problem of setting aside reserves for the remaining cases can be viewed as a problem in setting confidence limits for the expression (8), in which a, b, and the expectation are unknown.

5. The conputation of premiums

We now turn to some implications of our data analyses for credibility theory. In what follows we set aside questions of numbers of claims and (largely) questions of loadings. That is, we focus upon the "fair experience premium," especially as it applied to the reinsurer. Our expressions are to be viewed, at least in the workmen's compensation field, as "fair experience premiums" per injury or illness, or more generally per unit of experience.

Perhaps the best known of the credibility formulas is this. If total costs $x_1,\ldots,x_n,x_{n+1},\ldots$ are conditionally independent and identically distributed given $\underset{\sim}{\theta}$, and $\mu(\underset{\sim}{\theta}) = E(x_i|\underset{\sim}{\theta})$, then subject to the conditions of a theorem of Ericson (1970 -- see also Stone, 1963 and Bühlmann, 1970, Chapter 4),

$$E(\mu(\underset{\sim}{\theta})|x_1,\ldots,x_n) = \frac{\bar{x}\,\mathrm{Var}(\mu(\underset{\sim}{\theta})) + E(\mu(\underset{\sim}{\theta}))E(\mathrm{Var}(\bar{x}|\underset{\sim}{\theta}))}{\mathrm{Var}(\mu(\underset{\sim}{\theta})) + E(\mathrm{Var}(\bar{x}|\underset{\sim}{\theta}))} . \quad (10)$$

Think of $x_1,x_2,\ldots$ as realized total costs from a single policyholder. The expression (10) is then the fair experience premium for that policyholder for the period in which x_{n+1} will be observed. Realistic circumstances in which Ericson's theorem applies are those for which (i) x_i given $\underset{\sim}{\theta}$ is distributed as a member of the exponential family of distributions (ii) $\Sigma_1^n x_i$ is part of a finite dimensional sufficient statistic, and (iii) $\underset{\sim}{\theta}$ has a conjugate prior (unconditional) distribution.

Since the normal conditional distribution for x_i satisfies (i) and (ii) and the normal prior for μ is conjugate, (7) is also (as is well known) the wide sense (best linear least squares) conditional expectation of $\mu(\underset{\sim}{\theta})$ given $x_1,\ldots,x_n$ (see Doob, 1953, pages 75-78 and Bühlmann, loc. cit.).

The criteria (i) and (ii) imply in particular that given $\underset{\sim}{\theta}$, x_i has all moments (see Ferguson, 1967, page 129).

One instance in which (10) holds is suggested by our data. That is, x_1 given θ has an exponential distribution with expectation $1/\theta$, and θ has a gamma distribution, with density proportional to $\theta^{\alpha-1}e^{-\gamma\theta}$ $(\theta > 0)$, where $\alpha, \gamma > 0$. Here it is easily checked that (10) reduces to

$$\sum_1^n x_i + \gamma \Big/ n + \alpha - 1 \; . \tag{11}$$

If $\alpha \leq 2$, as our data suggest can occur, then $\mathrm{Var}(x_i)$ is not finite, and here more importantly neither is $\mathrm{Var}(\mu(\theta))$, so the right-hand side of (10) does not make sense. Still, the left-hand side continues to make sense and agrees with (11) provided the denominator of (11) is positive. It is therefore of interest to estimate the parameters α and γ of the prior distribution from previous data on the collective of policyholders, even when it is known that α may be not more than 2.

Previous data $w_1,\ldots,w_m$ from the collective may be assumed to have the common unconditional density of x_i,

$$\frac{\alpha\gamma^{\alpha}}{(\gamma + x)^{\alpha+1}} \qquad (x > 0) \; . \tag{12}$$

(Necessarily $\alpha > 1$ if $E(\mu(\theta)) < \infty$.) Maximum likelihood estimates cannot be computed in closed form. (The order statistics are minimal sufficient here - see Ferguson, 1967, page 132.) Still there is substantial information available about them. If L is the likelihood function, then

$$\frac{\partial \log L}{\partial \alpha} = \frac{n}{\alpha} + \Sigma \log\left(\frac{\gamma}{\gamma + w_i}\right) \tag{13}$$

$$\frac{\partial \log L}{\partial \gamma} = \frac{n\alpha}{\gamma} - (\alpha + 1)\,\Sigma\,\frac{1}{\gamma + w_i} \tag{14}$$

Thus, if γ is known, there is one dimensional sufficient statistic, and $\hat{\alpha}$ (the solution of (13) equals 0) is given by $-\hat{\alpha} = 1/\frac{1}{n}\Sigma \log\left(\frac{\gamma}{\gamma + w_i}\right)$. Likewise, if α is known then $\hat{\gamma}$ is the solution of

$$\frac{\alpha}{\alpha + 1} = \frac{1}{n}\Sigma\,\frac{\gamma}{\gamma + w_i}\,,$$

which is obtained easily by iteration. When neither is known a priori, then the method of scoring is available to find approximate maximum likelihood estimates - see Rao, 1965, page 305. Compute easily that if the parameter is written (α, γ) then the information matrix is

$$\begin{pmatrix} \frac{1}{\alpha^2} & -\frac{1}{\gamma(\alpha + 1)} \\ -\frac{1}{\gamma(\alpha + 1)} & \frac{\alpha}{\gamma^2(\alpha + 2)} \end{pmatrix}. \tag{15}$$

In order to complete Rao's program, we used only a point at which to begin the iteration. The method of moments is convenient here: Because $E(w_j) \equiv \gamma/\alpha - 1$, set

$$\bar{w} = \gamma/\alpha - 1\,, \tag{16}$$

pick an initial α subjectively, and solve (16) for the initial γ; our data suggest that $\alpha = 2$ may be a reasonable initial choice. For additional information on the method of maximum likelihood see Chapter 5 of Rao's book (1965). Of course, the user may on subjective grounds wish to alter any data-based estimates of α and γ.

The exponential-gamma example and our data bear upon

the computation of fair experience premiums in reinsurance. It is convenient to work with non-proportional reinsurance (see Bühlmann, 1970, pages 14 and 112), though qualitatively similar conclusions obtain in the proportional case as well. As before, we set aside questions of numbers of claims; our fair experience premiums should be viewed per case.

We suppose there exists $K > 0$ such that for any total cost X, the minimum of X and K is borne by the insurance carrier, and the maximum of $X - K$ and 0 by the reinsurer. For purposes of reinsurance, costs are distributed according to the unconditional distributions of the client companies of the reinsurer. Thus, for a random total cost X suppose now that for $x > K$

$$P(X > x \mid X > K \text{ and } \alpha) = (x/K)^{-\alpha}\,. \tag{17}$$

(This K exceeds the K of section 3.) We assume that $E(X) < \infty$ and therefore that $\delta \overset{\text{def}}{=} \alpha - 1 > 0$. Bayesian estimation of the conditional expectation of X given $X > k$, and δ, is discussed in Appendix III. The treatment there is for gamma prior distributions of δ, but can be extended easily to prior distributions which are convex combinations of gamma distributions, and therefore approximately to any prior distributions of δ. More precisely, we assume that δ has density proportional to $\delta^{\xi}e^{-d\delta}$ $(\delta > 0)$ for some $d > 0$ and $\xi > -1$. Since $E(X \mid X > K \text{ and } \delta) = K + K/\delta$, the fair experience premium per case, given previous total costs $x_1,\ldots,x_n$, is the posterior expectation of K/δ. It follows from (A5), Appendix III that the posterior expectation is always infinite unless $\xi > 0$, in which case (see (A7)) it is

$$K\,\frac{E\{\Gamma(B + \xi)/(d + \log C)^{B}\}}{E\{\Gamma(B + \xi + 1)/(d + \log C)^{B+1}\}}\,, \tag{18}$$

where $C = \prod_{i=1}^{n} x_i$, and B has a binomial distribution with parameters n and $\frac{1}{2}$, and the expectations are with respect to the distribution of B.

Compute that, given d and ξ, the conditional density of X given $X > K$ at x is

$$\frac{d^{\xi+1}K}{x^2[d + \log(x/K)]^{\xi+1}}\left\{\frac{\xi + 1}{d + \log(x/K)} + 1\right\} \quad (x > K) . \qquad (19)$$

Clearly when $\xi \leq 0$, $E(X|X > K) = \infty$; moreover, this follows from the foregoing remarks on the posterior expectation of K/δ. The variance of the density (19) is never finite. The case $\xi = 0$ is particularly interesting probabilistically. We explore thie special situation.

Feller ((1968), page 251) argues that long run averages are not what are important in the insurance industry. Even so, the notion of fair experience premium suggests that, for each client company of a reinsurer, average total costs and average fair experience premium should in the long run be approximately equal. When $\xi = 0$ it is possible to establish premiums in such a way that at any sufficiently remote fixed time in the future, average fair experience premium and average total cost are arbitrarlly close with arbitrarily high probability, although the chance that they remain close indefinitely is 0. More precisely, let $y_1, y_2, \ldots$ be indefinitely many independent, identically distributed random variables with density (19), where $\xi = 0$. For $n = 1,2,\ldots$ let

$$S_n = \sum_{i=1}^{n} y_i .$$

Furthermore, fix an arbitrary positive ε. Then

$$P\left\{\left|\frac{S_n}{n} - dK \log \log n\right| < \varepsilon\right\} \to 1 \quad \text{as} \quad n \to \infty . \qquad (20)$$

So in particular

$$P\left\{\left|\frac{S_n}{ndK \log \log n} - 1\right| < \varepsilon\right\} \to 1 \quad \text{as} \quad n \to \infty . \qquad (21)$$

Yet,

$$P\left\{\frac{S_n}{ndK \log \log n} \to 1 \text{ as } n \to \infty\right\} = 0 . \tag{22}$$

(21) is a consequence of Feller's general weak law of large numbers (see Feller, 1966, pages 232-234); (22) is an application of a theorem of Chow and Robbins (1961). While (21) suggests that $dKn \log \log n$ is the only fair experience premium for n total costs, the Chow-Robbins result implies that over the extended horizon nothing will suffice. Moreover, no loadings will rectify the problem. A reinsurance company whose gamma prior distribution for δ has $\xi = 0$ is very much like the proprietor of a St. Petersburg casino whose only game pays 2^r dollars to a player who tosses $r - 1$ "tails" before the first "head" in successive tosses of a fair coin (see Feller, 1968, Section X.4).

It is difficult to make inferences about d and ξ from a random sample distributed as (19). Again the order statistics are minimal sufficient. Closed form maximum likelihood estimates are not available. Indeed, if all x_i exceed eK, then the likelihood function does not have a maximum in the region $\xi + 1 + d > 0$. The information matrix has no simple expression, and therefore one seems reduced to numerical exploration of the likelihood surface. The observation that if $\tilde{X}$ has density (19) and $\xi > q$, then

$$E(\tilde{X}(d + \log \tilde{X} - \log K)^q) = Kd^q\left\{\frac{\xi + 1}{\xi + 1 - q} + \frac{d}{\xi - q}\right\} \tag{23}$$

makes the method of moments available. The case $q = 0$ is particularly simple, and leads to

$$\frac{d}{\xi} = \frac{\overline{X}}{K} - 1 . \tag{24}$$

It seems reasonable to pick one of d and ξ subjectively, solve (24) for the other, and use the resulting parameter point to begin exploration of the likelihood surface.

One practical message in our discussion of reinsurance is this. Data distributed as (19) are highly variable, and thus when (19) applies, total case costs to a reinsurer are either very difficult or impossible to control. Therefore, it is in the interest of the reinsurer to see that (19) is not a correct model, even if, as our data suggest, (17) is. Put another way, the reinsurer ought to conduct business so that nature's gamma prior distribution for δ does not describe its client companies. There are at least two ways to accomplish this. One involves examining a random sample of data on total case costs of a potential client: fix a number p near 0, a K, and a fixed threshold α_0 appreciably larger than 1; then test the hypothesis $\alpha > \alpha_0$ at level p, and if it is rejected do not reinsure the potential client. To be precise, pick a c for which $\Phi(c) = p$ ($\Phi(\cdot)$ is the standard, normal cumulative distribution function). Compute $\bar{Z}$ and S, the sample mean and sample standard deviation of the Z's, where Z is defined following (1). And decline the business if

$$\sqrt{n}/\sqrt{n}\,\bar{Z} - cS < \alpha_0 . \tag{25}$$

This procedure should be tried for various values of K, in part to see if (17) is applicable.

Another approach to the problem just considered does not involve examining data. Before describing it we note that data distributed according to (17) may be quite variable, but nevertheless typically less variable than data with density (19). The reinsurer can have (17) (for some α) governing its total case costs if effectively it has only one type of customer, that is, client companies which themselves have nearly identical cross-sections of customers. In conclusion, then, it appears to be in the best interest of a reinsurer to restrict the nature of its clients either to those whose total case costs are shown to be in reasonable control, or at the very least to a homogeneous collective.

Appendix I

B. Mandelbrot (1963) has advocated the use of stable distributions in analyses of economic data. That a random variable W has a stable distribution is characterized by the following property. If $W, W_1, W_2, \ldots$ are independent and identically distributed, then for every $n = 1, 2, \ldots$ there exist constants c_n and d_n such that $\sum_{k=1}^{n} W_k$ is distributed as $c_n W + d_n$. Necessarily $c_n = n^{1/\alpha}$ for $0 < \alpha \leq 2$; α is called the index of the stable distribution.

For detailed information concerning stable distributions see Feller (1966) and the references he cites. The normal distribution is the only stable distribution for which $\alpha = 2$. The Cauchy distribution is stable $(\alpha = 1)$ as is the distribution of the reciprocal of a chi-square variable with 1 degree of freedom $(\alpha = 1/2)$. If W is stable with index $\alpha < 2$, then

$$P(|W| > x)/x^{\alpha} \rightarrow \text{some constant as } x \rightarrow \infty, \qquad \text{(A1)}$$

and so W does not have a finite variance.

Typically stable distributions are parameterized by, in addition to α, a location parameter δ, a scale parameter c, and a parameter β which measures skewness; $-\infty < d < \infty$, $0 < c < \infty$, $-1 \leq \beta \leq 1$. Unless $\alpha < 1$ and $\beta = +1$ or $\beta = -1$, each stable distribution has support the entire real line.

Appendix II

Assume that $z, z_1, z_2, \ldots, z_m$ are independent and identically distributed, with distribution function

$$P(z|\alpha, \tau) = 1 - e^{-\alpha z - \tau z^2} \quad (z > 0).$$

The common density of the observations is

$$p(z|\alpha,\tau) = (\alpha + \tau z)e^{-\alpha z - \tau z^2} \qquad (z > 0) .$$

We fix $z > 0$ and study $\log p$ for $\alpha, \tau > 0$. Thus

$$\phi_\tau(z) \overset{\text{def}}{=} \left.\frac{\partial \log p}{\partial \tau}\right|_{\tau=0} = \frac{2z}{\alpha} - z^2 ;$$

$$\phi_\alpha(z) \overset{\text{def}}{=} \left.\frac{\partial \log p}{\partial \alpha}\right|_{\tau=0} = \frac{1}{\alpha} - z .$$

These are both Cramér functions (Neyman, 1959, Section 3). According to results of Neyman and of LeCam (see Neyman, 1959), with data $z_1,\ldots,z_m$ one asymptotically locally most powerful test of $H_0 : \tau = 0$ against $H_1 : \tau > 0$ is based on a statistic with numerator

$$\sum_{i=1}^{m} \phi_\tau(z_i) - a\phi_\alpha(z_i) , \tag{A2}$$

where $a = \mathrm{Cov}(\phi_\alpha(z),\phi_\tau(z))/\mathrm{Var}(\phi_\alpha(z))$, and, in practice, in the expression (A2) α is replaced by its maximum likelihood estimate $(\hat\alpha)$ under H_0. Now $\hat\alpha = 1/\bar z$, where $\bar z$ is the mean of the z's, and $\sum z_i - \bar z = 0$, so the required expression simplifies to $2m(\bar z)^2 - \sum z_i^2 = m((\bar z)^2 - s^2)$, where $s^2 = m^{-1} \sum_{i=1}^{m} (z_i - \bar z)^2$.

In order to find the denominator of the test statistic compute that under H_0, $\mathrm{Var}\left(\frac{2z}{\alpha} - z^2\right) = 8/\alpha^4$. Neyman's theory dictates that when H_0 obtains

$$\frac{m((\bar z)^2 - s^2)}{\sqrt{8m/\hat\alpha^4}} = \sqrt{\frac{m}{8}} \left(1 - \frac{s^2}{(\bar z)^2}\right) \tag{A3}$$

tends in distribution to the standard normal as $m \to \infty$, and that the cited asymptotically locally most powerful test of H_0 versus H_1 rejects H_0 for large values of the expression (A3).

Appendix III

Assume that the random variable X satisfies $P(X > x | X > K) = (x/K)^{-\alpha}$ for some $K > 0$ and $\alpha > 0$. Then the conditional density of X given $X > K$ is proportional to $\alpha/x^{\alpha+1}$. If X has a finite expectation then $\alpha > 1$. Suppose this to be the case. Suppose further that $x_1 \ldots x_n$ are independent observations distributed as X, and that each is larger than K. We discuss Bayesian estimation of the conditional expectation of X given $X > K$, and α.

The likelihood function is proportional to $\alpha^n/C^{\alpha+1}$, where $C = \prod_{i=1}^{n} x_i$. Put $\delta = \alpha - 1$, so $\delta > 0$. We choose to work with a gamma prior density for δ. Of course we are guided in part by computational considerations. Our computations make clear, however, what the corresponding answers are for priors which are convex combinations for gammas, and therefore approximately for any prior distribution of δ. Thus, let δ have density proportional to $\delta^{\xi}e^{-d\delta}$ $(\delta > 0)$, for some $d > 0$ and $\xi > -1$. The posterior distribution of δ is proportional to

$$\frac{(\delta + 1)^n}{C^{\delta+2}} \delta^{\xi}e^{-d\delta} \quad (\delta > 0),$$

that is, since in this computation C is a constant, proportional to

$$(\delta + 1)^n \delta^{\xi} e^{-(d+\log C)\delta} \quad (\delta > 0) . \tag{A5}$$

Now $(E(X|X > K \text{ and } \delta) = K + \frac{K}{\delta}$, so our credibility formulas require the posterior expectation of $K + \frac{K}{\delta}$, which in view of (A5) and the binomial theorem is, if $\xi > 0$,

$$K + K \frac{\int_0^\infty \sum_{j=0}^{n} \binom{n}{j} \delta^{j+\xi-1} e^{-(d+\log C)\delta} \, d\delta}{\int_0^\infty \sum_{j=0}^{n} \binom{n}{j} \delta^{j+\xi} e^{-(d+\log C)\delta} \, d\delta}$$

$$= K + K \frac{\sum_{j=0}^{n} \binom{n}{j} \Gamma(j + \xi)(d + \log C)^{-j}}{\sum_{j=0}^{n} \binom{n}{j} \Gamma(j + \xi + 1)(d + \log C)^{-j-1}}, \tag{A6}$$

where $\Gamma(\cdot)$ is the gamma function. Divide the numerator and denominator of (A6) by 2^n to see that expression as

$$K + K \frac{E\{\Gamma(B + \xi)/(d + \log C)^B\}}{E\{\Gamma(B + \xi + 1)/(d + \log C)^{B+1}\}}, \tag{A7}$$

where B has a binomial distribution with parameters n and $\frac{1}{2}$.

If $\xi \leq 0$, $E(K + \frac{K}{\delta} \mid x_1 \ldots x_n) = \infty$, the case $\xi = 0$ having been singled out for special mention in the text.

Discussion by Kenneth M. Levine of On the Distribution of Claim Costs

"On the Distribution of Claims Costs" by William H. DuMouchel and Richard A. Olshen is an attempt at employing advanced statistical techniques in the fitting of empirical compensation data to a theoretical distribution, this distribution to be used in insurance pricing. This attempt is well received by the practicing actuary as knowledge of this distribution (and of the underlying frequency distribution) allows him to obtain an estimator for functions of loss costs that has a smaller variance than the estimator that would be obtained through the use of total loss statistics. We congratulate the authors on their success in fitting the pareto distribution to the available compensation data and their analysis of the implications for excess of loss reinsurance, focusing our comments on explanation, as opposed to criticism. The reader may judge the usefulness or "realism" of the model for himself. We will comment briefly on the development of a posterior pareto distribution, (as the reader may not have seen this development before), on a comparison of some likely candidates for theoretical severity distributions, and on the use of frequency and severity distributions in insurance pricing.

1. We wish to show that an exponential distribution conditional on the mean with parameter θ distributed gamma implies unconditionally a pareto distribution.

pf: Let $p(x|\theta) = \theta e^{-\theta x} \qquad (x \geq 0)$

where $p(x|\theta) \equiv \text{Prob}(\xi \leq x|\theta)$

then $\mu(\xi|\theta) = 1/\theta$

$$\sigma^2(\xi|\theta) = 1/\theta^2 .$$

If

$$\mu(\theta) = \beta^\alpha \theta^{\alpha-1} e^{-\beta\theta} \Gamma^{-1}(\alpha)$$

then

$$\mu(1/\theta) = \frac{\beta}{\alpha - 1}$$

$$\sigma^2(1/\theta) = \frac{\beta^2}{(\alpha - 1)^2(\alpha - 2)} .$$

Then, by Bayes theorem,

$$P(x) = \frac{\alpha\beta^\alpha}{(\beta + x)^{\alpha+1}} , \ \mu(\xi) = \frac{\beta}{\alpha - 1} , \ \sigma^2(\xi) = \frac{\alpha\beta^2}{(\alpha - 1)^2(\alpha - 2)}$$

and if we take n observations $x_1, \ldots, x_n$ we update (α, β) to $(\alpha + n, \beta + \sum_1^n x_t)$.

The exponential prior being simple exponential and regular and the gamma being the natural conjugate, the credibility result is exact Bayesian as well.

2. We briefly compare, in tabular form, three likely candidates for severity distributions. (See Figure 1)

3. Although most non-life insurance pricing in the United States is based solely on the calculation of the mean there are instances of pricing being based upon other statistics. Consider the charge in the excess pure premium ratio for retrospectively rated risks, defined as

$$\phi_\mu(r) = \frac{1}{\mu} \int_{r_\mu}^{\infty} (x - r_\mu) d_x F$$

where

$$\mu(F) = \mu, \qquad 0 < r < \infty .$$

We find values of ϕ for each r (entry ratio) and μ (by premium size) by:

A. Setting frequency (i.e. negative binomial) and

Figure 1

	density	mean	variance	parameters
Log Normal	$\frac{1}{\sqrt{2\pi}\,x} e^{-(\log x-\mu)^2/\sigma^2}$	$e^{\mu+\sigma^2/2}$	$\text{mean}\cdot[e^{\sigma^2} - 1]$	$-\infty < \mu < \infty$ $0 < \sigma < \infty$
Weibull	$\alpha\beta x^{\alpha-1} e^{-\beta x^{\alpha}}$	$\beta^{-\alpha^{-1}} \Gamma\left(\frac{\alpha + 1}{\alpha}\right)$	$\beta^{-2\alpha^{-1}} \Gamma\left[\left(\frac{\alpha+2}{\alpha}\right) - \Gamma^2\left(\frac{\alpha+1}{\alpha}\right)\right]$	$0 < \alpha < \infty$ $0 < \beta < \infty$
Pareto	$\frac{\alpha\gamma^{\alpha}}{(\gamma + x)^{\alpha+1}}$	$\frac{\gamma}{\alpha - 1}$ $(\alpha > 1)$	$\frac{\gamma^2\alpha}{(\alpha-1)^2(\alpha-2)}$ $(\alpha > 2)$	$0 < \alpha < \infty$ $0 < \gamma < \infty$

Note: The weibull distribution has been successfully fitted to commercial property package claim distributions. The distributions are listed in increasing order of skewness (+) and intractability (sic).

severity (i.e. weibull) distributions, the relevant parameters being determined by the empirical data, per this paper.

B. "Simulating" the experience of many virtual risks and calculating ϕ for each pair (r,μ).

We believe this approach to give better estimates to ϕ than are given by taking actual loss ratios and calculating smoothed values of ϕ, Simon (1965).

Credibility in Group Experience Rating

William J. Falk and Howard J. Bolnick
Continental Assurance Company

1. Introduction

In the paper "Experience Rating Group Life Insurance" (1974) Howard Bolnick discussed the use of various techniques available to insurance companies in experience rating group insurance cases. The tools studied include step-loss pooling, contingency reserves, premium margins, deficit recovery charges, risk charges, retroactive rating agreements, and termination classes. An additional method that was only touched on in the paper is the use of credibility techniques to predict claim experience.

Many papers have been published about credibility theory since its initial development. For the most part these papers have concerned themselves with the derivation of methods of calculating credibility factors or with theoretical justifications of these methods as estimators for future claim experience. The one aspect lacking is an investigation of the financial effect that using a credibility formula will have on an insurer. There appears to have been a tacit assumption that using a theoretically correct estimator for each group's true claims level is beneficial to the insurer. It is this assumption that will be discussed here.

2. The goals of experience rating

In order to analyze the utility of any experience rating method, it is first necessary to determine the goals of the experience rating process. It is these goals against which the success of experience rating techniques must be measured.

The insurer has three main goals that an effective experience rating system should meet. First, the insurer must charge each policyholder an adequate, equitable premium. Second, the insurer desires to maximize the underwriting gain or minimize the underwriting loss from experience-rated cases. Underwriting gain or loss is defined as in "Experience Rating Group Life Insurance," that is the premium charge for claims less the sum of rate credits, claims, and change in contingency reserves. The third insurer goal is to arrive at an experience rating system that will minimize anti-selection. Antiselection can occur when groups with poor claim experience gravitate to insurers using lower credibility factors while groups with good claim experience seek insurers with more liberal formulas.

The policyholder also has goals for the experience rating system. As "Experience Rating Group Life Insurance" pointed out, these goals may be contrary to the insurer's goals. The policyholder's position should be considered in the determination of an experience rating system.

3. Credibility in experience rating

The goal of using a credibility formula has been expressed as "the estimation of the true claim level of a particular risk based on both the actual observed claim experience of that risk and the expected claim level that would be predicted for the risk," (Maguire, 1971). The most common formula used is

$$\text{True Claim Level} = Z(\text{Actual Claim Level}) + (1 - Z)(\text{Expected Claim Level})$$

where Z is the credibility factor. The use of a credibility formula to meet this goal has often been justified using various theoretical methods and under different sets of assumptions. These proofs have not examined the ability of a credibility formula to aid the insurer in attaining its goals.

The main deficiency in the proofs is that they take the credibility formula out of its working environment, the experience rating system. The validity of separating out for analysis any one technique is at best questionable. The actuary needs to analyze the impact of the entire group of procedures on the adequacy and equity of the premiums and on the underwriting gain or loss.

4. Analysis of credibility in experience rating

To examine the impact of credibility formulas on the achievement of the insurer's goals, the effects on three types of cases must be analyzed; these are:

(1) Cases whose true claim level equals the expected claim level, (true = expected),

(2) Cases whose true claim level is less than the expected claim level, (true < expected), and

(3) Cases whose true claim level exceeds the expected claim level, (true > expected).

Let's first examine these three types of cases in a situation limited to prospective rating. This is a pure insurance situation in which the future premium is a function of past experience. The insurer uses gains on some cases to offset losses on other cases.

For type (1) cases, (true = expected), the introduction of credibility factors greater than zero should not affect the expected underwriting gain. The use of credibility factors with type (2) cases, (true < expected), will affect the gain. As the credibility factor increases, the expected premium, and thus the expected underwriting gain, will decrease. The opposite is true for type (3) cases, (true >

expected). The expected loss will decrease until a gain (or at least a break-even point) is reached with full credibility.

When all three types of cases are combined in a company's portfolio, the effects of a credibility formula depends on the distribution of true claim levels about the expected claim level. The optimal credibility factor for a given case size is dependent upon the degree to which the lower expected gain on type (2) cases is offset by the lower expected loss on type (3) cases.

Next, we must look at these case types in a combination prospective - retrospective experience rating situation. If the insurer returns 100% of all surpluses to the policyholder, then an underwriting loss is expected for the portfolio of cases since there are no gains left to offset the losses. Instead, losses are carried forward to be recovered in the future.

Once again let's examine the effect of a credibility formula on the three case types. The impact of a credibility formula on type (1) cases, (true = expected), will be minimal. The increased expected loss on cases where premiums are lowered due to favorable claims should offset the decreased expected loss on cases where premiums are increased due to poor claims experience. For type (2) cases, (true < expected), an increase in the credibility factor will increase the expected loss. This occurs due to the lower margin contained in the lower expected premium. The opposite effect will occur in type (3) cases, (true > expected). The higher expected premiums will decrease the probability of and the average amount of losses.

These three types of cases would be combined in an actual portfolio of group insurance cases. Determining the optimum credibility factor for each case size requires analyzing the impact of the credibility factors on the trade off between the decreased losses on type (3) cases and the increased losses on type (2) cases. The distribution of true claim level about the expected claim level will affect the magnitude of the credibility factors what will minimiee the expected underwriting loss for the portfolio.

An additional consideration in all of the above situations is the effect that the credibility formula has on premium fluctuation. Obviously, if the factor is zero, there will be no chance fluctuation. Credibility factors greater than zero will produce fluctuation that for a given case size increases as the factor increases. For the same credibility factor and case size a shorter averaging period, e.g. one year versus five years, will produce greater chance fluctuation.

5. Simulation as a method of analyzing credibility

Computer simulation is one method the actuary can use to examine the impact of introducing a credibility formula into an experience rating system. By simulating the various combinations of techniques he should be able to select the combination or combinations that will best meet the goals of the insurer.

The multi-year program described in "Experience Rating in Group Life Insurance" was expanded to provide an example of what might be done in simulating the use of credibility formulas. The assumptions and parameters used for these simulations are summarized in Table I. The Appendix presents the underwriting gain (loss) as a percent of the expected claims for each simulation performed.

The initial simulations were run using prospective experience rating only. These simulations support the analysis in Section 4. The use of credibility factors under claim level situation (1), as described in Table I, had little effect on the underwriting gain. The use of zero credibility maximized the gain for all simulations of claim level situation (2). Portfolios with claim level distribution (3) incurred losses except with full credibility of either the one-year or five-year average types. For the mixed portfolios, the results are varied. Under claim level situations (4) and (5) full credibility of either type maximized the underwriting gain. For portfolios with claim level (6) the choice of formula has little impact on the gain. The results for portfolios distributed according to claim level (7) are mixed. Two trials indicate no credibility as the best choice; the other trial indicates full credibility.

A second set of simulations was run using a combination prospective-retrospective experience rating system with several other techniques included. The results of using credibility factors with portfolios with claim level (1) indicate that the factors can have a small effect on underwriting gain. In general for these portfolios the one year formula with thirty-three to sixty-seven percent factor was better than other formulas. The claim level (2) portfolios exhibit a greater sensitivity to credibility factors. For all case sizes, the zero to thirty-three percent factors minimized the losses. The average loss was minimized by one-year, full credibility factor for all portfolios distributed in accordance with claim level situation (3). The trade off effect in portfolios with claim level distributions (4) and (5) point to a one-year factor between sixty-seven and one hundred percent. The data on claim level situation (6) strongly suggest a one-year factor near sixty-seven percent. The claim level (7) trials also point to a sixty-seven percent, one-year factor for the two larger cases. The smallest case results indicated a factor closer to thirty-three percent.

One item of note is that contrary to the usual concept of lower credibility for smaller groups, the simulation data indicates that the use of lower credibility levels for smaller groups does not necessarily maximize the underwriting gain (minimize the underwriting loss) for the size class. The distribution of true claim levels is at least as significant as size for the range of case sizes studied.

6. Conclusion

In order to determine whether or not to adopt a credibility formula and, if so, what the factors should be, the actuary needs to look farther than the theoretical justifications and calculations. He should also examine the impact of the calculated formula within the context of the insurer's entire experience rating environment. This examination should be conducted with respect to the effects the formula might have upon the attainment of the corporation's goals for the experience rating procedure. The examination should also consider the impact upon policyholder goals. One possible method of conducting this examination is simulation. Other methods need to be developed before it can be said that the actuaries are able to develop experience rating procedures that best meet the goals of the companies and of the policyholders.

The data presented strongly suggest two considerations that the actuary should be aware of when developing an experience rating system. First, the success of the system is dependent on the proper determination of the expected claims as shown by the poor performance under claim level assumptions (4) and (5). Second, the traditional concept of lower credibility for smaller cases may not prove sound for some portfolios.

Table I

Simulation Parameters

I. Case sizes used: 490 Lives; 1,000 Lives; 2,000 Lives

II. Premium Margin: 5%

III. Credibility Factors:

Situation	Factor (Z)
1.	0%
2.	33% of 1 Year's Claims
3.	67% of 1 Year's Claims
4.	100% of 1 Year's Claims
5.	33% of 5 Year Average Claims
6.	67% of 5 Year Average Claims
7.	100% of 5 Year Average Claims

IV. Claim Level Distributions: Number of cases in each claim level

	Claim Level (% of Expected)						
Situation	70%	80%	90%	100%	110%	120%	130%
1.	0	0	0	100	0	0	0
2.	0	100	0	0	0	0	0
3.	0	0	0	0	0	100	0
4.	5	10	0	50	20	10	5
5.	2	5	10	15	25	43	0
6.	5	10	20	30	20	10	50
7.	50	0	0	0	0	0	50

V. Additional Parameters for Combination Prospective-Retrospective Simulations:

A. Deficit Recovery charge equal to 10% of the deficit
B. Maximal Contingency Reserve = Expected Claims
C. Maximum Annual Increase in Contingency Reserve = 25% of Premium
D. Overall Stop-loss pooling Level = Expected Claims plus Two Standard Deviations
E. Rate Credit: 100% of Surplus
F. Cancellation Distribution

Table I (continued)

V. (continued)

Level of Deficit (D)	Probability of Cancellation
$0 < D \leq \mu$	.05
$\mu < D \leq \mu + \sigma$	.20
$\mu + \sigma < D \leq \mu + 2\sigma$	.40
$\mu + 2\sigma < D \leq \mu + 3\sigma$	.70
$\mu + 3\sigma < D$	.95

Appendix. Simulation results

This appendix contains the results of the several simulation runs. There are six tables; three for prospective-only runs, and three for combination prospective-retrospective runs. The tables give the average underwriting gain (loss) per case-year as a percent of the tabular claims for the case size.

PROSPECTIVE ONLY

490 Lives

CREDIBILITY

Claim Level	Trial	0%	33%-1 Year	67%-1 Year	100%-1 Year	33%-5 Years	67%-5 Years	100%-5 Years
1	1	7.04%	6.34%	5.59%	6.45%	6.44%	5.18%	4.90%
	2	5.91	5.24	5.17	6.52	5.40	5.28	4.85
	3	5.11	5.83	5.43	7.00	5.56	5.14	5.20
2	1	27.84	18.84	11.52	6.83	19.12	12.15	4.71
	2	27.39	18.11	11.25	6.94	18.30	11.09	4.54
	3	28.30	18.90	11.42	7.02	19.40	11.54	4.90
3	1	(10.36)	(6.42)	(.34)	6.89	(6.58)	(.57)	5.90
	2	(11.47)	(7.67)	(.99)	6.69	(7.59)	(1.53)	4.80
	3	(12.95)	(7.84)	(1.09)	6.76	(7.89)	(1.23)	5.81
4	1	6.41	4.96	4.80	6.51	4.76	4.42	5.14
	2	7.05	4.59	4.96	6.81	4.73	5.14	5.02
	3	4.69	3.69	4.43	6.80	3.62	4.11	5.14
5	1	.77	.74	2.93	6.50	.59	3.03	5.47
	2	(1.24)	(.62)	2.70	6.73	(.75)	2.49	5.20
	3	(.28)	.09	2.77	7.18	.27	2.83	5.79
6	1	7.14	7.19	6.00	6.50	6.62	5.47	5.27
	2	6.44	6.01	5.46	6.76	5.99	5.47	4.79
	3	4.88	5.52	5.20	6.91	5.41	4.95	5.14
7	1	8.19	7.46	6.04	6.86	7.17	6.21	5.38
	2	2.77	3.75	4.63	6.76	3.18	4.41	5.06
	3	6.78	6.28	5.83	6.98	6.32	5.61	5.23

PROSPECTIVE ONLY

1,000 Lives

			CREDIBILITY					
Claim Level	Trial	0%	33%-1 Year	67%-1 Year	100%-1 Year	33%-5 Years	67%-5 Years	100%-5 Years
1	1	4.99%	5.14%	5.15%	5.08%	5.26%	5.23%	5.05%
	2	5.53	5.27	5.11	5.19	5.32	4.90	4.75
	3	5.54	5.37	5.14	5.13	5.28	5.19	4.71
2	1	24.79	18.38	11.43	4.97	17.93	11.06	4.41
	2	24.80	18.17	11.15	5.02	17.55	11.01	3.82
	3	25.80	18.64	11.39	5.17	18.98	11.99	4.51
3	1	(14.77)	(8.21)	(1.43)	5.79	(7.99)	(1.04)	5.36
	2	(15.35)	(8.36)	(1.09)	5.91	(8.45)	(1.32)	5.44
	3	(14.48)	(7.89)	(1.14)	5.56	(7.58)	(.89)	5.74
4	1	1.98	2.44	4.08	5.13	2.02	4.09	5.06
	2	3.73	4.24	4.55	5.04	4.05	4.54	4.68
	3	2.70	3.36	4.25	5.21	30.6	4.37	5.18
5	1	(3.77)	(1.53)	1.98	5.52	.95	2.15	5.12
	2	(3.68)	(.54)	2.01	5.63	1.10	2.00	5.12
	3	(1.97)	.48	2.80	5.32	.54	2.77	5.55
6	1	4.66	4.61	5.16	5.11	4.78	4.93	5.10
	2	5.77	5.38	5.29	5.05	5.22	5.04	4.48
	3	4.96	4.83	5.00	5.29	4.63	5.15	5.15
7	1	7.36	6.42	5.71	5.24	6.17	5.82	4.85
	2	2.45	3.16	4.11	5.44	3.15	4.41	4.82
	3	6.62	6.00	5.61	5.57	6.10	5.61	5.33

PROSPECTIVE ONLY

2,000 Lives

CREDIBILITY

Claim Level	Trial	0%	33%-1 Year	67%-1 Year	100%-1 Year	33%-5 Years	67%-5 Years	100%-5 Years
1	1	5.87%	5.63%	5.19%	5.00%	5.56%	5.43%	5.00%
	2	4.59	4.66	5.18	5.11	4.73	4.81	4.86
	3	5.85	5.29	5.34	4.95	5.20	5.15	4.89
2	1	23.66	18.64	11.29	4.44	18.12	11.09	4.31
	2	24.71	18.63	11.32	4.34	18.59	11.14	4.06
	3	24.74	18.48	11.53	4.52	18.50	11.50	4.53
3	1	(15.44)	(8.16)	(1.51)	5.51	(8.06)	(1.45)	5.50
	2	(15.99)	(8.09)	(1.05)	5.65	(8.18)	(1.08)	5.42
	3	(14.86)	(7.23)	(.98)	5.65	(7.25)	(.72)	5.77
4	1	1.97	3.23	4.33	5.05	3.44	4.38	5.13
	2	2.56	3.95	4.78	5.08	4.13	4.49	5.11
	3	2.73	3.65	4.63	4.98	3.71	4.27	5.09
5	1	(4.62)	(1.09)	2.19	5.29	1.03	2.23	5.24
	2	(4.88)	(.62)	2.34	5.15	(.56)	2.24	5.13
	3	(2.85)	.53	2.72	5.14	.67	2.73	5.33
6	1	5.06	4.87	5.13	5.06	5.19	5.00	5.09
	2	5.87	5.48	5.43	5.10	5.57	5.25	5.12
	3	6.07	5.48	5.50	5.00	5.42	5.21	5.23
7	1	5.97	5.59	5.33	4.97	5.52	5.22	4.70
	2	2.47	3.69	4.28	4.94	3.73	4.33	4.84
	3	5.92	5.85	5.46	4.96	5.78	5.45	4.99

PROSPECTIVE-RETROSPECTIVE

1,000 Lives

CREDIBILITY

Claim Level	Trial	0%	33%-1 Year	67%-1 Year	100%-1 Year	33%-5 Years	67%-5 Years	100%-5 Years
1	1	(4.90)%	(4.18)%	(3.45)%	(4.33)%	(4.70)%	(5.36)%	(7.72)%
	2	(4.89)	(3.35)	(3.02)	(4.10)	(4.15)	(4.63)	(5.86)
	3	(4.80)	(3.49)	(3.66)	(3.93)	(4.67)	(5.11)	(5.44)
2	1	(1.31)	(1.26)	(1.70)	(4.09)	(1.53)	(2.53)	(7.16)
	2	(1.36)	(1.12)	(1.70)	(3.73)	(1.20)	(2.92)	(5.53)
	3	(1.20)	(1.22)	(1.75)	(3.95)	(1.42)	(2.66)	(6.14)
3	1	(12.66)	(7.24)	(5.41)	(4.63)	(8.81)	(8.04)	(6.65)
	2	(13.48)	(9.95)	(5.57)	(3.91)	(10.58)	(8.78)	(7.27)
	3	(12.24)	(7.21)	(5.49)	(4.64)	(10.58)	(7.70)	(6.00)
4	1	(5.45)	(4.51)	(3.04)	(4.28)	(4.99)	(5.47)	(7.63)
	2	(5.47)	(3.80)	(3.35)	(4.23)	(4.35)	(4.94)	(7.17)
	3	(5.28)	(4.01)	(3.40)	(4.80)	(5.11)	(5.75)	(6.79)
5	1	(7.80)	(4.84)	(3.82)	(4.97)	(6.08)	(5.99)	(6.97)
	2	(8.40)	(6.14)	(4.01)	(4.14)	(7.10)	(6.41)	(6.63)
	3	(6.61)	(4.16)	(3.76)	(4.37)	(6.19)	(6.23)	(6.01)
6	1	(4.06)	(3.40)	(2.75)	(4.23)	(4.04)	(4.87)	(7.30)
	2	(4.76)	(3.46)	(3.14)	(4.32)	(3.92)	(5.11)	(7.27)
	3	(4.85)	(3.56)	(3.30)	(4.60)	(4.70)	(5.45)	(6.85)
7	1	(3.56)	(2.58)	(2.26)	(2.95)	(4.04)	(4.41)	(6.13)
	2	(5.12)	(3.91)	(3.10)	(4.36)	(4.60)	(4.75)	(6.92)
	3	(4.01)	(3.51)	(2.70)	(3.95)	(4.12)	(5.47)	(6.81)

PROSPECTIVE-RETROSPECTIVE

490 Lives

CREDIBILITY

Claim Level	Trial	0%	33%-1 Year	67%-1 Year	100%-1 Year	33%-5 Years	67%-5 Years	100%-5 Years
1	1	(8.99)%	(7.82)%	(7.14)%	(8.54)%	(8.53)%	(10.14)%	(12.56)%
	2	(8.03)	(6.39)	(6.61)	(8.16)	(7.93)	(10.38)	(13.69)
	3	(8.89)	(6.98)	(7.29)	(8.68)	(8.19)	(10.27)	(11.90)
2	1	(3.97)	(3.89)	(4.80)	(6.95)	(4.43)	(7.24)	(12.85)
	2	(4.24)	(3.37)	(4.73)	(7.60)	(4.44)	(7.47)	(18.86)
	3	(3.83)	(3.75)	(4.52)	(7.56)	(4.40)	(6.37)	(11.35)
3	1	(15.82)	(13.72)	(9.62)	(7.98)	(15.62)	(13.21)	(15.73)
	2	(17.81)	(12.85)	(10.46)	(9.44)	(15.07)	(14.77)	(15.89)
	3	(21.99)	(16.40)	(11.98)	(11.71)	(18.69)	(15.72)	(14.48)
4	1	(9.68)	(9.31)	(7.19)	(8.41)	(10.43)	(11.47)	(15.07)
	2	(7.96)	(6.18)	(6.00)	(8.21)	(8.05)	(11.17)	(13.06)
	3	(10.73)	(8.88)	(8.52)	(7.72)	(10.42)	(11.89)	(14.37)
5	1	(11.37)	(10.39)	(8.48)	(8.68)	(10.44)	(11.40)	(14.17)
	2	(10.09)	(8.54)	(8.12)	(8.00)	(9.89)	(12.94)	(14.18)
	3	(14.34)	(10.35)	(8.98)	(10.52)	(12.46)	(12.42)	(13.84)
6	1	(8.72)	(7.70)	(6.22)	(8.24)	(9.64)	(10.08)	(13.81)
	2	(7.73)	(6.26)	(5.68)	(8.20)	(7.23)	(10.41)	(13.40)
	3	(8.38)	(6.39)	(6.38)	(8.72)	(10.09)	(10.68)	(14.37)
7	1	(5.94)	(5.70)	(7.12)	(7.89)	(7.79)	(9.58)	(11.26)
	2	(7.97)	(6.47)	(7.00)	(7.24)	(7.94)	(10.36)	(13.81)
	3	(7.13)	(7.34)	(7.34)	(7.76)	(8.71)	(10.39)	(13.21)

PROSPECTIVE-RETROSPECTIVE

2,000 Lives

CREDIBILITY

Claim Level	Trial	0%	33%-1 Year	67%-1 Year	100%-1 Year	33%-5 Years	67%-5 Years	100%-5 Years
1	1	(2.14)%	(.92)%	(.92)%	(1.25)%	(1.32)%	(1.32)%	(1.86)%
	2	(2.11)	(1.41)	(.78)	(1.59)	(1.90)	(1.52)	(1.97)
	3	(1.67)	(.96)	(.68)	(1.32)	(1.23)	(1.33)	(1.83)
2	1	(.17)	(.22)	(.45)	(1.38)	(.25)	(.50)	(2.10)
	2	(.15)	(.12)	(.32)	(1.02)	(.24)	(.37)	(1.45)
	3	(.20)	(.15)	(.39)	(1.28)	(.33)	(.45)	(1.65)
3	1	(10.35)	(5.74)	(1.99)	(1.23)	(6.98)	(3.68)	(2.21)
	2	(10.88)	(6.03)	(1.90)	(1.12)	(7.63)	(3.68)	(1.96)
	3	(11.06)	(5.72)	(2.40)	(1.37)	(7.19)	(3.67)	(2.14)
4	1	(2.78)	(1.29)	(1.08)	(1.16)	(1.83)	(1.50)	(1.70)
	2	(2.29)	(1.72)	(1.23)	(1.37)	(1.93)	(1.75)	(1.65)
	3	(2.30)	(1.49)	(.89)	(1.27)	(1.74)	(1.25)	(1.67)
5	1	(4.39)	(2.34)	(1.33)	(1.54)	(3.15)	(2.46)	(1.99)
	2	(4.78)	(3.11)	(1.38)	(1.34)	(4.10)	(3.15)	(2.14)
	3	(3.91)	(2.40)	(1.32)	(1.52)	(2.86)	(2.19)	(1.86)
6	1	(2.29)	(1.23)	(.93)	(1.18)	(1.18)	(1.61)	(1.73)
	2	(1.73)	(1.29)	(1.12)	(1.39)	(1.33)	(1.56)	(1.66)
	3	(2.06)	(1.45)	(.94)	(1.16)	(1.80)	(1.34)	(1.63)
7	1	(2.27)	(1.68)	(.94)	(1.36)	(1.79)	(1.27)	(1.72)
	2	(2.97)	(2.44)	(1.30)	(1.21)	(2.56)	(1.80)	(1.92)
	3	(2.36)	(1.67)	(.92)	(1.34)	(1.78)	(1.34)	(1.62)

Discussion by Paul H. Jackson of Credibility and Group Experience

This paper discusses the desirability of having a correct estimate for each group's true claim level. The authors' results can be viewed as suggesting that where the actuary has set the expected level of claims on the high side, the insurance company will maximize profit if it uses the lowest credibility possible because that will minimize the return of surplus to policyholders. Conversely, where the actuary has set the expected claims on the low side, the insurance company will be better off with the highest possible credibility because that forces a re-rating of cases to the higher level and would recover deficiencies at the most rapid rate.

The authors set forth several goals for experience rating. Their first is that the insurar should charge an adequate and equitable premium, and in practice it is necessary for this standard to be applied on both a retrospective and prospective basis. If the premiums are set at such an ideal level, however, then anti-selection is automatically minimized and the authors' third goal is redundant. The second goal suggested is the maximization of underwriting gains but this must be on an absolute dollar basis because the possibility of cancellation increases as past profit increases as a percentage of premium. The authors' third goal is stated in terms of credibility factors, but in practice, individual groups do not base their decisions on anything so arcane as credibility factors (which indeed they rarely know) but rather on the net retention and prospective premium level and while these do vary with the selection of credibility factors, as a goal there would appear to be no difference between the authors' third goal and their first. Restated for practical application, the insurer's goal should be (1) to charge each case a fair premium prospectively, (2) to have retained a fair premium in retrospect, and (3) to maximize the dollars of profit over the long run.

In discussing the three types of cases, the authors observe that where the true claim level is less than the expected claim level, the expected underwriting gain will decrease as the credibility factor increases. As part and parcel of this process, however, the probability of cancellation also decreases as the credibility factor increases. Thus, the insurer who wishes to maximize dollar profit will not simply be able to use zero credibility for this class of case.

The simulation results are subject to many interpretations but offer an interesting array of numbers to study. First, on a prospective basis, it should be obvious that one hundred percent credibility will develop the most stable results under all claim levels because there is an implication that each case is then perfectly rated prospectively. Similarly, zero credibility develops the most inequitable results prospectively. The prospective-retrospective tables can be viewed as setting forth the minimum level of premium loading that must be added to expenses if the insurer wishes to break even after one year of operation. Subsequent profits would then arise from recovery of deficits. In all of these tables, the variation by credibility factors is considerably less than the variation "claim level" which, in reality, is the variation in the establishment of possible premium levels.

The authors observe that with zero credibility there is

no chance fluctuation in premium levels and present this as an additional consideration for the insurer. In reality, the fluctuation in premiums is totally irrelevant because the insurer is interested in the fluctuation in the quantity (premium-claim) and fluctuation in this quantity decreases with an increase in credibility.

In the final analysis, the data presented by the authors shows clearly that if the actuary is going to set an incorrect level of expected claims, the company is better off if he sets it on the high side. The authors appear to conclude that the traditional concept of low credibility for smaller cases is not true if the actuary consistently underestimates claim levels. High credibility, however, merely offers mechanical means for correcting the initial mistake in setting premiums as rapidly as possible. The prospective-retrospective results would have been more useful if a risk charge had been included to develop the insurer's profit goal, in lieu of a return credit of one hundred percent of surplus, and if the probability of cancellation had been assumed to increase with an increase in retention. Finally, the variation by size of case seems unnecessarily small (490, 1,000 and 2,000 lives) where a simulation process is being used and certainly, results for twenty-five or fifty lives would be necessary in order to draw any conclusions about the soundness of the traditional concept of lower credibility for "smaller" cases. The authors present a lot of numerical results, which are of course illuminating, but their interpretation in greater depth would have been helpful to the practitioner.

Statistical Decision Theory and Credibility Theory Procedures

Leonard Freifelder

1. Introduction

The purpose of this paper is to present some results in credibility theory developed, in part, from the concepts and procedures of statistical decision theory. In the interest of brevity the various results are presented without proof. Further details are available from my Ph.D. dissertation, soon to be published by the Huebner Foundation of The University of Pennsylvania.

Ten years ago Allan Mayerson (1964a) resurrected some earlier work of Arthur Bailey (1945) in which the basic credibility theory equation was developed from a principle now known as conjugate prior analysis. The Bayesian approach to credibility theory soon became a quite acceptable technique. Bailey's original result was generalized by Jewell (1974a) who showed that the basic equation $ZA + (1 - Z)B$ can be derived for many conjugate pairs, not just the Beta-Bernoulli or the Gamma-Poisson cases. It is not my intention to investigate these points again. Those readers who are interested in these areas should read the paper James C. Hickman included in this collection.

Currently credibility theory is viewed as a method for estimating various moments or parameters of the probability distribution of total losses. It does not matter very much whether one derives his estimates of these quantities from the classical insurance approach (Whitney (1918), etc.) or from Bayesian principles, because in the most important cases, the revised estimate has the familiar form $ZA + (1 - Z)B$. However, it is important to recognize that ultimately these credibility-adjusted values are used to tell the insurer what he should charge in the future.

As we all know, an insurance premium has three basic components: (1) a charge for expected dollar claims, (2) a charge for insurer expenses, and (3) a charge for risk. If item (2), the expense loading, is ignored, it is clear that current credibility procedures are fine for item (1) which involves only the calculation of an expected value. It is traditional in insurance ratemaking to base the risk charge on the expected value. Thus, the current credibility procedures are acceptable for anyone who believes that a constant percentage of the expected value is an accurate risk charge.

However, the expected value is not a measure of risk and a constant percentage of the expected value cannot and does not lead to accurate risk charges. Some might suggest instead that the risk charge be based on the variance. Unfortunately the variance is not always a good risk measure (Hanoch and Levy, 1969). The best method of measuring risk is through utility theory. By developing a corporate utility function, the company can determine an accurate charge for risk. This paper shows how credibility theory adjustments should be made, if the corporate utility function is known and the principles of statistical decision theory are used.

2. The corporate utility function

Those readers familiar with the literature in utility theory know that it is difficult to determine a corporate utility function. However, the problem is simplified substantially if a specific functional form can be assumed. For ratemaking decisions, the exponential utility function $u(x) = \frac{1}{r}(1 - e^{-rx})$ is a particularly good choice. x measures the insurer's wealth and r measures the company's aversion to risk.

The exponential utility function is selected, because it is the only utility function that satisfies the following proposed ratemaking standard, which suggest that,

> An insurance company should use ratemaking proceduces capable of pricing individual contracts, where the rates contain an appropriate risk charge, are fair to all insureds and are independent of all considerations except anticipated claims experience.

The term individual refers to the smallest unit for the type of coverage under consideration. This is not necessarily a single person or object. The risk charge is appropriate if it leads to rates that are adequate, but at the same time are also not excessive. The concept of fairness requires that the rate structure be designed to make <u>all</u> applicants and policyholders equally desirable. Finally, if rates are independent of all considerations except anticipated claims experience, the premium rate will not depend on the size of the portfolio or the order in which the contracts are issued.

The proposed ratemaking standard is translated into the following set of ratemaking axioms.

Axiom 1: Rates should be calculated on individual contracts and should be based on their probability of loss distribution.

Axiom 2: Rates should contain a risk charge and the premium rates should accurately reflect the company's preferences.

Axiom 3:
a. Rates should not discriminate among the policyholders within the same class or the policyholders of different classes.

b. If the losses on two contracts are independent

random variables, the premium rates should not depend on the order in which the policies enter the portfolio.

The only utility function satisfying Axioms 1-3 is the exponential utility function.

To calculate rates the following rule is used,

$$u(x) = \int u(x + P - z)dF(z) \tag{1}$$

where the utility of the current position, i.e. rejecting the application, is equated to the expected utility after accepting the policy. P is the premium and $F(z)$ is the probability distribution of total losses. The indifference relationship shown above is an accepted method for making utility theory decisions. For all utility functions except the exponential,[1] equation (1) will yield the correct rate only if it is assumed that there are no other contracts in the portfolio and that the company's wealth is known. There are no "portfolio" or "wealth" effects with an exponential utility function. What this means is that with an exponential utility theory ratemaking model, the decision maker does not have to know the exact characteristics of the company's portfolio or its wealth. In practical situations the above information is not generally available.

Two other properties of the exponential utility theory model are worth mentioning. The first concerns premium calculation. Substituting $u(x) = \frac{1}{r}(1 - e^{-rx})$ into equation (1), it is easy to derive the following equation for premium P.

---

[1]The linear utility function $u(x) = x$ is a special case of the exponential obtained as $\lim_{r \to 0} \frac{1}{r}(1 - e^{-rx})$.

$$P = \frac{1}{r} \ln \int e^{rz} \, dF(z) \tag{2}$$

(2) can be written as,

$$P = \frac{1}{r} \ln M_z(r) \tag{3}$$

since

$$\int e^{tz} \, dF(z) = M_z(t) \, .$$

The other property describes the relationship between class and individual premium rates. This result is stated as an easily-proven theorem.

Theorem 1. If premium rates are based on an exponential utility function, the total premium required for a class of independent contracts is equal to the sum of the premiums required for each of the contracts individually.

3. The true individual premium and the a priori premium

It is useful for the purposes of this paper to define and illustrate the three different types of insurance premiums. These are,

1. The True Individual Premium
2. The A Priori Premium
3. The Experience-Adjusted Premium

The last two are actually the same type of premium, but take different amounts of information into account. The first two are discussed in this section and the last in the next section.

The true individual premium represents the theoretically correct rate the company should charge to insure a given individual. To develop this exact rate, the company must know both the form of the probability distribution of total losses and the parameters of this distribution. If this information is available, the true individual premium can be calculated. It should also be noted that if the true individual premium is known, there would be no reason to make credibility theory adjustments, because the rate being charged is correct.

A basic assumption of credibility theory is that some of the above information is unavailable. Generally the actual values of the parameters of the probability distribution of total losses are unknown. In such cases the premium that the company charges is called the a priori premium. The a priori premium represents the decision maker's best estimate of the true individual premium. The a priori premium requires that the loss process probability distribution be known and that the company can define a probability distribution for the values of the unknown parameters of this loss process. Information about the probability distribution of the parameters and the loss process distribution is usually drawn from the data on a population of similar contracts.

Let us illustrate these ideas with an example. Suppose both the frequency and the severity of accidents are random variables. Let n = the number of claims, where $E(n) = \mu$ and let x = the size of a claim with $E(x) = 1/\lambda$. Assume the relevant distributions are as follows:

$$\begin{aligned} f(n|\mu) &= \mu^n e^{-\mu}/n!, \qquad n = 0,1,2,\ldots \\ f(x|\lambda) &= \lambda e^{-\lambda x}, \qquad x \geq 0 \end{aligned} \tag{4}$$

Let the random variable z = total contract losses. $z = \sum_{i=1}^{n} x_i$ and $z = 0$ if $n = 0$. If μ and λ are known, the true individual premium can be determined. $f(z|\mu,\lambda)$ is only important in order to determine the moment generating function of z. Let us use the notation $M_z(r)$ for the moment generating function of $f(z|\mu,\lambda)$.

$$M_z(r) = \exp(\mu r/\lambda - r) \tag{5}$$

Substituting into (3) gives

$$P(z|\mu,\lambda) = \mu/(\lambda - r) \tag{6}$$

as the true individual premium.

However, if either μ or λ is unknown $P(z|\mu,\lambda)$ cannot be determined. Suppose μ is unknown, but that μ has the probability distribution,

$$f(\mu|a,b) = \frac{b^a}{\Gamma(a)}\mu^{a-1}e^{-b\mu}, \qquad \mu > 0 \tag{7}$$

The a priori premium is found by determining the distribution of z unconditional of μ. This distribution is $f(z|\lambda,a,b) = \int f(z|\mu,\lambda)f(\mu|a,b)d\mu$. The calculation though somewhat lengthy is straightforward. Here again only the moment generating function $M'_z(r)$ is shown.

$$M'_z(r) = \left[\frac{b(\lambda - r)}{(b + 1)(\lambda - r) - \lambda}\right]^a \tag{8}$$

The premium $P'(z)$ is

$$P'(z) = \frac{a}{r}\ln\left(\frac{b(\lambda - r)}{(b + 1)(\lambda - r) - \lambda}\right) \tag{9}$$

The a priori premium $P'(z)$ is greater than the true individual premium $P(z)$. This is a general result and is proved by using Jensen's inequality. The result holds because the true individual premium contains only one risk charge, while the a priori premium contains two. If the insurer knows both the loss process and its parameters, he charges the true individual premium. The only information he doesn't know is actual claims and the risk charge compensates the insurer for this uncertainty. If the insurer doesn't know the loss process parameters, he charges the a priori premium. Of course, he is now uncertain about two things - the parameters of the loss process and the actual claims - and the risk charge must compensate for both. Another way of describing this situation is that when the parameter values are unknown, the insurer is uncertain about how much risk he has assumed. Consequently he is in a situation of greater uncertainty and he must charge more for risk.

To show these ideas more clearly a numerical example is given. Suppose expected severity is known and is \$2380.95 = $1/\lambda$. Suppose expected frequency is $E(\mu) = .15514$. To calculate the true individual premium we assume μ is known and equal to .15514. For the a priori premium a Gamma prior distribution with parameters $a = .99584$, $b = 6.41895$ is used. In Table 1 the two premiums are shown as a function of the corporation's risk aversion. The a priori premium exceeds the true individual when the company is averse to risk $(r > 0)$.

4. The experience-adjusted premium and credibility theory

The experience-adjusted premium is very similar to the a priori premium. The former, however, considers both the prior information about the parameters of the loss process and the actual loss experience observed during the policy period. A posterior probability distribution for the values of the unknown parameters is developed by combining both pieces of information - the prior or original distribution and the data on actual losses. The experience-adjusted premium is calculated from the posterior distribution in exactly the same way the a priori premium was calculated from the prior distribution.

A statistical decision theory procedure called terminal analysis is used to determine the experience-adjusted premium. Terminal analysis is, "...the evaluation of and choice among terminal acts after the experiment has (actually or hypothetically) already been conducted and the outcome y observed;..." (Raiffa and Schlaifer 1961). The "terminal act" in this case is the selection of the value for the experience-adjusted premium. The experiment is to insure one

Table 1

A Comparison of the True Individual Premium and the a Priori Premium as a Function of Corporate Risk Aversion

r	A priori Premium (9)	True Individual Premium (6)
.00025	$1036.50	$912.59
.00020	760.40	705.18
.00018	687.41	646.42
.00016	627.27	596.69
.00014	576.84	554.07
.00012	533.95	517.14
.00010	497.01	484.81
.00009	480.40	470.12
.00008	464.87	456.30
.00007	450.31	443.26
.00006	436.64	430.95
.00005	423.78	419.30
.00004	411.65	408.26
.00003	400.20	397.80
.00002	389.37	387.85
.00001	379.11	378.38
.00000	369.38	369.38

or more people and the outcome y is to observe the actual loss experience.

Terminal analysis can be illustrated by continuing the example that was developed earlier. Suppose an applicant whose loss distributions are as shown in (4) and (7) is offered and accepts insurance for $P'(z) = \frac{a}{r}\ln\left(\frac{b(\lambda - r)}{(b+1)(\lambda - r) - \lambda}\right)$. Now assume that in a period of time t, m accidents are observed.[2] The probability of this event is

$$f(m|\mu,t) = \frac{(\mu t)^m e^{-\mu t}}{m!} \qquad (10)$$

The posterior distribution of μ, $f''(\mu)$ for short, is derived by combining (7) and (10)

$$f''(\mu) = \frac{f(m|\mu,t)f'(\mu|a,b)}{\int_\mu f(m|\mu,t)f'(\mu|a,b)d\mu}$$

$$f''(\mu) = \frac{(b+t)^{a+m}}{\Gamma(a+m)}\mu^{a+m-1}e^{-(b+t)\mu}, \quad \mu > 0 \qquad (11)$$

The experience-adjusted premium is calculated from $f''(z|\lambda,a,b)$ using $f''(\mu)$, and is

$$P''(z) = \frac{a+m}{r}\ln\left[\frac{(b+t)(\lambda - r)}{(b+t+1)(\lambda - r) - \lambda}\right] \qquad (12)$$

Comparing (9) and (12) shows the similarity of the a priori premium and the experience-adjusted premium. $P''(z)$ represents the price for the next period.

An important credibility theory concept is the idea of partial credibility. The partial credibility a body of experience receives reflects the data's acceptability for ratemaking purposes and measures its reliability as a

---

[2] It is not important to know the value of $\sum_{i=1}^{m} m_i$, where x_i = the cost of claim i, because with λ known, the difference between m/λ and $\sum_{i=1}^{m} x_i$ is due entirely to chance.

basis for estimating the unknown premium.[3] The Bayesian approach does not have a concept analogous to partial credibility, although in many cases a simple weighting scheme is used to combine the observed data and the prior information. By using the terminal analysis procedure, the proper weighting for the partially credible data is automatically made and is reflected in the experience-adjusted premium.

In the problem we have been considering, $P'(z)$ is originally charged because μ is unknown. At this time μ is estimated to be $\frac{a}{b}$, the expected value from $f(\mu|a,b)$. After a period of experience, $P'(z)$ from $f''(\mu)$ is charged and the estimate of μ is $\frac{a+m}{b+t}$. A third estimate for μ, based on the actual data is $\frac{m}{t}$. The estimate $\frac{a+m}{b+t}$ is derived by combing the other two estimates. To find the weight assigned to each, write $\frac{a+m}{b+t}$ as a linear combination of $\frac{a}{b}$ and $\frac{m}{t}$

$$\frac{a+m}{b+t} = \frac{a}{b}(1 - Z) + \frac{m}{t}Z \qquad (13)$$

The solution to (13) is $Z = \frac{t}{b+t}$, $(1 - Z) = \frac{b}{b+t}$. Z and $(1 - Z)$ can be described as the partial credibility of the observed data and the prior information. The experience-adjusted premium is not, however, a linear combination of the a priori premium and a premium based on the actual data. The experience-adjusted premium is less than this linear combination (using $Z = \frac{t}{b+t}$), a result which can be proved in general by using Jensen's inequality.

Some values for the experience-adjusted premium are shown in Table 2.

[3] Two partial credibility formulas are now used in insurance. For a review of these procedures, the reader should see Longley-Cook (1962).

Table 2

The Experience-Adjusted Premium

Risk Aversion Constant		= .00004
Expected Claim Size		= \$2857.14
Expected Claim Frequency		= .15514 (from prior distribution)
Gamma Prior Distribution Parameters	a	= .99584
	b	= 6.41895

No. of Claims	No. of Years of Exposure	Experience-Adjusted Premium (12)
0	0.0	\$505.55
0	0.5	468.67
0	1.0	436.67
1	0.5	939.30
1	1.0	875.44
1	3.0	688.26
1	5.0	567.03
2	5.0	851.13

The prior distribution says that the company can expect 1 claim every 6.5 years on this policy.

If this is correct, the events 0 claims in .5 years, 0 claims in 1 year, or 1 claim in 5 years are not unusual and the experience-adjusted premium stays relatively the same. On the other hand, unlikely events, which imply μ is greater than .15514, do change the experience-adjusted premium substantially. However, the amount of the change does depend on the credibility of the actual experience. For example, 2 accidents in 5 years, implying $\mu = .4$, produces almost the same rate as 1 accident in 1 year, where the estimate for μ is $2\frac{1}{2}$ times greater. This is because the loss experience in the former case is more credible than the loss experience in the latter situation.

The final topic is that of full credibility. It is clear that theoretically no data deserve to be considered fully credible, i.e. $Z = 1$. Credibilities should asymptotically approach 1 as more data becomes available, as at the same time the experience-adjusted premium will approach the true individual premium. However, since the loss distributions a company faces are non-stationary because conditions change over time, I believe insurers do have reason to ignore information developed in previous years and base their ratemaking decisions on only recent data. A full credibility standard accomplishes this purpose by telling the company how much data must be collected before the experience of earlier periods can be ignored.[4]

Before presenting the definition of full credibility, some premium concepts must be developed. Let $P'(K)$ be the experience-adjusted premium as described earlier, where K represents the data that is to be observed. Let $P^*(K)$ be a special type of experience-adjusted premium, which is based on the data and a "no-information" prior distribution. When a company charges $P^*(K)$, the premium is based on the data alone for the "no-information" prior distribution assumes the company has no information about the possible values of the unknown parameters. The no information state is characterized by a uniform prior distribution, which implies all parameter values are equally likely.

Definition: Full Credibility of the Data K

The data K are said to be fully credible if

---

[4]Another method of handling this problem was presented at the conference by Dr. Greg Taylor. His approach involved modelling the process of change over time, and retaining all the loss experience.

$$|E_K(P'(K)) - E_K(P^*(K))| < \varepsilon$$

where ε is a small monetary amount (e.g. \$1.00, \$.10, or \$.01) and $P^*(K)$ is based on a uniform prior distribution.

A company using this standard will collect data until the expected no-information experience-adjusted premium has approximately the same value as the expected experience-adjusted premium when prior information is not ignored.

A statistical decision theory technique called pre-posterior analysis is used to determine the amount of data that satisfied the full credibility definition. The procedure has three steps:

1. Terminal analysis, to determine $P'(K)$ and $P^*(K)$.
2. Calculation of the probability distribution of K, $f(K) = \int f(K|\alpha)f(\alpha)d\alpha$, where α represents the loss process parameters.
3. Calculation of $E_K(P''(K))$ and $E_K(P^*(K))$, to establish the minimum size of an experiment deserving full credibility.

These three steps are shown below.

1. Terminal Analysis

The experience-adjusted premium is given by (12).

$$P'(m) = \frac{a + m}{r} \ln\left[\frac{(b + t)(\lambda - r)}{(b + t + 1)(\lambda - r) - \lambda}\right]$$

For $a = 1$, the Gamma prior distribution approaches the uniform as b approaches 0.

$$P^*(m) = \frac{1 + m}{r} \ln\left[\frac{t(\lambda - r)}{(t + 1)(\lambda - r) - \lambda}\right] \tag{14}$$

2. The Distribution of m

$$f(m) = \int f(m|\mu,t)f'(\mu|a,b)d\mu$$

$f(m|\mu,t)$ is a Poisson distribution and $f'(\mu|a,b)$ is a Gamma distribution. The result for $f(m)$ has been shown by many authors (Dropkin, 1959) and is

$$f(m) = \frac{\Gamma(a+m)}{m!\Gamma(a)} \left(\frac{b}{b+t}\right)^{a} \left(\frac{t}{b+t}\right)^{m}, \quad m = 0,1,\ldots \quad (15)$$

3. The Full Credibility Standard

$$E_m(P''(m)) = \frac{a + E(m)}{r} \ln\left[\frac{(b+t)(\lambda - r)}{(b+t+1)(\lambda - r) - \lambda}\right]$$

$$E_m(P^*(m)) = \frac{1 + E(m)}{r} \ln\left[\frac{t(\lambda - r)}{(t+1)(\lambda - r) - \lambda}\right]$$

Since $E(m) = at/b$,

$$\left|\frac{a(b+t)}{br} \ln\left[\frac{(b+t)(\lambda-r)}{(b+t)(\lambda-r)-\lambda}\right] - \frac{b+at}{r} \ln\left[\frac{t(\lambda-r)}{(t+1)(\lambda-r)-\lambda}\right]\right| < \varepsilon$$

is the full credibility standard.

Some interesting numerical results can now be presented. The calculation of $E_m(P''(m))$ and $E_m(P^*(m))$ is straightforward and Table 3 shows how ε changes as a function of t, the number of exposures. If $\varepsilon = \$1.00$, the insurer needs at least 3250 exposures to assure that the expected premium based on the data and a no-information prior is within \$1.00 of a similar expected value based on both the data and the prior. For $\varepsilon = \$.10$, t is 35000, while 300,000 exposures are needed for $\varepsilon = \$.01$. The expected number of claims is $.15514 = \frac{a}{b}$. The company would expect 504.2 claims for 3250 exposures; 5429.9 claims on 35000 exposures; and 46542 claims with 300,000 exposures.

Because these full credibility values are specific to this prior distribution and are a function of λ and r, Table 4 gives the reader some idea of the sensitivity of the full credibility value. ε is \$1.00.

Table 3

A Comparison of $E_m(P''(m))$ and $E_m(P^*(m))$ as a Function of the Number of Exposures

Parameters of Gamma Prior Distribution : a = .99584, b = 6.41895

Risk Aversion Constant = .00004

Expected Claim Size = $2857.14

Number of Exposures t	Expected Experience Adjusted Premium $E_m(P''(m))$	Expected No - Information Premium $E_m(P^*(m))$	$\lvert E_m(P''(m))-E_m(P^*(m))\rvert$ ε
50	$501.03	$565.70	$64.67
100	500.76	533.06	32.30
500	500.52	506.97	6.45
1000	500.49	503.71	3.22
2000	500.47	502.08	1.61
3000	500.46	501.54	1.08
3250	500.46	501.46	1.00
10000	500.46	500.78	.32
25000	500.45	500.58	.13
35000	500.45	500.55	.10
100000	500.45	500.49	.04
200000	500.45	500.47	.02
300000	500.45	500.46	.01

Table 4

The Sensitivity of the Full Credibility Value to Changes in the Basic Parameters

Prior Distribution Parameters a	Prior Distribution Parameters b	Expected Severity λ	Risk Aversion r	Expected Experience - Adjusted Premium $E_m(P'(m))$	No. of exposures t
.99584	6.41895	.00035	.00004	\$500.46	3250
|	|	.00042	.00004	408.27	2650
|	|	.00030	.00004	596.71	3850
|	|	.00035	.00003	484.02	3125
|	|	.00035	.00007	554.09	3550
|	|	.00035	.00015	775.76	5000

These results are fairly easy to interpret. The full credibility standard should increase with r, because r measures corporate risk aversion. The more risk averse a company is, the more conservative its decisions. In terms of full credibility standards this would mean the company would require more data before it is willing to discard the prior information. Changes in λ work the other way, because larger λ implies a lower average cost per claim. When the average cost per claim decreases, the insurer's risk diminishes. Raising λ thus has the same effect as lowering r and therefore the full credibility value varies inversely with λ.

5. Summary and conclusions

Credibility theory has been reexamined in this paper through a ratemaking model based on utility theory and statistical decision theory. By using the procedures outlined in the preceding section, the decision maker can make partial credibility adjustments and select full credibility values that are based on the premiums he is charging and which reflect the risk he feels he is assuming. The numerical illustrations indicate that all the procedures are easy to use in realistic situations.

The more familiar developments of credibility theory work with the moments of the probability distribution of total losses under the assumption that knowing the value of these moments is sufficient to lead to accurate ratemaking. Even in those special cases where the assumption is correct (e.g. for normally distributed loss distributions), traditional credibility theory provides no mechanism for adjusting the indicated values to account for differences in aversion to risk. Under traditional procedures, conservative and not-so-conservative companies must use the same credibility values.

The results presented in this paper were based on the use of an exponential utility function to describe the company's risk behavior. Although the procedures are not dependent on a particular utility function, the exponential utility function is a particularly tractable form. Mathematical simplicity was not the most compelling reason for selecting this utility function. It was chosen because the exponential utility function is the only utility function that satisfies a set of axioms that describe how insurance companies should and do make rates.

One other area was developed in the paper. This concerned the various types of premiums and the informational requirements for each. The true individual premium represents the proper rate for a given policy. Both the a priori premium and the experience-adjusted premium use varying amounts of information in an attempt to estimate the true individual premium. Table 1 showed a comparison of the a priori premium and the true individual premium.

Credibility Formulas of the Updating Type

Hans U. Gerber and Donald A. Jones
The University of Michigan

1. Introduction

Let $S_1, S_2, S_3, \ldots$ be a sequence of random variables, for which we know their joint distribution. We assume that the first two moments of these random variables exist. In applications of this model, S_n is interpreted as the claims produced by a given policyholder in year n (although in many applications S_n could be the loss ratio in year n or the time period could be other than a year).

The basic problem of credibility theory in prospective ratemaking is: Given the outcomes of $S_1, S_2, \ldots, S_n$ (the claims experience of the first n years), establish an appropriate premium P_{n+1} for year $n + 1$.

The most popular solutions to this problem can be devised by the method of least squares, in which P_{n+1} is defined as the random variable X that solves the problem

$$\text{Minimize} \quad E[(X - S_{n+1})^2] \tag{1}$$

subject to the constraint that X be a member of a given class of random variables, say H (which usually is a linear space of square integrable random variables that form a Hilbert-Space). The choice of H determines the resulting premium P_{n+1}, which is illustrated by the following three examples.

<u>Example 1.</u> Let H_1 be the set of all real numbers, i.e., we demand that the X in (1) be a constant.

By differentiating (1) with respect to X, we see that the resulting premium is:

$$P_{n+1} = E[S_{n+1}] \tag{2}$$

Example 2. Let H_2 be the set of all square-integrable functions of $S_1, S_2, \ldots, S_n$. The resulting premium is now the conditional expected value

$$P_{n+1} = E[S_{n+1} | S_1, \ldots, S_n] \tag{3}$$

Example 3. Let H_3 be the set of all square-integrable functions of $S_1, S_2, \ldots, S_{n+1}$. The resulting premium is obviously

$$P_{n+1} = S_{n+1} \tag{4}$$

The method of least squares dates back about two thousand years in Euclidean geometry where it may be represented graphically. The following substitutions allow us to utilize this representation to summarize the results of the three examples graphically in Figure 1.

H_1	- x-axis
H_2	- xy-plane
H_3	- xyz-three dimensional space
$\sqrt{E[(X - S_{n+1})^2]}$	- Euclidean distance between X and S_{n+1}
P_{n+1}	- orthogonal projection of S_{n+1} on H_i

2. Linear credibility formulas

Each of the preceding examples has its shortcomings. Example 1 ignores the available claims experience, while Example 3 requires the knowledge of S_{n+1}, which is of course unknown in advance! The premium of Example 2 is satisfactory in theory. However, it requires complete

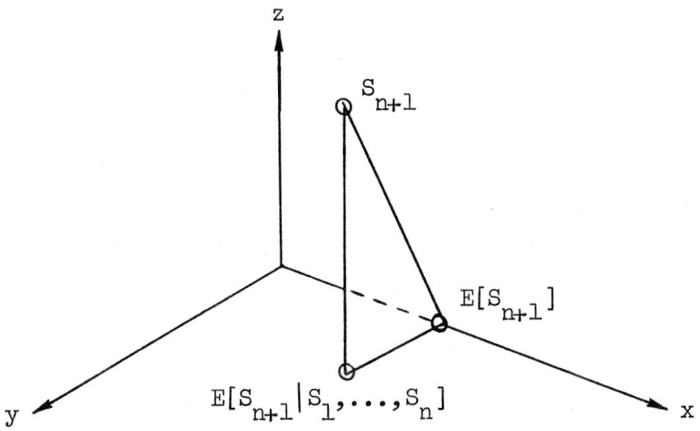

Figure 1

knowledge of the joint distribution of $(S_1,S_2,\ldots,S_{n+1})$, depends substantially on this distribution, and quite often is of an analytical form that has little appeal to the practitioner.

For these reasons most authors have assumed that H is the class of all linear functions of $S_1,\ldots,S_n$,

$$X = b_o + \sum_{i=1}^{n} b_i S_i \ . \tag{5}$$

In the following we shall adopt this assumption so problem (1) reduces to the minimization of

$$E\left[\left(b_o + \sum_{i=1}^{n} b_i S_i - S_{n+1}\right)^2\right]. \tag{6}$$

By definition of the class H, the resulting premium will be of the form

$$P_{n+1} = {}_na_o + \sum_{i=1}^{n} {}_na_i S_i \tag{7}$$

and therefore acceptable as far as simplicity is concerned.

A system of linear equations for the coefficients ${}_na_o, {}_na_1, \ldots, {}_na_n$ may be obtained by setting the $n + 1$ partial derivatives of (6) equal to zero. From the partial derivative with respect to b_o we get

$$ {}_n a_o + \sum_{i=1}^{n} {}_n a_i E[S_i] = E[S_{n+1}] \tag{8} $$

and from the other partial derivatives we obtain the equations

$$ {}_n a_o E[S_j] + \sum_{i=1}^{n} {}_n a_i E[S_i S_j] = E[S_j S_{n+1}] \tag{9} $$

for $j = 1,2,\ldots,n$. Furthermore, if we multiply the members of equation (8) by $E[S_j]$ and subtract it term by term from the corresponding equation (9), we get the equations

$$ \sum_{i=1}^{n} {}_n a_i \operatorname{Cov}[S_i, S_j] = \operatorname{Cov}[S_j, S_{n+1}] \tag{10} $$

for $j = 1,2,\ldots,n$. This is a linear system of n equations for the n credibility coefficients ${}_n a_1, {}_n a_2, \ldots, {}_n a_n$. In the sequel we shall assume that the matrix of this system, i.e., the covariance matrix of $(S_1,\ldots,S_n)$ is non-singular for every n (which guarantees a unique solution for these credibility coefficients). In turn, equation (8) may be solved for ${}_n a_o$.

3. Credibility formulas of the updating type

In the preceding section it was shown that linear credibility formula (7) require knowledge of only the first and second order moments of the distribution of total claims. We shall study the relationship between the expected value vector and the covariance matrix on the one side and the type of credibility formula on the other side.

Definition. A linear credibility formula is said to be of the updating type, if there is a sequence $Z_1, Z_2, \ldots$ of real numbers such that

$$ P_{n+1} = (1 - Z_n)P_n + Z_n S_n \, . \tag{11} $$

Remarks. A condition equivalent to (11) is that

$$ P_{n+1} - P_n = Z_n(S_n - P_n) \tag{12} $$

which shows that the premium adjustment from year n to year $n + 1$ is proportional to the excess of claims over premiums in year n.

The following two examples are of the updating type.

1) Geometric credibility weights. If $Z_n = Z$ (independent of n) repeated application of formula (11) shows that

$$ {}_na_i = Z(1 - Z)^{n-i} \tag{13} $$

for $i = 1,2,\ldots,n$.

2) Uniform credibility weights. If

$$ Z_n = \frac{W}{nW + V} \tag{14} $$

for $n = 1,2,\ldots,$ and certain constants $V > 0$, $W > 0$, repeated application of formula (11) shows that

$$ {}_na_1 = {}_na_2 = \cdots = {}_na_n = \frac{W}{nW + V} . \tag{15} $$

The following theorem characterizes the expected value vectors and the covariance matrices that lead to credibility formulas of the updating type.

Theorem 1. The credibility formula is of the updating type, if there exists a number μ and sequences $V_1, V_2, \ldots$ and $W_1, W_2, \ldots$ such that

$$ E[S_i] = \mu \tag{16} $$

$$ \mathrm{Cov}[S_i, S_j] = \begin{cases} V_i + W_i & \text{if } i = j \\ W_i & \text{if } i < j \end{cases} \tag{17} $$

for $j = i, i + 1, \ldots$ and $i = 1,2,\ldots$

Proof. 1) For a credibility formula of the updating type, we want to show the validity of formulas (16) and (17). Comparing equations (7) and (8) we see that $E[S_{n+1}] = E[P_{n+1}]$ for all n. From these equalities and those obtained by taking expected values in equation (11) it follows that $E[S_{n+1}] = E[S_n]$ for all n, which is equivalent to formula (16).

Formula (11) means that ${}_n a_n = Z_n$ and that

$$ {}_n a_j = (1 - Z_n)\, {}_{n-1}a_j \tag{18} $$

for $j = 0,1,\ldots,n - 1$. From these and formula (10), we get, for $j = 1,\ldots,n - 1$ and all n, that

$$ \begin{aligned} \mathrm{Cov}[S_j,S_{n+1}] &= \sum_{i=1}^{n} {}_n a_i \,\mathrm{Cov}[S_i,S_j] \qquad (19) \\ &= Z_n \,\mathrm{Cov}[S_n,S_j] + (1 - Z_n) \sum_{i=1}^{n-1} {}_{n-1}a_i \,\mathrm{Cov}[S_i,S_j] \\ &= Z_n \,\mathrm{Cov}[S_n,S_j] + (1 - Z_n)\,\mathrm{Cov}[S_j,S_n] \\ &= \mathrm{Cov}[S_j,S_n]. \end{aligned} $$

But this means precisely that the covariance matrix can be written in the form (17).

2) Now assume that equations (16) and (17) hold. We want to show the validity of formula (11), or equivalently that

$$ {}_n a_j = (1 - {}_n a_n)\, {}_{n-1}a_j \tag{20} $$

for $j = 0,1,\ldots,n - 1$. From equations (10) and (17) we get for $j = 1,2,\ldots,n - 1$, that

$$ \begin{aligned} \sum_{i=1}^{n-1} {}_n a_i \,\mathrm{Cov}[S_i,S_j] &= \mathrm{Cov}[S_j,S_{n+1}] - {}_n a_n \,\mathrm{Cov}[S_j,S_n] \\ &= (1 - {}_n a_n)\,\mathrm{Cov}[S_j,S_n]. \end{aligned} \tag{21} $$

Comparing this system of equations with

$$ \sum_{i=1}^{n-1} {}_{n-1}a_i \,\mathrm{Cov}[S_i,S_j] = \mathrm{Cov}[S_j,S_n] \tag{22} $$

we conclude that formula (20) holds for $j = 1,2,\ldots,n - 1$. Its validity for $j = 0$ follows from equations (8) and (16) Q.E.D.

The following result shows how the Z_n's can be obtained recursively from the elements of the covariance matrix.

<u>Theorem 2a.</u> Under the conditions of Theorem 1,

$$Z_1 = \frac{W_1}{W_1 + V_1} \quad \text{and} \tag{23}$$

$$Z_n = \frac{W_n - W_{n-1} + Z_{n-1}V_{n-1}}{W_n - W_{n-1} + Z_{n-1}V_{n-1} + V_n} \tag{24}$$

for $n = 2,3,\ldots$.

<u>Proof.</u> Formula (23) follows immediately from equation (10) for $n = j = 1$. Now, using equation (10) for $j = n$ and formula (18), we get

$$\text{Cov}[S_n, S_{n+1}] = Z_n \text{ Var}[S_n] + (1 - Z_n) \sum_{i=1}^{n-1} {}_{n-1}a_i \text{ Cov}[S_i, S_n]. \tag{25}$$

By equation (17), the last summation may be written as

$${}_{n-1}a_{n-1}\{\text{Cov}[S_{n-1}, S_n] - \text{Var}[S_{n-1}]\} + \sum_{i=1}^{n-1} {}_{n-1}a_i \text{ Cov}[S_i, S_{n-1}] \tag{26}$$

and then by equation (10) as

$$Z_{n-1}\{\text{Cov}[S_{n-1}, S_n] - \text{Var}[S_{n-1}]\} + \text{Cov}[S_{n-1}, S_n].$$

Substituting this in formula (25), we get in the notation of Theorem 1 that

$$W_n = Z_n(V_n + V_n) + (1 - Z_n)(W_{n-1} - Z_{n-1}V_{n-1}), \tag{27}$$

which may be solved for Z_n to obtain the recurrence relationship (24). Q.E.D.

In terms of an auxiliary sequence $U_1, U_2, \ldots,$ defined recursively by the formula

$$U_n = W_n - W_{n-1} + \frac{V_{n-1}U_{n-1}}{U_{n-1} + V_{n-1}} \tag{28}$$

with $U_1 = W_1$, Theorem 2a can be restated as follows:

<u>Theorem 2b.</u> For $n = 1,2,\ldots$

$$Z_n = \frac{U_n}{U_n + V_n} \tag{29}$$

Section 5 contains a natural interpretation for the U_n's.

4. A special family

Theorem 1 shows that the family of covariance matrices that leads to a credibility formula of the updating type is quite rich. While a rich family is sometimes advantageous (e.g., in marriage!), it can make statistical estimation more difficult.

In this section we will restrict ourselves to the three-parameter family of covariance matrices of the type (17), where

$$\begin{aligned} W_1 &= W > 0 \\ W_{j+1} - W_j &= \delta^2 \geq 0 \\ V_j &= V > 0 \,. \end{aligned} \tag{30}$$

Theorem 2a shows that in this case

$$Z = \frac{W}{W + V} \tag{31}$$

$$Z_n = F(Z_{n-1}) \tag{32}$$

where the function $F(x)$ is defined as

$$F(x) = \frac{\delta^2 + Vx}{\delta^2 + Vx + V} \,. \tag{33}$$

The resulting family of credibility formulas includes the two examples of the preceding section. For $\delta = 0$, formulas (31) and (32) lead to formula (14), and we are in the case of uniform credibility weights. This is not surprising, since in the case the covariance matrix is constant on the main diagonal and constant off the main diagonal. If δ is chosen such that

$$F(Z_1) = Z_1 \tag{34}$$

formula (32) shows that we arrive at geometric credibility weights.

Let us now consider the case of an arbitrary $\delta \neq 0$. From

$$F'(x) = \frac{V^2}{(\delta^2 + Vx + V)^2} \tag{35}$$

we see that $F'(x) < F'(0) < 1$ for $x > 0$. Since $F(0)$ is positive, the equation

$$F(x) = x \tag{36}$$

has a unique positive solution Z. Furthermore, the inequality $F(1) < 1$ implies that $Z < 1$.

Theorem 3. Suppose $\delta \neq 0$. Then Z_n converges monotonically to Z for $n \to \infty$.

Proof. From formula (32) and the above remarks it is evident that the standard argument for the convergence of the iterative algorithm of numerical analysis is applicable. This is best summarized by the following graph:

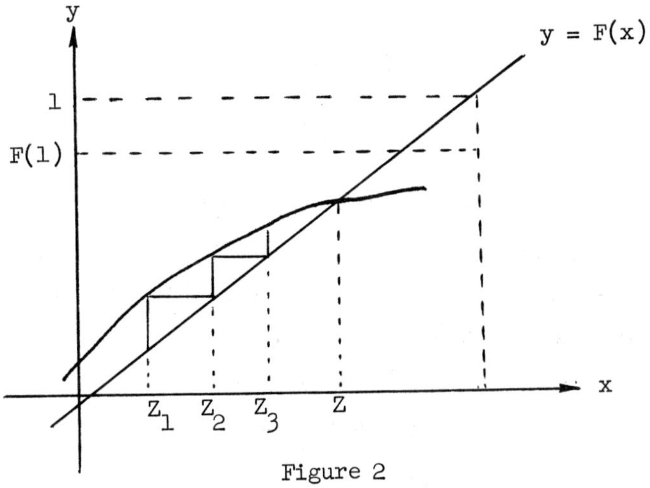

Figure 2

Remarks. 1) The sequence (Z_n) is increasing (decreasing), if and only if $Z_1 < Z$ $(Z_1 > Z)$. 2) If $\delta = 0$, the Z_n's converge obviously to 0. Formula (11) shows that

$$_na_{n-m} = (1 - Z_n)(1 - Z_{n-1}) \cdots (1 - Z_{n-m})Z_{n-m-1}. \tag{37}$$

Therefore, a by-product of Theorem 3 is that the credibility weights are asymptotically geometric:

Corollary. Suppose $\delta \neq 0$. Then for any m,

$$\lim_{n\to\infty} {}_n a_{n-m} = Z(1 - Z)^m. \tag{38}$$

5. The concept of risk parameters

In the case where $V_j > 0$ and $0 < W_j \leq W_{j+1}$ for $j = 1,2,\ldots,$ formulas (16) and (17) can be explained by the concept of risk parameters.

Suppose that the intrinsic (but not directly observable) quality of our policyholder is given by the random variables, $\theta_1,\theta_2,\theta_3,\ldots$ (the risk parameters). Intuitively, θ_n is the parameter that is effective for year n.

We require that the sequence $\{\theta_n\}$ has independent increments, with

$$E[\theta_{j+1} - \theta_j] = 0 \tag{39}$$

$$Var[\theta_{j+1} - \theta_j] = W_{j+1} - W_j \tag{40}$$

and set

$$E[\theta_1] = \mu, \quad Var[\theta_1] = W_1. \tag{41}$$

Furthermore, for given θ_j, S_j and all future claims S_{j+h} $(h = 1,2,\ldots)$ should be essentially independent. More precisely, we require that

$$E[S_j|\theta_j] = \theta_j \tag{42}$$

$$Var[S_j|\theta_j] = V_j \tag{43}$$

$$E[S_j S_{j+h}|\theta_j] = \theta_j^2. \tag{44}$$

From the assumptions (39), (41) and (42) we get that

$$E[S_j] = E[E[S_j|\theta_j]] = E[\theta_j] = \mu \tag{45}$$

which is equation (16). Next, using the well known decomposition formula for the variance, assumptions (40), (42) and (43) lead to

$$\begin{aligned} Var[S_j] &= E[Var[S_j|\theta_j]] + Var[E[S_j|\theta_j]] \\ &= V_j + Var[\theta_j] = V_j + W_j. \end{aligned} \tag{46}$$

Finally, for $h = 1,2,\ldots$

$$E[S_j S_{j+h}] = E[E[S_j S_{j+h} | \theta_j]] \tag{47}$$
$$= E[\theta_j^2] = Var[\theta_j] + \mu^2 = W_j + \mu^2$$

and therefore, $Cov[S_j, S_{j+h}] = W_j$.

Remarks about parametrization. 1) Under the additional assumption that the risk parameters $\theta_1, \theta_2, \theta_3, \ldots$ are normally distributed and also that the conditional distributions of the S_j's are normal, the Bayesian analysis can be carried out explicitly and leads to an identical result:

$$P_{n+1} = E[S_{n+1} | S_1, \ldots, S_n]. \tag{48}$$

Furthermore, the auxiliary parameter U_n of section 3 can now be interpreted as the conditional variance of θ_{n+1}, given the observations $S_1, S_2, \ldots, S_n$.

2) If the credibility formula should take into account only the frequency of the claims, one might assume that the conditional distribution of S_j is Poisson with parameter θ_j. Consequently, condition (43) would have to be replaced by

$$Var[S_j | \theta_j] = \theta_j . \tag{49}$$

In the following, only formula (46) has to be modified. It has to be replaced by

$$Var[S_j] = \mu + W_j . \tag{50}$$

It is remarkable that the resulting covariance matrix is still of the form (17), namely, now with $V_j = \mu$.

6. Reinterpretation of geometric credibility weights

In this section we shall present deterministic and probabilistic properties of

$$P_{n+1} = (1 - Z)^n \mu + \sum_{i=1}^{n} Z(1 - Z)^{n-i} S_i \tag{51}$$

with $0 < Z < 1$. These properties motivate the use of such a formula even in cases where the underlying model does not justify it on statistical grounds.

First let $P_{n+k}(S_n)$ denote the part of P_{n+k} that is due to the occurence of S_n $(k = 1,2,\dots)$. From formula (51)

$$P_{n+k}(S_n) = Z(1 - Z)^{k-1}S_n , \tag{52}$$

therefore

$$\sum_{k=1}^{\infty} P_{n+k}(S_n) = S_n . \tag{53}$$

Thus, regardless of what the claims of year n are, they will be fully repaid by future premiums. This and the following arguments are particularly meaningful if the S_n's are measured in indexed monetary units.

Now consider the loss (or gain) of the insurer, say L_n, for the n year period,

$$L_n = \sum_{i=1}^{n} (S_i - P_i) ,$$

which may be rearranged as

$$L_n = \sum_{i=1}^{n} (1 - Z)^{n-i}S_i - \frac{\mu}{Z} [1 - (1 - Z)^n] . \tag{54}$$

This shows that a great degree of financial stability can be accomplished by the use of geometric credibility weights. Suppose that $S_1, S_2, \dots$ are independent and identically distributed with $E[S_n] = \mu$, and $Var[S_n] = \sigma^2$. From formula (54)

$$E[L_n] = 0 \tag{55}$$

$$Var[L_n] = \frac{1 - (1 - Z)^{2n}}{1 - (1 - z)^2} \sigma^2 . \tag{56}$$

As $n \to \infty$,

$$Var[L_n] \to (2Z - Z^2)^{-1}\sigma^2 . \tag{57}$$

Furthermore, the distribution of L_n converges to the distribution of the random variable L, where

$$L = \sum_{i=0}^{\infty} (1 - Z)^i S_{i+1} - \frac{\mu}{Z} \tag{58}$$

which can be interpreted as a discounted sum. On the other

hand, a purely statistical argument would have led to constant premiums, $P_n' = \mu$ for all n, with resulting aggregate losses

$$L_n' = \sum_{i=1}^{n} S_i - \mu n. \quad (59)$$

While the expected value of the loss at any time is still zero, we see that

$$\mathrm{Var}[L_n'] = \sigma^2 n \quad (60)$$

which implies divergence of its variance and consequently of its distribution.

As an illustration, we have simulated the outcomes of 100 periods under the assumption that the S_n's were independent and identically distributed each assuming only the values 0 or 2 with equal probabilities. Figure 3 compares the aggregate losses as a function of time under three different credibility formulas. The formulas are:

Formula 1: $P_n = 1$ for all n (purely statistical approach)

Formula 2: P_n according to formula (51) with $Z = .1$

Formula 3: P_n according to formula (51) with $Z = .2$

As expected, Formula 3 produced the most stable result for the insurance company.

7. Analogy with the theory of Brownian motion

The Ornstein-Uhlenbeck theory of Brownian motion is concerned with the velocity $V(t)$ and the position $X(t)$ of a particle as a function of time t. Then, from physics, the Langevin equation is

$$dV(t) = -bV(t)dt + dW(t), \quad b > 0 \quad (61)$$

where $W(t)$ denotes a Wiener process. (Without the last term, we would have merely a deterministic slow down of the particle; the purpose of the last term is to make the motion oscillate.) Formal integration of the last equation leads to

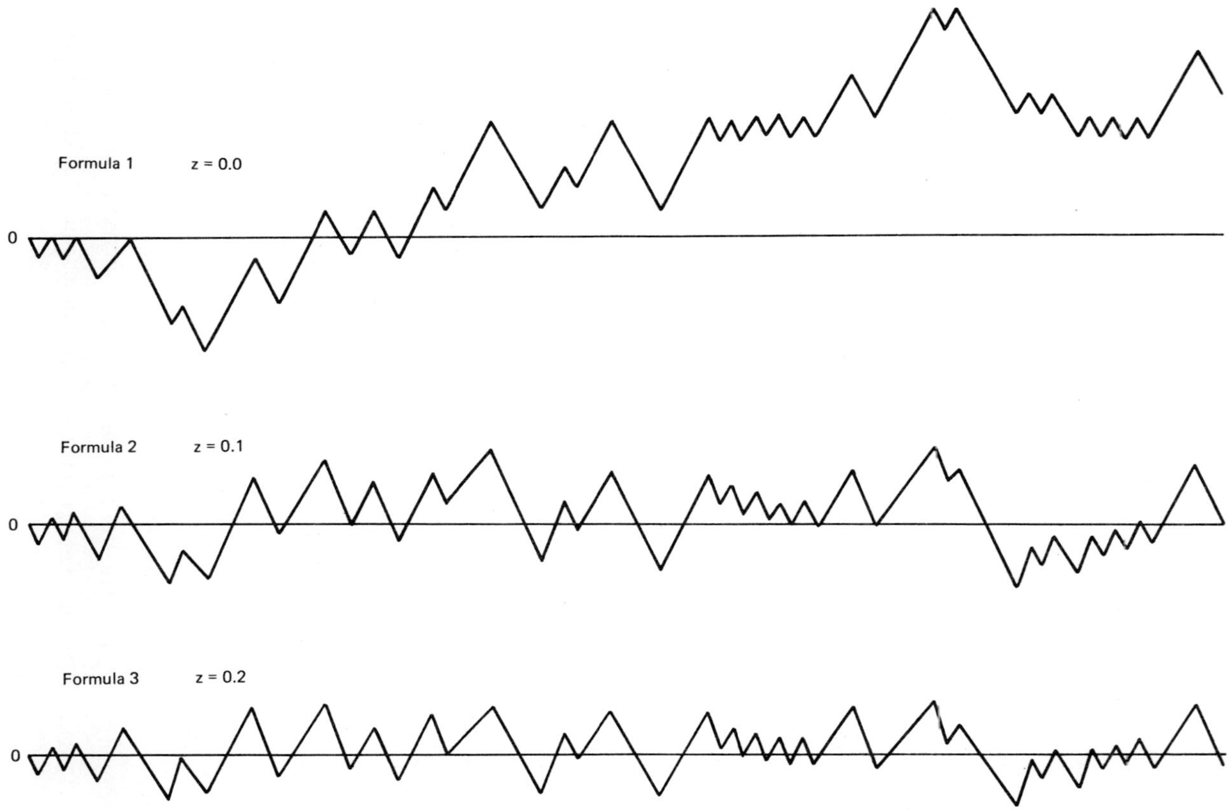

Figure 3

Simulated Sample Paths of the Aggregate Losses

$$V(t) = e^{-bt}V(0) + \int_0^t e^{b(t-s)}dW(s) \tag{62}$$

and from this we get

$$X(t) = X(0) + \int_0^t V(s)ds . \tag{63}$$

Interestingly enough, the same construction is followed when a formula of type (51) is applied. Assuming a continuous time model, the analogue of the difference equation (12) with Z_n = constant is

$$dP(t) = c[dS(t) - P(t)dt] \tag{64}$$

where $P(t)$ is the premium density at time t, $S(t)$ the aggregate claims at time t and $c > 0$. Obviously equation (64) is of the form (61). The only difference is now that the Wiener process has been replaced by the aggregate claims process $S(t)$ (for example, a compound Poisson process). Formal integration of the stochastic equation (64) leads to

$$P(t) = e^{-ct}P(0) + c\int_0^t e^{-c(t-u)}dS(u) . \tag{65}$$

Finally, the aggregate loss at time t is

$$L(t) = \int_0^t e^{-c(t-u)}dS(u) - \frac{P(0)}{c}(1 - e^{-ct}) . \tag{66}$$

The last two formulas should be viewed as the continuous analogues of formulas (51) and (54).

Appendix. Credibility formulas of the updating type in the light of functional analysis

The purpose of this appendix is to present an alternative proof for Theorem 1 by use of Hilbert space techniques. Intuitively, a Hilbert space is an infinite dimensional generalization of Euclidean space of finite dimension. The concepts of distance and orthogonality carry over into Hilbert space theory and, of course, then so do projections and the theory of least squares. The idea that Hilbert space methods might have applications in credibility theory is not new, but their actual use has not appeared. Thus the raison d'etre for this appendix.

Let H be a Hilbert space with elements ("vectors") $\vec{a}, \vec{b}, \vec{c}, \ldots$ For any $\vec{a}, \vec{b} \in H$ an inner product $(\vec{a}, \vec{b})$ is defined. Let U be a given subspace of H and let $\vec{x}$ and $\vec{y}$ be any two vectors in H. We denote by V the subspace that is spanned by U and $\vec{x}$ (i.e., the smallest subspace of H that contains U and $\vec{x}$), and by T_1 and T_2, the projection operators onto U and V, respectively.

Theorem 4. There is a real number Z such that

$$T_2\vec{y} = Z\vec{x} + (1 - Z)T_1\vec{x} \tag{67}$$

if and only if

$$(\vec{a}, \vec{y}) = (\vec{a}, \vec{x}) \tag{68}$$

for all $\vec{a} \in U$.

Proof. 1) Assume that there is a constant Z such that equation (67) holds. Since $\vec{y} - T_2\vec{y}$ is orthogonal to V, we get for any $\vec{a} \in V$ that

$$\begin{aligned} 0 &= (\vec{a}, \vec{y} - T_2\vec{y}) \\ &= (\vec{a}, \vec{y}) - Z(\vec{a}, \vec{x}) - (1 - Z)(\vec{a}, T_1\vec{x}). \end{aligned} \tag{69}$$

Especially this is true for all $\vec{a} \in U \subseteq V$. But for $\vec{a} \in U$, $(\vec{a}, T_1\vec{x}) = (\vec{a}, \vec{x})$, and therefore

$$0 = (\vec{a}, \vec{y}) - (\vec{a}, \vec{x}) \tag{70}$$

which shows the validity of (68).

2) Now assume that (68) holds. Since $T_2\vec{y} \in V$, it is of the form

$$T_2\vec{y} = Z\vec{x} + \vec{u} \tag{71}$$

for some constant Z and some vector $\vec{u} \in U$. The difference $\vec{y} - T_2\vec{y}$ is orthogonal to V. Thus for any $\vec{a} \in U$, we get

$$
\begin{aligned}
0 &= (\vec{a},\vec{y} - T_2\vec{y}) \\
&= (\vec{a},\vec{y}) - Z(\vec{a},\vec{x}) - (\vec{a},\vec{u}) \qquad (72) \\
&= (1 - Z)(\vec{a},\vec{x}) - (\vec{a},\vec{u})
\end{aligned}
$$

It follows that $\vec{u} = (1 - Z)T_1\vec{x}$. Q.E.D.

For the alternative proof of Theorem 1, let the Hilbert space H be the set of all square-integrable random variables, with the inner product defined as

$$(X,Y) = E[XY] \ . \qquad (73)$$

Let U be the subspace that is spanned by

$$S_o = 1, S_1, \ldots, S_n \qquad (74)$$

(Thus, U is the set of all random variables of the form (5).) The roles of $\vec{x}$ and $\vec{y}$ are played by S_{n+1} and S_{n+2}. Since P_{n+1} is the projection of S_{n+1} on U, and P_{n+2} the projection of S_{n+2} on V, statement (67) reads that there is a constant Z (call it Z_{n+1}), such that

$$P_{n+2} = Z_{n+1}S_{n+1} + (1 - Z_{n+1})P_{n+1} \qquad (75)$$

The equivalent condition (68) now reads

$$E[S_i \ S_{n+1}] = E[S_i \ S_{n+2}] \qquad (76)$$

for $i = 0,1,\ldots,n$. For $i = 0$ this gives us

$$E[S_{n+1}] = E[S_{n+2}] \qquad (77)$$

Because of that, the equations for $i = 1,\ldots,n$ become

$$\mathrm{Cov}[S_i,S_{n+1}] = \mathrm{Cov}[S_i,S_{n+2}] \qquad (78)$$

Theorem 1 is now an immediate application of Theorem 4.

Discussion by James C. Hickman and Robert B. Miller of Credibility Formulas of the Updating Type.

Cramér (1930) has given the classic definition of risk theory: "The object of the theory of risk is to give a mathematical analysis of the random fluctuations in an insurance business and to discuss the various means of protection against their inconvenient effects." The subject of this conference might be stated as the adaptive estimation of the parameters of risk theory models. Estimation is of obvious importance to any discussion of "means of protection against the inconvenient effects" of deviations from expected results.

Gerber and Jones have contributed to the solution of this estimation problem. They have adopted a general multivariate model and have developed in detail the linear least square method of estimating conditional means. Rather than embellish their impressive results, we would like to raise some questions about their basic model.

Other things being equal, simple models are to be preferred to complex models. Yet it seems to us that the appealing simplicity of the multivariate model for the random vector of claims used by Gerber and Jones may be somewhat illusory. Their model requires the estimation of a great many covariances. Because of the obvious impossibility of iterating a sequence of claims results for a particular case, it seems clear that satisfactory estimates will require the use of prior and ancillary information. Since credibility theory is devoted to the adaptive estimation of risk parameters, it does not seem inappropriate to consider at this conference somewhat more elaborate models in which the steps in the estimation procedure are indicated. Consequently, our discussion will consider the formulation of a multivariate model that is suggested by plausible economic assumptions and which explicitly requires the introduction of ancillary information as well as past claims for the particular case under consideration into the parameter estimation process.

We have been impressed with the efficient market theory developed to study price changes in speculative markets. One form of this theory postulates that in a market where the participants have access to a common body of information, and where transaction and information costs are insignificant, current prices fully reflect all information and one may expect price changes to be independently distributed, see Fama (1970). There is an impressive amount of statistical evidence that the commodity and common stock markets are approximately efficient.

Efficient market theory has led to new insights into many markets; may it be applied to help us understand the insurance market? We aren't certain of the answer to this question. Nevertheless, we would like to suggest that in an efficient insurance market, a common pool of economic and risk classification information, plus competitive pressures, will tend to produce pure premiums (expected claims) such that deviations from expected claims will be mutually independent. If the deviations from expected claims are not independent, there will be dependencies in the distribution that could be exploited by the insurance company or the insured to take advantage of the other party to the contract. Observed dependencies should be a signal to management to update its estimates of the risk model parameters, or to improve its classification system, or to take both actions.

Let us illustrate our idea with an example that employs the tractable multinormal distribution (see Anderson, 1953). An element S_i of the random vector $\underset{\sim}{S} = (S_1, S_2, \ldots, S_{n+1})'$ may be interpreted as the aggregate claims in year i. Given the risk parameters $\underset{\sim}{\theta} = (\theta_1, \theta_2, \ldots, \theta_{n+1})'$, we will assume that $\underset{\sim}{S}$ has a multinormal distribution with mean vector $h\underset{\sim}{\theta}$, and variance-covariance matrix $r^2 \underset{\sim}{I}_{(n+1,n+1)}$, where $\underset{\sim}{I}_{(n+1,n+1)}$ is the $(n+1, n+1)$ identity matrix. The constants h and r^2 are identified with the particular case under study. They adjust the risk parameters for the level and variability of claims experience for the case under consideration. Note that, given the risk parameters $h\underset{\sim}{\theta}$, the elements of $\underset{\sim}{S}$ are mutually independent. Thus our model assumes that the insurance market is efficient.

In addition, we will assume that all prior and ancillary information about the risk parameters $\underset{\sim}{\theta}$ has been summarized in a conjugate multinormal distribution with mean vector $\underset{\sim}{\mu}$ and variance-covariance matrix, see DeGroot (1970). For example, broad economic trends, such as inflation induced shifts in claims amounts, might be reflected in the vector $\underset{\sim}{\mu}$ and the fact that these shifts are not independent over time would be reflected in $\underset{\sim}{A}$. The determination of the distribution of $\underset{\sim}{\theta}$ might well involve a time series analysis of a broadly based claims index.

From the distribution assumptions made about $\underset{\sim}{S}$ and $\underset{\sim}{\theta}$, it may be shown that $(\underset{\sim}{\theta}, \underset{\sim}{S})'$ has a multinormal distribution with mean vector $(\underset{\sim}{\mu}, h\underset{\sim}{\mu})'$ and variance-covariance matrix

$$\begin{pmatrix} \underset{\sim}{A} & \underset{\sim}{A} \\ \underset{\sim}{A} & \underset{\sim}{A} + r^2 \underset{\sim}{I} \end{pmatrix}.$$

It may also be shown that the distribution of S_{n+1}, given $S_1, S_2, \ldots, S_n$, $\underset{\sim}{\mu}$, h, r^2, and $\underset{\sim}{A}$, is normal with mean

$$h\mu_{n+1} + \underset{\sim}{\Delta}'(\underset{\sim}{A} + r^2\underset{\sim}{I})^{-1}_{(n,n)}(\underset{\sim}{S} - h\underset{\sim}{\mu})_{(n,1)}$$

and variance

$$(a_{(n+1,n+1)} + r^2) - \underset{\sim}{\Delta}'(\underset{\sim}{A} + r^2\underset{\sim}{I})^{-1}_{(n,n)}\underset{\sim}{\Delta},$$

where

$$\underset{\sim}{\Delta}' = (a_{n+1,1}, a_{n+1,2}, \ldots, a_{n+1,n}).$$

In each of these expressions $a_{i,j}$ is an element of the matrix $\underset{\sim}{A}$.

This model incorporates ideas from efficient market theory and permits broad economic information, as well as claims data for the particular case, to enter into the parameter estimation process. It is contemplated that tests of independence on the sequence of claims amounts would be periodically performed as a general test of the adequacy of the model, and the quality of the parameter estimates and the classification system. We are not so naive as to believe that all claims distributions are normal. We cheerfully acknowledge that other multivariate distributions should be explored. Nevertheless, we believe that even the crude probability statements available from the normal distribution would be useful in many risk management problems.

Credibility and Profitability

David J. Grady
The Travelers Insurance Company

For the casualty actuary, credibility is a fundamental component of the rating process. Profitability provides a measure of how well he has accomplished his task of pricing the product.

This paper explores the classical relationship between full credibility and profitability in an attempt to focus on a problem for which a reasonable solution has been known to casualty actuaries for over forty years. In spite of this, the solution has remained unemployed and is apparently unemployable. The purpose of this paper is:

1. To reformulate the classical approaches to full crediblity and insurer's risk so that their juxtaposition may point up the problem,
2. To provide numerical results for selected major lines of business,
3. To investigate the paradox from the related viewpoints of theory and practice.

The Classical Theory of Credibility

Let n represent the total number of identical units of exposure for a particular line of business of an insurer during a specified period of time. Let the random variable X_i denote the losses generated by the ith unit of exposure during this time. The X_i's are assumed to be independent, homogeneous and stationary over time, and to have identical means, μ, and identical variances, σ^2. Then the total losses of the insurer over this time period may be represented by

$$T = \sum_{i=1}^{n} x_i$$

The insurer's expected losses for the time period is given by

$$\mu_T = E\{T\} = n\mu .$$

The variance of the losses for this time period is

$$\sigma_T^2 = E\{(T - \mu_T)^2\} = n\sigma^2$$

and the standard deviation is

$$\sigma_T = \sqrt{n}\,\sigma .$$

Let the random variable

$$z = \frac{\sum_{i=1}^{n} x_i - n\mu}{\sqrt{n}\,\sigma} .$$

Then, by the Central Limit theorem, $\lim_{n\to\infty} f(z) = N(0,1)$.

We may then construct a probability statement with critical region of size α for a two-sided interval to contain $\sum_{i=1}^{n} x_i$:

$$\Pr\left\{n\mu - z_{1-\frac{\alpha}{2}}\sqrt{n}\,\sigma < \sum_{i=1}^{n} x_i < n\mu + z_{1-\frac{\alpha}{2}}\sqrt{n}\,\sigma\right\} = 1 - \alpha$$

Dividing each of the components of the interval by $n\mu$, we have:

$$\Pr\left\{1 - z_{1-\frac{\alpha}{2}}\frac{\sigma}{\sqrt{n}\,\mu} < \frac{\sum_{i=1}^{n} x_i}{n\mu} < 1 + z_{1-\frac{\alpha}{2}}\frac{\sigma}{\sqrt{n}\,\mu}\right\} = 1 - \alpha .$$

Since $\sum_{i=1}^{n} x_i$ represents the actual claims experience during and $n\mu$ denotes the total pure premium charged by the insurer for that time period, the endpoints of the interval are expressed in terms of percentage deviations of actual losses about expected losses. For example, if we wish the actual claims experience to fall within 5% of expected losses 90% of the time, the probability statement would read:

$$\Pr\left\{1 - 1.645\,\frac{\sigma}{\sqrt{n}\,\mu} < \frac{\sum_{i=1}^{n} x_i}{n\mu} < 1 + 1.645\,\frac{\sigma}{\sqrt{n}\,\mu}\right\}$$

$$= \Pr\left\{1 - K < \frac{\sum_{i=1}^{n} x_i}{n\mu} < 1 + K\right\}$$

$$= \Pr\left\{0.95 < \frac{\sum_{i=1}^{n} x_i}{n\mu} < 1.05\right\}$$

$$= 0.90\,.$$

Hence,

$$Z_{0.95}\,\frac{\sigma}{\sqrt{n}\,\mu} = 0.05\ .$$

Since μ and σ are treated as known parameters in this formulation, we may solve the equation for n. Thus, if the insurer has at least

$$n = \frac{Z_{0.95}}{(0.05)^2} \cdot \frac{\sigma^2}{\mu^2}$$

units of exposure in the line of business, he believes his loss experience in the line will not usually vary drastically from the total pure premium he has charged. Hence, he judges the experience of the line to be fully credible within the limits of the two arbitrary parameters $\alpha = 0.10$ and $K = 0.05$.

Two comments may be made concerning the standard formula

$$n = \frac{Z^2_{1-\frac{\alpha}{2}}}{K^2} \cdot \frac{\sigma^2}{\mu^2}$$

which underlies the determination of full credibility requirements.

1. The parameters μ and σ are actually unknown. However, since we are only concerned with their relativity and since we usually derive their estimates from large volumes of data, it is generally believed that an adequate representation of the true population parameters is achieved.
2. The standard formulas for full credibility currently in use for most casualty lines do not estimate the required number of exposures but instead provide us with the required number of claims. This outcome is a direct result of the assumption that claim frequency is appropriately represented by the Poisson distribution.

The transition which the formula for full credibility undergoes under the Poisson assumption may be summarized as follows:

Let μ = mean pure premium

σ = standard deviation of the pure premium distribution

λ = mean claim frequency

λ_2 = variance of the claim frequency distribution

θ = mean claim amount

θ_2 = variance of the distribution of claim amounts.

Let X denote a random variable possessing the claim amount distribution. Let N denote the mean number of claims arising from n identical units of exposure.

Then:

$$n = \frac{Z^2_{1-\frac{\alpha}{2}}}{K^2} \cdot \frac{\sigma^2}{\mu^2}$$

$$= \frac{Z^2_{1-\frac{\alpha}{2}}}{K^2} \cdot \frac{\theta_2\lambda + \theta^2\lambda_2}{(\theta\lambda)^2}$$

$$= \frac{Z^2_{1-\frac{\alpha}{2}}}{K^2} \cdot \frac{\theta_2\lambda + \theta^2\lambda}{\theta^2\lambda^2}$$

Since $\lambda = \lambda_2$ for the Poisson distribution

$$= \frac{Z^2_{1-\frac{\alpha}{2}}}{K^2} \cdot \frac{\theta_2 + \theta^2}{\theta^2\lambda}$$

$$= \frac{Z^2_{1-\frac{\alpha}{2}}}{K^2} \cdot \frac{(\theta_2 + \theta^2)n}{\theta^2 N}$$

$$N = \frac{Z^2_{1-\frac{\alpha}{2}}}{K^2} \cdot \frac{\theta_2 + \theta^2}{\theta^2}$$

$$\text{(I)} \quad N = \frac{Z^2_{1-\frac{\alpha}{2}}}{K^2} \cdot \frac{E[X^2]}{(E[X])^2}$$

This is essentially identical to Perryman's formula for full credibility of the pure premium (see Perryman, 1932).

$$N = \frac{zf(P)^2\left(1 + \frac{S^2}{M^2}\right)}{K^2}$$

$$= \frac{Z^2_{1-\frac{\alpha}{2}}}{K^2}\left(1 + \frac{\theta_2}{\theta^2}\right)$$

Perryman's formula expresses the required number of claims in terms of the coefficient of variation of the claim severity distribution, while formula (I) is simply a more efficient calculating formula for the same factor.

Two basic arguments have been lodged against the Perryman formula for full credibility of the pure premium:

1. The Poisson assumption is inappropriate since the variance of the claim frequency distribution

generally exceeds the mean.

2. The pure premium distribution is so violently skewed that higher moments must be taken into account.

Mayerson, Jones and Bowers (1968) calculated three examples which utilized the Cornish-Fisher expansion to determine N. The procedure indicated that the Poisson assumption had relatively little impact on the determination of full credibility requirements. This follows immediately from an examination of the variance of the pure premium distribution:

$$\sigma = \theta_2\lambda + \theta^2\lambda_2 .$$

Since the claim amount distribution for a line of insurance generally demonstrates marked positive skewness, the square of the mean of the distribution is overshadowed by its variance. Therefore, the variance of the claim frequency distribution is the coefficient of a much smaller quantity than that to which the mean claim frequency is applied.

In a discussion of the Mayerson, Jones and Bowers paper, McIntosh showed that the third and higher moments of the claim amount distribution have an almost negligible effect on full credibility requirements when compared with the impact of the variance.

Since the coefficient of variation of the claim severity distribution was shown to be a major factor in determining full credibility for the pure premium, there would seem to be ample justification for employing the Perryman formula in rate-making. But in the six years since the publication of the Mayerson, Jones and Bowers paper, no further mention has been made of the Perryman approach, and the dust that has surrounded it since 1932 has begun to settle again.

The classical theory of insurer's risk

The classical concept of insurer's risk may be developed in a manner completely analogous to that of credibility. Retaining the notation of the previous section, we may construct a probability statement for a one-sided interval containing $\sum_{i=1}^{n} x_i$:

$$\Pr\left\{ \sum_{i=1}^{n} x_i < n\mu + Z_{1-\frac{\alpha}{2}} \sqrt{n}\,\sigma \right\} = 1 - \frac{\alpha}{2} .$$

The quantity $Z_{1-\frac{\alpha}{2}} \sqrt{n}\,\sigma$ is known as insurer's risk and is defined to be adverse deviation from expected loss experience. Insurer's risk increases as the size of the idealized portfolio increases, but insurer's risk increases at a decreasing rate. Chart I provides a graphical representation of the utilization of this measure of insurer's risk. For the idealized portfolio, an insurer's actual total annual losses will be normally distributed about his expected total annual losses. Since the expected annual losses represent the total pure premium included in the rates, the graph illustrates that even under ideal conditions, the total pure premium will be inadequate half the time. Since an insurer cannot afford to participate in a business in which rate inadequacy is a common state of affairs, a contingency margin must be incorporated in the rates. The measure of insurer's risk allows us to set an upper boundary to the losses to be covered by the contingency margin. The losses above this boundary must be covered by policyholder's surplus in conjunction with reinsurance arrangements. Chart II illustrates the effect which excess-of-loss reinsurance has on a positively skewed distribution of actual total annual losses. This type of contract tends to restore the normality assumption implicit in the classical treatment of insurer's risk.

The probability statement for insurer's risk may be developed in a manner similar to that of the preceding section. We have the following statement for a single insured:

$$\Pr\left\{\frac{\bar{x}}{\mu} < 1 + Z_{1-\frac{\alpha}{2}} \frac{\sigma}{\sqrt{n}\,\mu}\right\} = 1 - \frac{\alpha}{2}$$

where $Z_{1-\frac{\alpha}{2}} \frac{\sigma}{\sqrt{n}\,\mu}$ expresses the size of the contingency margin as a percentage of the pure premium to be charged for each unit of exposure.

Finally, under the Poisson assumption for claim frequency, we have:

$$\Pr\left\{\frac{\bar{x}}{\mu} < 1 + Z_{1-\frac{\alpha}{2}} \frac{\sqrt{E[X^2]}}{\sqrt{N}\,E[X]}\right\} = 1 - \frac{\alpha}{2}\,.$$

Letting K denote the size of the contingency margin:

$$\text{(II)} \qquad K = Z_{1-\frac{\alpha}{2}} \frac{\sqrt{E[X^2]}}{\sqrt{N}\,E[X]}\,.$$

Formula (II), of course, is simply a restatement of formula (I). However, the preceding discussion has developed K as the contingency margin to be incorporated in the rates. K is no longer simply an arbitrary parameter.

Numerical results

The current standard for full credibility for the automobile liability lines is 1,084 claims while the standard for general liability lines is 683 claims.

The standard profit and contingencies provisions for casualty-property lines are shown in Exhibit I. The margin for casualty lines is generally 5% of the premium dollar while the comparable provision for property lines is 6% of premium. The line of workmen's compensation provides a significant exception to the general rule: the social and compulsory nature of this covsrage has acted to limit the P & C margin to 2.5% of premium.

Two comments may be made about current P & C provisions:

1. They are expressed in terms of the total premium dollar. Therefore, if we wish to compare the total possible contingency margin with that derived from classical theory, we should divide K by the permissible loss ratio.
2. Since both profit and contingencies share a fixed portion of the premium dollar, and since this percentage is relatively invariant over the different lines of business, they exist as complements in the rate structure. As a result, profit currently varies inversely with the risk assumed while logic would seem to dictate that profit should vary directly with risk.

The complementary nature of profit and contingencies provides us with an indirect test of potential profitability. To the extent credibility requirements are deficient, the margin for contingencies must increase. Comparing the margin for contingencies produced by formula (II) with the current combined P & C margin for a particular line provides a rough estimate of its profitability.

We examined the relationship between credibility and insurer's risk for four major lines of business separately for three accident years of experience. The accident years 1968-1970 were selected since they provide reasonably mature data at this point in time. The lines of business studied are:

1. Private Passenger Automobile Bodily Injury Liability
2. Commercial Automobile Bodily Injury Liability
3. Workmen's Compensation

4. General Liability - Bodily Injury.

Bickerstaff (1971) uses data on \$50 deductible collision claims were utilized for comparative purposes.

Full credibility for $\alpha = 0.10$, $K = 0.05$ and the calculated contingency margin for $\alpha = 0.05$, $N = 1,082$ are shown in Exhibit II. The results are reasonably stable over the short time span involved and are graduated downward in the following order:

1. Private Passenger Auto - B.I.
2. General Liability - B.I.
3. Commercial Auto - B.I.
4. Workmen's Compensation
5. Private Passenger Auto - Collision

It must be stated that these results could be improved by a proper stratification of the lines of business involved in the study. For example, private passenger auto B.I. should be analyzed according to limits, general liability by subline, commercial auto by coverage and workmen's compensation by type of injury.

Conclusions

Formulas (I) and (II) produce the following interpretations:

1. Low credibility may be compensated for by a high contingency margin.
2. Low contingency margins require high full credibility standards.

However, the insurance industry is currently operating under low standards for both full credibility and contingency margins. It would appear that an increase in both requirements could benefit the industry at this time.

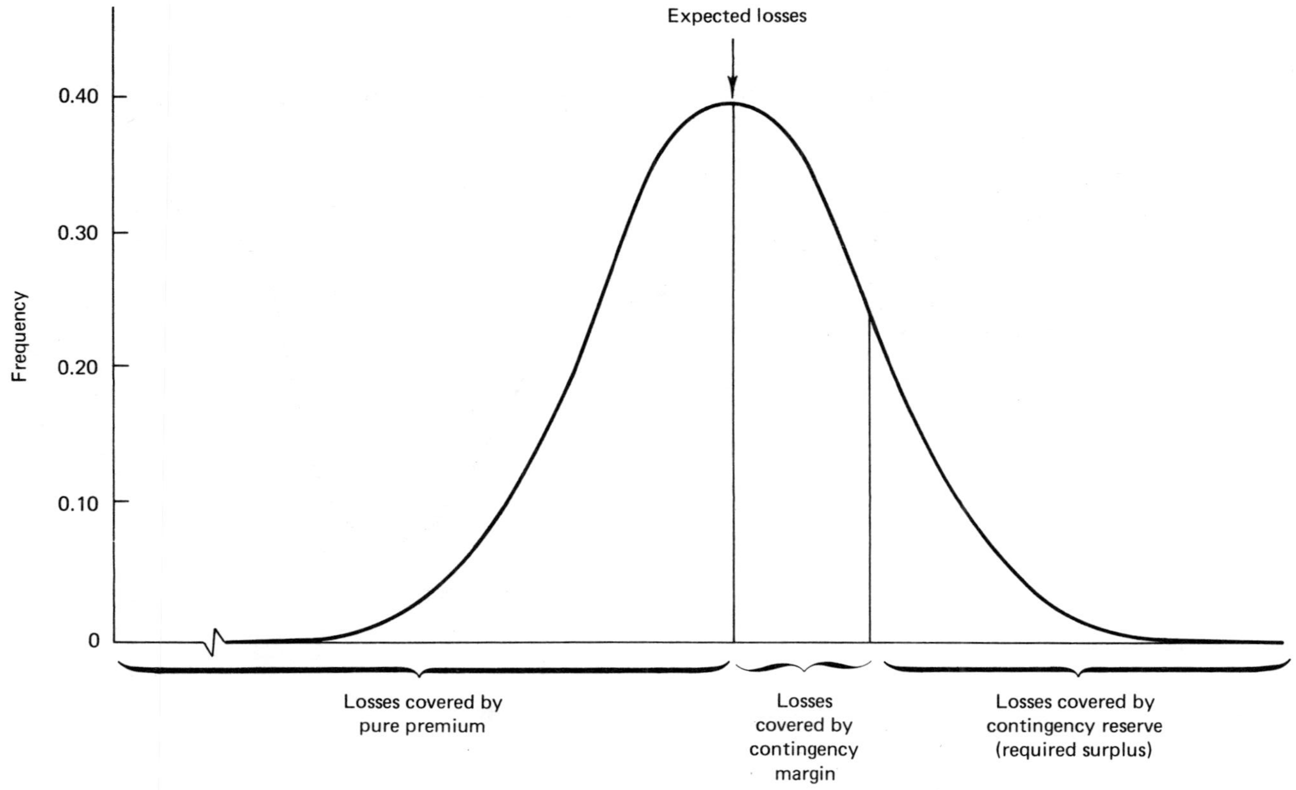

Chart I: Distribution of Total Annual Losses

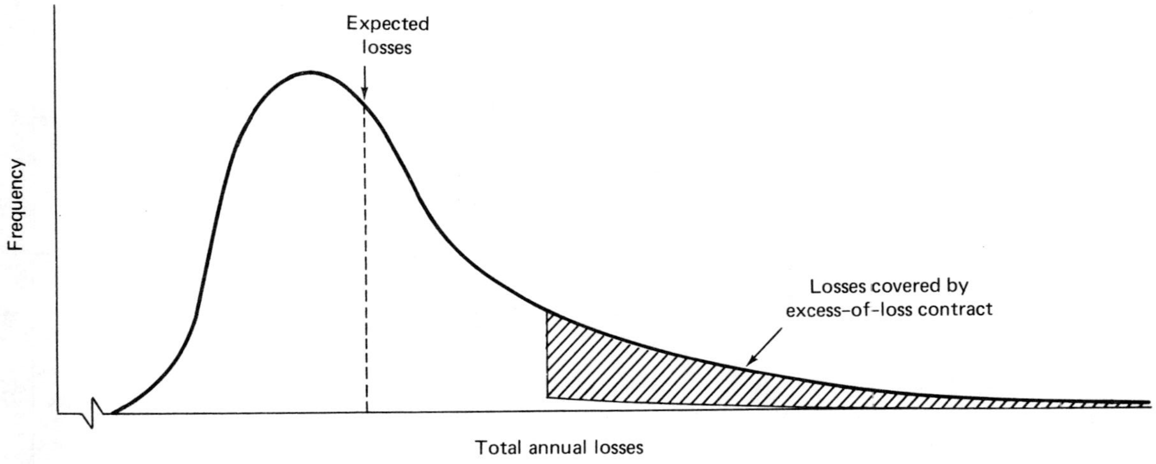

Chart II: Impact of Excess-of-Loss Reinsurance on Total Annual Losses

Exhibit I
Standard Provisions for Underwriting Profit and Contingencies

Line of Business	Standard P&C Provision*	Relativities†
1. Private Passenger Automobile	5.0%	1.00
a. Bodily Injury Liability	5.0	1.00
b. Property Damage Liability	5.0	1.00
c. Collision	5.0	1.00
d. Comprehensive	5.0	1.00
2. Personal Liability	5.0	1.00
3. Homeowners Multiple Peril	6.0	1.20
4. Workmen's Compensation	2.5	0.50
5. Commercial Automobile	5.0	1.00
a. Bodily Injury Liability	5.0	1.00
b. Property Damage Liability	5.0	1.00
c. Collision	5.0	1.00
d. Comprehensive	5.0	1.00
6. General Liability (B.I. and P.D.)	5.0	1.00
a. Owners, Landlords and Tenants	5.0	1.00
b. Manufacturers and Contractors	5.0	1.00
c. Products	5.0	1.00
d. Professional	5.0	1.00
e. Composite Rated	5.0	1.00
7. Burglary	5.0	1.00
8. Glass	5.0	1.00
9. Boiler and Machinery	5.0	1.00
10. Fire	6.0	1.20
11. Allied Lines	5.0	1.00
12. Inland Marine	6.0	1.20
13. Ocean Marine	6.0	1.20
14. Commercial Multiple Peril	6.0	1.20

*Expressed as a percentage of premium

†Using Private Passenger Automobile Bodily Injury Liability as a base

Exhibit II
Comparison of Full Credibility Requirements
and Indicated Contingency Margins
for Selected Lines

Line of Business	Accident Year	Full Credibility N for $\alpha = 0.10$, $K = 0.05$	Contingency Margin K for $\alpha = 0.05$, $N = 1,082$
Personal Auto B.I.	1968	56,252	0.219
	1969	56,003	0.219
	1970	52,932	0.213
Commercial Auto B.I.	1968	16,309	0.118
	1969	14,319	0.111
	1970	17,618	0.123
Workmen's Compensation	1968	11,383	0.099
	1969	13,613	0.108
	1970	11,963	0.101
General Liability - B.I.	1968	30,005	0.160
	1969	31,609	0.164
	1970	24,690	0.145
Personal Auto Collision	1971	2,876	0.050

Discussion by Clarence R. Atwood of Credibility and Profitability.

This paper explores the relationship between full credibility and profitability. Mr. Grady begins this exploration by reviewing the classical theory of credibility. However, he attempts to introduce standards for full credibility related to number of exposure units rather than number of claims. To accomplish this he assumes the random variable X_i denotes the loss generated by the ith unit of exposure unit. His model has a loss produced by each exposure unit, and this means that he conceives the case of no loss as equal to the random variable X_i assuming a value of zero. When Grady calculates the mean and variance of X he uses exposure rather than number of claims for "n". This causes the variance and mean to be affected by the size of claim as well as the existence of a claim.

The formula for the variance of the distribution of total losses as outlined on page 179 of Mayerson, Jones and Bowers (1968) is as follows:

$$E\{(T - m_T)^2\} = \mu_2\lambda + \mu^2\lambda_2 \tag{1}$$

where T = Total Losses

m_T = mean of total losses

μ_2 = variance of loss amount distribution

μ = mean of loss amount distribution

λ = mean of claim frequency distribution

λ_2 = variance of claim frequency distribution

and if we assume the frequency is constant becomes:

$$E\{(T - m_T)^2\} = \mu_2\lambda$$

which is similar to Grady's formula except "n" in Grady's formula represents the exposure rather than the claim count and the variance of Grady's formula differs by the number of exposure units with zero loss values.

Grady derives the formula for the number of exposure units required for full credibility from the moments of the claim amount distribution which again includes a claim for every exposure unit. The Mayerson, Jones and Bowers formula (E) on page 180 is:

$$\lambda = \frac{Z_e^2}{k^2}\left(\frac{\lambda_2}{\lambda} + \frac{\mu_2}{\mu^2}\right) \qquad (3)$$

where,

$Z_e = 100\left(\frac{1 + P}{2}\right)$ percentile of standard normal distribution with P and k equal assumed values, usually P = .90 and k = .05

and, reduces to the following form, similar to Grady's formula, if the frequency is assumed to be constant;

$$\lambda = \frac{Z_e^2}{k^2}\left(\frac{\mu_2}{\mu^2}\right) \qquad (4)$$

The author then separates the frequency distribution and the claim amount distribution to produce the classical Perryman formula for full credibility (using the claim amount moments and assuming the frequency distribution approximates a Poisson). The author ends his exploration of classical theory with a commentary on how little the fundamental theories of Perryman have been applied in recent years. I share the author's concern and can see no practical or theoretical reason for lack of progress in this important area.

The remainder of the paper is devoted to equating the

standard contingency margin of casualty insurance ratemaking to the value of "k" in the standard formula for full credibility. As normally conceived, "k" is a parameter chosen to represent a judgment decision as to the fluctuation above or below the mean to be allowed. Just because a given class, territory, or state is small in terms of number of claims does not imply the risk is greater for the individual exposure unit and consequently requires a higher contingency margin. This particular concept of "k" is in conflict with the purpose of credibility as through credibility standards we normally merge the prior experience with the new (and probably more indicative) experience. Grady's concept of "k" would require the ratemaker to discard all prior knowledge and possibly raise the contingency margin if the number of losses in the latest experience is small. It would be impossible to market insurance policies rated on this basis let alone have them approved by the regulator.

The author compares the standard profit and contingency margins included in the ratemaking process for a number of lines of business. He concludes from the illustration in his Exhibit I that contingency margins do not vary with the risk involved. Its difficult to see how he reached this conclusion since:

1. The standard P & C provision in Exhibit I should have been related to the permissible loss ratio as stated in his paper.
2. Many of the riskier lines of business develop additional contingency margin through investment income on the loss reserves, and this additional income was not considered in Exhibit I.

This paper presents an interesting exploration of

classical credibility theory but needs refinement as respects profit and contingency margins and their relationship to credibility.

Credibility for Regression Models with Application to Trend

Charles A. Hachemeister
Prudential Reinsurance Company

Introduction

Inflation has moved from a minor annoyance to a major element in Casualty insurance rate making. Twenty years ago it was sufficient to adjust automobile rate levels without any trend of loss severity or frequency. Presently, this minor annoyance has become a major element in the rate making process. This development has led to the necessity of estimating these trends by state. However, no standards have been specifically developed for evaluating credibility of state trend line versus country wide trend lines.

Standards for developing credibility adjusted state trend lines are developed in this paper. The general approach is a direct extension of the Bühlmann & Straub (1970), "Credibility for Loss Ratios." The results obtained apply to much more general models than simple linear trend. In fact, credibility standards have been developed for arbitrary linear regression models.

Expected Severity Over Time

To put our thoughts into perspective, let us consider a concrete example of estimating expected severity over time for total private passenger BI total limits severity.[1]

---

[1] The Automobile Bodily Injury data in this paper has been supplied by the Insurance Services Office.

FIGURE 1

State #1
Private Passenger
Bodily Injury
Total Limits Severities

Time Period	t	# of Claims P_{t1}	Observed Severity x_{t1}
7-9/70	12	7861	1738
10-12/70	11	9251	1642
1-3/71	10	8706	1794
4-6/71	9	8575	2051
7-9/71	8	7917	2079
10-12/71	7	8263	2234
1-3/72	6	9456	2032
4-6/72	5	8003	2035
7-9/72	4	7365	2115
10-12/72	3	7832	2262
1-3/73	2	7849	2267
4-6/73	1	9077	2517

Figure 1 shows Private Passenger Automobile data from a particular state giving a number of claims in each calendar quarter along with the observed severity. Time is denoted by an index, t, for which observations are available from time n to time 1. Time runs backwards for reasons of computational ease below. In figure 1, we also introduce notation P_{ts} as the number of claims, and x_{ts} as the observed severity in time period t and state s.

It is our objective to estimate the expected value of x over time given s:

$$E(x_{ts}) = \mu_{ts}$$

Two competing choices for a model to estimate μ_{ts} are time series analysis, where the major emphasis lies on the interdependence of the x_{ij} for various i and j, and the regression model, where μ_{ts} is considered a linear combination of other observed variables. These two approaches are not entirely independent since it is possible to create a model which contains both the elements of interdependence of the x_{ij} and also a mean value μ_{ts} which is dependent upon observed values of other variables. The problem of dealing with such a model is the practical one of producing estimates of the auto-covariance function of the x_{ij} for different i and j at the same time as estimating the regression coefficients. However, the results of the analysis below will follow in large measure for either choice of model.

The Classical Trend and Regression Model

We will make the particular choice to model this expected value as a linear trend:

$$\mu_{st} = a_s + b_s t$$

If we introduce the two column matrices,

$$\beta_s = \begin{pmatrix} a_s \\ b_s \end{pmatrix}; \quad Y_{ts} = \begin{pmatrix} 1 \\ t \end{pmatrix}$$

then we will be able to write the expected value of x_{ts} in matrix form,

$$\mu_{ts} = Y'_{ts}\beta_s$$

Notice that this matrix formulation of μ_{ts} is not limited to a simple trend, but would apply also for models where

$$\mu_{ts} = \sum_{i=1}^{r} \beta_{si} y_{sti}$$

In this case,

$$\beta_s = \begin{pmatrix} \beta_{s1} \\ \beta_{s2} \\ \vdots \\ \beta_{sr} \end{pmatrix}$$

and the r by 1 matrix of independent variables is

$$Y_{ts} = \begin{pmatrix} y_{st1} \\ y_{st2} \\ \vdots \\ y_{str} \end{pmatrix} .$$

While we will only discuss the trend model in the numerical example given below, all the theoretical results follow for this more general model.

For development of the classical regression results, it will be necessary to deal with our data in matrix formulation. We will refer to the column matrix of severities for a given state as

$$X_s = \begin{pmatrix} x_{ns} \\ x_{n-1,s} \\ \vdots \\ x_{1s} \end{pmatrix} .$$

For each state we will also refer to the n by r matrix of independent variable observations over time as

$$Y_s = \begin{pmatrix} Y'_{ns} \\ Y'_{n-1,s} \\ \vdots \\ Y'_{1,s} \end{pmatrix} .$$

For our trend model this is a 12 by 2 matrix. The first column of which is all 1's; the second column of which has entries which go from 12 to 1.

With regard to the number of claims, it will be valuable to introduce an n by n square matrix with zeros in the nondiagonal elements and with the number of claims for each time period going down the main diagonal:

$$P_s = \begin{pmatrix} P_{ns} & & & \bigcirc \\ & P_{n-1,s} & & \\ & & \ddots & \\ \bigcirc & & & P_{1s} \end{pmatrix}$$

We will also find it necessary to refer to the mean value of the process for various time periods for a given state,

$$\mu_s = \begin{pmatrix} \mu_{ns} \\ \mu_{n-1,s} \\ \vdots \\ \mu_{1s} \end{pmatrix}$$

for which

$$\mu_s = Y_s \beta_s$$

now follows.

Time Series Implications

In a time series model one does not usually consider that the mean value μ_{ts} as dependent upon other variables, Y_{ts}. The direction of the investigation in such models is concerned with the n by n autocovariance matrix

$$C_s = E[X_s X_s'] - \mu_s \mu_s'$$

It is not the intention of this paper to pursue the time series direction of analysis. However, the results developed in this paper hold in large measure with an arbitrary autocovariance matrix.

We will follow the Bühlmann, Straub formulation in which the variance of x_{ts} is proportional to the number of claims:

$$E(x_{ts}^2) - \mu_{ts}^2 = \frac{\sigma_s^2}{P_{ts}}$$

and the severity x_{ts} is independent from time period to time period:[2]

$$E(x_{is}x_{js}) - \mu_{is}\mu_{js} = 0 \qquad i \neq j$$

This is, of course, an over simplification of the real world. With these assumptions we find the $n \times n$ auto-covariance matrix in terms of matrix P_s, defined above, as

$$C_s = \sigma_s^2 P_s^{-1}$$

Basic Summary Statistics

There will be certain statistics which will arise frequently in our discussion of the trend example. Figure 2 defines the summary statistics that we will need below. Note, of course, that only those statistics which involve x_{ts} are random variables.

FIGURE 2

Basic Summary Statistics

$$P_{.s} = \sum_{t=1}^{n} P_{ts} \qquad P_{..} = \sum_{s=1}^{N} P_{.s}$$

$$\bar{t}_s = \sum_{t=1}^{n} P_{ts}t/P_{.s} \qquad \bar{t} = \sum_{s=1}^{N} P_{.s}\bar{t}_s/P_{..}$$

$$\overline{t^2_s} = \sum_{t=1}^{n} P_{ts}t^2/P_{.s} \qquad \overline{t^2} = \sum_{s=1}^{N} P_{.s}\overline{t^2_s}/P_{..}$$

$$\bar{x}_s = \sum_{t=1}^{n} P_{ts}x_{ts}/P_{.s} \qquad \bar{x} = \sum_{s=1}^{N} P_{.s}\bar{x}_s/P_{..}$$

$$\overline{xt}_s = \sum_{t=1}^{n} P_{ts}tx_{ts}/P_{.s} \qquad \overline{xt} = \sum_{s=1}^{N} P_{.s}\overline{xt}_s/P_{..}$$

---

[2]Note particularly that this last assumption implies that there are no seasonal factors affecting the data.

FIGURE 2 (continued)

$$\sigma^2_{ts} = \overline{t^2_s} - \bar{t}^2_s \qquad \sigma^2_t = \overline{t^2} - \bar{t}^2$$

$$\sigma_{txs} = \overline{xt}_s - \bar{x}_s \bar{t}_s \qquad \sigma_{tx} = \overline{xt} - \bar{x}\,\bar{t}$$

$$\sigma^2_{xs} = \overline{x^2_s} - \bar{x}^2_s \qquad \sigma^2_x = \overline{x^2} - \bar{x}^2$$

State Wide Full Credibility Trend Estimates

Were we to follow the classical generalized least squares estimation procedures for β_s, we would find in terms of the matrices defined above

$$\hat{\beta}_s = (Y'_s C_s^{-1} Y_s)^{-1} Y'_s C_s^{-1} X_s$$

For our particular trend example these results become:

$$\hat{a}_s = \bar{x}_s - \bar{t}_s \hat{b}_s$$

and

$$\hat{b}_s = \sigma_{txs}/\sigma^2_{ts}$$

Pooled Data

Figure 3 compares the private passenger BI severity experience from state to state. Figure 4 contains the values for the summary statistics needed to calculate the estimates of slopes and intercepts contained on Figure 3. For our purposes we will consider that these five states make up the entire country. However, the analysis can be generalized to any number of states. Accordingly, we will refer below to N states. The right-hand two columns of this figure show the pooled data being the sum of the data elements from the five states for comparable time periods.

FIGURE 3

Private Passenger
Bodily Injury
Total Limits Severities
by State

		1		2		3		4		5		"Countrywide"	
Time Period	t	# of Claims P_{t1}	Severity x_{t1}	# of Claims P_{t2}	Severity x_{t2}	# of Claims P_{t3}	Severity x_{t3}	# of Claims P_{t4}	Severity x_{t4}	# of Claims P_{ts}	Severity x_{ts}	# of Claims $P_{t.}$	Severity $x_{t.}$
7-9/70	12	7861	1738	1622	1364	1147	1759	407	1223	2902	1456	13939	1623
10-12/70	11	9251	1642	1742	1408	1357	1685	396	1146	3172	1499	15918	1579
1-3/71	10	8706	1794	1523	1597	1329	1479	348	1010	3046	1609	14952	1690
4-6/71	9	8575	2051	1515	1444	1204	1763	341	1257	3068	1741	14703	1882
7-9/71	8	7917	2079	1622	1342	998	1674	315	1426	2693	1482	13545	1827
10-12/71	7	8263	2234	1602	1675	1077	2103	328	1532	2910	1572	14180	2009
1-3/72	6	9456	2032	1964	1470	1277	1502	352	1953	3275	1606	16324	1836
4-6/72	5	8003	2035	1515	1448	1218	1622	331	1123	2697	1735	13764	1853
7-9/72	4	7365	2115	1527	1464	896	1828	287	1343	2663	1607	12738	1893
10-12/72	3	7832	2262	1748	1831	1003	2155	384	1243	3017	1573	13984	2024
1-3/73	2	7849	2267	1654	1612	1108	2233	321	1762	3242	1613	14174	2027
4-6/73	1	9077	2517	1861	1471	1121	2059	342	1306	3425	1690	15826	2157
Intercept	$\hat{a}_s$		2470		1621		2096		1538		1676		2148
Slope	$\hat{b}_s$		- 62.39		- 17.14		- 43.32		- 27.81		- 11.87		- 43.35

FIGURE 4

Values of Summary
Statistics by State

State:	1	2	3	4	5	"Countrywide"
$P_{.s}$	100,155	19,895	13,735	4,152	36,110	174,047
$\bar{t}_s$	6.54972	6.41171	6.69982	6.66089	6.43725	6.52511
$\overline{t^2}_s$	54.88889	53.22398	56.91824	56.79143	53.75876	54.66964
$\bar{x}_s$	2,060.92	1,511.22	1,805.84	1,352.98	1,599.83	1,865.40
$\overline{xt}_s$	12,750.36	9,481.90	11,577.80	8,666.54	10,152.19	11,647.75
σ^2_{ts}	11.99009	12.11393	12.03068	12.42402	12.32061	12.09264
σ_{txs}	-748.09102	-207.62975	-521.01641	-345.04749	-146.30085	-524.21257
σ^2_{xs}	55,881.	18,725.	60,776.	68,275.	7,573.	99807

Just as we have a need to be able to refer to all the data within a state in a concise fashion, we will have a need to refer to all of the data country wide in a concise fashion. To this end for severities we define the $n \times N$ by 1 column of severities as

$$X = \begin{pmatrix} X_1 \\ X_2 \\ \vdots \\ X_N \end{pmatrix},$$

the $n \times N$ by r matrix of independent variable observations as

$$Y = \begin{pmatrix} Y_1 \\ Y_2 \\ \vdots \\ Y_N \end{pmatrix},$$

and the super matrix of numbers of claims matrices as the $n \times N$ matrix

$$P = \begin{pmatrix} P_1 & & & O \\ & P_2 & & \\ & & \ddots & \\ O & & & P_N \end{pmatrix}.$$

Also, we will consider the $n \times N$ by 1 column matrix of mean values:

$$E(X) = \mu = \begin{pmatrix} \mu_1 \\ \mu_2 \\ \vdots \\ \mu_N \end{pmatrix}$$

It will also be necessary for us to use the autocovariance

matrix of all of the severities country wide:

$$E[XX'] - \mu\mu' = C = \begin{pmatrix} C_1 & & & & \bigcirc \\ & C_2 & & & \\ & & \cdot & & \\ & & & \cdot & \\ \bigcirc & & & \cdot & C_N \end{pmatrix}$$

It is important to note that since this "super" autocovariance matrix is made up of the state autocovariance matrices down the super diagonal with zero elements elsewhere, this model specifically considers that the observations from one state are independent of those from another state.

In terms of these super matrices, the pooled "country wide" estimates of β become:

$$\hat{\beta} = (Y'C^{-1}Y)^{-1}Y'C^{-1}X$$

<u>State Versus "Countrywide" Trend</u>

The estimates of the intercept and slope of the trend line shown on figure 3 vary substantially from state to state. Without credibility the only two alternatives available to the decision maker is whether to consider the data from the other states to be from the same basic population as the state in question, and therefore use the country wide estimate; or to consider that the state data was sufficiently different, and therefore throw out the data from other states using only the state estimate. Figure 5 compares the country wide severity data with that of state #4. Notice that the country wide data lies more closely about the least squares trend line, although the country wide line lies substantially above the state line. One is not exactly happy with the trend line estimate for the state because of the very wide variation of the data points about that line. In this instance, one might be more ready to accept the country wide versus the state trend.

Figure 5

State no. 4 vs "Countrywide"

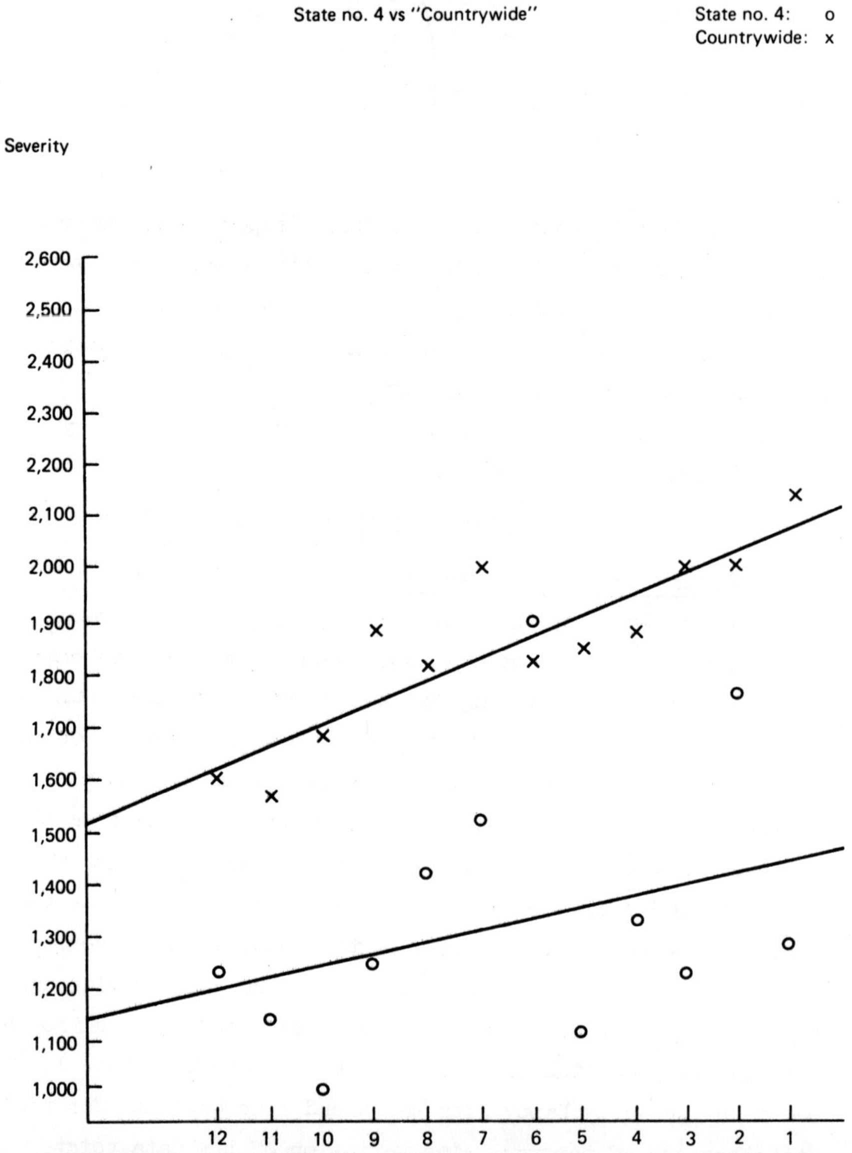

However, state versus country wide are not the only two choices. If one were to believe that the distribution of x_{ts} varied from state to state and had to choose an optimal decision over all of the states, a compound decision problem, then it is not clear whether the choice should be a state wide or a country wide trend. The exact solution of this problem, produces a credibility weighting between the two trends, as will be seen below.

Alternatively, if one is only making a single decision for one state but if it is believed that the distribution of x is a random pick from some set of distributions governed by an index, say θ_s, then the result is the same as the compound decision.

Figure 6 contains the estimated trend lines for each of our five states and the heavier line as that for country wide. It is clear from looking at this figure that the slopes and intercepts vary from state to state. In the compound problem of trying to choose a set of trend lines for all of the states to optimize the total trend choice, one should act as if the slopes and intercepts do have a distribution which is reflected in these differences.

With the introduction of an index θ_s to describe these distributions, we need to reformulate the state data in terms of this index. First of all, the β_s become functions of θ_s

$$\beta_s = B(\theta_s)$$

as does the expected value of x_{ts} given θ_s

$$E[x_{ts}|\theta_s] = \mu_{ts}(\theta_s) = Y'_{ts}B(\theta_s)$$

The autocovariance matrix is in general a matrix function of θ_s

$$C_s = C_s(\theta_s)$$

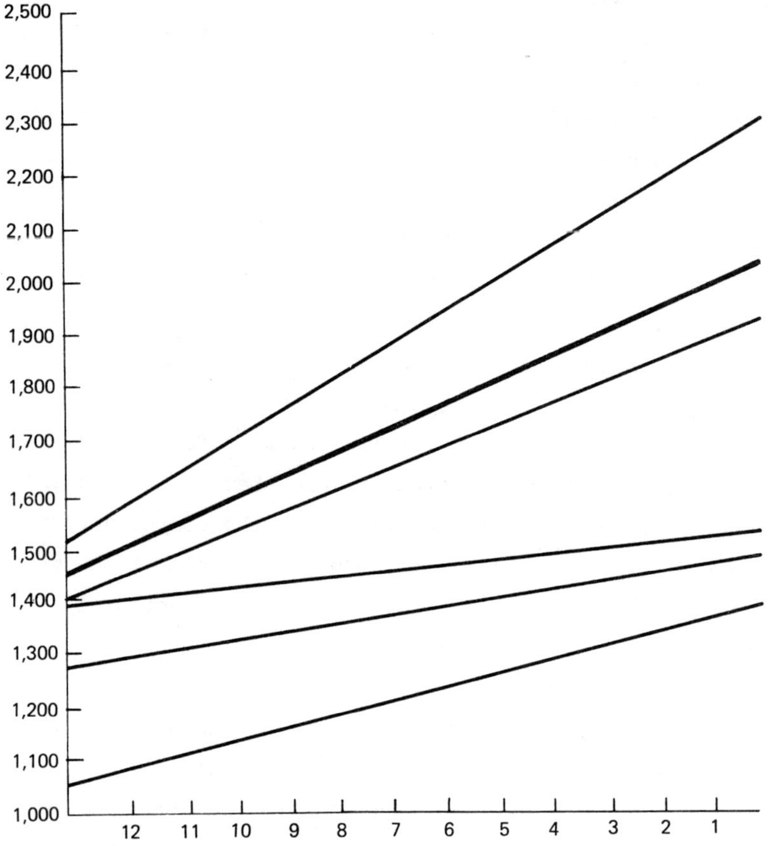

Figure 6

Comparison of Observed State Trends

In this paper we will pursue the case of where the autocovariance matrix is known up to a scalar multiplier, the variance of x_{ts} which is a function of θ_s:

$$C_s(\theta_s) = \sigma^2(\theta_s)P_s^{-1}$$

Expected Values Over θ

It will be necessary below to take expected values of various functions of θ.

$B(\theta)$:

The expected value of the column matrix B is equal to a column matrix β without subscripts

$$E[B(\theta)] = \beta .$$

The covariance matrix of the $B(\theta)$ will be denoted by the r by r matrix:

$$E[B(\theta_s)B'(\theta_s)] - \beta\beta' = \Gamma_{rxr} .$$

μ:

The expected value of μ_{ts} is now:

$$E[\mu_{ts}(\theta_s)] = Y'_{ts}\beta$$

With a natural extension to the column matrix μ_s within a state and then country wide to μ as:

$$E[\mu_s(\theta_s)] = Y_s\beta \quad \text{and} \quad E[\mu(\theta_1,\ldots,\theta_N)] = Y\beta$$

We will also find it necessary to refer below to the column matrix of autocovariances between a particular mean value and that of all other mean values:

$$E[\mu\mu_{tk}(\theta_k)] - Y_h\beta\beta' Y_{tk} = \begin{pmatrix} Y_1\Gamma Y_{tk}\delta_{1k} \\ Y_2\Gamma Y_{tk}\delta_{2k} \\ \vdots \\ Y_N\Gamma Y_{tk}\delta_{Nk} \end{pmatrix}$$

where δ_{ij} is the Kronecker delta:

$$\delta_{ij} = \begin{cases} 1 & i = j \\ 0 & i \neq j \end{cases}$$

The autocovariance matrix of the mean values is a super matrix of $n \times n$ matrices down the super diagonal with zero elements clscwhere:

$$E[\mu\mu'] - E[\mu]E[\mu'] = \begin{pmatrix} Y_1 \Gamma Y_1' & & & \bigcirc \\ & Y_2 \Gamma Y_2' & & \\ & & \ddots & \\ \bigcirc & & & Y_N \Gamma Y_N' \end{pmatrix}$$

$\sigma_s^2(\theta_s)$:
The state variance is also a variable now, which depends upon θ_s. The expected value of the autocovariance matrix for a given state is denoted by:

$$E[C_s(\theta_s)] = V_s$$

However, in our case we will take:

$$V_s = \sigma^2 P_s^{-1}$$

The extension of this to the country wide autocovariance matrix is:

$$E[C] = V = \begin{pmatrix} V_1 & & & \bigcirc \\ & V_2 & & \\ & & \ddots & \\ \bigcirc & & & V_N \end{pmatrix} = \sigma^2 P^{-1}$$

Estimation of $\mu_{ij}(\theta_j)$

With this preliminary background, it is now possible to consider estimates of the mean value of the trend line at any point of time. We take the usual conditions of unbiasedness and minimum variance:

$$E\hat{\mu}_{ij} = E\mu_{ij}(\theta_j)$$

$$E\{(\hat{\mu}^*_{ij} - \mu_{ij}(\theta))^2\} \leq E\{\hat{\mu}_{ij} - \mu_{ij}(\theta))^2\} \tag{1}$$

where we will accept the estimator μ^*_{ij} as the optimal estimator, if (1) holds for all possible estimators $\hat{\mu}_{ij}$.

Following Bühlmann and Straub, we will consider estimators of the form:

$$\hat{\mu}_{ij} = \alpha_0 + \sum_{s=1}^{N} \sum_{t=1}^{n} \alpha_{ts} x_{ts} = \alpha_0 + X'A$$

Where we introduce the column vector of coefficients for state and country wide as

$$A_s = \begin{pmatrix} \alpha_{1s} \\ \alpha_{2s} \\ \vdots \\ \alpha_{ns} \end{pmatrix} \quad \text{and} \quad A = \begin{pmatrix} A_1 \\ A_2 \\ \vdots \\ A_N \end{pmatrix}$$

While we require our estimator to be unbiased, this will happen automatically because of the inclusion of the additive constant of α_0 in the estimator. Accordingly, to determine our estimator we will minimize:

$$\Phi_{ij} = E[\{\alpha_0 + X'A - \mu_{ij}(\theta_j)\}^2]$$

To do this, we take the partial derivative of Φ_{ij} with respect to α_0 set to 0

$$\frac{\partial\Phi_{ij}}{\alpha_0} = 2E[\alpha_0 + X'A - \mu_{ij}(\theta_j)] = 0$$

to find:

$$\alpha_0 = E[\mu_{ij}(\theta_j)] - E[\mu']A = \beta'[Y_{ij} - Y'A]$$

The column vector of partial derivatives of Φ_{ij} with respect to A is set equal to 0,

$$\frac{\partial\Phi_{ij}}{\partial A} = 2E[XX'A + X(\alpha_0 - \mu_{ij}(\theta_j))] = 0$$

finding:

$$E[(C + \mu\mu')A + \mu\alpha_0] = E[\mu\mu_{ij}(\theta_j)]$$

after taking conditional expectations holding the θ_s for $s = 1$ to N, constant and rearranging terms. Carrying out the expectation over the θ_s, we find:

$$[V + E(\mu\mu') - E(\mu)E(\mu')]A = E[\mu\mu_{ij}(\theta_j)] - E[\mu]E[\mu_{ij}(\theta_j)]$$

To this point the analysis has been quite general without depending upon the form of V or of the form of the autocovariance matrix of the μ. To proceed it is necessary for us to assume V and the autocovariance matrix of μ to be comprised of n by n matrices of state data down the super diagonal with zeros elsewhere. If this is the case for each state, we may now write:

$$(V_s + Y_s\Gamma Y_s')A_s = Y_s\Gamma Y_{ij}\delta_{sj} \tag{2}$$

which immediately indicates that

$$A_s = 0 \quad \text{for} \quad s \neq j$$

If we premultiply (2) for state j by $Y_j'V_j^{-1}$, we find:

$$(I + Y_j'V_j^{-1}Y_j\Gamma)Y_j'A_j = Y_j'V_j^{-1}Y_j\Gamma Y_{ij}$$

Anticipating later results, let us pause for a moment to define:

$$K_j = P_{.j}(Y_j'V_j^{-1}Y_j\Gamma)^{-1}$$

and the credibility matrix:[3]

$$Z_j = P_{.j}(P_{.j}I + K_j)^{-1}$$

---

[3]The K_j matrix only exists if Γ is positive definite. However, the Z_j matrix always exists even when K_j does not; and may be written in the form:

$$Z_j = Y_j'V_j^{-1}Y_j\Gamma(I + Y_j'V_j^{-1}Y_j\Gamma)^{-1}$$

This immediately yields:

$$Y_j' A_j = Z_j Y_{ij}$$

Combining this with (2), we now find:

$$A_j = V_j^{-1} Y_j \Gamma [I - Z_j] Y_{ij}$$

Premultiplying this by X_j' and rearranging terms, since

$$Y_j' V_j^{-1} Y_j \Gamma [I - Z_j] = Z_j$$

we find:

$$X_j' A_j = \hat{\beta}_j' Z_j Y_{ij}$$

for the case where C_j is known up to a scalar multiplier[4] which depends upon θ_j. Recall that in the case of greatest interest to us $C_j = \sigma^2(\theta_j) P_j^{-1}$. Now since

$$\alpha_0 = \beta' [I - Z_j] Y_{ij}$$

we can finally write our estimator as:

$$\hat{\mu}_{ij} = [\hat{\beta}_j' Z_j + \beta' (I - Z_j)] Y_{ij}$$

It is particularly interesting and satisfying to note that this estimator holds for any Y_{ij}. In other words, we have credibility adjusted the regression coefficients.

Relation to the Bühlmann, Straub Model

The form of the estimator in the Bühlmann, Straub model was:

$$\hat{\mu}_{ij} = X' A$$

[4] If C_j is some more complex function of θ_j, $\hat{\beta}_j$ becomes a function of θ_j such that in general

$$E\hat{\beta}_j \neq (Y_j' V_j^{-1} Y_j)^{-1} Y_j' V_j^{-1} X_j$$

without an additive constant. If this model were followed through for the regression case, one would find:

$$\hat{\mu}_{ij} = [\beta'_j Z_j + d\beta'(I - Z_j)]Y_{ij}$$

which is the same as the estimator above, except for d, which is equal to the expression:

$$d = \sum_{s=1}^{N} \hat{\beta}'_s Z_s \Gamma^{-1}\beta / \sum_{s=1}^{N} \beta' Z_s \Gamma^{-1}\beta .$$

In the univariate case of Bühlmann and Straub the parameter equivalent of β cancelled entirely from the estimator. However, in the multivariate case, this is not so; so that there is no benefit to using the estimator without the additive constant.

Parameter Estimation

To apply our credibility model to real data, we need to be in a position to estimate the various elements which are not directly observable within it. Up to this point we have been able to be very general in the form of the autocovariance matrix within a given state. At this point, we sacrifice this generality to be able to produce unbiased estimators of the parameters in question. The easiest parameter to deal with is the column matrix β. The least squares estimate of β, using pooled data, is unbiased:

$$E(\hat{\beta}) = E[(Y'PY)^{-1}Y'PX] = \beta$$

For an estimator of expected value of the state variance σ^2, let us consider the mean square error for a given state:

$$\hat{\sigma}^2_s = \frac{1}{n - r} \sum_{t=1}^{n} P_{ts}(x_{ts} - \hat{\mu}_{ts})^2 .$$

In matrix terms this becomes:

$$\hat{\sigma}^2_s = \frac{1}{n - r} (X'_s P_s X_s - X'_s P_s Y_s (Y'_s P_s Y_s)^{-1} Y'_s P_s X_s)$$

Following the classical evaluation of the expected value of the mean square error as outlined in Goldberger,[5] we note that the above matrix is a 1 by 1 matrix and further that the trace of any two matrices is independent of the order of multiplication:

$$tr(AB) = tr(BA)$$

so that we may evaluate the expected value of $\hat{\sigma}_s^2$ as:

$$(n - r)E(\hat{\sigma}_s^2) = E\ tr[P_s(I - Y_s(Y_s' P_s Y_s)^{-1} Y_s' P_s) X_s X_s']$$

since

$$I - Y_s(Y_s' P_s Y_s)^{-1} Y_s' P_s \quad \text{annihilates} \quad Y_s B(\theta_s) B'(\theta_s) Y_s'$$

this becomes:

$$(n - r)E(\hat{\sigma}_s^2) = tr[P_s(I - Y_s(Y_s' P_s Y_s)^{-1} Y_s' P_s) V_s]$$

or

$$E(\hat{\sigma}_s^2) = \frac{1}{n - r}\{trI_{n\times n} - tr\ I_{r\times r}\}\sigma^2 ,$$

so that $\hat{\sigma}_s^2$ is an unbiased estimator of σ^2. We shall take the unweighted average of these state mean square errors as our overall estimator of σ^2:

$$\hat{\sigma}^2 = \frac{1}{N} \sum_{s=1}^{N} \hat{\sigma}_s^2$$

which is clearly unbiased.

The estimator of the covariance matrix of the $B(\theta)$ is somewhat more difficult to find an estimator for. First of all, consider:

$$G = \sum_{s=1}^{N} (Y' PY)^{-1}(Y_s' P_s Y_s)(\hat{\beta}_s - \hat{\beta})(\hat{\beta}_s - \hat{\beta})' .$$

To evaluate the expected value of G, let us first consider expected values of matrices of estimators of the $\hat{\beta}_s$. In

---

[5] "Econometric Theory"; John Wiley & Sons, Inc. - Page 166

particular, we note:

$$\hat{\beta}_j\hat{\beta}'_s = (Y_jP_jY_j)^{-1}Y'_jP_jX_jX'P_sY_s(Y'_sP_sY_s)^{-1} ,$$

so that:

$$E(\hat{\beta}_j\hat{\beta}'_s) = \beta\beta' + [\Gamma + \sigma^2(Y'_sP_sY_s)^{-1}]\delta_{js} .$$

At this point we now wish to consider the expected value of $\hat{\hat{\beta}}\hat{\beta}'_s$. To evaluate this expected value, we will assume:

$$\hat{\hat{\beta}}\hat{\beta}'_s = \sum_{j-1}^{N} (Y'PY)^{-1}(Y'_jP_jY_j)\hat{\beta}_j\hat{\beta}'_s$$

Using this relationship, we find:

$$E(\hat{\hat{\beta}}\hat{\beta}'_s) = \beta\beta' + (Y'PY)^{-1}(Y'_sP_sY_s)\Gamma + (Y'PY)^{-1}\sigma^2$$

Using a similar analysis for $\hat{\hat{\beta}}\hat{\hat{\beta}}'$ yields:

$$\hat{\hat{\beta}}\hat{\hat{\beta}}' = \sum_{j=1}^{N} \hat{\hat{\beta}}\hat{\beta}'_j(Y'_jP_jY_j)(Y'PY)^{-1} \quad \text{and}$$

$$E(\hat{\hat{\beta}}\hat{\hat{\beta}}') = \beta\beta' + \sum_{j=1}^{N} (Y'PY)^{-1}(Y'_jP_jY_j)\Gamma(Y'_jP_jY_j)(Y'PY)^{-1} + \\ + (Y'PY)^{-1}\sigma^2$$

Combining our results we find:

$$E(G) = \left[I - \sum_{s=1}^{N} (Y'PY)^{-1}(Y'_sP_sY_s)(Y'PY)^{-1}(Y'_sP_sY_s)\right]\Gamma \\ + (N - 1)(Y'PY)^{-1}\sigma^2$$

If we introduce the r by r matrix

$$\Pi = I - \sum_{s=1}^{N} (Y'PY)^{-1}(Y'_sP_sY_s)(Y'PY)^{-1}(Y'_sP_sY_s) ,$$

an unbiased estimator for Γ is

$$H = \Pi^{-1}(G - (N - 1)(Y'PY)^{-1}\hat{\sigma}^2) .$$

However, since Γ is symmetric we will take our estimator as

$$\hat{\Gamma} = \tfrac{1}{2}(H + H')$$

Form of the Estimators for the Trend Example

To put the above theoretical results into perspective, let us translate them into the trend example. The 2 by 2 matrix of weighted independent variables becomes:

$$Y_s' P_s Y_s = P_{.s} \begin{pmatrix} 1 & \bar{t}_s \\ \bar{t}_s & \overline{t^2_s} \end{pmatrix}$$

The slope and intercept are:

$$\hat{\beta}_s = \begin{pmatrix} \hat{a}_s \\ \hat{b}_s \end{pmatrix} = \begin{pmatrix} \bar{x}_s - \bar{t}_s \, \sigma_{txs}/\sigma^2_{ts} \\ \sigma_{txs}/\sigma^2_{ts} \end{pmatrix}$$

The estimate of average variance is:

$$\hat{\sigma}^2 = \frac{1}{N(n-2)} \sum_{s=1}^{N} P_{.s}(\sigma^2_{xs} - \sigma^2_{txs}/\sigma^2_{ts})$$

The elements of $\hat{\Gamma}$ are denoted as:

$$\hat{\Gamma} = \begin{pmatrix} \hat{\sigma}^2_a & \hat{\sigma}_{ab} \\ \hat{\sigma}_{ab} & \hat{\sigma}^2_b \end{pmatrix}$$

The K matrix within the credibility form then becomes:

$$\hat{K}_s = \begin{pmatrix} \hat{k}_{s11} & \hat{k}_{s12} \\ \hat{k}_{s21} & \hat{k}_{s22} \end{pmatrix}$$

$$= \frac{\hat{\sigma}^2}{\sigma^2_{ts}(\hat{\sigma}^2_a \hat{\sigma}^2_b - \hat{\sigma}^2_{ab})} \begin{pmatrix} \hat{\sigma}^2_b \overline{t^2_s} + \hat{\sigma}_{ab}\bar{t} & -\hat{\sigma}^2_b \bar{t} - \hat{\sigma}_{ab} \\ \hat{\sigma}_{ab}\overline{t^2} - \hat{\sigma}^2_a \bar{t} & \hat{\sigma}_{ab}\bar{t} + \hat{\sigma}^2_a \end{pmatrix}$$

Thus the credibility formula becomes:

$$Z_s = \frac{P_{.s}}{P_{.s}^2 + (\hat{k}_{s11} + \hat{k}_{s22})P_{.s} + \hat{k}_{s11}\hat{k}_{s22} - \hat{k}_{s12}\hat{k}_{s21}} \times \begin{pmatrix} P_{.s} + \hat{k}_{s22} & -\hat{k}_{s12} \\ -\hat{k}_{s21} & P_{.s} + \hat{k}_{s11} \end{pmatrix}$$

Using the data shown in figure 4 these estimators take on the values as shown in figure 7.

Figure 7

Numerical Value of the estimates

$$\Pi = \begin{pmatrix} .61017 & -.00468 \\ -.00066 & .60537 \end{pmatrix}$$

$$\hat{\Gamma} = \begin{pmatrix} 241,550 & -13,819 \\ -13,819 & 805 \end{pmatrix}$$

$$K_1 = \begin{pmatrix} -49,179 & 9,073 \\ -874,219 & 160,327 \end{pmatrix}$$

$$K_2 = \begin{pmatrix} -48,080 & 9,097 \\ -854,430 & 160,691 \end{pmatrix}$$

$$K_3 = \begin{pmatrix} -49,479 & 8,914 \\ -879,957 & 157,592 \end{pmatrix}$$

$$K_4 = \begin{pmatrix} -47,466 & 8,664 \\ -844,260 & 153,154 \end{pmatrix}$$

$$K_5 = \begin{pmatrix} -47,194 & 8,923 \\ -838,835 & 157,632 \end{pmatrix}$$

$$G - (N-1)(Y'PY)^{-1}\hat{\sigma}^2 =$$

$$= \begin{pmatrix} 147,451 & -8,415.88 \\ -8,544.26 & 496.3438 \end{pmatrix}$$

$$\hat{\sigma}^2 = 44,057,744$$

$$Z_1 = \begin{pmatrix} 1.2489 & -.0435 \\ 4.0219 & .2444 \end{pmatrix}$$

$$Z_2 = \begin{pmatrix} 1.3871 & -.0699 \\ 6.4852 & -.2165 \end{pmatrix}$$

$$Z_3 = \begin{pmatrix} 1.3680 & -.0712 \\ 7.0261 & -.2854 \end{pmatrix}$$

$$Z_4 = \begin{pmatrix} 1.1083 & -.0610 \\ 6.0202 & -.3052 \end{pmatrix}$$

$$Z_5 = \begin{pmatrix} 1.2376 & -.0570 \\ 5.5842 & -.0708 \end{pmatrix}$$

Using these numerical values, we find the credibility adjusted slopes and intercepts. These are compared with the state and country wide slopes and intercepts on figure 8.

FIGURE 8

State			State Data	Credibility Adjusted Data	Countrywide Data
1	Intercept:	a	2470	2473	2148
	Slope:	b	-62.39	-61.98	-43.35
2	Intercept:	a	1621	1587	2148
	Slope:	b	-17.14	-12.19	-43.35
3	Intercept:	a	2096	2077	2148
	Slope:	b	-43.31	-39.64	-43.35
4	Intercept:	a	1538	1566	2148
	Slope:	b	-27.81	-10.85	-43.35
5	Intercept:	a	1676	1740	2148
	Slope:	b	-11.87	-18.68	-43.35

Figure 9 compares the state trend line denoted by S and the country wide trend line denoted by C with the credibility adjusted trend line denoted by A. In all of the states, except state # 4, the credibility adjusted trend line is virtually the same as the state trend line. However, in state #4, with a smaller claim volume, the credibility adjusted trend line is such different from the state trend line. State #4 trend lines clearly point out a distressing aspect of the credibility adjusted trend line. The credibility adjusted trend line has a lower trend than both the country wide and state trend lines. In fact, a closer examination of the other state trend line graphs will show that the credibility adjusted trend for state #2 is also lower than both state and country wide. In state #1 the credibility adjusted slope is less than for the state but the credibility adjusted trend line lies above both the state and country wide lines for the

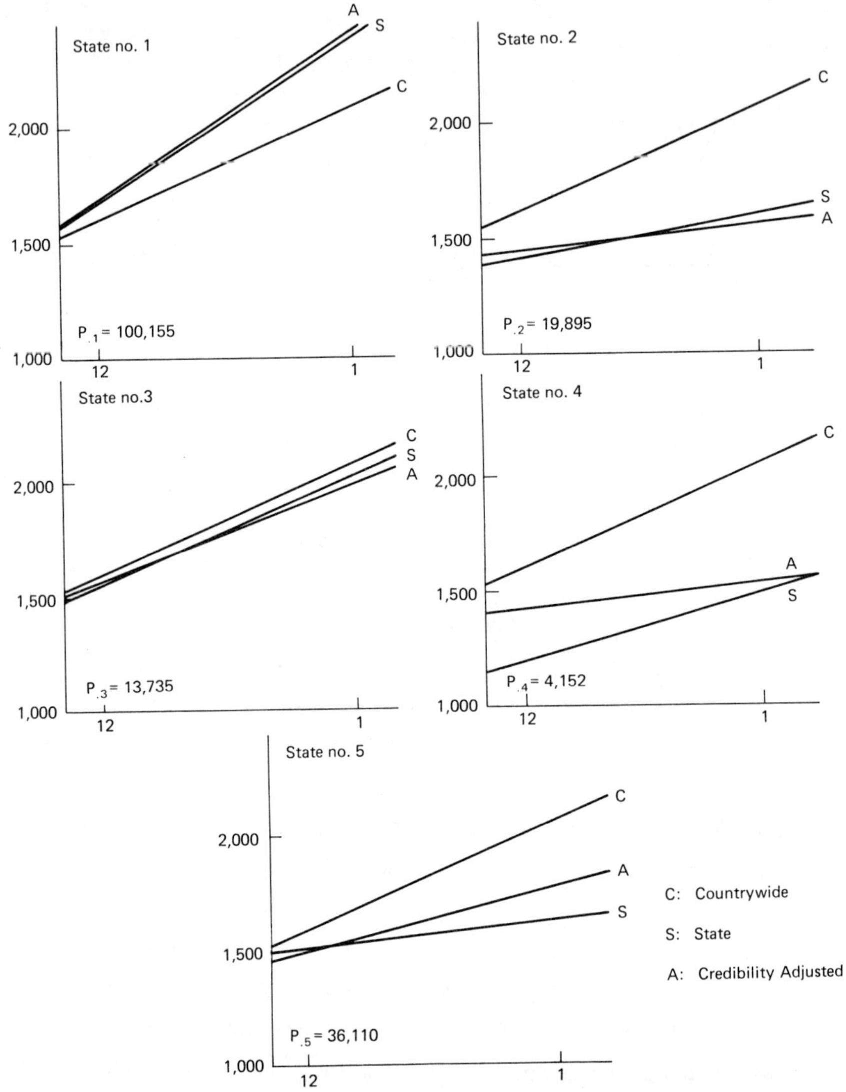

Figure 9

Comparison of
Credibility Adjusted Trend Lines
with State and Countrywide Lines

time period from our observed values were taken.

These strange results arise from our choice of model. That is, we have assumed that not only can the trend for a given state be considered as being a pick from a distribution of trends, but also that the level of severity for a random pick over some distribution of average severity levels. However, if we were to reflect upon what a proper model for trend would be, it is fairly easy to conclude that the level of severity as embodied by the intercept, a_s in the trend line, is distinctly different from state to state and should not be credibility adjusted for.

It is possible to alleviate this defect by changing the basic credibility model. In order to more adequately discuss this, it is necessary for us to first discuss the effect of linear transformations of the independent variables on our credibility estimate, $\hat{\mu}_{ij}$.

Invariance of $\hat{\mu}_{ij}$ Under Transformations of the Independent Variables

The column matrix Y_{ts} describes the values of r variables which are observed at time t. Such that

$$\mu_{ts} = Y'_{ts}\beta_s$$

This mean value could just as well be described by a linear combination of transformed variables Y^*_{ts}

$$\mu_{ts} = Y^{*\prime}_{ts}\beta^*_s$$

The easiest example of this is simple scaling and translation of each of the independent variables. In our case we would define time about an origin and with a scale such that the weighted average of the scaled times was zero and the sample variance of the scaled times was equal to one. This transformation would be accomplished by a matrix:

$$T_s = \begin{pmatrix} 1 & 0 \\ -\bar{t}_s/\sigma_{ts} & 1/\sigma_{ts} \end{pmatrix}$$

This matrix can be considered a mapping of Y_{ts} to Y^*_{ts}:

$$Y_{ts} = \begin{pmatrix} 1 \\ t \end{pmatrix} \xrightarrow[T_s]{} Y^*_{ts} = \begin{pmatrix} 1 \\ \dfrac{t - \bar{t}_s}{\sigma_{ts}} \end{pmatrix}$$

However, it is not necessary to merely consider simple locations scaling transformations; but any arbitrary linear transformation on Y_{ts} will not affect the credibility estimate $\hat{\mu}_{ts}$.

An arbitrary transformation T_s will generate:

$$Y^*_{ts} = T_s Y_{ts}$$

from which

$$Y^*_s = Y_s T'_s$$

and

$$Y^{*\prime}_s P_s Y^*_s = T_s Y'_s P_s Y_s T'_s$$

follow immediately.

In order that the mean value estimate still holds, the inverse transformation must be applied to β_s

$$\mu_{ts} = Y'_{ts}\beta_s = Y^{*\prime}_{ts}\beta^*_s \Rightarrow \beta^*_s = T'^{-1}_s \beta_s$$

Similarly, if the mean value were to hold using the countrywide β, this same transformation needs to be applied:

$$\beta^*_s = T'^{-1}_s \beta$$

With regard to the transformed estimates of β_s, it follows from the above that:

$$\hat{\beta}^*_s = T'^{-1}_s \hat{\beta}_s$$

With regard to the countrywide estimates $\hat{\beta}$, a transformed estimate will be denoted as:

$$\hat{\beta}_s^* = T_s'^{-1}\hat{\beta}$$

The transformed β_s will now generate a transformed Γ matrix which varies by state, denoted by:

$$\Gamma_s^* = T_s'^{-1}\Gamma T_s^{-1}$$

This will lead to a transformed credibility matrix:

$$Z_s^* = T_s Z_s T_s^{-1}$$

combining these elements to find the transformed estimate:

$$\mu_{ts}^* = [\hat{\beta}_s^* Z_s^* + \hat{\beta}_s^*(I - Z_s^*)]Y_{ts}^*$$

It is immediately clear that this estimate is identical with the original untransformed estimate.

<u>Origin and Scale Transformations for the Trend Model</u>

One of the immediate implications of the above results is that the credibility results found above would have been the same if our time data had been transformed to have zero mean and unit variance. Using the result of this transformation

$$Y_{ts}^* = \begin{pmatrix} 1 \\ \dfrac{t - \bar{t}_s}{\sigma_{ts}} \end{pmatrix}$$

simplifies the credibility form since

$$Y_s^{*\prime} P_s Y_s^* = P_{.s} I$$

However, now the Γ matrix varies from state to state. Explicitly

$$\Gamma_s^* = \begin{pmatrix} \sigma_{as}^2 & \sigma_{abs} \\ \sigma_{abs} & \sigma_{bs}^2 \end{pmatrix}$$

$$= \begin{pmatrix} \sigma_a^2 + 2\sigma ab\bar{t}_s + \bar{t}_s^2\sigma b^2 & \sigma_{ts}(\sigma_{ab} + \bar{t}_s\sigma b^2 \\ \sigma_{ts}(\sigma_{ab} + \bar{t}_s\sigma b^2) & \sigma_{ts}^2\sigma b^2 \end{pmatrix}$$

The transformed credibility constant K_s^* now takes on the simple form:

$$K_s^* = \sigma^2\Gamma_s^{*-1}$$

The transformed credibility matrix:

$$Z_s^* = P_{.s}(P_{.s}I + K_s^*)^{-1}$$

still has the same general form as in the untransformed case. The $\hat{\beta}_s^*$, $\hat{\hat{\beta}}_s^*$ and estimated values of Γ_s^*, K_s^* and Z_s^* are shown in figure 10 by state for the scale and location transformation.

Mixed Models

The upsetting results for the credibility adjusted trend line shown above in figure 9 came about because the mean value μ_{ts} is modeled in the same fashion for each state, specifically assuming that both slopes and intercepts were distributed about some mean value slope b and mean value intercept a. If we were to pause for a moment to think about our personal model of the trend situation; we would be more inclined to believe that while the avarage dollar at any point and time would vary substantially from state to state, the rate of change in the average dollar would tend to be the same from state to state. The modeling implication of this is, first of all, not to use a trend line; but to use an exponential trend. We will not pursue this direction in this paper. However, this analysis will be carried out in further research on this subject.

FIGURE 10

Estimates for Scaled t

State	Transformed State Coefficients	Transformed Countrywide Coefficients	Transformed Γ	Transformed K	Transformed Credibility Matrix
s	$\hat{\beta}_s^*$	$\hat{\hat{\beta}}_s^*$	Γ_s^*	K_s^*	Z_s^*
1	$\begin{pmatrix} 2,061 \\ -216.04 \end{pmatrix}$	$\begin{pmatrix} 1,864 \\ -150.11 \end{pmatrix}$	$\begin{pmatrix} 95,058 & -29,596 \\ -29,596 & 9,651 \end{pmatrix}$	$\begin{pmatrix} 10,244 & 31,415 \\ 31,415 & 100,904 \end{pmatrix}$	$\begin{pmatrix} .9494 & -.1483 \\ -.1483 & .5213 \end{pmatrix}$
2	$\begin{pmatrix} 1,511 \\ -59.66 \end{pmatrix}$	$\begin{pmatrix} 1,870 \\ -150.88 \end{pmatrix}$	$\begin{pmatrix} 97,433 & -30,135 \\ -30,135 & 9,751 \end{pmatrix}$	$\begin{pmatrix} 10,244 & 31,661 \\ 31,661 & 102,367 \end{pmatrix}$	$\begin{pmatrix} .9068 & -.2348 \\ -.2348 & .2235 \end{pmatrix}$
3	$\begin{pmatrix} 1,806 \\ -150.21 \end{pmatrix}$	$\begin{pmatrix} 1,858 \\ -150.36 \end{pmatrix}$	$\begin{pmatrix} 92,511 & -29,227 \\ -29,227 & 9,684 \end{pmatrix}$	$\begin{pmatrix} 10,244 & 30,919 \\ 30,919 & 97,868 \end{pmatrix}$	$\begin{pmatrix} .8911 & -.2469 \\ -.2469 & .1915 \end{pmatrix}$
4	$\begin{pmatrix} 1,353 \\ -98.01 \end{pmatrix}$	$\begin{pmatrix} 1,860 \\ -152.80 \end{pmatrix}$	$\begin{pmatrix} 93,168 & -29,811 \\ -29,811 & 10,000 \end{pmatrix}$	$\begin{pmatrix} 10,244 & 30,539 \\ 30,539 & 95,443 \end{pmatrix}$	$\begin{pmatrix} .8251 & -.2530 \\ -.2530 & .1193 \end{pmatrix}$
5	$\begin{pmatrix} 1,600 \\ -41.68 \end{pmatrix}$	$\begin{pmatrix} 1,869 \\ -152.16 \end{pmatrix}$	$\begin{pmatrix} 96,991 & -30,318 \\ -30,318 & 9,917 \end{pmatrix}$	$\begin{pmatrix} 10,244 & 31,320 \\ 31,320 & 100,194 \end{pmatrix}$	$\begin{pmatrix} .9222 & -.2119 \\ -.2119 & .3136 \end{pmatrix}$

Restricting our thinking to the trend line model, the credibility model which is most meaningful would be one in which only the slope is considered to be a variable from state to state, but where the intercept is a constant:

$$\mu_{ts}(\theta_s) - a_s + b(\theta_s)t$$

This sort of model is directly analogous to the Bühlmann, Straub introduction of treaty conditions in their paper, which allow the severities to be modified by some function before entering the credibility formula.

We have shown above that scale and translation formulation will not affect our final credibility estimate. For ease of exposition in this section, we will assume that the time values in our trend line have been chosen so that the weighted average of observed times is zero and the weighted sample variance is equal to one. The modifications to our basic credibility model, because of the constant values a_s within the mean value μ_{ts} formula, are fairly simple. For the regular credibility model β_s was the same function of θ_s for all states. In our mixed model this function varies from state to state:

$$B_s(\theta_s) = \begin{pmatrix} a_s \\ b(\theta_s) \end{pmatrix}$$

The expected value of this function varies from state to state:

$$E[B_s(\theta_s)] = {}_s\beta = \begin{pmatrix} a_s \\ b \end{pmatrix}$$

We have chosen to denote this expected value as ${}_s\beta$ to avoid confusion with the function of θ, β_s. The covariance matrix Γ_s^* is:

$$E[B_s(\theta_s)B'(\theta_s)] - {}_s\beta_s\beta' = \Gamma_s^* = \begin{pmatrix} 0 & 0 \\ 0 & \sigma_{bs}^2 \end{pmatrix}$$

with the only non-zero entry being σ_b^2.

If we introduce for state j

$$K_{bj} = \sigma^2/\sigma_{bj}^2$$

to define:

$$Z_{bj} = P_{.j}/(P_{.j} + K_{bj})$$

The credibility matrix for our mixed model becomes:

$$Z_j = \begin{pmatrix} 0 & 0 \\ 0 & Z_{bj} \end{pmatrix}$$

Using the same theoretical development as in the regular credibility model, for the mixed model leads to:

$$\hat{\mu}_{ij} = [\hat{\beta}'_j Z_j + {}_j\beta'(I - Z_j)]Y_{ij}$$

The only difference is this estimate is that ${}_j\beta'$ replaces β'.[6] This estimate may be written for the trend case without recourse to matrices simply as:

$$\hat{\mu}_{ij} = a_j + [\hat{b}_j Z_{bj} + \hat{b}(1 - Z_{bj})]i$$

Using the formulas for the mixed model, the constant K, the credibility and finally the credibility adjusted slopes are shown on figure 11. For this mixed model, our credibility results are much more pleasing since the credibility adjusted

---

[6]It is important to note that this result holds for any mixed model, not just for out trend case. The most general mixed model, of course, allows arbitrary elements of β_s to be considered independent of θ_s.

FIGURE 11

Credibility Adjusted Slopes
Without Intercept Adjustments

State	Number of Claims Over 3 Years		Credibility	Transformed State Slope	Transformed Credibility Adjusted Slope	Transformed Countrywide Slope
s	$P_{.s}$	K_{bs}	Z_{bs}	$\hat{b}^*$	$\tilde{b}^*$	$\hat{\hat{b}}^*$
1	100,155	4,565	.9564	-216.04	-213.17	-150.11
2	19,895	4,518	.8149	- 59.66	- 76.54	-150.88
3	13,735	4,550	.7512	-150.21	-150.21	-150.36
4	4,152	4,406	.4852	- 98.01	-126.22	-152.80
5	36,110	4,443	.8904	- 41.68	- 53.79	-152.16

slope must lie between the state and countrywide slopes. Further, some general observations can be made concerning the relative size of credibility to be given to state data. With this five state base as countrywide for most states, the number of claims that are observed show extremely high credibility. Only for the smallest state #4, with 4,152 claims observed over three years is credibility lower than .5. Of course, for practical application, the credibility standard should be developed using all of the states not just five.

Discussion by Al Quirin of Credibility for Regression Models with Application to Trend

This paper considers an arbitrary linear regression model, incorporates the Bühlmann Straub formulation of the model, extends the estimator form considered in the Bühlmann Straub model, exhibits the relationship between the least squares estimators, and finally derives computational results involving simple linear trend.

Arbitrary Linear Regression Model Considered	$E(x_{ts}) = u_{ts} = y'_{ts}\beta_s$	(1)
Bühlmann-Straub Formulation Incorporated	$E(x_{ts}^2) - u_{ts}^2 = \sigma_s^2/\rho_{ts}$	(2)
	$E(x_{is}x_{js}) - u_{is}u_{js} = 0, \ i \neq j$	(3)
Bühlmann-Straub Estimator Form	$\hat{u}_{ts} = x' A$	(4a)
Extended to	$\hat{u}_{ts} = \alpha_0 + x' A$	(4b)

Relationship of Least Squares Estimators

using (4b) $\quad \hat{u}_{ts} = [\hat{\beta}'_s z_s + \beta'(I - z_2)]y_{ts}$

using (4a) $\quad \hat{u}_{ts} = [\hat{\beta}'_s z_s + \beta'(I - z_2)]y_{ts}$

$$\text{Where} \quad d = \frac{\sum_s \beta'_s z_s \Gamma^{-1} \beta}{\sum_s \beta' z_s \Gamma^{-1} \beta}$$

Adequate accountability for inflation has become the single most important need in Property and Casualty insurance ratemaking today. In response to this need, Mr. Hachemeister's paper developing credibility standards for arbitrary linear regression models and in particular, developing credibility adjusted state trend lines, should prove to be invaluable.

In his Introduction, the author mentions that "no standards have been specifically developed for evaluating (the) credibility of state trend lines vs. countrywide trend lines." Although not specifically developed for analyzing trend, a credibility procedure has been used for some time by the Insurance Services Office (ISO) in their trend calculations, at least in private passenger automobile insurance. In each state, the determination of the average annual change in paid claim costs and claim frequencies is accomplished by credibility weighing the state and countrywide average annual changes. These average annual changes are taken from linear and exponential least squares trend lines for paid claim costs and claim frequencies, respectively. The credibility weights assigned are based on the latest year ending number of claims. Unfortunately, the theoretical justification for this approach is no deeper than assuming the number of claims has a Poisson distribution, and approximating probabilities by the use of the normal distribution. The standard for full credibility is 10,623 claims and reflects a probability of .99 that the number of claims will be within ±2.5% of the expected number of claims (on the assumption that the mean is equal to the variance). Partial credibilities are obtained using the formula $Z^2 = \frac{P}{10,623}$, where P is the latest year ending number of claims needed for partial credibility Z. The theoretical soundness of this procedure has been proven deficient by several authors, but up until this point in time, the theoretical advantages of alternative procedures do not seem to outweigh the practical advantage of simplicity (both in explanation to state insurance departments and in mathematical computation) present in the current procedure. From my own point of view, even though I feel that simplicity is a much overrated virtue in the very technical business of insurance ratemaking and that theoretical soundness should be of primary importance, I am convinced that any alternative credibility procedure will face the rather strict test of practical expediency before being implemented by those in the business of pricing insurance. With regard to Mr. Hachemeister's paper, it is precisely its simplicity in practical application (as well as its theoretical validity) which leads me to believe that it will someday soon become extensively utilized in calculating trend.

In the first half of the paper, the author states the problem of state vs. countrywide trend, introduces notation, displays data for a computational example, presents basic summary statistics, and reviews the classical and generalized linear regression model. Although the author has made mention to the point, it should be reiterated that even though the form of the estimator

$$\hat{\beta}_s = (y_s' c_s^{-1} y_s)^{-1} y_s' c_s^{-1} x_s$$

follows that obtained in classical generalized least squares estimation and that the theoretical results hold in general for the positive-definite matrix C_s, the assumption made regarding autocorrelation in deriving numerical results is not that of generalized least squares. In particular, recall that the classical generalized least squares formulation of the state s trend model is

i) $E(x_{ts}) = u_{ts} = a_s + b_s t \qquad t = 1,\ldots,n$

ii) $E(x_{ts}^2) - u_{ts}^2 = c_{ts} = \sigma_s^2/\rho_{ts} \qquad s = 1,\ldots,N$

The $n \times n$ positive definite matrix C_s allows for both heteroscedasticity and autocorrelation, i.e., for both

iii) $E(x_{ts}^2) - u_{ts}^2 = \sigma_s^2, \qquad \forall t$

and

iv) $E(x_{is}x_{js}) - u_{is}u_{js} = 0, \qquad i \neq j$

not holding. However, in deriving numerical results, Hachemeister disallows autocorrelation by assuming that iv) holds. In other words, should these problem be found to occur in trend data, further computational refinements will become necessary in practical application.

An approach to the solution of the problem of state vs. countrywide trend, is then formulated as a compound decision problem. In particular, the mean value μ_{ts} of a "credibility adjusted state s trend line" is modeled as

v) $\mu_{ts}(\theta_s) = a_t(\theta_s) + b_t(\theta_s)t$

where for each state s and each time period t, one acts as if the slopes and intercepts were distributed about some mean slope $E[b_t(\theta_s)]$ and some mean intercept $E[a_t(\theta_s)]$. Best linear unbiased estimators (BLUE) are then considered of the form

vi) $\hat{\mu}_{ts} = \alpha_0 + \sum_{s=1}^{N} \sum_{t=1}^{n} \alpha_{ts}x_{ts} = \alpha_0 + x'A$

and are found to be

vii) $\hat{\mu}_{ts} = [\hat{\beta}_s z_s + \beta'(I - z_s)]y_{ts}$

The application of this result to real data requires that estimates be made of various parameters not directly observable within the credibility model (e.g. z_s in vii) is a function of K_s which in turn depends on estimates of σ^2, v, and Γ). Because of the need for these estimates, assumptions iii) and iv) are made to simplify the derivation of numerical results.

The invariance property of $\hat{\mu}_{ts}$ for any linear transformation of the independent variables follows in a straightforward manner. Using this result, Hachemeister performs a scaling and translation on the linear trend model so that the weighted average (using # claims as weights) of scaled times in zero and the sample variance of scaled times is equal to unity. Finally, a mixed model is employed, to avoid the distressing results obtained when state intercepts are credibility adjusted, so that the final model chosen is

$$\mu_{ts}(\theta_s) = a_s + b(\theta_s)t \ .$$

Note that in this model the intercept varies by state but is assumed constant over all time periods. For each state s and each time period t the slope is still considered to be distributed about some mean slope. The effect of the estimated form in this mixed model is that slopes are credibility adjusted while intercepts are not.

To investigate the credibility standards developed and to evaluate the procedure finally decided upon in credibility adjusting state trend lines, consider the transformed simple linear trend model which credibility adjusts slopes without intercept adjustments.

Here,

$$u_{ts}(\theta_s) = a_s + b(\theta_s)t$$

where

$$\beta_s(\theta_s) = \begin{pmatrix} a_s \\ b(\theta_s) \end{pmatrix}$$

and

$$E[\beta_s(\theta_s)] = s^{\beta} = \begin{pmatrix} a_s \\ b \end{pmatrix} \ .$$

The estimator becomes for state s

$$\begin{aligned} \hat{u}_{ts} &= [\hat{\beta}'_s z_s + s^{\beta'}(I - z_s)]y_{ts} \\ &= a_s + [\hat{b}_s z_{bs} + \hat{b}(1 - z_{bs})]t \end{aligned}$$

where

$$z_{bs} = p_{.s}/(p_{.s} + K_{bs})$$

and

$$K_{bs} = \sigma^2/\sigma_{bs}^2 \ .$$

Note that the credibility parameter K_{bs} satisfies the general definition demonstrated by Bühlmann that it be equal to

$$\frac{\text{expected value of process variance } (= \sigma^2)}{\text{variance of the hypothetical means } (= \sigma_{bs}^2)} \ .$$

The K_{bs}'s vary by state but a single constant K value could be adopted should the K_{bs}'s developed for all states show the same stability (centered around 4,500) as those developed for the five selected states.

Credibility for the Layman

Charles C. Hewitt, Jr.

The Committee has had the foresight not to provide me with a blackboard -- Hans Bühlmann they give a blackboard with four boards three rows deep. Therefore, the nature of this address will be nontechnical.

Before I begin I think it is appropriate at this time that we acknowledge the contributions of certain individuals who are at the head table. Our Co-Chairmen who have made all the arrangements and established the agenda -- Paul Kahn and Charlie Hachemeister. Another gentleman we should recognize had the lack of foresight to arrange to take his sabbatical year at the time of this conference. I wonder if all of you realize that Bill Jewell has come all the way back from Vienna solely to help us run this meeting.

Finally, and I don't believe any applause is necessary, I would like to acknowledge an individual who got us started on these conferences who is not with us -- Ed Lew.

Bridging the gap

I feel rather strongly that at the present time in the history of our civilization we have a cultural gap between what is sometimes referred to as a civilized survival society and a civilized identity society. Because of this gap which is more than just a generation gap I feel that those of us who understand the differences between these two types of society have an obligation to bridge the gap and increase the understanding among peoples in both groups.

On a more mundane level I have recently attended an annual meeting of the American Risk Insurance Association at the Greenbrier in which I tried to explain to these professors of insurance what it is that casualty actuaries do and to highlight some of the differences between life and casualty actuaries.

Within the actuarial profession we have "pure" actuaries and "lay" actuaries as Matt Rodermund so aptly described in an address prepared for the Fiftieth Anniversary celebration of the Casualty Actuarial Society. My "bag" is being able to communicate with actuaries in both camps. I am considered a pure actuary by the lay actuaries and a lay actuary by the pure actuaries. The penalty for trying to bridge this gap within our profession is that I am not accepted by either group as a member of that particular group. In this respect I am in the same position as President Ford with his proposal for amnesty which pleases neither the draft evaders or deserters because it is "conditional" and does not please the families of dead, wounded and missing in action servicemen because it is too liberal.

At this particular meeting I think it is appropriate in attempting to bridge the gap between pure actuaries and lay actuaries to attempt to show why the public accepts the notion of credibility and therefore why it works.

<u>Three "theories-in-practice" challenges for the casualty actuary</u>

In my career lifetime in the casualty actuarial profession I have seen three major challenges for putting into practice some of the theoretical ideas that are appropriate in solving the problems which we encounter.

The first and most important of these challenges is the subject of credibility -- the reason for this conference --

and I shall defer further discussion on this topic for the major portion of this address.

The second challenge is to make use of what I call the "force of selection." I use the term selection in the purest Darwinian sense in that species and characteristics survive as a result of a selection process in nature. The process has two parts. First the organism must be strong enough to survive to the point of mating and second must be attractive enough to the opposite sex to reproduce itself. This idea also has application in which I have chosen to call the force of mortality, a subject about which I wrote a paper fifteen years ago. It would appear that we can derive actuarial information by recognizing that certain infants and juveniles have a lesser ability to survive and that therefore a force of selection exists which results in the medically strong reaching maturity.

In casualty insurance this is also recognized in papers dealing with automobile merit rating where classes of risk are created on the basis of individuals who have had no accidents in five years, one accident in five years, two accidents in five years, and so forth.

The third major challenge is to make use of utility theory in decision making. The insurance customer, through the very act of buying an insurance policy uses utility theory because he pays more for the policy than the pure loss cost. The direct insurer does exactly the same thing when he purchases reinsurance. I have presented to the Society of Actuaries at a joint seminar session a short paper in which the use of utility theory in the purchase of reinsurance is illustrated.

Credibility for the layman

In the remainder of these remarks when I talk about

credibility I am referring to one dimensional linear credibility. It is an interesting commentary on how far we have gone in the last five or six years that I need to distinguish between this simplest form and multi-dimensional or nonlinear credibility.

Credibility in its simplest form represents a compromise between a hypothesis and an observation or series of observations. The individual making a judgment feels intuitively that the best estimate must lie somewhere between the original hypothesis and the observation. Linear credibility meets this condition and therefore is understandable and acceptable to the underwriter, who in casualty insurance is often more important than the actuary and also to the general public -- the consumer.

During one part of my career I had the responsibility of explaining experience rating and credibility in workmen's componsation insurance to insurance buyers and I can assure you that although the customer does not always like the result he does understand the process and feels that the linear credibility approach is a rational one. Also, credibility has the value of giving us a single answer to the question and not a range of answers, another fact which the public appreciates.

The Bühlmann restatement of credibility gives us an appreciation of the fact that credibility depends upon three principal factors and I shall discuss each of these in order:

1. Amount of exposure
2. Variance of the risk process
3. Variation in hypotheses

In discussing each of these three factors I will try to make use of everyday illustrations, practical insurance illustrations and then mention basically what steps the insurance business has taken to adjust for or allow for the insufficiency of information available for making a judgment.

In illustrating the first factor -- amount of exposure -- I am reminded of a story which I will tell with a brief preface, although the preface is not essential to the story itself. Sometime in the 1920's the author Sinclair Lewis was receiving an award as a distinguished alumnus of Yale University. In accepting the award, Lewis took the occasion to assert his known atheism. "I do not believe there is a God," said Lewis, "If in fact there is one, let him strike me down here and now." And of course nothing happened.

However, several days later the noted columnist Arthur Brisbane took Lewis to task. "Lewis, you poor fool," said Brisbane, "You remind me of the ants who lived along the right-of-way of the Atchison, Topeka and Santa Fe Railroad. This colony of ants depended for its existence on the crumbs thrown from the dining cars as they passed. However, the ant colony came upon hard times because through chance no crumbs were thrown out near their particular place along the right-of-way. The situation became desperate and the colony decided to hold a meeting. It was suggested that they all pray to the President of the Atchison, Topeka and Santa Fe Railroad to send more dining cars so that crumbs would be thrown off in their area. So they did pray and the following day they waited and no crumbs were thrown off where they lived. So the ants concluded that there was no such person as the President of the Atchison, Topeka and Santa Fe Railroad."

This illustrates the making of a decision on the basis of insufficient information -- perhaps if the ants had waited several more days they would have changed their thinking.

At the opposite end we have an illustration of waiting for sufficient observations to affirm a conclusion. I am reminded of a family experience. We knew a 95-year-old gentleman who had just lost his 71-year-old son. When he was consoled by people on the loss, he stated shaking his head rather sadly, "I always said I never would raise that boy."

In the insurance business we have the extremes of class-rated risks where there is not sufficient information on the individual insured to produce an experience rating (no credibility) and at the opposite extreme the extremely large risks which are totally self-rating and where credibility theory is not really necessary at all.

The normal remedy that the insurance industry uses for insufficient exposure is to wait for more experience before making a decision if it is possible to put off such a decision.

Less understood by the casualty actuary is the importance of recognizing the variation in results of the risk process as an indicator for credibility. Again as illustration for the layman I am reminded of the story of the four boys who decided one morning to play hooky from school because they knew they were going to get a test. About 10:30 a.m. their consciences got the better of them and they decided they better show up. When they reached the classroom about 11:00 a.m. they explained to the teacher that they had been on their way to school in a car and that they had gotten a flat tire and they were late because they had stopped to have the tire fixed. The teacher indicated that there was no problem, that he would give them a make-up examination during their lunch hour and told them to report to a particular room. At lunch time when they reported to the room in question he had each of them sit in the four opposite corners of the room. "There is only one question on this test," said the teacher, "Which tire was flat?"

If there was no variation in the results, then credibility of the four boys would have been considerable. In the world of everyday illustrations at the opposite end we have innumerable events in nature which occur with such constancy that we give complete credibility. I am thinking of the forecasting of the time of sunrise and sunset, the temperature at which water boils and freezes, etc.

This idea unfortunately is not carried over into the practice of insurance to the extent which it might be. Intuitively actuaries recognized that taking such measures as limiting the value of individual losses as they enter experience does produce greater consistency and hence a more credible insurance base. But I think you will agree that much more could be done in this area.

Finally the third factor in credibility which is most difficult to understand and least recognized is the importance of the variation in the hypotheses from which we start our judgment. We recognize that the term credibility applies to the observations but we often forget that the hypothesis itself is not a completely credible starting point but rather a judgment sometimes uncertain. An everyday illustration of the effect of no variation of hypotheses upon the judgment of an individual is the type of person whom all of us has met or knows -- the individual who believes in religious miracles. This individual may never have seen a miracle and may never see one and yet his faith is so unshakable (no variation in hypothesis) that the fact that a miracle has never been observed has no effect upon his belief.

Because we live in a relatively advanced civilization, it is difficult to postulate situations in which we do not have any collateral information upon which to base hypotheses before an observation is made. Therefore let me take this back to the time of the caveman and let's suppose the individual has lived his entire life in the darkness of a cave and has finally emerged at the mouth of the cave during night. When the sun first comes up he is astounded. He doesn't know whether the earth or the sun is on fire or the world is about to come to an end. As the day progresses he may even assume that the day will go on forever. But when the sun sets, he is now in a position to make a judgment on the length of the following day if the sun does rise again and that judgment must be that the second day will be the same as the first because the caveman had no hypothesis (infinite variation) to begin with when the sun first rose.

An illustration from workmen's compensation insurance is appropriate. Two classifications which come to mind are breweries and construction. Most breweries are quite similar in hazard and therefore we would expect the individual risks in this classification to produce substantially similar experience. Therefore under the Bühlmann restatement of credibility we would not give the individual results much credibility relative to the class rate. On the other hand construction work, either road construction or building type construction, takes on an almost infinite variety. We would therefore expect individual construction risks to differ substantially one from the other and accordingly there would be a wide variation in the hypothesis with respect to individual risk performance. Hence these risks would expect to receive greater credibility proportionately.

Again casualty actuaries perhaps intuitively have recognized this factor by attempting to create risk classifications which are as homogeneous as possible and hence require little credibility in order to establish a correct rate for the individual risk.

Summary

In order that I have made myself clear and have not left us in the position of having said two different things which conflict in your minds, I would like to summarize. In so doing I want to avoid the experience of the widow who decided to erect a tombstone on her husband's grave and to say something appropriate. She first had inscribed, "May he rest in peace." Then she decided to add as a second thought, "Until we meet again." Now taken separately these are two very fine expressions but when joined together they create a misunderstanding in the mind of the reader.

The three factors which I have discussed are that we must recognize the "credibility" of our starting point or hypothesis. We have to ask ourselves how sure are we of the original point from which we begin to make our judgment. Second we must look at the consistency of our observations. If they are relatively similar we are prepared to assign a higher degree of credibility than if there is a considerable variation in the results. And similarly we must allow for the increase or decrease in experience or exposure in making our judgment. The more the experience the more we believe the observations. The less the experience the more we believe the hypothesis.

This is "credibility for the layman" and I thank you for your close attention.

Introduction and Historical Overview of Credibility

James C. Hickman
University of Wisconsin, Madison

1. Introduction*

"Experience keeps a dear school, but fools will learn in no other."

- Benjamin Franklin

Credibility theory is a collection of ideas concerning the systematic adjustment of insurance premiums as claims experience is obtained. This preliminary definition is probably too broad to be useful, for it encompasses almost all activity involving the analysis of insurance data and the subsequent use of these analyses in adjusting insurance prices. On a more operational level Hewitt (1970) defines credibility "as a linear estimate of the true (inherent) expectation derived as a result of a compromise between hypothesis and observation."

An idea or concept with a catchy name is more likely to capture attention and influence practice than one with an esoteric label. Credibility is a word that is frequently used in everyday conversation. In the press of the United States it has been used in relation to the political problems of the current and immediate past Presidents. In politics it appears that one starts with a reservoir of credibility which decreases as executive experience is compiled. Within

*Sections 1 and 2 draw heavily on Section 1 of "Credibility Theory and Bayesian Estimation," by R. B. Miller and J. C. Hickman (to appear).

insurance, on the other hand, the conventional models behave in the reverse fashion. That is, credibility increases as the amount of experience increases.

The appeal of the word "credibility" is a bit of an obstacle in the study of methods for analyzing insurance claims data and adjusting premiums. Attempts to classify contributions to the theory are partially frustrated by the existence of ideas for analyzing insurance data that use the language of credibility theory but do not employ the distinctive weighted average characteristic of conventional credibility models.

As a practical tool, credibility is largely an invention of North American actuaries. However, the roots go deep into the basic economic theory of risk and into statistical estimation. In its present formulation, credibility theory was developed about the time of World War I in connection with premium adjustment systems in workmen's compensation insurance. In that new and rapidly expanding field, some industrial companies with a large number of employees and favorable safety records pressed for recognition in their insurance premiums of their apparently superior claims records.

It is instructive to quote from a paper by A. H. Mowbray (1914) which appeared in the first volume of the Proceedings, Casualty Actuarial Society.

> "A dependable pure premium is one for which the probability is high, that it does not differ from the true pure premiums by more than an arbitrary limit."

It would be difficult to form a more succinct statement of the objective of credibility theory. Mowbray's paper dealt with workmen compensation premiums and established a theme that persisted throughout the early volumes of the Proceedings.

It is particularly appropriate to quote from one of Mowbray's pioneering papers at this Conference. Mowbray served for many years on the faculty of our host institution, the University of California, Berkeley.

Because credibility theory concerns models for the adaptive response of insurance price systems to their dynamic environment, this theory pervades most of actuarial science. Credibility theory is an attempt to create a model by which we may learn about the world in which insurance systems operate. Learning and adaptation are necessary for any successful system.

It is instructive to record a few specific instances, outside the usual domain of credibility theory, where applications have been suggested and in some cases developed.

(1) Jackson and Hamilton (1968) in discussing the valuation of pension fund assets point out that several of the valuation methods involving a blend of initial cost and current market value may be usefully viewed as applications of credibility theory.

(2) In its Preliminary Report, May 1974, the Society of Actuaries Committee on Cost Comparison Methods and Related Issues (1974) wrestled with the problem of evaluating non-guaranteed cash flows, such as policy dividends, within a cost comparison index. One of the suggestions was to apply a credibility factor to dividend illustrations before the value of such dividends are included in the calculation of a cost comparison index.

(3) Within individual life insurance, the adaptive economic behavior which credibility theory facilitates is perhaps best illustrated in dividend

determination. The language used to describe the process by which dividend interest and expense rates are thought of as a blend between initial assumptions and recent results is very reminiscent of credibility theory. Kimeldorf and Jones (1967) have developed a mortality table graduation method in which the weighted average aspect of credibility theory is explicitly used.

2. Two approaches

> "Factual science may collect statistics and make charts. But its predictions are, as has been well said, but past history reversed."
>
> \- John Dewey

Establishing a classification system for ideas is a hazardous business. The divisions among the principal schools of thought on any subject are seldom unambiguous. In addition, one runs the risk that he has misunderstood the intentions of the contributors to the theory. Despite these possible pitfalls, we shall proceed on the assumption that one may classify contributions to credibility theory on the basis of whether the credibility model proposed views the parameters of the claims process as fixed constants or as random variables. If the parameters are viewed as fixed parameters, to be estimated using only relevant insurance data, the model is consistent with the traditional or sampling theory view of statistics. On the other hand, if the parameters that define the claims process are viewed as random variables generated by a process that the investigator will seek to understand using an amalgamation of prior and current information, the model is consistent with the Bayesian approach to statistics. Jones (1965) has introduced North American actuaries to this approach.

The first, in terms of when it had an impact on practical

insurance affairs, is the class of traditional methods in which the risk parameters are viewed as constants. This method requires as a first step fixing the size of an insurance experience to which complete credibility will be attached for rate making purposes. Once this anchor is fixed, the problem becomes that of establishing, in some reasonable fashion, partial credibility weights which will be applied to smaller amounts of insurance data. The adjusted estimate of claims, to be used in setting premiums in the next accounting period is

$$Z(t) \cdot y + (1 - Z(t)) \cdot m',$$

where y is some measure of actual claims, m' is a prior estimate of expected claims, and $Z(t)$ is the credibility factor. The credibility factor is a function of t, a measure of the size of the insurance experience that generated the claims measured by y.

In the first method a value of t_0, such that it is agreed as a practical matter to let $Z(t_0) = 1$, must be determined. A classic example found in Longley-Cook's monograph (1962) and the paper by Mayerson, Bowers, and Jones (1968), involves estimating the parameter (λt) of a Poisson distribution. We seek, in this method the value of t_0 such that

$$\Pr[(1 - k)E[\tilde{x}] \leq \tilde{x} \leq (1 + k)E[\tilde{x}]] \geq p$$

where $\tilde{x}$ is the total number of claims in the group under consideration. The distribution of $\tilde{x}$ depends on the index of group size t. In our particular example $\tilde{x}$ has a Poisson distribution. If $k = .05$ and $p = .9$, this requirement for full credibility may be rewritten as

$$\Pr\left[\frac{-.05\ E[\tilde{x}]}{\sigma_{\tilde{x}}} \leq \frac{\tilde{x} - E[\tilde{x}]}{\sigma_{\tilde{x}}} \leq \frac{.05\ E[\tilde{x}]}{\sigma_{\tilde{x}}}\right] \geq .9$$

$$\Pr\left[-.05\sqrt{\lambda t} \le \frac{\tilde{x} - \lambda t}{\sqrt{\lambda t}} \le .05\sqrt{\lambda t}\right] \ge .9 .$$

If we are to use x as an estimate of $E[\tilde{x}]$, subject to these specifications, we may use the fact that $(\tilde{x} - \lambda t)/\sqrt{\lambda t}$ has an approximate normal distribution, mean zero, variance one $(N(0,1))$ to find that we must have $x \approx 1{,}084$ before the specifications are satisfied. Following this approach to credibility, one would now state that $Z(1084) = 1$, where the size of the experience is measured in terms of the number of claims incurred. Other examples were $\tilde{x}$ is total claims rather than simply the number of claims are possible (Mayerson, Jones and Bowers, 1968).

This approach leaves open the assignment of $Z(t)$ for values $t < t_0$. Typical choices have been $Z(t) = \sqrt{t}/\sqrt{t_0}$ and $Z(t) = tc/(t + h)$ where $c = (t_0 + h)/t_0$, $t \le t_0$. Besides all the usual problems in selecting a sufficiently realistic model for the insurance claims process, this approach also leaves to the decision maker the assignment of the specification parameters k and p.

The second school of thought might be described as the Bayesian school. Within this school the expected claims for a group is viewed as being generated by a random process that may not be completely known. Prior and collateral information about expected claims is summarized in the form of a prior distribution. As the claims experience unfolds Bayes' Theorem is used to find the posterior distribution of the process generating the parameters of the claims distribution. Since conventional insurance theory uses other methods for introducing risk and profit margins, the posterior mean of the process generating expected claims is the usual output of a Bayesian credibility analysis.

The Bayesian approach does not require the premium decision maker to specify an error rate, k, or a precision probability, p, for the purpose of defining the volume of experience needed for credibility one. Partial credibility is no problem within the Bayesian approach for the weighting of the claims data and the prior mean to produce the posterior mean is handled automatically. The price for this convenience is the need to specify a prior distribution or at least enough parameters of the prior to make least squares approximation of the posterior mean possible.

The Bayesian approach was brought to the attention of practicing actuaries in a series of remarkable papers by Arthur L. Bailey (1945), (1950). Before the foundations of Bayesian statistics were widely understood, Bailey formed some eloquent criticisms of classical statistics and developed an openly Bayesian approach to credibility. Bailey's work was related to modern Bayesian statistics by Mayerson (1964a).

Mayerson was also intrigued by least squares approximations to posterior means. Bühlmann (1967) was also interested in the idea of approximating a posterior mean by a linear function of the prior mean and the mean of the claims data. When using least squares lines, this led to credibility factors of the form

$$Z(t) = \frac{\mathrm{Var}'(\tilde{\mu})}{\mathrm{Var}'(\tilde{\mu}) + E'_{\mu}\,\mathrm{Var}(\tilde{\bar{x}}|\mu)}$$

where $\mathrm{Var}'(\tilde{\mu})$ is the variance of the prior distribution of $\tilde{\mu}$, the expected claims, and E'_{μ} denotes an expectation operator with respect to the prior distribution. Of course, Bailey and others had already found credibility factors of this form for beta-binomial, gamma-Poisson, and normal-normal Bayesian models.

3. Credibility theory's role in practice

"Models are to be used, but not to be believed."

- Henri Theil

In order to place credibility theory in a proper perspective, it is useful to review the steps in managing a financial system with explicit risk components. The steps in this process are exhibited in Table 1.

1. Selection of a risk model. This is by far the most important and most perplexing step. Keeping Theil's admonition in mind, the actuary must humbly remember that he can never capture reality in his models. On the other hand, only by the use of models can he plan.
2. Obtain initial estimates of the parameters of the model. In science one sometimes engages in unsystematic data snooping in search of patterns that may lead to insights. It is inconceivable that an insurance system would be proposed without some prior feeling for the magnitude of the parameters.
3. Use the model and the initial parameter estimates to compute premiums and reserves. For many years the attention of practicing actuaries was riveted on this step. A second aspect of this step is to use the model to establish risk management policy (selection standards, reinsurance policy, etc.)
4. Collect information on the operation of the system.
5. Analyze the information obtained with the objective of possibly modifying the basic model. More likely the application of the new information will be in revising the estimates of the parameters of the model. From the revised estimates, adjustments in

Table 1

Steps in the Management of a Risk Process

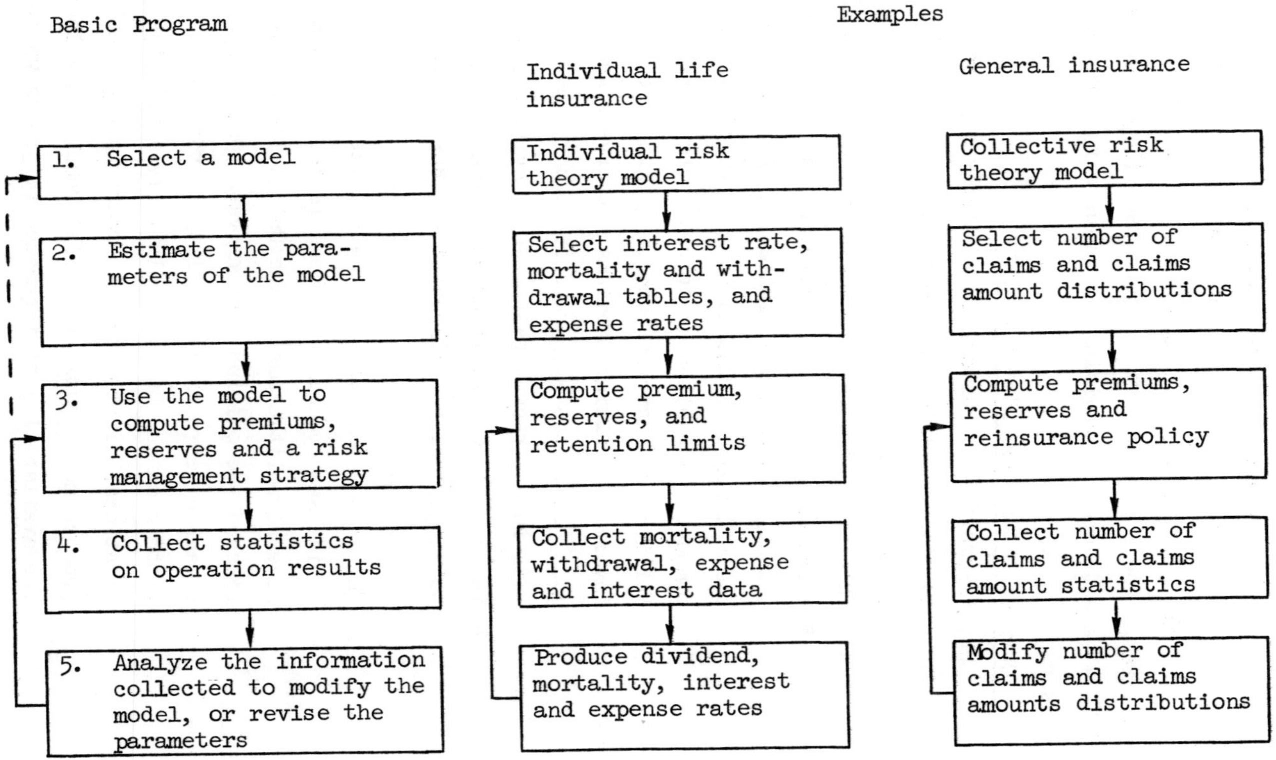

Basic Program
Examples
Individual life insurance
General insurance
1. Select a model
2. Estimate the parameters of the model
3. Use the model to compute premiums, reserves and a risk management strategy
4. Collect statistics on operation results
5. Analyze the information collected to modify the model, or revise the parameters
Individual risk theory model
Select interest rate, mortality and withdrawal tables, and expense rates
Compute premium, reserves, and retention limits
Collect mortality, withdrawal, expense and interest data
Produce dividend, mortality, interest and expense rates
Collective risk theory model
Select number of claims and claims amount distributions
Compute premiums, reserves and reinsurance policy
Collect number of claims and claims amount statistics
Modify number of claims and claims amounts distributions

the price structure and in the risk management strategy are possible. It is in this step that credibility procedures play a key role.

Table 1 contains two examples of the application of this program. The important papers by Jackson (1953) and Bolnick (1974) are devoted to revising the price structure in group insurance.

4. Current importance of credibility

Why is credibility theory a singularly appropriate topic for an actuarial research conference in 1974? The answer comes in three parts.

1. The first part relates to the state of actuarial science. Because of fundamental scientific advances, actuaries have a rich selection of basic models at their disposal. Thanks in part to the increase in computing capabilities attributable to the availability of electronic computers, the problems involved in fixing premiums, reserves, and a risk management strategy are under much tighter control than in the recent past. The remaining problems are in the area of analyzing and using insurance data to successfully modify an insurance system as its dynamic environment is revealed.
2. The second part of the answer relates to current social and economic problems in the United States. Several politicians in the United States have expressed the opinion that private companies may have attached too much credibility to the experience (both good and bad) of relatively small risk classifications. In this view, broader groups would produce more stable financial results and increase the availability of insurance to groups where the

lack of insurance seems to be impeding economic development. Although this issue has important social and political aspects, it would seem that credibility theory could contribute to the resolution of the issues involved.

3. The third part of the answer relates to dissatisfaction within the insurance industry with what is deemed by many to be excessive volatility of insurance financial results. It would seem that the successful application of credibility theory would improve the ability of insurance companies to modify their price structures as the economic environment changes and thereby produce less variable financial results.

5. Future directions

In the program of this conference, both the current state of credibility theory as well as directions for future research will be presented. For the benefit of those who would like to join in advancing this work, it might be helpful to indicate the principal areas in which additional work is needed.

1. It is almost trite to repeate once more that statistical analysis of real claims data to measure the validity of some of the models proposed is needed. However, trite statements are often true and this is one of those situations.
2. Conventional credibility theory has focused on estimating, for price purposes, future claims. Perhaps credibility theory may be included within a comprehensive premium determination system that is consistent with decision theory. Bühlmann (1970) has been very active in developing this idea.

3. The third area where additional work will be rewarded may be classed as partially administration and partially research. Within this area the objective will be to develop and implement statistical systems which will provide a deeper understanding of the insurance process under study and facilitate the systematic adjustment of premiums.

Model Variations in Credibility Theory

William S. Jewell
The University of California, Berkeley

Abstract

Classical credibility theory is a linearized Bayesian forecasting method, in which the expected value of the next observation is obtained as a mixture of a prior mean and the sample mean of observed data. In this paper, we consider a variety of extensions to this model which appear to have practical importance. The main tool is least-squares theory.

After giving the general results for a time-varying, multi-dimensional risk, we find closed-term results for the stationary case in a matrix notation which is similar to the one-dimensional case. We also look at the problem of using data from non-predicted components which might be available in advance. In another section, we solve a particular time-varying model which arises in practice, and show its relation to the use of conditional distributions and "as-if" statistics in forecasting.

In the next variation, we give a different interpretation to the multidimensional data by assuming it comes from different, but related units; certain of the covariance terms drop out, and it is possible to get further closed-form results. If the units are total uncorrelated, then the cohort data is not used in our linear prediction; however, it is possible to force its use by using a proportional predictor, and this case is examined in detail in the next section.

Finally, some preliminary evolutionary models are

examined, in which the risk parameter itself may undergo some change over time.

1. Introduction

The efficient use of available data to forcast future performance is one of the central problems of modern business. In the casualty and health insurance fields, especially, profit or loss depends upon charging the correct premium for the individual risks underwritten.

When a new contract is signed, the insurer may know very little about the individual characteristics of the insuree, and the manual fair premium must be based upon prior statistics gather from a large collective of similar, but somewhat heterogeneous contracts grouped together under the same manual classification to "spread the risk." However, as the individual contract continues over several years, experience data can be gathered, and the premium can be experience-rated to more nearly reflect the individual risk characteristics.

A simple but effective approach to estimating the experience-rated fair premium of such a risk was developed by American actuaries in the 20's. It was called credibility theory - presumably because the problem was seen to be how much credibility to attach to the small amount of individual experience versus the mass of data from the collective. For many years, the basic ad hoc credibility formula, and its various elaborations worked very well, even though there was little agreement as to why they were correct, and practically no interest from the statistical community.

However, beginning with the resurgence of Bayesian techniques in the 60's, a succession of important papers has put credibility theory on firm mathematical footing, by showing that the basic credibility formula is an exact Bayesian result in many cases, or a very good least-squares approximation in others. Extensions have been made to multi-dimensional problems, special data structures, and to the problem of estimating the distribution of experience-rated risk.

The purpose of this paper is to provide a general framework in which to examine these extensions, along with other credibility model variations which suggest themselves either mathematically, or from insurance applications. Particular emphasis will be placed on various interpretation of multi-dimensional problems, and upon the non-stationary cases which can be explicitly solved.

Although credibility theory has its origins in actuarial mathematics, it is mathematically a method of making linearized Bayesian forecasts. For this reason, we believe these actual variations to have other important statistical applications.

2. Basic credibility results

First, let us consider the Bayesian and classical forms of the one-dimensional time-homogeneous forecast.

Let ξ be a discrete or continuous random variable (the risk), depending upon a parameter θ (the risk parameter) through a likelihood density $p(\cdot|\theta)$; a prior density $u(\theta)$ is assumed known. If n independent risk samples, $\underline{x} = \{\xi_t = x_t;\ t = 1,2,\ldots,n\}$ (the experience data), are drawn, then the Bayesian forecast of the mean risk next period (the experience-rated fair premium) is just the conditional mean:

$$E\{\xi_{n+1}|\underline{x}\} = \iint yp(y|\theta)dy \frac{\prod_{t=1}^{n} p(x_t|\theta)}{\int \prod_{t=1}^{n} p(x_t|\phi)u(\phi)d\phi} u(\theta)d\theta \qquad (2.1)$$

Practically speaking, this expression can only be evaluated with the aid of a computer, or by using natural conjugate prior families (DeGroot, 1970 and Jewell, 1973c) of likelihood and prior to carry out the updating.

Based on practical arguments, American actuaries in the 1920's proposed forecasting the mean risk through the credibility formula:

$$E\{\xi_{n+1} | \underline{x}\} \approx f(\underline{x}) = (1 - Z) \cdot m + Z\left(\frac{1}{n} \sum_{t=1}^{n} x_t\right), \qquad (2.2)$$

$$Z = \frac{n}{N + n} .$$

Here, $m = E_\theta m(\theta) = E_\theta E\{\xi | \theta\}$ is the prior mean (the manual fair premium), and N is a time constant chosen heuristically. Z is called the credibility factor, which increases to unity with increasing data. The most interesting feature of (2), as contrasted with (1), is the linear dependence of $f(\underline{x})$ on the data, through the sample mean $\frac{1}{n} \Sigma x_t$. The credibility method of experience rating has worked well in the insurance industry for over 40 years.

In the 1950's, Bailey (1950) and Mayerson (1964a) showed that (2) was, in fact, the exact Bayesian result (1) for the Beta-Binomial, Gamma-Poisson, and Normal-Normal conjugate prior-likelihood families. Bühlmann (1967) then showed that $f(\underline{x})$ was the minimum least-squares linear estimator for arbitrary priors and likelihood, provided that $N = E_\theta V\{\xi | \theta\} / V_\theta E\{\xi | \theta\}$. A fuller historical discussion may be found in Jewell (1973a).

In Jewell (1973b), the author showed that $f(\underline{x})$ was also exact for the simple (or linear) exponential family (with natural parameterization):

$$p(x | \theta) = \frac{a(x) e^{-\theta x}}{c(\theta)} , \qquad (x \in X) \qquad (2.3)$$

provided that the natural conjugate prior,

$$u(\theta) \propto [c(\theta)]^{-n_0} e^{-\theta x_0}, \qquad (\theta \in \Theta) \qquad (2.4)$$

is used over the complete parameter space θ, and that $u(\theta) \rightarrow 0$ at both ends of the range (Jewell, (1974b)). It turns out that the hyperparameter n_0 is the time constant N of Bühlmann, while $x_0 = m \cdot N$. Credibility also holds, in an extended sense, for exponential families with different sufficient statistics (Jewell, (1973b)) and there are exact credibility results in the multidimensional case (Jewell, (1974d)).

To develop non-stationary and multidimensional credibility formulae related to (2), it is first appropriate to review some least-squares theory.

3. Least-squares theory

Suppose we have a vector-valued random variable $\underline{\xi}$ from whose observations $\underline{x}$ we are trying to predict another random variable η through a forecast function $f(\underline{x})$. Assuming we have the joint distribution $P(y,\underline{x}) = \Pr\{\eta \leq y;\ \underline{\xi} \leq \underline{x}\}$, the classical means of evaluating the forecast function is the mean-square error:

$$I = \int (y - f(\underline{x}))^2 dP(y,\underline{x}) \ . \tag{3.1}$$

It is known that the integrable function f^0 which minimizes (3.1) at value I^0 is the conditional mean:

$$f^0(\underline{x}) = E\{\eta | \underline{\xi} = \underline{x}\} \ , \tag{3.2}$$

where E is defined with respect to the measure P. However, in many cases the exact conditional calculation is too difficult and an approximate forecast function f is sought. Since completion of the square shows that

$$\begin{aligned} I &= I^0 + \int (f^0(\underline{x}) - f(\underline{x}))^2 dP(\underline{x}) \\ I^0 &= E_{\underline{\xi}} V\{\eta|\underline{\xi}\} = V\{\eta\} - Vf^0(\underline{\xi}) \end{aligned} \tag{3.3}$$

for any f, then the approximate forecast is also a least-square fit to the conditional mean, and one may select arbitrary parameters in the approximation to make the integral in (3.3) as small as possible, or work directly with (3.1).

A typical choice of an approximate forecast is a linear function

$$f(\underline{x}) = a_0 + \Sigma a_j x_j \, . \qquad (3.4)$$

In this case it is well known that the optimal parameters a_j^* $(j \neq 0)$ are given by solutions of linear equations of the form:

$$\sum_{j \neq 0} C\{\xi_i, \xi_j\} \cdot a_j^* = C\{\eta; \xi_i\} \qquad (\forall\, i \neq 0) \qquad (3.5)$$

with a_0^* selected so as to make the average forecast $E\{f(\underline{\xi})\}$ unbiased, e.g.,

$$E\{f(\underline{\xi})\} = E\{\eta\}; \; a_0^* = E\{\eta\} - \sum_{j \neq 0} a_j^* E\{\xi_j\} \, . \qquad (3.6)$$

The prior variance of the optimal linear forecast is:

$$V\{f(\underline{\xi})\} = \sum_{i,j \neq 0} \sum a_i^* a_j^* C\{\xi_i, \xi_j\} = \sum_{j \neq 0} a_j^* C\{\eta; \xi_j\} \, , \qquad (3.7)$$

and the approximation error is:

$$I - I^0 = Vf^0(\underline{\xi}) - \sum_{j \neq 0} a_j^* C\{\eta; \xi_j\} \, . \qquad (3.8)$$

As before, all operators are defined on the measure $P = P(y, \underline{x})$.

In some applications, it is sometimes felt that only proportional functions should be allowed, i.e., $a_0^* \equiv 0$. In this case (3.5) is replaced by:

$$\sum_{j \neq 0} E\{\xi_i \cdot \xi_j\} \cdot a_j^* = E\{\eta \cdot \xi_i\} \qquad (\forall\, i \neq 0) \qquad (3.9)$$

and the average value of the forecast function is, in general, now biased, and the mean-square error will be larger.

One can remove the bias, at the price of further error, by constraining the optimal a_j^*. This is most conveniently accomplished by adding $\mu E\{\xi_i\}$ to the RHS of (3.9), and then adjusting μ, the Lagrange multiplier, until

$E\{\eta\} = \Sigma\, a_j^* E\{\xi_j\}$. After some reduction we find

$$\sum_{j\neq 0} C\{\xi_i,\xi_j\} \cdot (a_j^* - a_j^0) = \mu E(\xi_i) \qquad (\forall\, i \neq 0) \quad (3.10)$$

where a_j^0 is now the best linear solution (3.5) (3.6).

One can also replace the linear functions of observables in (3.4) by linearly-weighted functionals of observables, but this apparently more general theory is already contained in the above by redefinition of the ξ_i.

We shall now apply the above theory to a variety of multidimensional credibility problems with the slight difference that the observables constitute a matrix, and differing interpretations will be placed on the various components of this matrix. The development of various models based upon a collective of risks will lead to special forms for the moments in (3.5) (3.6), enabling us to solve (3.5) or (3.10) in closed form.

4. Multidimensional independent observations of a single risk

4.1 Model

In our first model variation, we assume that multidimensional, possibly nonstationary observations are made of a single risk.

As before we assume that the variation of performance over the collective of risks is described by a (possibly vector-valued) parameter θ. Given that we collect data from a single risk (i.e., given θ), we suppose that m different random variables $(\xi_{1t},\xi_{2t},\ldots,\xi_{mt})$ can be observed at a certain epoch t. We suppose that the joint distribution of this vector $\underline{\xi}_t$ is known for each θ, viz:

$$\Pr\{\underline{\xi}_t \leq \underline{x}_t \mid \theta\} = P_t(\underline{x}_t \mid \theta) \qquad (4.1)$$

and that the $\underline{\xi}_t$ are mutually independent, given θ. If the cdf prior, $U(\theta)$, is known, then the distribution of an observation vector $\underline{x}$ picked "at random" from the collective at time t is

$$E_\theta P_t(\underline{x}|\theta) = \int P_t(\underline{x}|\theta)dU(\theta) . \tag{4.2}$$

Now suppose that a sequence of n independent experience observations are made on the vector of random variables generated by a specific risk contract $(\underline{\xi}_1, \underline{\xi}_2, \ldots, \underline{\xi}_t, \ldots, \underline{\xi}_n)$; this will generate a matrix of observations $X = \{x_{it}|(i = 1,2,\ldots,m)\ (t = 1,2,\ldots,n)\}$ with probability distribution

$$\Pr\{\Xi \leq X|\theta\} = \Pr\{\underline{\xi}_t \leq \underline{x}_t (t = 1,\ldots,n)|\theta\} = \prod_{t=1}^{n} P_t(\underline{x}_t|\theta). \tag{4.3}$$

Suppose we wish to forecast the next observation of a selected observable component $i = s$, i.e., $\eta = \xi_{s,n+1}$. Then, by use of the least-squares technique described above, we see that the problem is to find a best linear approximation to $E\{\xi_{s,n+1}|\Xi = X\}$ by means of the formulae given there. Assuming that $\xi_{s,n+1}$ (or $\underline{\xi}_{n+1}$) will also be an independent draw from the same risk, we see that the appropriate measure, referred to section 3 as $P(y,\underline{x})$, will be:

$$P(y,X) = E_\theta\left\{P_{s,n+1}(y|\theta) \prod_{t=1}^{n} P_t(\underline{x}_t|\theta)\right\} \tag{4.4}$$

since the optimization will have to be over all prior possible families of $\{\underline{\xi}_{n+1}; \Xi\}$. Here $P_{s,n+1}(\cdot|\cdot)$ is the sth marginal distribution of $P_{n+1}(\cdot|\cdot)$.

The optimal solution to the best linear forecast of $E\{\xi_{s,n+1}|X\}$ is given by the corresponding generalization of (3.5), which is to find coefficients

$$\left\{a_0;\ a_{it}\begin{pmatrix} i = 1,\ldots,m \\ t = 1,\ldots,n \end{pmatrix}\right\} \text{ in } f(X) = a_0 + \sum_{i=1}^{m}\sum_{t=1}^{n} a_{it}x_{it}$$

by solving:

$$\sum_{j=1}^{m}\sum_{u=1}^{n} C\{\xi_{it};\ \xi_{ju}\}\cdot a_{ju} = C\{\xi_{it};\ \xi_{s,n+1}\} \quad \begin{pmatrix} i = 1,\ldots,m \\ t = 1,\ldots,n \end{pmatrix}, \tag{4.5}$$

and

$$a_0 = E\{\xi_{s,n+1}\} - \sum_{i=1}^{m} \sum_{t=1}^{n} a_{it} E\{\xi_{it}\} . \qquad (4.6)$$

The problem is now to define and calculate the above means and covariances using the measure (4.4).

4.2 Moment Notation and Results

In what follows, $i,j = 1,2,\ldots,m$; and $t,u = 1,2,\ldots, n, n+1$. Define

$$m_{it}(\theta) = E\{\xi_{it}|\theta\} = \int x_i dP_{it}(x_i|\theta) , \qquad (4.7)$$

and

$$m_{it} = E\{\xi_{it}\} = E_\theta E\{\xi_{it}|\theta\} = E_\theta m_{it}(\theta) = \int m_{it}(\theta) dU(\theta), \quad (4.8)$$

as the mean ith observation at epoch t for an individual risk, or for observations from the collective, respectively. In this notation, (4.6) reads:

$$a_0 = m_{s,n+1} - \sum_i \sum_t a_{it} m_{it} . \qquad (4.6')$$

For higher order moments, it depends whether the draw is from the same or different time periods. For the same time period, define:

$$C_{it,jt}(\theta) = C\{\xi_{it}; \xi_{jt}|\theta\} = \iint x_i x_j dP_t(\cdot\cdot x_i, x_j \cdot\cdot|\theta) - (m_{it}(\theta))(m_{jt}(\theta)) . \qquad (4.9)$$

However, for different time periods, we see that

$$C\{\xi_{it}, \xi_{ju}|\theta\} \equiv 0 \qquad (t \neq u) \qquad (4.10)$$

because of the independence assumption. To get the total covariance over the collective, we need to define the mean covariance:

$$E_{it,jt} = E_\theta[C_{it,jt}(\theta)] = E_\theta C\{\xi_{it}, \xi_{jt}|\theta\} ; \qquad (4.11)$$

$$E_{it,ju} \equiv 0 \qquad (t \neq u) \qquad (4.12)$$

as well as the covariance of the means:

$$D_{it,ju} = C_\theta[m_{it}(\theta); m_{ju}(\theta)] = C_\theta[E\{\xi_{it}|\theta\}; E\{\xi_{ju}|\theta\}]. \qquad (4.13)$$

The total covariance is just the sum of these two terms. This latter term is often overlooked in applications, since it is perfectly possible to have independence in successive time intervals (or even among observable components) for a given risk, and yet have collective variability over the performance parameter θ.

The coefficients in the least-squares solution covariance matrix (4.5) have two forms:

$$C\{\xi_{it};\ \xi_{ju}\} = \begin{cases} E_{it,jt} + D_{it,jt} & (t = u) \\ D_{it,ju} & (t \neq u)\ . \end{cases} \tag{4.14}$$

On the other hand, since prediction epoch $n + 1$ is distinct from the experience interval, the RHS of (4.5) has coefficients:

$$C\{\xi_{it};\ \xi_{s,n+1}\} = D_{it;s(n+1)}\ . \tag{4.15}$$

Note that E and D are both symmetric functions of their subscript pairs.

Unfortunately, the above analysis does not simplify the solution of (4.5) much, so we now examine a specific submodel which has great practical importance. We will return to the nonstationary case in Section 6.

4.3 Time-homogeneous risks submodel

In many cases, one can assume that underlying distributions (4.1) and the various moments do not depend on t, either because the risk process is assumed stationary, or because certain transformations are available so that "as if" stationary statistics can be derived. This model was first described in (Jewell, (1973a)).

In this case, the moments defined in section 4.2 reduce to the families $\{m_i\}$, $\{E_{ij}\}$ and $\{D_{ij}\}$, and (4.14) and (4.15) become:

$$C\{\xi_{it};\ \xi_{ju}\} = \begin{cases} E_{ij} + D_{ij} & (t = u) \\ D_{ij} & (t \neq u) \end{cases} \qquad (4.16)$$

and

$$C\{\xi_{it};\ \xi_{s,n+1}\} = D_{is}\ . \qquad (4.17)$$

By examining the equations (4.5) for the same i and different t, we deduce

$$a_{it} = a_i \ \text{(say) for all } t = 1,2,\ldots,n \quad \text{for each } i = 1,\ldots,m \qquad (4.18)$$

so that the predicting linear form:

$$f(X) = a_0 + \sum_{i=1}^{m} a_i \sum_{t=1}^{n} x_{it} \qquad (4.19)$$

weights all observed values for a given component the same, as we might expect. The revised optimal solution conditions (4.5) and (4.6) now read:

$$\sum_{j=1}^{n} (E_{ij} + nD_{ij})a_j = D_{is} \qquad (i = 1,\ldots,n) \qquad (4.20)$$

$$a_0 = m_s - n \sum_{j=1}^{m} a_j m_j\ . \qquad (4.21)$$

Various general results can be proven about the solutions to the above, but first it is convenient to change to a vector notation which will relate more clearly to the classical one-dimensional theory.

First, let us recognize explicitly that (4.19) predicts the mean of component s, and rewrite it as:

$$E\{\xi_{s,n+1}|X\} \approx f_s(X) = a_{so} + \sum_{j=1}^{m} Z_{sj}\left(\frac{1}{n}\sum_{t=1}^{n} x_{jt}\right), \qquad (4.19')$$

with f and a_o being given an additional subscript, and Z_{sj} being n times the a_j found in (4.20).

Now, if we allow s to range over all components, we get a vector forecast versus of (4.19).

$$\underline{f}(X) = \underline{a}_o + Z\left(\frac{1}{n}\sum_{t=1}^{n} \underline{x}_t\right) \qquad (4.19'')$$

where the $m \times 1$ vectors $\underline{f}$ and $\underline{a}_o$ are defined in the obvious way, and Z is the $m \times m$ matrix of credibility coefficients $\{Z_{sj}\}$, which measures the contribution of the vector sample mean to the vector forecast.

Then defining vector and matrix moments $\underline{m}$, E, and D in the obvious way, we see that (4.20) and (4.21) becomes:

$$Z(E + nD) = nD \, , \tag{4.22}$$

and

$$\underline{a}_o = \underline{m} - Z\underline{m} \, , \tag{4.23}$$

using the fact that E and D are symmetric.

Now assume that D is positive definite, and define an $m \times m$ matrix of time constants $\{N_{ij}\}$

$$N = ED^{-1} \tag{4.24}$$

(If D is only non-negative definite, then with probability one some $m_i(\theta)$ lies in some hyperplane for all θ, and at least one dimension of the forecast problem is uninteresting). We see that the credibility matrix satisfies:

$$Z = n(N + nI)^{-1}; \quad (I - Z) = \frac{1}{n} ZN \tag{4.25}$$

and the vector forecast (4.19″) has the solution:

$$\underline{f}(X) = (I - Z)\underline{m} + Z\left(\frac{1}{n} \sum_{t=1}^{n} \underline{x}_t\right) \tag{4.26}$$

The comparison with the one-dimensional case (2.2) is immediate, once we define $E_{11} = E_\theta V\{\xi_1|\theta\}$, $D_{11} = V_\theta E\{\xi_1|\theta\}$, and $N = E_{11}|D_{11}$. Explicit formulae for $m = 2$ are in (Jewell, 1973a).

In certain respects, the time-homogeneous multidimensional solution (4.25) (4.26) is very much like the classical one-dimensional solution (2.2). When $n = 0$, the non-data iniital forecast is the collective mean $\underline{m}$. And, if the eigenvalues of N are $\{\upsilon_i\}$ and distinct, then the eigenvalues of Z are $\{n/(n + \upsilon_i)\}$ and also distinct, and one can show that $\lim_{n\to\infty} Z = I$; thus, in the limit, each component of risk is estimated only through its own sample mean, which then become "fully-credible," as in the one-dimensional case.

However, for a finite number of data points, it can be seen that Z is in general a full matrix, indicating that all the component sample means are used to forecast any one component, thus obtaining as much information as possible through intercomponent dependency. Further, one can show that the optimal credibility coefficients need not be monotone, or even positive! This is in definite contrast to the one-dimensional result. Numerical results for the "problem of severity" are given in (Jewell, 1973a).

If we indicate the forecast for period $n + 1$ by $\underline{f}^{n+1}$, we can easily illustrate an interactive premium calculation method for (4.19"). Since the optimal coefficients are different in different epochs, we first calculate an iteractive principle for the credibility coefficients Z^n, Z^{n+1} from (4.25):

$$\frac{Z^{n+1}}{n+1} = \frac{Z^n}{n}\left(I - \frac{Z^n}{n}\right)^{-1} \tag{4.27}$$

and then find

$$\underline{f}^{n+1} = \left(I - \frac{Z^{n+1}}{n+1}\right)\underline{f}^n + \frac{Z^{n+1}}{n+1}\underline{x}_{n+1}\,. \tag{4.28}$$

This illustrates clearly how decreasing weight is placed on the last observation, as the number of observations increases, and we place increasing credibility on the forecast already obtained.

5. Use of future data from nonpredicted components

5.1 Model

Not all of the components of $\underline{\xi}_t$ may become known at the same point in time. In particular, certain of the values $x_{i,n+1}$ $(i \neq s)$ may be known at the moment of forecasting. For example, the exposure under a given contract may be a random variable from year to year, but known for the year in question before the losses are. This knowledge provides additional predictive support.

For simplicity, assume the future values of all components except the predicted one are available. We can then imagine that the matrix X of observations described in section 4.1 is augmented to a matrix X^+ which has an additional incomplete column of helper components $\xi_{i,n+1} = x_{i,n+1}$ $(i \neq s)$. The problem is then to find the best forecast to $E\{\xi_{s,n+1} | X^+\}$ through a linear form

$$f(X^+) = a_o + \sum_{i=1}^{m} \sum_{t=1}^{n} a_{it} x_{it} + \sum_{\substack{i=1 \\ i \neq s}}^{m} a_{i,n+1} x_{i,n+1} \,. \tag{5.1}$$

Retaining the assumption of independence between successive observations, we see that the appropriate generalization of the measure (4.4) is:

$$P(y, X^+) = E_\theta P_{n+1}(\underline{x}_{n+1} | \theta) \prod_{t=1}^{n} P_t(\underline{x}_t | \theta) \tag{5.2}$$

where y replaces the variable $x_{s,n+1}$. (4.5) and (4.6) are then extended in the obvious manner.

5.2 General results

In the general case, additional means $m_{i,n+1}$ are defined, and (4.6) becomes

$$a_o = m_{s,n+1} - \sum_{\forall i} \sum_{t=1}^{n} a_{it} m_{it} - \sum_{\forall i \neq s} a_{t,n+1} m_{i,n+1} \,. \tag{5.3}$$

Extending also the definitions of $E_{it,jt}$ and $D_{it,jt}$ to include time indices $n + 1$, we see that (4.14) still applies for the new $(mn + m - 1)$-square matrix of coefficients in the generalization of (4.5). On the right-hand side, however, the time indices are identical between the predictor and the new data, so that (4.15) must be changed to:

$$C\{\xi_{it}, \xi_{s,n+1}\} = \begin{cases} D_{it;s,n+1} & (\forall i, t = 1,2,\ldots,n) \\ E_{i,n+1;s,n+1} + D_{i,n+1;s,n+1} & (\forall i \neq s). \end{cases} \tag{5.4}$$

5.3 Time-homogeneous risks

Following the simplifications introduced in section 4.3 we use time-homogeneous moments m_i, E_{ij}, D_{ij}, and note that (4.18) still applies for $t \neq n + 1$. Using the credibility coefficients Z_{sj} and a_{so} from (4.19) and changing the $a_{i,n+1}$ in (5.1) to Y_{sj} to reflect the dependence on the predicted component, we rewrite (5.1) and (5.3) as:

$$f_s(X^+) = a_{so} + \sum_{j=1}^{n} Z_{sj}\left(\frac{\sum_{t=1}^{n} x_{jt}}{n}\right) + \sum_{\substack{j=1 \\ j\neq s}}^{m} Y_{sj}(x_{j,n+1}) \quad (5.5)$$

and

$$a_{so} = m_s - \sum_j Z_{sj} \cdot m_j - \sum_{j\neq s} Y_{sj} m_j \, . \quad (5.6)$$

These new credibility coefficients are now given by the $(2m - 1)$ square system:

$$\sum_j (E_{ij} + nD_{ij})Z_{sj} + \sum_{j\neq s} nD_{ij}Y_{sj} = nD_{is} \qquad (i = 1,2,\ldots,m)(5.7)$$

$$\sum_j D_{ij}Z_{sj} + \sum_{j\neq s} (E_{ij} + D_{ij})Y_{sj} = E_{is} + D_{is} \qquad (\forall i \neq s) \qquad (5.8)$$

These equations are somewhat difficult to solve because of the missing terms: $\{Y_{ss}\}$.

We temporarily indicate dependence of the solution on n thus: $Z_{sj}(n)$, $Y_{sj}(n)$, and $a_{so}(n)$. There are two special cases of interest.

5.3.1 n = 0 (no historical data)

If no experience data is available, the $Z_{sj}(0) \equiv 0$ for all s, j, and all predictive help comes from other first-period components, assumed known. The coefficients are given by the $(m - 1)$-square system

$$\sum_{j\neq s} (E_{ij} + D_{ij})Y_{sj}(0) = E_{is} + D_{is} \, . \qquad (\forall i \neq s) \qquad (5.9)$$

This is just classical $(m - 1)$-variable regression, with $E_{ij} + D_{ij}$ as the total variance of the various ξ_i on ξ_j.

$a_{so}(0)$ makes the forecast unbiased, via (5.6).

5.3.2 $n \to \infty$ ("fully credible" observations)

As n gets very large, only the terms in D_{ij} remains in (5.7). By subtraction, we get the $(m - 1)$-square system:

$$\sum_{j \neq s} E_{ij} Y_{sj}(\infty) = E_{is} \qquad (\forall i \neq s) \tag{5.10}$$

which is again a classical $(m - 1)$-variable regression, now using just the expected covariance between components.

Further, from the dominant part of (5.7), we get:

$$D_{is} Z_{ss}(\infty) + \sum_{j \neq s} D_{ij}(Y_{sj}(\infty) + Z_{sj}(\infty)) = D_{is} \qquad (\forall i) \tag{5.11}$$

By examining the dependencies in the matrix of coefficients, we see the only possible solutions are then:

$$Z_{ss}(\infty) = 1; \quad Z_{sj}(\infty) = -Y_{sj}(\infty) \quad (j \neq s); \quad a_{so}(\infty) = 0. \tag{5.12}$$

In other words, as $n \to \infty$, we have, approximately:

$$f_s(X^+) \approx \left(\frac{1}{n} \sum_{t=1}^{n} x_{st}\right) + \sum_{j \neq s} Y_{sj}(\infty)\left(X_{j,n+1} - \frac{1}{n} \sum_{t=1}^{n} x_{j,t}\right) \tag{5.13}$$

So that data cotemporal with the prediction is always used, in addition to the "fully credible" sample mean.

5.3.3 Arbitrary n

Explicit solutions to the transient behavior of (5.7) (5.8) seem quite difficult. If s and n are fixed, one can define reduced coefficients

$$e_{ij} = \frac{E_{ij}}{E_{is}}; \quad f_{ij} = \frac{E_{ij} + (n+1)D_{ij}}{E_{is} + (n+1)D_{is}}, \tag{5.14}$$

and solve two $(m - 1)$-square systems:

$$\sum_{j \neq s} e_{ij}[nY_{sj}(n) - Z_{sj}(n)] = n + Z_{ss}(n) \qquad (i \neq s) \tag{5.15}$$

$$\sum_{j \neq s} f_{ij}[Y_{sj}(n) + Z_{sj}(n)] = 1 - Z_{ss}(n) \qquad (i \neq s) \tag{5.16}$$

for the combinations of variables inside the square brackets, starting with some initial value of $Z_{ss}(n)$, say $Z^o_{ss} = nD_{ss}/(nD_{ss} + E_{ss})$.

Then from those solutions a new value of Z_{ss} is formed from:

$$Z_{ss}(n) = Z^o_{ss} - \frac{\sum_{j\neq s} [nD_{sj}Y_{sj}(n)+(E_{sj}+nD_{sj})Z_{sj}(n)]}{E_{ss} + nD_{ss}} \tag{5.17}$$

The computation should converge quickly.

6. Time-dependent observations and conditional distributions

6.1 One-dimensional forecasts with separable mean

Certain special cases of the general time-dependent model (4.5) can be solved explicitly, and have important application. First, assume we have a one-dimensional problem, with given m_{1t}, $D_{1t,1u}(t,u = 1,t,\ldots,n + 1)$ and $E_{1t,1t}(t = 1,2,\ldots,n)$, as defined in section 4.2. The equations for the $n + 1$ unknown coefficients now read $(s = 1)$:

$$a_o = m_{1,n+1} - \sum_{t=1}^{n} a_{1t}m_{1t} \tag{6.1}$$

and

$$(E_{1t,1t} + D_{1t,1t})a_{1t} + \sum_{u\neq t} D_{1t,1u}a_{1u} = D_{1t,1(n+1)} \qquad (t = 1,2,\ldots,n) \tag{6.2}$$

which gives an $n \times n$ general system to solve.

In many applications, it is possible to find constants k_{1t} and a function $m_1(\theta)$ such that:

$$m_{1t}(\theta) = k_{1t}m_1(\theta) \qquad \forall t\,,\ \forall\theta\,, \tag{6.3}$$

i.e., with the time-dependency and risk variation separable, at least in the mean. It follows that:

$$m_{1t} = E_\theta m_{1t}(\theta) = k_{1t} \cdot m_1, \quad \text{with} \quad m_1 = E_\theta m_1(\theta)\,, \tag{6.4}$$

and

$$D_{1t,1u} = C_\theta\{m_{1t}(\theta),m_{1u}(\theta)\} = k_{1t}k_{1u} \cdot D_{11}\,, \quad \text{with } D_{11} = V_\theta\{m_1(\theta)\}\,. \tag{6.5}$$

($E_{1t,1t}$ is still arbitrary in t.) Equation (4.6) becomes

$$a_o = k_{1n+1} \cdot m_1 - \sum_{t=1}^{n} a_{1t}k_{1t} \cdot m_1 \, , \tag{6.6}$$

and the remaining coefficients are given by the system:

$$(E_{1t,1t} + k_{1t}^2 D_{11})a_{1t} + \sum_{t \neq u} k_{1t}k_{1u}D_{11}a_{1u} = k_{1t}k_{1n+1}D_{11} \quad (t = 1,\ldots,n) \, . \tag{6.7}$$

Dividing equation t by $k_{1t}D_{11}$, and comparing successive equations, we find $E_{1t,1t}a_{1t}/k_{1t}$ is a constant for all t, and finally:

$$a_{1t} = \left(\frac{k_{1n+1}k_{1t}D_{11}}{E_{1t,1t}} \right) \frac{1}{1 + D_{11} \sum_u (k_{1u}^2/E_{1u,1u})} \quad (t = 1,\ldots,n) \, . \tag{6.8}$$

We can see the relationship to regular credibility more clearly if we define a time-weighted expected covariance:

$$e_{11}(t) = \frac{E_{1t,1t}}{k_{1t}^2} \, , \qquad (t = 1,\ldots,n) \tag{6.9}$$

a time-varying "time constant,"

$$N_{11}(t) = e_{11}(t)/D_{11} \qquad (t = 1,\ldots,n) \tag{6.10}$$

and a normalized per-observation crediblity factor:

$$z_{11}(t) = \frac{k_{1t}}{k_{1,n+1}} a_{1t} \, . \qquad (t = 1,\ldots,n) \tag{6.11}$$

In this new notation, the forecast function becomes

$$f_1(\underline{x}) = k_{1,n+1}\left[\left(1 - \sum_t z_{11}(t)\right)m_1 + \sum_t z_{11}(t) \frac{x_{1t}}{k_{1t}}\right] \tag{6.12}$$

with per-observation credibility factors:

$$z_{11}(t) = \left\{N_{11}(t)\left[1 + \sum_u (N_{11}(u))^{-1}\right]\right\}^{-1} . (t = 1,2,\ldots,n) \tag{6.13}$$

In other words, each observation is normalized with respect to time dependency, weighted with a varying credibility, added to a term which keeps the forecast unbiased, and then "re-inflated" to period $n + 1$. If we compare (6.13) with the classical formula for Z, we see that when the time-dependency is completely removed, z_{11} becomes Z/n, thus giving a sample mean in (6.12).

6.2 One-dimensional "as-if" forecast

A special case of the above occurs if the distribution of risk varies by a known scale factor in each time period, such as inflation, or known changes in observation techniques. Then, for example, each ξ_{1t}/k_{1t} has the same distribution as some "base" r.v. ξ_1, and (6.4), (6.5) hold, together with

$$E_{1t,1t} = E_\theta V\{\xi_{1t}|\theta\} = k_{1t}^2 E_{11} , \qquad \text{with } E_{11} = E_\theta V\{\xi_1|\theta\} . \tag{6.14}$$

$e_{11}(t)$ and $z_{11}(t)$ now become time-invariant, with $z_{11} = Z/n$, and we have a classic credibility formula, with each observation x_{1t} weighted by $(1/k_{1t})$. In this case, the observations are said to be normalized to the base distribution on an "as-if" basis.

6.3 Use of conditional distributions in forecasting

One of the problems with the use of multi-dimensional data is the fact that it is difficult to decide, a priori, what transformations or combinations of the observations are appropriate for a linear model.

One possible way to get such natural transfunctions is to use the distribution of the desired component, conditioned on the secondary data $\{x_{it}|\forall i \neq s\}$, given for $t = 1,2,\ldots,n$ or $t = 1,2,\ldots,n+1$. In this way, the forecasting problem reduces to a one-dimensional problem solvable by (6.2) and only the use of a linear form of the $\{x_{st}\}$ can be considered to be an approximation to the exact predictor. This approach was suggested by a special model of Bühlmann and Straub (see Bühlmann, 1971 and Bühlmann and Straub, 1970), given below in section 6.3.2.

There are two different models, depending on whether or not secondary data from period $n + 1$ is available.

6.3.1 Future data available

For concreteness, suppose $s = 1$, and assume that future values of the secondary variables are given. Let X^+, referred to in section 5, be decomposed into a $1 \times n$ and an $(m - 1) \times (n + 1)$ matrix, labelled:

$$\underline{x}^1 = \{x_{1t} | t = 1,2,\ldots,n\};$$
$$X^{\pm} = \{x_{it} | i = 2,\ldots,m;\ t = 1,2,\ldots,n + 1\} . \tag{6.15}$$

The use of conditional distributions can be explained as the forecast of $E\{\xi_{1,n+1} | X^+\}$ using the conditional measure $P(y,\underline{x}^1 | X^{\pm})$.

Switching to densities, and with a slight abuse of notation, we see that the conditional density is:

$$p(y,\underline{x}^1 | X^{\pm}) = \frac{E_\theta \prod_{t=1}^{n+1} p_t(x_{1t} | x_{2t},\ldots,x_{mt};\ \theta)\cdot p(X^{\pm} | \theta)}{E_\theta p(X^{\pm} | \theta)} \tag{6.16}$$

with $y = x_{1,n+1}$ and where:

$$p_t(x_{1t} | x_{2t},\ldots,x_{mt};\ \theta) = \frac{p_t(x_{1t},x_{2t},\ldots,x_{mt} | \theta)}{\int p_t(x_{1t},x_{2t},\ldots,x_{mt} | \theta)dx_{1t}} ,$$

$$(t = 1,2,\ldots,n + 1)$$

$$p(X^{\pm} | \theta) = \prod_{t=1}^{n+1} \int p_t(x_{1t},x_{2t},\ldots,x_{mt} | \theta)dx_{1t} .$$

As usual, the vector of samples in each time period is independent. Letting $m_{1t}(x_{2t},x_{3t},\ldots,x_{mt};\ \theta)$ and $v_{1t}(x_{2t},x_{3t},\ldots,x_{mt};\ \theta)$ be the mean and variance, respectively, of the conditional density $p_t(x_{1t} | x_{2t},\ldots,x_{mt};\ \theta)$, we find

$$m_{1t}(X^{\pm}) = E\{\xi_{1t} | X^{\pm}\} = \frac{E_\theta\{m_{1t}(x_{2t},\ldots,x_{mt};\ \theta)\cdot p(X^{\pm} | \theta)\}}{E_\theta p(X^{\pm} | \theta)} = \tag{6.17}$$

$$= \frac{C_\theta\{m_{1t}(x_{2t},\ldots,x_{mt};\ \theta);\ p(X^\pm|\theta)\}}{E_\theta p(X^\pm|\theta)} + E_\theta m_{1t}(x_{2t},\ldots,x_{mt};\ \theta) \qquad (6.17)$$

$$(t = 1,2,\ldots,n+1)\ .$$

Proceeding in a similar manner with $C\{\xi_{1t},\xi_{1u}|X^\pm\}$ we see we can define functions equivalent to those used in (6.2), as:

$$E_{1t,1t}(X^\pm) = \frac{C_\theta\{v_{1t}(x_{2t},\ldots,x_{mt};\ \theta);\ p(X^\pm|\theta)\}}{E_\theta p(X^\pm|\theta)} + E_\theta v_{1t}(x_{2t},\ldots,x_{mt};\ \theta) \qquad (t = 1,\ldots,n) \qquad (6.18)$$

$$\begin{aligned} D_{1t,1u}(X^\pm) = {} & \frac{C_\theta\{m_{1t}(x_{2t},\ldots,x_{mt};\theta)\cdot m_{1u}(x_{2t},\ldots,x_{mt};\theta);p(X^\pm|\theta)\}}{E_\theta p(X^\pm|\theta)} \\ & + C_\theta\{m_{1t}(x_{2t},\ldots,x_{mt};\theta);m_{1u}(x_{2t},\ldots,x_{mt};\theta)\} \\ & + [E_\theta m_{1t}(x_{2t},\ldots,x_{mt};\theta)][E_\theta m_{1u}(x_{2t},\ldots,x_{mt};\theta)] \\ & - m_{1t}(X^\pm)\cdot m_{1u}(X^\pm) \qquad (t,u = 1,\ldots,n+1)\ . \qquad (6.19) \end{aligned}$$

In principle, we now have the necessary coefficients to solve a one-dimensional, time-varying system using (6.1) and (6.2). Admittedly, the computational labor implied in the above is considerable; however, special forms of dependence, with $m = 2$ or 3 might simplify things further.

6.3.2 Future data unavailable

If the future values of the nonpredicted components are unavailable, then we decompose the data X into $1 \times n$ and $(m - 1) \times n$ matrices.

$$\underline{x}^1 = \{x_{1t}|t = 1,2,\ldots,n\};$$
$$X^- = \{x_{it}|i = 2,\ldots,m;\ t = 1,2,\ldots,n\} \qquad (6.20)$$

and forecast $E\{\xi_{1,n+1}|X\}$ using the conditional measure

$P(y,\underline{x}^1|X^-)$, with density

$$p(y,\underline{x}^1|X^-) = \frac{E_\theta p_{1,n+1}(y|\theta) \prod_{i=1}^{n} p_t(x_{1t}|x_{2t},\ldots,x_{mt};\theta)\cdot p(X^-|\theta)}{E_\theta p(X^-|\theta)} . \tag{6.21}$$

It can be seen that all of the equations of the last subsection still apply with $X^\pm$ replaced by X^-, and an obvious redefinition of $p(X^-|\theta)$ and of the $(n+1)$st components involving the mean; viz:

$$m_{1,n+1}(X^-) = \frac{C_\theta\{m_{1,n+1}(\theta);\ p(X^-|\theta)\}}{E_\theta p(X^-|\theta)} + m_{1,n+1} \tag{6.22}$$

$$\begin{aligned} D_{1t,1,n+1}(X^-) = {} & \frac{C_\theta\{m_{1t}(x_{2t},\ldots,x_{mt};\ \theta)\cdot m_{1,n+1}(\theta);\ p(X^-|\theta)\}}{E_\theta p(X^-|\theta)} \\ & + C_\theta\{m_{1t}(x_{2t},\ldots,x_{mt};\ \theta);\ m_{1,n+1}(\theta)\} \\ & + [E_\theta m_{1t}(x_{2t},\ldots,x_{mt};\ \theta)]\cdot m_{1,n+1} \\ & - m_{1t}(X^-)\cdot m_{1,n+1}(X^-) \qquad (t = 1,2,\ldots,n) . \end{aligned} \tag{6.23}$$

It should perhaps be re-emphasized that, even if the underlying process is stationary, a general time-dependent model usually results because of the dependency of the conditional mean and variance (stationary in form) upon the time-varying observations X^-.

6.3.3 Independent collective variations of secondary variables

An important special case of the above occurs when the secondary variables vary across the collective in a manner independent from the variation in the predicted component. In other words, we assume that the risk parameter, now a vector, has two components $\underline{\theta} = \{\theta^1;\ \theta^2\}$ with independent priors, such that conditional densities used above have separate risk parameter variations:

$$\begin{aligned} p_t(x_{1t}|x_{2t},\ldots,x_{mt};\ \theta) &= p_t(x_{1t}|x_{2t},\ldots,x_{mt};\ \theta^1) \\ p_t(x_{2t},\ldots,x_{mt}|\underline{\theta}) &= p_t(x_{2t},\ldots,x_{mt}|\theta^2) \\ p(X^{\pm}|\underline{\theta}) &= p(X^{\pm}|\theta^2) \\ p(X^{-}|\underline{\theta}) &= p(X^{\pm}|\theta^2) \\ p_{1,n+1}(y|\underline{\theta}) &= p_{1,n+1}(y|\theta^1) \end{aligned} \tag{6.24}$$

as needed, and over the approximate range of t in the models using $X^{\pm}$ or X^{-}.

An even more strigent assumption might be that the secondary observations represent external factors which affect every member of the collective in the same way, such as economic externalities. In this case θ^2 does not exist, and $p(X^{\pm}|\underline{\theta}) = p(X^{\pm})$, and so forth.

In either case, the formulae of the last two subsections simplify dramatically, with the following moments used in (6.1), (6.2):

$$\left.\begin{array}{l} m_{1t}(X^{\pm}) \\ m_{1t}(X^{-}) \end{array}\right\} = E_\theta m_{1t}(x_{2t},\ldots,x_{mt};\ \theta) \qquad (t = 1,2,\ldots,n)$$

$$m_{1,n+1}(X^{\pm}) = E_\theta m_{1,n+1}(x_{2t},\ldots,x_{mt};\ \theta) \qquad (t = n+1) \tag{6.25}$$

$$m_{1,n+1}(X^{-}) = E_\theta m_{1,n+1}(\theta)$$

$$E_{1t,1t} = E_\theta v_{1t}(x_{2t},\ldots,x_{mt};\ \theta) \qquad (t = 1,2,\ldots,n)$$

$$\left.\begin{array}{l} D_{1t,1u}(X^{\pm}) \\ D_{1t,1u}(X^{-}) \end{array}\right\} = C_\theta\{m_{1t}(x_{2t},\ldots,x_{mt};\ \theta);m_{1u}(x_{2t},\ldots,x_{mt};\ \theta)\}$$
$$(t,u = 1,2,\ldots,n) \tag{6.26}$$

$$D_{1t,1,n+1}(X^{\pm}) = C_\theta\{m_{1t}(x_{2t},\ldots,x_{mt};\ \theta);m_{1,n+1}(x_{2t},\ldots,x_{mt};\ \theta)\}$$
$$D_{1t,1,n+1}(X^{-}) = C_\theta\{m_{1t}(x_{2t},\ldots,x_{mt};\ \theta);m_{1,n+1}(\theta)\}$$
$$(t = 1,2,\ldots,n) \tag{6.27}$$

All of the values of θ above are in fact θ^1, so that all dependence on θ^2 vanishes.

Note that if the original m-dimensional problem is stationary, and the dependency on θ factors out of $m_1(x_{2t},\ldots,x_{mt};\theta)$, then the resulting forecasting problem will be of the separable-mean type analyzed in section 6.1.

6.3.4 Forecasting claim rate, given exposure or volume

To illustrate the above, we consider a special case analyzed by Bühlman (1971) and Bühlmann and Straub (1970), in which ξ_{1t} is the claim rate (total \$ claims per unit exposure or volume of business) in year t, and $\xi_{2t} > 0$ is the exposure or volume in the same year. The joint claims-volume process is assumed stationary in time. Then, from elementary considerations,

$$E\{\xi_{1t} \mid \xi_{2t} = x_{2t};\ \theta\} = m_{1t}(\theta) = m_o(\theta) \quad (\forall t), \qquad (6.28)$$

$$V\{\xi_{1t} \mid \xi_{2t} = x_{2t};\ \theta\} = v_{1t}(\theta) = \frac{v_o(\theta)}{x_{2t}} \quad (\forall t), \qquad (6.29)$$

where $m_o(\theta)$ and $v_o(\theta)$ are moments associated with unit exposure or volume. First, assume that the experience random variable x_{2t} has a distribution $p(x_{2t}|\theta)$ depending on θ, and $x_{2,n+1}$ is known. Then

$$p(X^{\pm}|\theta) = \prod_{t=1}^{n+1} p(x_{2t}|\theta), \qquad (6.30)$$

the mean is stationary,

$$m_{1t}(X^{\pm}) = \frac{C_\theta\{m_o(\theta);p(X^{\pm}|\theta)\}}{E_\theta p(X^{\pm}|\theta)} + E_\theta m_o(\theta) = m_1(X^{\pm}), \qquad (6.31)$$

$$\text{say,} \quad (t = 1,2,\ldots,n+1)$$

and the covariance components become

$$E_{1t,1t}(X^{\pm}) = \frac{C_{\theta}\{v_o(\theta);p(X^{\pm}|\theta)\}}{x_{2t}\cdot E\ p(X^{\pm}|\theta)} + \frac{1}{x_{2t}} E_{\theta}v_o(\theta) = \frac{E_{oo}(X^{\pm})}{x_{2t}},$$

$$\text{say,} \quad (t = 1,2,\ldots,n) \tag{6.32}$$

$$D_{1t,1u}(X^{\pm}) = \frac{C_{\theta}\{(m_o(\theta))^2;p(X^{\pm}|\theta)\}}{E_{\theta}p(X^{\pm}|\theta)} + V_{\theta}m_o(\theta)$$

$$+ (E_{\theta}m_o(\theta))^2 - (m_1(X^{\pm}))^2 = D_{11}(X^{\pm}), \tag{6.33}$$

$$\text{say,} \quad (t = 1,2,\ldots,n) \quad (u = 1,2,\ldots,n+1).$$

Note that the functions defined above all depend on $X^{\pm}$, and hence implicitly on n; however (6.31) is of separable mean form with $k_{1t} = 1$, and has a solution given by (6.10).

For fixed n, we find

$$f = m_1(X^{\pm}) \cdot Z_o + \frac{1}{n}\sum_{t=1}^{n} z_{1t}x_{1t}, \tag{6.34}$$

with

$$z_{1t} = \frac{n \cdot x_{2t}}{N_{oo}(X^{\pm}) + \sum_{u=1}^{n} x_{2,u}} \quad (t = 1,2,\ldots,n);$$

$$Z_o = \frac{N_{oo}(X^{\pm})}{N_{oo}(X^{\pm}) + \sum_{u=1}^{n} x_{2,u}} \tag{6.35}$$

and

$$N_{oo}(X^{\pm}) = \frac{E_{oo}(X^{\pm})}{D_{11}(X^{\pm})}. \tag{6.36}$$

We see that the forecast (6.34) of claim rate is actually made in terms of an average of $x_{1t} \cdot x_{2t}$, i.e., in terms of the total claim amount; this function is then a more natural predictor than using claim rate and exposure separately. Notice also that operational time for credibility is total volume, rather than n.

The future volume, $x_{2,n+1}$ enters only into calculation of the mean $m_1(X^{\pm})$ and "time constant" $N_{oo}(X^{\pm})$. If this volume were not available, then the model of subsection 6.3.2 would merely substitute $m_1(X^-)$ and $N_{oo}(X^-)$, with obvious modifications of (6.30) - (6.33). In either case, as experience data is accumulated, and n becomes $n + 1$, these parameters must be updated using the new value $x_{2,n+2}$ (or $x_{2,n+1}$). Possible simplifications in the updating might occur by using conjugate prior families of exponential type.

If we now assume that x_{2t} has independent variation across the collective, as in section 6.3.3, then we have one of the models analyzed by Bühlmann and Straub (1970), with the following additional simplifications:

$$\begin{aligned} m_1(X^{\pm}) &= m_1(X^-) = m_1 = E_\theta m_o(\theta) , \\ E_{oo}(X^{\pm}) &= E_{oo}(X^-) = E_{oo} = E_\theta v_o(\theta) , \\ D_{11}(X^{\pm}) &= D_{11}(X^-) = D_{11} = V_\theta m_o(\theta) \end{aligned} \tag{6.37}$$

and we see that (6.34) and (6.35) apply with time constant

$$N_{oo}(X^{\pm}) = N_{oo}(X^-) = N_{oo} = \frac{E_\theta v_o(\theta)}{V_\theta m_o(\theta)} \tag{6.38}$$

which does not change with n. Thus, in this special case, the future value of exposure, $x_{2,n+1}$ has no predictive value, whether it is available or not!

We see this peculiar result will occur for all models where section 6.3.3 applies, and where the conditional mean is "unbiased" by knowledge of the other component values. Only $E_{1t,1t}$ is then time-varying, and does not use future values.

It is also possible to take a combined linear-nonlinear approach to forecasting. For example, if only certain conditional relationships between components were simple, then the approach of this section might be used for those secondary variables, the rest being used as in the original linear multi-dimensional model. The result would be a reduced dimension, time-dependent case. Alternatively, it may be necessary to use a credibility approximation based on secondary data to get approximations to the conditional moments.

6.4 m-dimensional forecasts with separable mean

We conclude by indicating briefly how the assumption of a separable mean simplifies also the m-dimensional time-dependent forecast, reducing it to finding the inverse of $n+1$ matrices of order $m \times m$.

Suppose that the general time-dependent mean defined in (4.8) can be written in separable fashion as

$$m_{it}(\theta) = k_{it} \cdot m_i(\theta) \qquad (\forall i,t,\theta) \tag{6.39}$$

thus giving

$$m_{it} = k_{it} \cdot m_i, \quad \text{with} \quad m_i = E_\theta m_i(\theta) , \tag{6.40}$$

and

$$D_{it,ju} = k_{it} \cdot k_{ju} \cdot D_{ij}, \quad \text{with} \quad D_{ij} = C_\theta\{m_i(\theta), m_j(\theta)\} \tag{6.41}$$

Equation (4.6) becomes:

$$a_o = k_{s,n+1} \cdot m_s - \sum_{i=1}^{m} m_i \sum_{t=1}^{n} k_{it} a_{it} , \tag{6.42}$$

with the coefficients $[a_{it}]$ given by the (mn)-square system:

$$\sum_{j=1}^{m} E_{it,jt} \cdot a_{jt} + k_{it} \sum_{j=1}^{m} D_{ij} \sum_{u=1}^{n} k_{ju} a_{ju} = k_{it} k_{s,n+1} D_{i,s} \qquad (\forall i,t) . \tag{6.43}$$

Define a time-weighted expected covariance matrix $e(t)$ similar to (6.9)

$$e_{ij}(t) = \frac{E_{it,jt}}{k_{it} \cdot k_{jt}} \qquad \begin{matrix} (i,j = 1,2,\ldots,m) \\ (t = 1,2,\ldots,n) \end{matrix} \tag{6.44}$$

and normalized per-observation credibility factors:

$$z_{s,j}(t) = \frac{k_{jt}}{k_{s,n+1}} a_{jt} \ . \qquad (6.45)$$

Then (6.43) can be written in matrix form as:

$$z(t) \cdot e(t) + \left(\sum_{u=1}^{n} z(u) \right) \cdot D = D \ . \qquad (t = 1,2,\ldots) \ (6.46)$$

By defining the time-varying matrix of time constants

$$N(t) = e(t)D^{-1} \qquad (6.47)$$

and noticing that $z(t) \cdot e(t)$ is a constant for all t, we finally obtain

$$z(t) = \left\{ N(t) \left[1 + \sum_{u} (N(u))^{-1} \right] \right\}^{-1} \qquad (6.48)$$

which should be compared with (6.13).

The forecast functions are:

$$f_s(X) = k_{s,n+1} \left\{ \left[m_s - \sum_t \sum_j z_{sj}(t) m_j \right] + \sum_t \sum_j z_{sj}(t) \frac{x_{jt}}{k_{st}} \right\} (6.49)$$

6.5 m-dimensional "as-if" forecasts

Following the model of section 6.2 for m-dimensions, then for every t, ξ_{it}/k_{it} will have the same distribution as some base r.v. ξ_i, $(i = 1,2,\ldots,m)$. We find that

$$e_{ij}(t) = E_\theta C\{\xi_i; \xi_j | \theta\} = E_{ij}, \ \text{say} \qquad (6.50)$$

and one may then verify that one obtains again, in slightly different form, the m-dimensional credibility coefficients of section 5.3, with the exception that the observations x_{it} are weighted by $(1/k_{it})$, i.e., they are normalized to the base distributions on an "as-if" basis.

7. Concurrent observations of related multiple risks

7.1 Model

We now give a different interpretation to the matrix of random variables $\{\xi_{it}\}$ by assuming that it represents successive samples at epochs $t = 1,2,\ldots,n$ from different, but related risks $i = 1,2,\ldots,m$, from a collective specified by a parameter θ_i for each i. We have two insurance examples in mind: in the first, the different dimensions might represent different pure risks in the same policyholder, such as occurs in a comprehensive automobile or homeowner's policy. Here the distributions of each dimension are different, and the different θ_i are probably strongly related to one another through the fact that they describe different attributes of the same automobile and drivers, the same house, etc. However, given θ_i, risk i is independent of different attributes of the others.

The other application might be simply to describe a cohort, or finite population, of individual risks which are identical, given $\underline{\theta} = \{\theta_1, \theta_2, \ldots, \theta_m\}$. However, for reasons which are examined further in section 7.7, it may be that the multidimensional prior $U(\theta_1, \theta_2, \ldots, \theta_m)$ shows independence among the risk parameters. In this variation, we are probably mostly interested in identical risk likelihoods, and the prior representing exchangeable variables with weak coupling. Again, given $\underline{\theta}$, the actual risk histories of each individual are independent.

For the likelihood, we assume $m \times (n + 1)$ distributions are given:

$$\Pr\{\xi_{it} \le x_{it} | \underline{\theta}\} = \Pr\{\xi_{it} \le x_{it} | \theta_i\} = P_{it}(x_{it} | \theta_i). \qquad (7.1)$$
$$(i = 1,2,\ldots,m) \quad (t = 1,2,\ldots,n + 1)$$

The vector of observations $\underline{x}_t$ in a single period is simply

$$\Pr\{\underline{\xi}_t \le \underline{x}_t | \underline{\theta}\} = \prod_{i=1}^{m} P_{it}(x_{it} | \theta_i), \quad (t = 1,2,\ldots) \qquad (7.2)$$

a prior, no-observation forecast.

$$\Pr\{\underline{\xi}_t \le \underline{x}_t\} = E_\theta \Pr\{\underline{\xi}_t \le \underline{x}_t | \theta\} = \iiint \prod_i P_{it}(x_{it} | \theta_i) dU(\underline{\theta}). \qquad (7.3)$$

As before, the problem is to predict the next observation

of a selected risk $i = s$, i.e., $\eta = \xi_{s,n+1}$ as a linear function of the matrix of observations X. From the above, it can be seen that the appropriate measure for the calculation of the coefficients in (4.5), (4.6) will be

$$P(y, X) = E_{\underline{\theta}} P_{s,n+1}(y|\theta_s) \prod_{t=1}^{n} \prod_{i=1}^{m} P_{it}(x_{it}|\theta_i) \,. \tag{7.4}$$

7.2 Moment notation and results

As before, the mean of (7.1) is:

$$m_{it}(\theta_i) = E\{\xi_{it}|\theta_i\} = \int x dP_{it}(x|\theta_i) \qquad (i = 1,2,\ldots,m) \quad (t = 1,2,\ldots) \tag{7.5}$$

$$m_{it} = E_{\underline{\theta}} m_{it}(\theta_i) = E_{\theta_i} m_t(\theta_i) \,. \tag{7.6}$$

Now because of the assumed independence between risks, and between time periods, given the parameters, the covariance

$$C\{\xi_{it};\, \xi_{ju}|\underline{\theta}\} = \begin{cases} V\{\xi_{it}|\theta_i\} = v_{it}(\theta_i) & (i = j;\ t = u) \\ 0 & \text{otherwise} \end{cases} \tag{7.7}$$

is null except when both risk and time-period coincide.

Then in a manner parallel with section 4.2, we define:

$$E_{it,ju} = E_{\underline{\theta}} C\{\xi_{it};\, \xi_{ju}|\underline{\theta}\} = \begin{cases} E_{\theta_i}\{v_{it}(\theta_i)\} & (i = j;\ t = u) \\ 0 & \text{otherwise}, \end{cases} \tag{7.8}$$

and

$$D_{it,ju} = C_{\underline{\theta}}[m_{it}(\theta_i);\, m_{ju}(\theta_j)] = \begin{cases} C_{\theta_i,\theta_j}[m_{it}(\theta_i);\, m_{ju}(\theta_j)] & (i \neq j) \\ C_{\theta_i}[m_{it}(\theta_i);\, m_{iu}(\theta_i)] & (i = j)\,. \end{cases} \tag{7.9}$$

Perhaps it is worth remarking that one of the forms in (7.9) uses a two-dimensional marginal of $U(\ldots)$, while the other uses a one-dimensional marginal. The general form of (4.5) for this model of related risks will then be

$$E_{it,it}a_{it} + \sum_{j=1}^{m} \sum_{u=1}^{n} D_{it,ju}a_{ju} = D_{it;s,(n+1)} \quad \forall(i,t) \qquad (7.10)$$

with a_o given by (4.6').

7.3 Time-homogeneous related risks

If the risk process is homogeneous in time, then the moments defined in the last section reduce to the familiar $\{m_i\}\{E_{ii}\}$ and $\{D_{ij}\}$. It follows that $a_{it} = a_i \ \forall t$, $(i = 1,\ldots,m)$, the predictor is given by (4.19), a_o is given by (4.21), and (7.10) becomes

$$E_{ii}a_i + n \sum_{j=1}^{m} D_{ij}a_j = D_{ia} \quad (i = 1,\ldots,m) . \qquad (7.11)$$

By comparison with (4.16), we see that all of the results of section 4.3 apply in this case, by setting $E_{ij} = 0$ $(i \neq j)$, and of course using the correct moment definitions. In particular, since E is diagonal,

$$(N^{-1})_{ij} = \frac{D_{ij}}{E_{jj}} \quad (i,j = 1,\ldots,m) \qquad (7.12)$$

which saves one inversion in calculating

$$Z = nN^{-1}(I + nN^{-1})^{-1} . \qquad (7.13)$$

7.3.1 Weak coupling solution

In most applications of the cohort model D_{ij} $(i \neq j)$ will be small compared to D_{ii} and D_{jj} in (7.9).

If $D_{ij} = 0$ $(i \neq j)$, there is no correlation between the different risks, and N and Z are diagonal, say

$$N^o_{ij} = \begin{cases} E_{ii}/D_{ii} & (i = j) \\ 0 & (i \neq j) \end{cases} ; \qquad (7.14)$$

$$Z^o_{ij} = \begin{cases} nD_{ii}/(E_{ii} + nD_{ii}) & (i = j) \\ 0 & (i \neq j) \end{cases} ,$$

which is one-dimensional credibility.

By expanding (7.12)

$$N^{-1} = (N^{o})^{-1} + \Delta; \ \Delta_{ij} = \begin{cases} 0 & (i = j) \\ D_{ij}/E_{jj} & (i \neq j) \end{cases} \tag{7.15}$$

and neglecting terms of order Δ^2 or higher, we can find an approximate solution to (7.13):

$$Z \approx Z^{o} + \frac{1}{n} \cdot Z^{o}N^{o}\Delta N^{o}Z^{o} \tag{7.16}$$

or

$$Z_{ij} \approx \begin{cases} Z_{ii} & (i = j) \\ \dfrac{nE_{ii}D_{ij}}{(E_{ii} + nD_{ii})(E_{jj} + nD_{jj})} & (i \neq j) \end{cases},$$

which reveals the exact nature of the weak coupling.

7.3.2 Homogeneous exchangeable related risks

In the cohort interpretation of this model, all risks have identical distributions, given $\underline{\theta}$, and $\underline{\theta}$ consists of exchangeable random variables, i.e., all marginals of U are identical.

This simplifies the moments to:

$$\begin{aligned} m_i &= m_1 \\ E_{ii} &= E_{11} \end{aligned} \qquad (i = 1,2,\ldots,m) \tag{7.18}$$

and

$$D_{ij} = \begin{cases} D_{11} & (i = j) \\ D_{12} & (i \neq j) \end{cases}. \tag{7.19}$$

This leads to only two kinds of credibility factors

$$Z_{sj} = \begin{cases} Z_{11} & (s = j) \\ Z_{12} & (s \neq j) \end{cases} \tag{7.20}$$

gotten by solving:

$$nD_{12}Z_{11} + [E_{11} + nD_{11} + n(m-2)D_{12}]Z_{12} = nD_{12}$$
$$(E_{11} + nD_{11})Z_{11} + n(m-1)D_{12}Z_{12} = nD_{11} \tag{7.21}$$

This system is most conveniently solved by defining:

$$N_{11} = E_{11}/D_{ii}; \quad d = D_{12}/D_{11} \tag{7.22}$$

and two new time constants

$$N_1 = N_{11}/(1-d); \quad N_o = N_{11}/[1 + (m-1)d] , \tag{7.23}$$

together with their associated credibility forms, $Z_i = n/(n + N_i)$ $(i = 0,1)$. In this new notation, we get a forecast function:

$$f_s(X) = (1 - Z_o)m_1 + \left(1 - \frac{N_o}{N_1}\right)(1 - Z_1)Z_o\left(\frac{\sum_{i=1}^{m}\sum_{t=1}^{n} x_{it}}{mn}\right) + Z_1\left(\frac{1}{n}\sum_{t=1}^{n} x_{st}\right) . \tag{7.24}$$

We see that in addition to the usual blend of m_1 and the sample mean of the selected experience data, we also get a term which includes the grand sample mean of all cohort data. Eventually, of course, $\lim_{n\to\infty} Z_1 = 1$, and we attach full credibility only to the selected risk data.

As the coupling between members of the cohort vanishes, $d \to 0$, and $N_o = N_1 = N_{11}$, $Z_o = Z_1 = Z_{11} = n/(n + N_{11})$, and (7.24) reduces to the usual one-dimensional credibility formula. Thus, when risks are independent, all cohort data is thrown away. (But see section 8 for a different model).

On the other hand, if there is perfect correlation between components of $\underline{\theta}$, i.e., $\theta_1 = \theta_2 = \cdots \theta_m$, then $d \to 1$, $N_1 \to \infty$, $N_o = N_{11}/m$, and the forecast uses all the data in the grand sample mean to forecast any one component:

$$f_1(X) = (1 - Z_{oo})m_1 + Z_{oo}\left(\frac{\sum_i\sum_t x_{it}}{mn}\right) \tag{7.25}$$

with a credibility factor which has operational time mn, and time constant N_{11}:

$$Z_{oo} = mn/(mn + N_{11}) . \qquad (7.26)$$

7.4 Time-dependent related risks with separable mean

Another case in which (7.10) can be solved more simply as when the risk parameter and time-dependence are separable in the mean, as in the model of section 6.4.

Since $e(t)$ in (6.44) is diagonal, only one inversion is needed. Defining:

$$A_{ij} = \delta_{ij} + D_{ij} \sum_{u=1}^{n} \left(\frac{1}{e_{jj}(u)} \right); \quad \delta_{ij} = \begin{cases} 1 & (i = j) \\ o & (i \neq j) \end{cases} \qquad (7.27)$$

we see from rearranging (6.48) that the per-observation credibility factors are

$$z_{ij}(t) = \sum_k (A^{-1})_{ik} D_{kj} / e_{jj}(t) \quad (t = 1,2,\dots) \qquad (7.28)$$

Once $z_{ij}(1)$ is calculated, the rest follow easily, and the forecast function (6.49) is used.

7.4.1 Weak coupling solutions

If the coupling between risks is small, then D_{ij} $(i \neq j)$ is small compared to the diagonal terms, and one can use the methods of section 7.3.1 to get explicit solutions to (7.28). After some algebra, we find:

$$z_{ij}(t) \approx \begin{cases} \dfrac{(D_{ii}/e_{ii}(t))}{A_{ii}} & (i = j) \\[2ex] \dfrac{D_{ij}/e_{jj}(t)}{A_{ii} \cdot A_{jj}} & (i \neq j) \end{cases} \qquad (7.29)$$

which should be compared with 7.17, after noting that in the time homogeneous case, $e_{ii}(t) = E_{ii}$, and $A_{ii} = 1 + (nD_{ii}/E_{ii})$.

7.4.2 Homogeneous exchangeable related risks

When the assumptions of section 7.3.2 are satisfied,

then simplified moments are obtained as in (7.18) (7.19). However, the notation now refers to the time-dependency "deflated" moments defined in (6.39) and (6.41), except that $k_{it} = k_t$, $(i = 1,2,\ldots,m)$.

There are now two normalized per-observation credibility factors analogous to (6.45) and (7.20),

$$\frac{k_t}{k_{n+1}} a_{jt} = \begin{cases} z_{11}(t) & (j = s) \\ z_{12}(t) & (j \neq s) \end{cases} \tag{7.30}$$

and it is necessary to define time-varying expected covariance and time-constants:

$$e_{11}(t) = \frac{E_{1t,1t}}{k_{1t}^2}; \quad N_{11}(t) = e_{11}(t)/D_{11} . \tag{7.31}$$

For the solution of (6.43), we get a result similar to (7.21):

$$nD_{12}z_{12}(t) + [e_{11}(t) + nD_{11} + n(m-2)D_{12}]z_{12}(t) = D_{12}$$

$$(t = 1,2,\ldots) \tag{7.32}$$

$$(e_{11}(t) + nD_{11})z_{11}(t) + n(m-1)D_{12}z_{12}(t) = D_{11} ,$$

which suggests we define new time-varying "time-constants":

$$N_1(t) = N_{11}(t)/(1-d); \quad N_0(t) = N_{11}(t)/[1 + (m-1)d] \tag{7.33}$$

and associated per-observation credibilities; $z_i(t) = (n + N_i(t))^{-1}$ $(i = 0,1)$.

Then, we get a result analogous to (6.49), but in the format of (7.24)

$$f_s(X) = k_{n+1}\left\{m_1\left[1 - \sum_u z_0(u)\right] + \frac{d}{1+(m-1)d} \cdot \left[1 - \sum_u z_1(u)\right] \sum_{i=1}^{m} \sum_{t=1}^{n} z_0(t)\left(\frac{x_{it}}{k_t}\right) + \sum_{t=1}^{n} z_1(t)\left(\frac{x_{st}}{k_t}\right)\right\}. \tag{7.34}$$

The analogies with previous cases should be clear.

7.5 Use of future observations of related risks

As in section 5, it may be that "early returns" are available from related risks, and these may help in the prediction process. We assume, for comparison purposes that all such $\xi_{i,n+1} = x_{i,n+1}$ $(i \neq s)$ data is available and seek to predict $E\{\xi_{s,n+1} | X^{+}\}$ through (5.1). By examining the extension of measure (7.4) in a manner similar to (5.2), we see that the key point in transferring in the results of section 5.2 to the related risks model is the fact already discovered in (7.8), namely:

$$E_{it,ju} = \begin{cases} E_{it,it} = E_{\theta_i}\{v_{it}(\theta_i)\} & (i = j, t = u)\ (i = 1,2,\ldots,m)\ (t = 1,2,\ldots) \\ 0 & \text{otherwise.} \end{cases} \tag{7.35}$$

In particular the right-hand side coefficients (5.4) have no E components. We now examine the two special cases likely to be of practical importance.

7.5.1 Time-homogeneous related risks

The essential simplification applied to (5.7) and (5.8) gives:

$$E_{ii}Z_{si} + \sum_{j} nD_{ij}Z_{sj} + \sum_{j \neq s} nD_{ij}Y_{sj} = nD_{ij} \tag{7.36}$$
$$(i = 1,2,\ldots,m)$$

$$\sum_{j} D_{ij}Z_{sj} + E_{ii}Y_{si} + \sum_{j \neq s} D_{ij}Y_{sj} = D_{is} \quad (\forall i \neq s) \tag{7.37}$$

By subtraction, we obtain the interesting result

$$Z_{sj}(n) = nY_{sj}(n)\,, \quad (j \neq s) \tag{7.38}$$

valid for all n.

For $n = 0$, not much simplification results. $Z_{sj}(0) = 0$ for all s, j and the prediction comes from the prior and the first-period helper components with coefficients:

$$E_{ii}Y_{si}(0) + \sum_{j \neq s} D_{ij}Y_{sj}(0) = D_{is} \quad (\forall i \neq s) \tag{7.39}$$

However, for $n \to \infty$,

$$Z_{sj}(\infty) = \begin{cases} 1 & (j = s) \\ 0 & (j \neq s) \end{cases} \tag{7.40}$$

$$Y_{sj}(\infty) = 0 \qquad (\forall j \neq s) .$$

This behavior is in contrast with that of section 5.3, where related observations cotemporal with the predicted value continues to be used for all n. Furthermore from (5.10) we see that the essential reason this does not happen in the related risks model is because $E_{ij} = 0$ $(i \neq j)$, i.e., because the risks are unrelated, given the parameters.

For arbitrary n and fixed s, one can define coefficients:

$$g_{ij} = \begin{cases} \dfrac{D_{ij}}{D_{is}} & (i \neq j) \\ \dfrac{E_{ii} + (n+1)D_{ii}}{(n+1)D_{ij}} & (i = j) \end{cases} \tag{7.41}$$

and then solve an $(m - 1)$ system

$$\sum_{j \neq s} g_{ij} Z_{sj}(n) = \frac{n(1 - Z_{ss}(n))}{n + 1} \qquad (i \neq s) \tag{7.42}$$

with $Z_{ss}(n)$ checked by a simplification of (5.17).

$$Z_{ss}(n) = Z_{ss}^{o} - \frac{(n + 1) \sum_{j \neq s} D_{sj} Z_{sj}(n)}{E_{ss} + nD_{ss}} ,$$

and $Y_{sj}(n) = Z_{sj}(n)/n$.

7.5.2 Homogeneous exchangeable related risks

One can also apply the special condition of section 7.3.2 to the problem of future observations, and one finds that only three distinct types of variables remain, Z_{11}, Z_{12}, and $Y_{12} = Z_{12}/n$. The solution is similar to (7.24) but messier because of the unequal numbers of observations in the various parts of X^{+}. We omit the details.

7.6 Use of conditional distributions for related risks

One can also use the ideas of section 6.3 to analyze the related risks model. First, given the (vector) parameter $\underline{\theta}$, the joint density in each time period is the product of each component, (7.2). Thus, in the notation of section 6.3, the conditional density (6.16) becomes

$$p_t(x_{1t} | x_{2t}, \ldots, x_{nt}; \underline{\theta}) = p_{1t}(x_{1t} | \theta_i) \tag{7.44}$$

and the secondary data has density:

$$p(X^{\pm} | \underline{\theta}) = \prod_{t=1}^{n+1} \prod_{i=2}^{m} p_{it}(x_{it} | \theta_i) , \tag{7.45}$$

and the appropriate measure (6.16) is just:

$$p(y, \underline{x}^1 | X^{\pm}) = \frac{E_{\underline{\theta}} \prod_{t=1}^{n+1} p_t(x_{1t} | \theta_1) \cdot p(X^{\pm} | \underline{\theta})}{E_{\underline{\theta}} p(X^{\pm} | \underline{\theta})} . \tag{7.46}$$

The conditional means and variances of (7.44) are just the $m_{1t}(\theta_1)$ and $v_{1t}(\theta_1)$ defined in (7.5) and (7.7), and the equivalent (conditional) mean needed in (6.1) becomes:

$$m_{1t}(X^{\pm}) = \frac{C_{\underline{\theta}}\{m_{2t}(\theta_1); \, p(X^{\pm} | \underline{\theta})\}}{E_{\underline{\theta}} p(X^{\pm} | \underline{\theta})} + E_{\theta_1} m_{1t}(\theta_1) \tag{7.47}$$

$$(t = 1, 2, \ldots, n + 1) .$$

The conditional covariance breaks up into:

$$E_{1t,1t}(X^{\pm}) = \frac{C_{\underline{\theta}}\{v_{1t}(\theta_1); \, p(X^{\pm} | \theta)\}}{E_{\underline{\theta}} p(X^{\pm} | \underline{\theta})} + E_{\theta_1} v_{1t}(\theta_1) \tag{7.48}$$

$$(t = 1, 2, \ldots, n)$$

and

$$D_{1t,1u}(X^{\pm}) = \frac{C_{\underline{\theta}}\{m_{1t}(\theta_1)m_{1u}(\theta_1);\ p(X^{\pm}|\underline{\theta})\}}{E_{\underline{\theta}}p(X^{\pm}|\underline{\theta})} + C_{\underline{\theta}}\{m_{1t}(\theta_1);\ m_{1u}(\theta_1)\}$$

$$+ [E_{\theta_1}m_{1t}(\theta_1)][E_{\theta_1}m_{1u}(\theta_1)] - m_{1t}(X^{\pm}) \cdot m_{1u}(X^{\pm})$$

$$(t,u = 1,2,\ldots,n+1)\ . \qquad (7.49)$$

In particular, note that secondary data enters only through the function $p(X^{\pm}|\theta)$. The assumption of time-homogeneity, or of factorable $m_{1t}(\theta_1)$ further simplifies the analysis, following the results in section 6.1. However, since the appropriate moments still depend on $X^{\pm}$, the results (6.12) or (4.26) are valid only for fixed n. Similar remarks apply when using only X^{-}.

Note that the model of section 6.3.3 is not appropriate here, since this would eliminate any use of secondary data, because of the very nature of the related risks model. Similarly, loss of correlation between the components of $\underline{\theta}$ would reduce the problem to a standard one-dimensional model.

7.7 An externalities model of related risk

It is not immediately obvious how a multi-dimensional prior $U(\ldots)$ might arise in practice, since individual risks are usually considered to be unrelated individuals or properties. However, suppose that these risks operate in a common environment, in which there is a random external factor influencing the choice of parameters, such as nature, fire protection, geological factors, etc. Then mathematically speaking, we might model this externality by a different parameter ϕ, and assume that each risk prior has ϕ as a hyperparameter, viz.

$$\Pr\{\text{parameter}_i \leq \theta_i|\phi\} = U_i(\theta_i|\phi) \qquad (7.50)$$

giving a joint prior

$$U(\theta_1,\theta_2,\ldots,\theta_m) = E_\phi \prod_{i=1}^{m} U_i(\theta_i|\phi) , \qquad (7.51)$$

providing one can also specify a (hyper-) prior distribution on the external parameter. This model is probably not appropriate for time-varying externalities, such as the stock market, or traffic volume, but might explain more continuing regional differences between risk collectives caused by local environment. For instance the distribution of automobile accident proneness parameters in a collective may be pretty well determined by the underwriting rules of the company, but there may be geographical traffic conditions affecting all members of the pool, which are not described in the make-up of the group.

For this model, one could define

$$m_{it}(\theta_i;\ \phi) = E\{\xi_{it}|\theta_i,\phi\};\ v_{it}(\theta_i;\ \phi) = V\{\xi_{it}|\theta_i,\phi\} \qquad (7.52)$$

and thus obtain moments conditional on the external parameters:

$$\begin{aligned} M_{it}(\theta) &= E_{\theta_i|\phi} m_{it}(\theta_i|\phi) = \int m_{it}(\theta_i;\ \phi)dU_i(\theta_i|\phi) \\ U_{it}(\theta) &= E_{\theta_i|\phi} v_{it}(\theta_i;\ \phi);\ F_{it,iu}(\theta) \qquad (7.53) \\ &= C_{\theta_i|\phi}\{m_{it}(\theta_i,\phi);\ m_{iu}(\theta_i;\ \phi)\} . \end{aligned}$$

By the usual conditional arguments we then get

$$m_{it} = E_{\phi,\theta_i} E\{\xi_{it}|\theta_i,\phi\} = E_\phi M_{it}(\phi) \qquad (7.54)$$

and

$$C\{\xi_{it},\xi_{ju}\} = \begin{cases} E_\phi U_{it}(\phi)+E_\phi F_{it,it}(\phi)+V_\phi M_{it}(\phi) & \binom{i\,=\,j}{t\,=\,u} \\ E_\phi F_{it,iu}(\phi)+C_\phi(M_{it}(\phi);\ M_{iu}(\phi)) & \binom{i\,=\,j}{t\,\neq\,u} \\ C_\phi(M_{it}(\phi);\ M_{ju}(\phi)) & \text{otherwise} . \end{cases} \qquad (7.55)$$

We see that this external parameter introduces another source of variation and complication into our model, and additional simplifying assumption on the form of this dependence would be needed. The key coupling between individual risks is seen to be through the dependence of $M_{it}(\phi)$ on ϕ.

8. Use of concurrent observations in proportional forecasts

8.1 Model

In section 7, models of homogeneous, exchangeable related risks led to prediction formulae with two parts: one part, which was the data from the predicted risk $\{x_{st}\}$ in a classic credibility form, and another part which used all the data available X, grouped together with similar weights. (See (7.24), (7.34) and section 7.5.2.) However, as the coupling between risks vanishes, this second part tends towards zero. This is, of course, because completely independent observations of other risks do not help in the prediction of the selected contract. However, many people still feel that a large amount of cohort data will somehow be representative of collective statistics and should be included in any forecast.

One way to force the use of independent cohort data is to restrict the forecast form to a proportional function of the $\{x_{it}\}$, by setting $a_o \equiv 0$, and following the analysis suggested in (3.8). If we take the general related risks equation (7.10) and assume that the risks are independent, then from (7.9):

$$D_{it,ju} = 0 \qquad (i \neq j)\,, \tag{8.1}$$

and we would solve the $m(n \times n)$-systems

$$E_{it,it}a_{it} + \sum_{u=1}^{n} D_{it,it}a_{iu} = \mu m_{it} + \begin{cases} D_{st;s,n+1} & (i=s) \\ 0 & (i \neq s) \end{cases} \forall (i,t) \tag{8.2}$$

for a value of μ such that

$$m_{s,n+1} = \sum_{i=1}^{m} \sum_{t=1}^{n} m_{it}a_{it}\,. \tag{8.3}$$

For a linear forecast, $\mu = 0$ in (8.2), and we would

get, say

$$a_{it}^{o} = \begin{cases} a_{st}^{o} & (i = s) \\ 0 & (i \neq s) , \end{cases} \tag{8.4}$$

thus ignoring the cohort data, and the constant term a_o would make the forecast unbiased.

But in a proportional forecast, μ would in general be nonzero, and $a_{it} - a_{it}^{o}$ would be the nonzero solution of (8.2) with only the first term on the RHS. This second solution would substitute for the constant term to make the forecast unbiased.

This approach was suggested by a similar analysis in Bühlmann (1971) and Bühlman and Straub (1970) for the model discussed in section 6.3.4. In certain cases, as we shall see below in section 8.2.1, there is another advantage to this approach in that the collective mean completely factors out of the formulae, leaving only second moments to be estimated.

For the moment, we assume cohort risks may be different, though independent.

8.2 Time-dependent independent risks with separable mean

Although (8.2) can be solved as a sequence of $(n \times n)$ linear systems, we shall only consider the case where the time-dependency is separable in the mean, i.e., where there exists functions k_{it}, m_i, D_{ii} such that (6.40) and (6.41) hold. (8.2) then becomes

$$E_{it,it}a_{it} + k_{it}D_{ii} \sum_{u} k_{iu}a_{iu} = \mu k_{it}m_i + \begin{Bmatrix} k_{st}k_{s,n+1}D_{ss} & (i=s) \\ 0 & (i \neq s) \end{Bmatrix} \tag{8.5}$$

Making the usual definitions (6.44) and (6.45), we obtain the equations for the per-observation credibility coefficients

$$e_{ii}(t)z_{si}(t)+D_{ii}\sum_{u=1}^{n} z_{si}(u) = \mu m_i + \begin{cases} D_{ss} & (i=s) \\ 0 & (i\neq s) \end{cases} \qquad (t=1,2,\ldots) \quad (8.6)$$

For $\mu = 0$, the solution $z^o_{si}(t)$ is particularly simple: (compare (7.29))

$$z^o_{si}(t) = \begin{cases} \dfrac{D_{ss}/e_{ss}(t)}{1 + D_{ss}\sum\limits_u (1/e_{ss}(u))} & (s = i) \\ 0 & (s \neq 1) \end{cases} \quad (8.7)$$

for each risk separately.

Letting $y_{si}(t) = z_{si}(t) - z^o_{si}(t)$, we solve:

$$e_{ii}(t)y_{si}(t) + D_{ii}\sum_u y_{si}(u) = \mu m_i \qquad (\forall i) \quad (8.8)$$

by dividing by $e_{ii}(t)$, summing on t, and then back substituting in (8.8), obtaining:

$$y_{si}(t) = \frac{\mu m_i}{e_{ii}(t)} \cdot \frac{1}{1 + D_{ii}\sum\limits_u \left(\frac{1}{e_{ii}(u)}\right)}, \quad (8.9)$$

in terms of the unknown LaGrange multiplier. To find μ, we use (8.3), written as:

$$m_s = \sum_{i=1}^{m}\sum_{t=1}^{n} m_i z_{si}(t) = m_s \sum_t z^o_{ss}(t) + \sum_i\sum_t m_i y_{si}(t) \quad (8.10)$$

from which, finally

$$\mu = \frac{m_s}{1 + D_{ss}\sum\limits_u e^{-1}_{ss}(u)} \left[\sum_{j=1}^{m} \frac{m_j^2 \sum\limits_u e^{-1}_{jj}(u)}{1 + D_{jj}\sum\limits_u e^{-1}_{jj}(u)} \right]^{-1} . \quad (8.11)$$

Introducing the notation:

$$Z^o_{ii} = \sum_{t=1}^{n} z^o_{ii}(t) = \frac{D_{ii}\sum\limits_t e^{-1}_{ii}(t)}{1 + D_{ii}\sum\limits_u e^{-1}_{ii}(u)}, \quad (8.12)$$

we finally express the proportional forecast for this model as:

$$f_s(X) = k_{s,n+1}\left[m_s(1 - Z^o_{ss}) \cdot \left\{\frac{\sum_{i=1}^{m}\sum_{t=1}^{n}\left(\frac{m_i}{D_{ii}}\right) z_{ii}(t)\left(\frac{x_{it}}{k_{it}}\right)}{\sum_j \frac{m_j^2}{D_{jj}} Z^o_{jj}}\right\} + \sum_{t=1}^{n} z_{sj}(t)\left(\frac{x_{st}}{k_{st}}\right)\right] \tag{8.13}$$

which should be compared with the linear forecasts (6.12) (where $s = 1$), (6.49) and (7.34). In particular, we see that the linear equivalent (6.12) has a constant term in which the expression in braces above is replaced by unity. For a large enough sample of unrelated risks we expect its value in (8.13) to approach unity, and taking expectations, we see that this is so, almost surely.

8.2.1 Identical unrelated risks

If the individual risks are identically distributed and have their parameters selected identically, then:

$$z_{si}(t) = z_{11}(t);\; Z^o_{ss} = Z^o_{11};\; m_i = m_1;\; k_{it} = k_{1t};\; D_{ii} = D_{11} \tag{8.14}$$

and (8.13) becomes

$$f_s(X) = k_{1,n+1}\left[(1 - Z^o_{11})\left\{\sum_{t=1}^{n}\frac{z_{11}(t)}{Z^o_{11}}\left(\frac{1}{n}\sum_{i=1}^{m}\frac{x_{it}}{k_{1t}}\right)\right\} + \sum_{t=1}^{n} z_{11}(t)\left(\frac{x_{st}}{k_{1t}}\right)\right] \tag{8.15}$$

with simplified coefficients:

$$\frac{z_{11}(t)}{Z^o_{11}} = \frac{e^{-1}_{11}(t)}{\sum_u e^{-1}_{11}(u)} = \frac{k^2_{1t}/E_{1t,1t}}{\sum_u (k^2_{1u}/E_{1u,1u})}\,. \tag{8.16}$$

We see that the collective mean m_1 has vanished from (8.15), which now only requires knowledge of D_{11}, and the n

values of $e_{11}(t)$. In fact, the expression in braces in (8.15) is the cohort estimate of the collective mean m_1 which would replace it in the linear model (6.12).

8.2.2 Time-invariant mean

A different simplification results of $k_{it} = 1$ $(\forall i,t)$. In this case, $e_{11}(t) = E_{1t,1t}$, but the credibility coefficients $z^o_{ii}(t)$ in (8.7) are still time-varying. The only simplification in (8.13) is a deletion of all the k_{it}, with a further simplification if all the means, m_i, are identical.

A model of this type occurs if each risk is governed by a conditional distribution whose parameters are observations of secondary variables, but such that the mean of the risk random variable is "unbiased" by knowledge of the other variables, as discussed in section 6.3.4. The model of Bühlmann (1971) and Bühlmann and Straub (1970) is of this type, for instance.

8.2.3 Stationary, identical independent risks

In the simplest proportional model, all risks are identically distributed and stationary, so that

$$nz^o_{ii}(t) = Z^o_{ii} = Z_{11} = \frac{nD_{11}}{E_{11} + nD_{11}} \qquad (\forall i), \qquad (8.17)$$

and

$$f_s(X) = (1-Z_{11})\left\{\frac{1}{mn}\sum_{i=1}^{m}\sum_{t=1}^{n} x_{it}\right\} + Z_{11}\left(\frac{1}{n}\sum_{t=1}^{n} x_{st}\right). \qquad (8.18)$$

Here the collective mean is approximated by the grand sample mean of all available data.

8.3 General remarks

One can also analyze problems in which some dependence remains between the risks. For example, a proportional model of related risks with separable mean can be attacked using the methods of sections 7.3.1 and 7.4.1. We omit the details.

Why would one use a proportional model, when it is

known that its mean-square error must be larger than a linear one? Bühlmann and Straub's answer is that very often one has to begin with the data X, and from it develop also the collective statistics; if natural forms for these estimates can be developed as a by-product of the forecasting process, then surely these are more desirable than an unrelated prior estimate of the statistics. We do not get much help of this kind for our general model (8.13), but in the special cases of section 8.2.1 and 8.2.3 estimates of the mean are automatically provided by the forecast, leaving one with the separate task of estimating the variance components. A possible approach to this for their special model is given by Bühlmann and Straub, op. cit.

Another tacit reason for wanting to have all values of X in a forecast, even a linear one, may be the suspicion that the independent sampling from a collective is in fact, not from that collective for which the statistics were gathered. This could happen, for instance, because of a shift in external factors, or because the choice of the θ_i are somehow being biased by the method of sampling, the population characteristics, etc. A better way to handle this concern would be to construct a different model, perhaps along the lines of the externalities model discussed in section 7.7, which is essentially a collective of collectives. However, this only enlarges the estimation problem.

9. Evolutionary models for a single risk

9.1 Model

In our previous models, the risk parameter θ was assumed to be chosen once and for all for one or more risks, and we referred to nonstationary models in which the underlying distribution changed by known forms over time. In contrast, we shall use the word evolutionary to refer to models in which θ itself undergoes some random change over time; the underlying distribution can be of fixed form or may be nonstationary. We shall discuss only the single risk case.

As before, let $\underline{\xi}_t = \underline{x}_t$ $(t = 1,2,\ldots,n)$ be the m-vectors of experience data, drawn independently from $p_t(\underline{x}_t|\theta_t)$, once the value of the risk parameter, θ_t, is known for period t. The evolutionary mechanism, so to speak, is specified in the joint distribution $U(\theta_1,\theta_2,\ldots,\theta_t,\ldots)$ of the risk parameter history $\underline{\theta} = \{\theta_1,\theta_2,\ldots,\theta_t,\ldots\}$. Various special forms are of practical interest. (For reference, in our previous single-risk model U was degenerate, with identical marginals $U_1(\theta_1)$, and $\theta_1 = \theta_2 = \cdots$).

Defining:

$$m_{it}(\theta_t) = E\{\xi_{it}|\underline{\theta}\}; \quad C_{it,jt}(\theta_t) = C\{\xi_{it};\xi_{jt}|\underline{\theta}\} \qquad (i = 1,\ldots,m) \quad (t = 1,\ldots,n+1) \tag{9.1}$$

we see we get a structure of collective moments:

$$m_{it} = E_{\theta_t} m_{it}(\theta_t) \tag{9.2}$$

$$E_{it,ju} = \begin{cases} 0 & (t \neq u) \\ E_{\theta_t}\{C_{it,jt}(\theta_t)\} & (t = u) \end{cases} \tag{9.3}$$

and

$$D_{it,ju} = \begin{cases} C_{(\theta_t,\theta_u)}\{m_{it}(\theta_t);\ m_{ju}(\theta_u)\} & (t \neq u) \\ C_{\theta_t}\{m_{it}(\theta_t);\ m_{jt}(\theta_t)\} & (t = u) \end{cases} \tag{9.4}$$

Note that only the various marginals $U_t(\theta_t)$ of $U(\underline{\theta})$ are needed, except for $D_{it,ju}$ $(t \neq u)$, when two-dimensional marginals are required. The credibility forecast then follows directly from (4.5).

Incidentally, although we seem to imply that θ_t is a scalar making up a vector history $\underline{\theta} = \{\theta_1, \theta_2, \ldots\}$, there is no reason why θ_t itself could not be a vector, with one or more components for each component ξ_i $(i = 1, \ldots, m)$. Models in this and previous sections are not limited to one-parameter families!

Evolutionary models have not net been explored in any great detail. We give three special examples to show possible variations.

9.2 Exchangeable risk parameters

A first sample model might be a stationary onc in which the marginal priors $U_t(\theta_t)$ are the same for every t, and that all joint probabilities needed in (9.4) are the same for all t, u. In other words, we assume the θ_t are exchangeable random variables; thus we think of the risk as making random, but correlated, shifts in parameters, none of which are a priori distinguishable from one another.

Thnn we have, simply,

$$m_{it} = m_i \qquad (\forall t) \tag{9.5}$$

$$E_{it,ju} = \begin{cases} 0 & (t \neq u) \\ E_{ij} & (t = u) \end{cases} \tag{9.6}$$

but there are two types of covariance of means:

$$D_{it,ju} = \begin{cases} D_{ij}^{12} & (t \neq u) \\ D_{ij}^{11} & (t = u) \end{cases} \tag{9.7}$$

Clearly, the optimal coefficients are time invariant, and we use a forecast function:

$$\underline{f}(X) = (I - Z)\underline{m} + Z\left(\frac{1}{n} \sum_{t=1}^{n} \underline{x}_t\right)$$

in which the credibility coefficients are the solution of

$$Z(E + D^{11} + (n-1)D^{12}) = nD^{12} \ . \tag{9.9}$$

For n large, the solution behaves like classic credibility, with time constant $N \approx E(D^{12})^{-1}$. However, if the shifts in θ_t become more and more random, then the coupling D^{12} approaches zero, and we see that little credibility is given to observations.

9.3 Independent increments to location parameters

The following interesting model was suggested by Gerber and Jones (1973). Suppose that $\underline{\theta}$ and the underlying distributions are such that the covariance is stationary:

$$E_{it,jt} = E_{ij} \qquad (\forall t) . \tag{9.10}$$

However, we suppose that the evolutionary mechanism is one which gives a sequence of independent shifts to the location parameters at the end of each time period. In other words, $\underline{\theta}$ behaves as if there is a sequence of independent, identically distributed random m-vectors $\underline{\eta}_t = \{\eta_{it} | i = 1,2,\ldots,m\}$ such that

$$\underline{m}_t(\theta_t) = \underline{m}_{t-1}(\theta_{t-1}) + \underline{\eta}_t \tag{9.11}$$

with $\{\underline{\eta}_t, \underline{\eta}_{t+1}, \ldots\}$ and θ_{t-1} mutually independent $(t = 2,\ldots)$. Assume further that the moments of these independent shifts are known:

$$E\{\eta_{it}\} = s_i; \qquad (i = 1,2,\ldots,n) \tag{9.12}$$

$$C\{\eta_{it}; \eta_{ju}\} = \begin{cases} 0 & (t \neq u) \\ F_{ij} & (t = u) \end{cases} . \tag{9.13}$$

Then it follows that:

$$m_{it} = m_{i,t-1} + s_i \tag{9.14}$$

and

$$D_{it,jt} = D_{i(t-1),j(t-1)} + F_{ij} . \tag{9.15}$$

Since from (9.11),

$$\underline{m}_u(\theta_u) = \underline{m}_t(\theta_t) + \underline{\eta}_{t+1} + \eta_{t+2} + \cdots \underline{\eta}_u \tag{9.16}$$

and all terms on the right are mutually independent; then:

$$D_{it,ju} = D_{it,jt} \qquad (t \leq u) . \tag{9.17}$$

Referring everything to period one, we then finally obtain

$$m_{it} = m_{i1} + (t - 1)s_i \tag{9.18}$$

and

$$D_{it,ju} = D_{i1,j1} + [\min(t,u) - 1]F_{ij} , \tag{9.19}$$

for all $i,j = 1,\ldots,m$, and $t = 1,2,\ldots,n + 1$. From (9.10), (9.18), and (9.19), one can in principle solve for (time-varying) coefficients in (4.5).

In the one-dimensional case, Gerber and Jones show that the successive forecasts $f^1,f^2,\ldots,f^t$ obey a simple iterative formula, and that the weights attached to successive observations are ultimately geometric, with the latest observation getting the largest weight. This clearly occurs because of the spreading variance term (9.19) which makes earlier observations less credible. This is in contrast to the non-evolutionary case studied in section 4.3.

9.4 Known discontinuity in risk

Suppose that it is known that at a certain epoch T, there is a sudden change in the factors influencing a risk. In an insurance setting this may reflect the installation of a sprinkler system, a change in management operating policy, a new speed limit, etc.

Therefore, there are only two risk parameters, θ^1 and θ^2 for this individual:

$$\theta_t = \begin{cases} \theta^1 & (t = 1,2,\ldots,T) \\ \theta^2 & (t = T + 1,\ldots) \end{cases} , \tag{9.20}$$

two means for each component,

$$m_{it} = \begin{cases} m_i^1 & (t = 1,2,\ldots,T) \\ m_i^2 & (t = T + 1,\ldots) \end{cases} , \qquad (i = 1,2,\ldots,m) \tag{9.21}$$

and two groups of expected covariances,

$$E_{it,jt} = \begin{cases} E^{11}_{ij} & (t = 1,2,\ldots,T) \\ E^{22}_{ij} & (t = T + 1,\ldots) \end{cases} \quad (i,j = 1,\ldots,m) . \qquad (9.22)$$

corresponding to the two different regions.

There are three types of covariance of means

$$D_{it,ju} = \begin{cases} D^{11}_{ij} & (t,u = 1,2,\ldots,T) \\ D^{12}_{ij} = D^{21}_{ji} & (t = 1,2,\ldots,T,\ u = T + 1,\ldots), \\ D^{22}_{ij} & (t,u = T + 1,\ldots) \end{cases} \qquad (9.23)$$

with the coupling between the old and new risk parameters reflected only in $D^{12}_{ij} = D^{21}_{ji}$.

If $n \leq T$, the problem reduces to one of ordinary multidimensional credibility, as in (4.19), (4.22), (4.23). But if $n > T$, it is clear there are two matrices of credibility coefficients $\{Z^1_{sj}\}$, $\{Z^2_{sj}\}$, which are used in a forecast function,

$$\underline{f}(X) = \underline{a}_o + Z^1\left(\frac{1}{T}\sum_{t=1}^{T} \underline{x}_t\right) + Z^2\left(\frac{1}{n - T}\sum_{t=T+1}^{n} \underline{x}_t\right) \qquad (9.24)$$

and whose solution is given by the matrix equations:

$$Z^1(E^{11} + T\cdot D^{11}) + Z^2(T\cdot D^{21}) = TD^{21} \qquad (9.25)$$

$$Z^1((n - T)\cdot D^{12}) + Z^2(E^{22} + (n - T)D^{22}) = (n - T)D^{22}$$

and normalized by:

$$\underline{a}_o = \underline{m}^2 - Z^1\underline{m}^1 - Z^2\underline{m}^2 . \qquad (9.26)$$

Notice that the solution behaves as expected: if $D^{12} = D^{21} = 0$, then $Z^1 = 0$, and only the most recent observations are used. But if $E^{11} = E^{22}$ and $D^{11} = D^{22} = D^{12} = D^{21}$, then $Z^1 = (T/n)Z$ and $Z^2 = \left(\frac{n - T}{n}\right)Z$, where Z is given by (4.22), and we have the usual non-evolutionary case.

The one-dimension explicit solution of the above is interesting. Letting $Z^{11} = TD^{11}/(E^{11} + TD^{11})$ and $Z^{22} = (n - T)D^{22}/(E^{22} + (n - T)D^{22})$, and suppressing the lower indices 11, we get the (scalar) results.

$$Z^1 = \frac{r_1[Z^{11}(1 - Z^{22})]}{\Delta} ; \quad Z^2 = \frac{Z^{22}(1 - r_1 r_2 Z^{11})}{\Delta} \qquad (9.27)$$

where $r_1 = D^{12}/D^{11}$, $r_2 = D^{12}/D^{22}$ and $\Delta = 1 - r_1 r_2 Z^{11} Z^{22}$.

Other variations, such as multiple changes in θ, or changes at some random epoch are easy to formulate, but difficult to solve in closed form.

10. Summary

The various extensions of credibility explored in this paper reflect nothing more than the repeated use of the least-squares theory of section 3, together with various special cases of the collective model of risk described in section 4.

These results are interesting for two reasons: they provide specific cases in which the covariance matrix can be inverted, or at least reduced to a smaller-dimensional problem, and they show how persistent is the basic credibility concept of mixing a prior estimate and a sample mean of derivations. This enables us to develop intuition about model variations, and reinforces the idea that in a linearized Bayesian analysis, only prior estimates of the moments m, D, and E are needed.

Clearly the theory has already outstripped the application, and we must now re-examine the possible application in insurance and decision theory to gain further insight into the next group of problem areas.

Discussion by Erwin Straub of Model Variations in Credibility Theory

This paper covers a great number of problems and aspects, it contains many different models and ideas on credibility so that it is virtually impossible to review it in only a few minutes in any exhaustive way. Therefore I confine myself to a few marginal remarks.

Let us consider the multidimensional credibility formula, i.e.

in Jewell's notation:

$$\underline{f}(X) = Z\left[\frac{1}{n}\sum_{t=1}^{n}\underline{X}_t\right]+(I-Z)\underline{\mu}$$

with $Z = nD(E + nD)^{-1}$

in Bühlmann's notation:

$$\hat{\mu}_k = \Gamma_k\underline{X}_{\cdot k}+(I-\Gamma_k)\underline{\tilde{X}}$$

with $\Gamma_k = P_{\cdot k}W(V+P_{\cdot k}W)^{-1}$

and $\underline{\tilde{X}} = \Gamma^{-1}\sum_{j=1}^{N}\Gamma_{\cdot j}\underline{X}_{\cdot j}$

In order to compare these two formulae we may use the following dictionary:

English language	Jewell's language	Buhlmann's language
estimator for mean vector of a specific risk or risk category	$\underline{f}(X)$	$\hat{\underline{\mu}}_k$
credibility matrix	Z	Γ_k
individual claims experience	$\frac{1}{n}\sum_{t=1}^{n}\underline{X}_t$	$\underline{X}_{\cdot k} = \sum_{t=1}^{n}\frac{P_{tk}}{P_{\cdot k}}\underline{X}_{tk}$
overall mean/experience	$\underline{\mu}$ (or $\underline{m}$)	$\tilde{X}$
no. of risk units observed in n years	n	$P_{\cdot k}$

mean of conditional covariances	$\frac{1}{n} E$	$\frac{1}{P._k} V$
covariances of conditional means	D	W

The main difference between the two above formulae is that the one on the left hand is inhomogeneous whereas the other is homogeneous. Besides that there is another rather minor difference: within the Bühlmann concept there are any number P_{tk} of risks in category k at time t whereas $P_{tk} = 1$ at least up through section 4 of Jewell's paper in this collection.

This minor difference, the two different notations and a recent discussion with Hans Bühlmann lead me to the following comment (in Bühlmann's notation). The concept of the structure function is difficult to understand and it seems to me that one could get around it by redefining the underlying model as follows:

Portfolio consists of N

homogeneous classes	$C_1 \; C_2 \ldots C_N$
characterized by parameters	$\vartheta_1 \; \vartheta_2 \ldots \vartheta_N$
and containing	$P._1 \; P._2 \ldots P._N$ risk units

And do not think of the $\vartheta_1, \vartheta_2, \ldots, \vartheta_N$ as random variables (because this is unnecessary and difficult to understand) but as characterizing parameters with unknown values.

Consequently, define

$$\mu = \sum_{j=1}^{N} \frac{P._j}{P} \mu(\vartheta_j)$$

$$V = \sum_{j=1}^{N} \frac{P._j}{P} \sigma^2(\vartheta_j)$$

$$W = \sum_{j=1}^{N} \frac{P._j}{P} [\mu(\vartheta_j) - \mu)^2] .$$

Note that knowledge of the individual parameter values

is not required (only V and W are needed), and we know how to estimate them from the observations.

Further, the structure of the portfolio is fully described by

$$\upsilon_1, \upsilon_2, \ldots, \upsilon_N$$

and

$$P._1, P._2, \ldots, P._N$$

or rather by

$$\mu(\upsilon_1), \delta^2(\upsilon_1); \ \mu(\upsilon_2), \delta^2(\upsilon_2); \ \ldots \ \mu(\upsilon_N), \delta^2(\upsilon_N)$$

and

$$P._1 \qquad P._2 \qquad \ldots \qquad P._N$$

The structure function $U(\upsilon)$ is essentially superfluous.

Insurance Credibility Theory and Bayesian Estimation

Robert B. Miller and James C. Hickman
The University of Wisconsin

1. Introduction

Credibility theory is a collection of ideas concerning the systematic adjustment of insurance premiums as claims experience is obtained. This preliminary definition is perhaps too broad to be useful, for it encompasses almost all activity involving the analysis of insurance data and the subsequent use of these analyses in adjusting insurance prices. On a more operational level, credibility theory may be thought of as involving the development of a system of weights, which are functions of the size of the insurance experience available, for estimating future claims cost as a weighted average of the actual claims for the group under consideration and the expected claims based on prior or ancillary experience.

As a practical tool, credibility is largely an invention of North American actuaries. However, the roots go deep into the fundamental economic theory of risk and into statistical estimation theory. In its present formulation, it arose initially in workmen's compensation insurance where some industrial companies with large numbers of employees and favorable safety records pressed for recognition in their insurance premiums of their apparently superior claim records.

There are several school of thought about credibility. Attempts to classify the contributions to the theory are partially frustrated by the existence of ideas that use the language of credibility theory for claims analysis methods that do not involve the distinctive weighted average characteristic of conventional credibility theory. However, if one strives to identify the most comprehensive schools of thought, two are easy to establish.

The first, in terms of when it had an impact on practical insurance affairs, is the class of methods that initially requires fixing the size of an insurance experience to which complete credibility will be attached for ratemaking purposes. Once this anchor is fixed, the problem becomes that of establishing, in some reasonable fashion, partial credibility weights which will be applied to smaller amounts of insurance data. The adjusted estimate of claims, to be used in setting premiums in the next accounting period is

$$Z(t) \cdot y + (1 - Z(t)) \cdot m' ,$$

where y is some measure of actual claims, m' is a prior estimate of expected claims, and $Z(t)$, $0 \leq Z(t) \leq 1$, is the credibility factor. The credibility factor is a function of t, a measure of the size of the insurance experience that generated the claims measured by y.

In the first method a value of t_o, such that it is agreed as a practical matter to let $Z(t_o) = 1$, must be determined. A classic example found in Longley-Cook's monograph (1962) and the paper by Mayerson, Bowers, and Jones (1968), involves estimating the parameter (λt) of a Poisson distribution. We seek, in this method, the value of t_o such that

$$\Pr[(1 - k)E[\tilde{x}] \leq \tilde{x} \leq (1 + k)E[\tilde{x}]] \geq p$$

where $\tilde{x}$ is the total number of claims in the group under consideration. The distribution of $\tilde{x}$ depends on the index of group size t. In our particular example $\tilde{x}$ has a Poisson distribution. If $k = .05$ and $p = .9$, this requirement for full credibility may be rewritten as

$$\Pr\left[\frac{-.05\, E[\tilde{x}]}{\sigma_{\tilde{x}}} \leq \frac{\tilde{x} - E[\tilde{x}]}{\sigma_{\tilde{x}}} \leq \frac{.05\, E[\tilde{x}]}{\sigma_{\tilde{x}}}\right] \geq .9$$

$$\Pr\left[-.05\sqrt{\lambda t} \leq \frac{\tilde{x} - \lambda t}{\sqrt{\lambda t}} \leq .05\sqrt{\lambda t}\right] \geq .9 .$$

If we are to use an observed x as an estimate of $E[\tilde{x}]$, subject to these specifications, we may use the fact that $(\tilde{x} - \lambda t)/\sqrt{\lambda t}$ has an approximate normal distribution, mean zero, variance one $(N(0,1))$ to find that we must have $x \approx 1{,}084$ before the specifications are satisfied. Following this approach to credibility, one would now state that $Z(1084) = 1$, where the size of the experience is measured in terms of the number of claims incurred. Other examples where $\tilde{x}$ is total claims rather than simply the number of claims are possible (Mayerson, Jones, and Bowers, 1968).

This approach leaves open the assignment of $Z(t)$ for values $t < t_o$. Besides all the usual problems in selecting a sufficiently realistic model for the insurance claims process, this approach leaves to the decision maker the assignment of the specification parameters k and p.

The second school of thought might be described as the Bayesian school. Within this school the expected claims for a group is viewed as being generated by a random process that may not be completely known. Prior and collateral information about expected claims is summarized in the form of a prior distribution. As the claims experience unfolds Bayes' Theorem is used to find the posterior distribution of the process generating the parameters of the claims distribution. Since conventional insurance theory uses other methods for introducing risk and profit margins, the posterior mean of the process generating expected claims is the usual output of a Bayesian credibility analysis.

The Bayesian approach does not require the premium decision maker to specify an error rate, k, or a precision probability, p, for the purpose of defining the volume of experience needed for credibility one. Partial credibility is no problem within the Bayesian approach for the weighting of the claims data and the prior mean to produce the posterior mean is handled automatically. The price for this convenience is the need to specify a prior distribution or at least enough parameters of the prior to make least squares approximation of the posterior mean possible.

The Bayesian approach was brought to the attention of practicing actuaries in two remarkable papers by Arthur L. Bailey (1945, 1950). Before the foundations of Bayesian statistics were widely understood, Bailey formed some eloquent criticisms of classical statistics and developed an openly Bayesian approach to credibility. Bailey's work was related to modern Bayesian statistics by Mayerson (1964).

Mayerson was intrigued by least squares approximations to posterior means. Bühlmann (1967) was also interested in the idea of approximating a posterior mean by a linear function of the prior mean and the mean of the claims data. When using least squares lines, this led to credibility factors of the form

$$Z(t) = \frac{\mathrm{Var}'(\tilde{\mu})}{\mathrm{Var}'(\tilde{\mu}) + E'_{\mu}\ \mathrm{Var}(\tilde{x}|\mu)}$$

where $\mathrm{Var}'(\tilde{\mu})$ is the variance of the prior distribution of $\tilde{\mu}$, the expected claims, and E'_{μ} denotes an expectation operator with respect to the prior distribution. Of course, Bailey and others had already found credibility factors of this form for beta-binomial, gamma-Poisson, and normal-normal Bayesian models. Ericson (1970) has shown that for a fairly broad class of conjugate distributions, posterior means may be expressed in this form. Recently Jewell (1973) has asserted that for the linear multivariate exponential family, with suitably enriched natural conjugate priors, the same result is obtained.

In this paper we will adopt a Bayesian view. We do this without apology. It seems almost inconceivable that a decision about insurance prices could be made without prior information. The requirement to quantify this information in the form of a distribution for the parameters of the claims process would seem to be an exercise that would clarify thought in any situation. Since some type of model must be adopted in order to have a coherent procedure for premium adjustment, it seems to us that the adoption of a Bayesian approach adds no undue burdens. The Bayesian approach does not compel the semi-arbitrary determination of the size of the experience needed to achieve credibility one and it yields dividends by making it possible to find the predictive distribution for claims.

2. The collective risk model

We will adopt the collective risk model (Bohman and Esscher, 1963; Cramér, 1955) for the insurance claims process. This decision was made because the collective risk model is at the same time one of the most general and one of the most highly developed models for insurance claims. Within this paper, credibility theory will mean the Bayesian estimation of certain parameters of a collective risk process.

Within the collective risk model the cumulative distribution of $\tilde{x}$, the total claims within a group whose size is indexed by t, is given by

$$F(x,t) = \sum_{n=0}^{\infty} P_n(t)V^{n^*}(x), \quad x > 0,\ t > 0$$
$$= 0 \qquad\qquad \text{otherwise.}$$

In this expression

$P_n(t)$ is the probability of n claims in a group of size t,

$V^1(x)$ is the cumulative distribution function given one claim has occurred and

V^{n^*} is the nth convolution of $V^1(x)$ with itself.

That is, V^{n^*} is the cumulative distribution of $\tilde{x}_1 + \tilde{x}_2 + \dots + \tilde{x}_n$, where the components of the sum are mutually independent and each has distribution $V^1(x)$. $V^{0^*}(x)$ is a step function with a step of one at zero. In this model the distribution of each $\tilde{x}$ is independent of $\tilde{n}$, the number of claims. The moments of the distribution $V^1(x)$ will be denoted by

$$c_i = \int_0^{\infty} x^i \, dV^1(x) ,$$

and the moment generating function (assumed to exist) will be denoted by

$$M(\theta) = \int_0^{\infty} e^{\theta x} \, dV^1(x) .$$

In many applications it is reasonable to assume that $\tilde{n}$ has a Poisson distribution with parameter λt. In this case the size parameter t may be interpreted as a number of policies. A policy in force for the entire accounting period adds one to t and policies in force for a part of a period will add a fraction to t.

For the resulting compound Poisson process it may be confirmed that the moment generating function of $\tilde{x}$ is $e^{\lambda t[M(\theta)-1]}$, $E[\tilde{x}] = \lambda tc_1$, and $Var(\tilde{x}) = \lambda tc_2$.

For the standardized random variable

$$\tilde{z} = \frac{\tilde{x} - \lambda t c_1}{\sqrt{\lambda t c_2}},$$

it may be shown that

$$\underset{t \to \infty}{\text{Limit}}\ E[e^{\theta \tilde{z}}] = e^{\theta^2/2},$$

or that $\tilde{z}$ has an approximate $N(0,1)$ distribution when t is large. Consequently, $\tilde{x}$ has an approximate distribution which is $N(\lambda t c_1, \lambda t c_2)$, and $\tilde{y} = \tilde{x}/t$, the average claims payment per policy, has an approximate distribution which is $N(\lambda c_1, \lambda c_2/t)$.

An alternative assumption, to make explicit allowance for a lack of homogeneity with respect to risk characteristics within an insurance group, is that

$$P_n(t) = \int_0^\infty \frac{(\lambda t)^n e^{-\lambda t}}{n!} \frac{\beta^\alpha}{\Gamma(\alpha)} \lambda^{\alpha-1} e^{-\beta\lambda}\, d\lambda$$

$$0 < \alpha .$$

$$0 < \beta .$$

Then

$$P_n(t) = \frac{\Gamma(n+\alpha)}{\Gamma(n+1)\Gamma(\alpha)} \left(\frac{\beta}{t+\beta}\right)^\alpha \left(\frac{t}{t+\beta}\right)^n,$$

which is a negative binomial distribution. Then the moment generating function of $\tilde{x}$ becomes $1/[1 + (\beta^{-1} - M(\theta)\beta^{-1})t]^\alpha$, $E[\tilde{x}] = \alpha t c_1/\beta$, and $\text{Var}(\tilde{x}) = \alpha t[\beta c_2 + t c_1^2]/\beta^2$.

For this model defining the random variable

$$\tilde{\omega} = \frac{\tilde{x}}{t\alpha c_1/\beta},$$

it may be shown that

$$\underset{t \to \infty}{\text{Limit}}\ E[e^{\theta \tilde{\omega}}] = \frac{1}{(1 - \theta/\alpha)^\alpha}$$

or that $\tilde{\omega}$ has an approximate gamma distribution with parameters α and α when t is large. This means that

$\tilde{y} = \tilde{x}/t$, the average claims payment per policy, has an approximate gamma distribution with parameters α and β/c_1.

In the parlance of general insurance, the expected claims payments per policy, λc_1 in the Poisson case, $\alpha c_1/\beta$ in the negative binomial case, is called the pure premium. One objective of credibility theory from a Bayesian viewpoint is to find the posterior distribution of the pure premium.

3. Credibility without sufficient statistics

Because of the assumed independence between the number of claims and the individual claim amount distributions, it would seem natural to proceed to the Bayesian estimation of the parameters of each distribution. Once the posterior distribution of the expected number of claims and the expected claims amount are available, this strategy would call for the determination of the posterior distribution of the pure premium.

At times the data needed to estimate the parameters of each of the distributions are not available. For example, only total claims $\tilde{x}$, and number of policies t, might be known. In such a case a Bayesian approach to credibility theory would use the approximate distribution of $\tilde{y} = \tilde{x}/t$ for the likelihood.

For example, if $P_n(t)$ is a Poisson probability function, we have shown that $\tilde{y}$ has an approximate $N(\lambda c_1, \lambda c_2/t)$ distribution. We then adopt a conventional Bayesian analysis using for convenience conjugate prior distributions. Let the prior distribution of λc_1, given $\lambda c_2 = 1/r$ be $N(\mu', 1/r\tau')$ and the marginal distribution of $1/\lambda c_2$ be gamma with parameters α' and β'. Then the posterior distribution of λc_1, the pure premium, has a non-standard student t distribution with mean

$(\tau'\mu' + ty)/(\tau' + t)$. The credibility factor is $Z(t) = t/(t + \tau')$. The remaining parameters, as defined by DeGroot (1970), of the posterior distribution of λc_1 are

$$\alpha'' = \alpha' + \tau'/2$$

$$\beta'' = \beta' + \frac{\tau' t(y - \mu)^2}{\alpha(\tau' + t)} .$$

Defining the parameters $h'' = \frac{\alpha''\tau'}{\beta''}$ and $\mu'' = (\tau'\mu' + \tau y)/(\tau' + t)$, we may write the probability density function of this posterior distribution as

$$p''(\mu|\alpha'',\beta'',\tau',\mu'') \propto [1 + (\tfrac{1}{2}\alpha'')(\alpha''\tau'/\beta'')(\mu - \mu'')^2]^{-\frac{1}{2}(2\alpha''+1)} .$$

It is clear that the random variable $\sqrt{h''}\,(\tilde{\mu} - \mu'')$ has a central t distribution with $2\alpha''$ degrees of freedom, and hence probability statements about $\tilde{\mu}$ may be made using standard t tables.

If $P_n(t)$ is a negative binomial probability function, our limiting distribution result does not lead to such an attractive result. In this case $\tilde{y} = \tilde{x}/t$ has an approximate gamma distribution with parameters α and β/c_1, which are free of t. Therefore, it appears impossible to develop an approximate credibility factor that will tend to one as t, the number of policies, increases.

4. Bayesian credibility with sufficient statistics

If we assume that the prior distributions of $E[\tilde{n}|t = 1]$ and $E[\tilde{x}|n = 1]$ are independent, we may proceed to Bayesian estimation of each of these risk parameters. We will make this independence assumption for it seems that knowledge of the distribution of the expected number of claims per policy would not influence the distribution of the average claims amount. Then for our collective risk model the posterior expected pure premium, $E''[E[\tilde{n}|t = 1] \cdot E''[\tilde{x}|n = 1]]$, where

E" denotes an expectation with respect to the posterior distribution, is $E''[E[\tilde{n}|t = 1]]E''[E[\tilde{x}|n = 1]]$. Of course, it may be much more convenient to take as a point estimate of the pure premium the posterior mode.

In this section we will proceed to the computation of the components of the pure premium by Bayesian analysis of some commonly assumed distributions in risk theory. The first two examples are simple applications of Ericson's Theorem (1970) about posterior means.

a. Poisson distribution for number of claims

The amalgamation of a Poisson distribution with parameter λt for the number of claims and a conjugate prior gamma distribution to produce a posterior gamma distribution is a classic example of Bayesian credibility. The posterior probability density function of λ, with n claims observed is given by

$$p''(\lambda|n,t,\alpha',\beta') \propto \frac{(\lambda t)^n}{n!} e^{-\lambda t} \lambda^{\alpha'-1} e^{-\beta'\lambda} . \qquad (1)$$

The posterior mean is

$$\frac{n + \alpha'}{t + \beta'} = \frac{n}{t}\left(\frac{t}{t + \beta'}\right) + \frac{\alpha'}{\beta'}\left(\frac{\beta'}{t + \beta'}\right) ,$$

so the credibility factor is given by

$$Z(t) = \frac{t}{t + \beta'} .$$

b. Exponential distribution for claim amount

Lundberg's (1909) original example of collective risk theory used an exponential distribution for claim amount, that is

$$\frac{dV^1(x)}{dx} = \left(\frac{1}{\delta}\right)e^{-x/\delta}, \quad 0 < x,\ 0 < \delta .$$

A conjugate prior has a probability density function given by

$$p'(\delta) \propto \left(\frac{1}{\delta}\right)^{n'} e^{-\frac{s'}{\delta}}, \quad 0 < s',\ 2 < n',\ 0 < \delta .$$

This prior is also called the inverse chi-square distribution and is often mentioned in connection with the Bayesian analysis of a normal distribution whose variance is assumed to be a random variable. The present parameterization is chosen, instead of the more conventional one, to assist in interpretation. The parameter n' may be interpreted as the number of prior "claims" observed and s' as the sum of prior "claims." Tables of the chi-square distribution may be used to make probability statements about $\tilde{\delta}$, for the random variable $2s'/\tilde{\delta}$ has a $\chi^2[2(n' - 1)]$ distribution. Hence if $\Pr[\tilde{\delta} \geq \Delta] = .05$, then $\Pr[(2s'/\Delta) \geq (2s'/\tilde{\delta})] = .05$ showing that $2s'/\Delta$ must the 5th percentile of chi-square distribution with $2(n' - 1)$ degrees of freedom. Similar calculations yield other percentiles of the inverse chi-square distribution.

The posterior distribution of $\tilde{\delta}$, given that n claims have occurred with total amount $s = x_1 + x_2 + \cdots + x_n$, is given by

$$p''(\delta | n + n' = n'', s + s' = s'') \propto \left(\frac{1}{\delta}\right)^{n''} e^{-\frac{s''}{\delta}} . \qquad (2)$$

The posterior mean of δ is

$$\frac{s''}{n'' - 2} = \frac{s}{n}\left(\frac{n}{n + n' - 2}\right) + \left(\frac{s'}{n' - 2}\right)\left(\frac{n' - 2}{n + n' - 2}\right),$$

so the credibility factor is

$$Z(n) = \frac{n}{n + n' - 2} = \frac{n}{n'' - 2} .$$

5. Gamma distribution for claim amount

Although it leads to convenient computations, the use of the exponential distribution for claim amount is frequently criticized for its presumed lack of flexibility. Therefore, let us examine a more general gamma distribution for claim amount. That is let us study the gamma density

$$\frac{dV^1(x)}{dx} = \frac{\gamma^\gamma x^{\gamma-1}}{\delta^\gamma \Gamma(\gamma)} e^{-\frac{\gamma}{\delta} x}, \quad 0 < x, \delta, \gamma . \qquad (3)$$

We select this parameterization because, among other things, $E[\tilde{x}] = \delta$. It should be noted that this parameterization does not satisfy the hypotheses of Ericson's (1970) or Jewell's (1973) results.

A conjugate prior for the parameters $(\tilde{\gamma}, \tilde{\delta})$ has a density function given by

$$p'(\gamma, \delta | n', p', s') \propto \Gamma(\gamma)^{-n'} \left(\frac{\gamma}{\delta} \right)^{n'\gamma+1} p'^{\gamma-1} e^{-\frac{\gamma}{\delta} s'} .$$

Then the posterior distribution of $(\tilde{\gamma}, \tilde{\delta})$ given that n claims have occurred with total amount s and $p = \Pi_1^n x_i$, has a density given by

$$p''(\gamma, \delta | n' + n = n'', p'p = p'', s' + s = s'')$$

$$\propto \Gamma(\gamma)^{-n''} \left(\frac{\gamma}{\delta} \right)^{n''\gamma+1} p''^{\gamma-1} e^{-\frac{\gamma}{\delta} s''} .$$

It is clear that exhibiting the marginal posterior distribution of δ will be more complicated than in the previous case.

An examination of likelihood contours of Equation (3) leads to the conjecture that perhaps a satisfactory approximation to the posterior marginal distribution might be obtained by replacing γ by its modal value, $\hat{\gamma}$. That is

$$p''(\delta | n'', p'', s'') \propto [\Gamma(\hat{\gamma})^{-n''} \hat{\gamma}^{n''\hat{\gamma}+1} (p'')^{\hat{\gamma}-1}][\left(\frac{1}{\delta} \right)^{n''\hat{\gamma}+1} e^{-\frac{\gamma}{\delta} s''}]$$

$$\propto \left(\frac{1}{\delta} \right)^{n''\hat{\gamma}+1} e^{-\frac{\hat{\gamma}}{\delta} s''} \qquad (4)$$

where the symbol $\propto$ is to be read "approximately proportional to." This approximation depends on the ability of the cross section of the bivariate density at the mode to summarize the shape of the marginal density of $\tilde{\delta}$. If the contours studied are at all typical, the approximation should be good.

In fact an examination of the information matrix

associated with the distribution displayed in Equation (3) shows that asymptotically $\tilde{\gamma}$ and $\tilde{\delta}$ are normally distributed and independent. See the appendix. This means that the principal axes of the contours will tend toward being parallel with the coordinate axes. This lends considerable support to the conjecture that for a reasonable number of claims, the shape of the bivariate distribution of $(\tilde{\gamma},\tilde{\delta})$ will permit the use of the approximate integration trick we propose.

The joint mode of the bivariate posterior distribution of $(\tilde{\gamma},\tilde{\delta})$ may be found by solving simultaneously

$$-\delta(n''\gamma + 1) + \gamma s'' = 0$$

and

$$-n''\psi(\gamma) + n''\ln\gamma - n''\ln\delta + \ln p'' + \gamma^{-1}(n''\gamma + 1) + \delta^{-1}s'' = 0 ,$$

where $\psi(\gamma)$ is the digamma function. This leads to the approximate solution

$$\hat{\delta} = s''(n'' + \hat{\gamma}^{-1})^{-1}$$

$$\hat{\gamma} = [(n'' + 2)/2][n''(\ln\hat{\delta} - 1) - \ln p'' + s''\hat{\delta}^{-1}]^{-1} ,$$

which must be solved iteratively. This approximation is based on two terms of an asymptotic expansion of $\psi(\gamma)$.

In Table 1 some values of the cumulative distribution function of $\tilde{\delta}$, computed "exactly" by numerical integration and using the approximation in equation (4), are presented. The selection of the parameters here was motivated by an example presented by Mayerson, Jones, and Bowers (1968). In their example of automobile property damage insurance the expected claims amount was \$89.92 while the variance of claims amount was 26,080 squared dollars.

Table 2 shows similar results for parameter values motivated by a California Workmens' Compensation insurance example presented by Dropkin (1964). In several cases

Table 1. "Exact" and approximate value of the posterior cumulative distribution function* of $\tilde{\delta}$ for three cases. (In each case $\hat{\gamma} = .3$ and $\hat{\delta} = 90.$)

$n'' = 10$, $s'' = 1200$, $\ell np'' = 22.0053$			$n'' = 50$, $s'' = 4800$, $\ell np'' = 109.6930$			$n'' = 100$, $s'' = 9300$, $\ell np'' = 220.0528$		
δ	"Exact"	Approx.	δ	"Exact"	Approx.	δ	"Exact"	Approx.
			45.80	.0006	.0004	59.85		.0039
			74.33	.1315	.1315	78.03		.1468
180.00	.6803	.6767	102.86	.5707	.5705	96.21	**	.5492
360.00	.9160	.9197	131.39	.8565	.8569	114.39		.8495
540.00	.9641	.9698	159.92	.9572	.9584	132.57		.9617

*The values for which the function is tabulated are approximately at $E''(\tilde{\delta})$, $E''(\tilde{\delta}) \pm \sqrt{Var''(\tilde{\delta})}$, and $E''(\tilde{\delta}) \pm 2\sqrt{Var''(\tilde{\delta})}$.

**"Exact" values are not available because the magnitude of the numbers caused overflow in the computer.

Table 2. "Exact" and approximate values of the posterior cumulative distribution function* of $\tilde{\delta}$ for three cases. (In each case $\hat{\gamma} = 2.18$ and $\hat{\delta} = 13{,}688$.)

$n'' = 10$, $s'' = 143{,}159$, $\ell np'' = 92.779$			$n'' = 50$, $s'' = 690{,}679$, $\ell np'' = 463.895$			$n'' = 100$, $s'' = 1{,}375{,}079$, $\ell np'' = 927.791$		
δ	"Exact"	Approx.	δ	"Exact"	Approx.	δ	"Exact"	Approx.
8,260	.0040	.0019	11,246		.0121	11,934		.0152
11,632	.1395	.1414	12,593		.1556	12,874		.1572
15,004	.5596	.5580	13,941	**	.5254	13,814	**	.5179
18,376	.8521	.8523	15,289		.8437	14,754		.8425
21,747	.9544	.9601	16,637		.9679	15,694		.9704

*The values for which the function is tabulated are approximately at $E''(\tilde{\delta})$, $E''(\tilde{\delta}) \pm \sqrt{Var''(\tilde{\delta})}$, and $E''(\tilde{\delta}) \pm 2\sqrt{Var''(\tilde{\delta})}$.

**"Exact" values are not available because the magnitude of the numbers caused overflow in the computer.

"exact" results were not obtainable because the magnitude of the numbers created "overflow" in the computer. In the cases where "exact" and approximate results were obtainable, the two corresponded very closely.

6. Posterior distribution of the pure premium

As pointed out in Section 2, in actuarial nomenclature $E[\tilde{n}]E[\tilde{x}|n = 1]/t$, the expected claims payments on a single policy during the policy period according to the collective risk model, is called a pure premium. The posterior distribution of this quantity will summarize all available information about the risk parameters that determine the pure premium.

Initially we will consider the simplest case where the number of claims per policy has a Poisson distribution with parameter $\tilde{\lambda}$ and the claim amount has an exponential distribution with parameter $\tilde{\delta}$. We will let $\tilde{\mu} = \tilde{\lambda}\tilde{\delta}$ and combine Equations (1) and (2) and our assumption of independence between the distributions of $\tilde{\lambda}$ and $\tilde{\delta}$ to exhibit the joint posterior density function of $\tilde{\lambda}$ and $\tilde{\delta}$:

$$p''(\delta,\lambda|n,t,\alpha',\beta',n'',s'') \propto \left(\frac{1}{\delta}\right)^{n''} e^{-\frac{s''}{\delta}} \lambda^{n+\alpha'-1} e^{-(t+\beta')\lambda} . \tag{5}$$

The marginal distribution of $\tilde{\mu}$ has a density function given by

$$p''(\mu|n,t,\alpha',\beta',n'',s'') \propto \frac{\mu^{n+\alpha'-1}}{[s'' + (t + \beta')\mu]^{n''+n+\alpha'-1}} .$$

The posterior mean of $\tilde{\mu}$ is

$$\left(\frac{n + \alpha'}{t + \beta'}\right)\left(\frac{s''}{n'' - 2}\right), \tag{6}$$

and the posterior mode is

$$\left(\frac{n + \alpha' - 1}{t + \beta'}\right)\left(\frac{s''}{n''}\right) .$$

The distribution, along with the familiar F distribution, is a member of the Pearson Type VI family of distributions.

See Johnson and Katz (1970).

If a two parameter gamma distribution is used for the claim amount distribution, it is interesting to develop an approximate distribution for the pure premium. Using the approximate posterior distribution for $\tilde{\delta}$ (Equation (4)), the approximate posterior density function of $\tilde{\lambda}$ and $\tilde{\delta}$ is

$$p''(\delta,\lambda|n,t,\alpha',\beta',n'',s'',\hat{\gamma}) \propto [(\frac{1}{\delta})^{n''\hat{\gamma}+1} e^{-\frac{\gamma}{\delta}s''}] \times [\lambda^{n+\alpha'-1} e^{-(t+\beta')\lambda}] . \qquad (7)$$

Then the approximate posterior marginal distribution of $\tilde{\mu} = \tilde{\lambda}\tilde{\delta}$ has a density function given by

$$p''(\mu|n,t,\alpha',\beta',n'',s'',\hat{\gamma}) \propto \frac{\mu^{n+\alpha'-1}}{[s''\hat{\gamma} + (t + \beta')\mu]^{n''\hat{\gamma}+n+\alpha'}} , \qquad (8)$$

This distribution will have a mean given by Equation (6) with s'' replaced by $s''\hat{\gamma}$ and n'' by $n''\hat{\gamma} + 1$.

Table 3 contains some values of the cumulative distribution, associated with the approximated posterior martinal distribution of $\tilde{\mu}$, with density function given by Equation (8). The parameters used in this illustration are consistent with those used in Table 1 with the modal value of $\tilde{\lambda}$ taken as .15, a fairly typical value for automobile property damage insurance.

In this section we have developed the posterior distribution for the pure premium for what is probably the simplest example of a collective risk model. The development of the posterior distribution for the pure premium for the richer model built on a two parameter gamma distribution for claim amount involved a rather standard approximation trick. The really important point is that with high speed computing to do the integration and graphical displays to guide the selection of prior distributions for parameters, the

Table 3. Some values of the posterior cumulative distribution function* of $\tilde{\mu}$ for three cases. (In each case $\hat{\gamma} = .3$ and the mode of the distribution of $\tilde{\mu}$ is 13.50.)

$n'' = 10,\ s'' = 1200$		$n'' = 50,\ s'' = 4800$		$n'' = 100,\ s'' = 9300$	
$n = 0,\ t = 0$		$n = 40,\ t = 267$		$n = 90,\ t = 600$	
$\alpha' = 25,\ \beta' = 10$		$\alpha' = 25,\ \beta' = 10$		$\alpha' = 25,\ \beta' = 10$	
μ	Cumulative Probability	μ	Cumulative Probability	μ	Cumulative Probability
		4.82	.0002	8.26	.0037
		10.30	.1051	11.42	.1457
45.00	.6582	15.78	.5723	14.58	.5485
105.38	.9248	21.26	.8558	17.74	.8489
165.76	.9737	26.74	.9706	20.90	.9615

*The values for which the function is tabulated are approximately at $E''(\tilde{\mu})$, $E''(\tilde{\mu}) \pm \sqrt{Var''(\tilde{\mu})}$, and $E''(\tilde{\mu}) \pm 2\sqrt{Var''(\tilde{\mu})}$

development of the posterior distribution of the pure premium could be developed for many reasonable distribution assumptions.

7. The predictive distribution

One of the distinct advantages of a Bayesian approach is that it leads naturally to a predictive distribution. After a model for the probability distribution of claims is selected, $f(x|\underline{\theta},t)$, and a joint distribution for $\underline{\tilde{\theta}}$ specified, integration will produce a predictive density function for a single claim amount $\tilde{x}$. That is

$$p(x) = \int f(x|\underline{\theta},\ t=1)p''(\underline{\theta})d\underline{\theta}$$

The distribution of $\underline{\theta}$ will usually be the posterior distribution with respect to previous years and will summarize all available information about the risk parameters. This distribution summarizes not only the random nature of the claims process, but the current uncertainty in the estimates of the parameters of the claims process.

Thus if one elects to introduce a security loading to augment the pure premium by either the variance or standard deviation loading principles, (Bühlmann, 1970, Chap. 4), it would seem natural to use the variance of the predictive distribution in the loading. This parameter would capture the essence of the total risk borne by the insurer.

For example, if we adopt the collective risk model, Poisson distribution for number of claims, exponential distribution for claim amount, the security loaded pure premium would be

$$E''[\tilde{\lambda}]E''[\tilde{\delta}] + k_1\sqrt{Var(\tilde{x})}$$

if one adopted a standard deviation loading principle or

$$E''[\tilde{\lambda}]E''[\tilde{\delta}] + k_2\ Var(\tilde{x})$$

if one adopted a variance loading principle. The constants k_1 and k_2 may vary with the risk capacity and attitude toward risk of the insurance company. In these expressions $\mathrm{Var}(\tilde{x})$ is the variance of the predictive distribution and for our Poisson-exponential example

$$\mathrm{Var}(\tilde{x}) = \mathrm{Var}''(\widetilde{\lambda\delta}) + E''(\tilde{\lambda}c_2)$$

$$= \frac{\alpha' s''^2(\alpha' + n'' - 2)}{\beta'^2(n'' - 2)^2(n'' - 3)} + \frac{2\alpha' s''}{\beta'(n'' - 2)} .$$

Of course if no actual insurance experience is available, $n = 0$, $s'' = s'$ and $n'' = n'$.

Bühlmann (1970) discusses the issues involved in this type of security loading under the title "the credibility premium."

It should be clearly understood that these issues go beyond the problem of fixing the security loading so as to hold the probability of adverse financial deviations on the line of policies under consideration to a suitably small, management selected, number. If this were the sole consideration, the standard deviation principle, coupled with an estimate of the number of policies expected to belong to the group, would seem most reasonable. This argument is not entirely convincing because of the many non-normal claims distributions.

Nevertheless, such loadings have the additonal advantage of being linear under proportional changes in claims distributions. On the other hand, variance loadings are linear with respect to the addition of independent risks and correspond with premium results if insurance customers' utility functions are approximated by a quadratic function.

For short term cash flow planning, the predictive distribution of total claims would be of interest. To fix this distribution a count of the number of policies t would be needed. In our simple Poisson-exponential example, this change in objective would simply replace the density $f(x|\lambda, \delta, t = 1)$ with the more general $f(x|\lambda, \delta, t)$ in the definition of the predictive distribution. The predictive mean and variance of $\tilde{x}$, total claims, become in this example

$$t\left(\frac{n + \alpha'}{n + \beta'}\right)\left(\frac{s''}{n'' - 2}\right)$$

and

$$\frac{t^2 s''^2(\alpha' + n'' - 2)\alpha'}{\beta'^2(n'' - 2)^2(n'' - 3)} + \frac{2t\alpha' s''}{\beta'(n'' - 2)} .$$

As a final example of the application of predictive distribution, recall that in the collective risk model, Poisson distribution of claims, $\tilde{x}$, the total claims, has an approximate $N(\lambda tc_1, \lambda tc_2)$ distribution. If the distribution of λtc_1, given $\lambda tc_2 = 1/r$, is $N(\mu'', 1/r\tau'')$, and the marginal distribution of $1/\lambda tc_2$ is gamma with parameters α'' and β'', then the approximate predictive distribution of total claims will be non-standard t (DeGroot, 1970, p. 170) with $2\alpha''$ degrees of freedom, location parameter μ'', and precision $\alpha''\tau''/\beta''$. The double primes are used on the parameter symbols to indicate that they are posterior to all available relevant insurance experience. This fairly "dangerous" distribution could be used for short term financial planning.

Once again the results obtained using these simple distribution assumptions are intended to be suggestive of the utility of Bayesian analysis of risk problems.

8. Summary

In this paper we have illustrated the use of Bayesian estimation methods for the parameters of a collective risk insurance claims process. It is our position that this leads to a reasonable method of adjusting insurance premiums as claims experience is obtained. The predictive distribution may be used to develop very comprehensive security loading factors either for short term individual premiums or for the entire process.

Appendix

In this appendix we develop the information matrix based on the distribution with probability density function

$$\frac{dV^1(x)}{dx} = \begin{cases} [\Gamma(\gamma)]^{-1}(\delta^{-1}\gamma)^{\gamma}\, x^{\gamma-1}\, e^{-\delta^{-1}\gamma x}, & x > 0,\ \delta > 0,\ \gamma > 0 \\ 0 & , \text{otherwise.} \end{cases}$$

The natural logarithm of the probability density function is

$$\ell(\delta,\gamma) = \gamma \ell n \quad - \gamma \ell n \delta - \ell n \Gamma(\gamma) + (\gamma - 1)\ell n x - (\delta^{-1}\gamma)x \ .$$

Thus

$$\frac{\partial \ell(\delta,\gamma)}{\partial \gamma} = 1 + \ell n \gamma - \ell n \delta - \psi(\gamma) + \ell n x - \frac{x}{\delta} ,$$

$$\frac{\partial^2 \ell(\delta,\gamma)}{\partial \gamma^2} = \frac{1}{\gamma} - \psi'(\gamma) ,$$

$$\frac{\partial \ell(\delta,\gamma)}{\partial \delta} = - \frac{\gamma}{\delta} + \frac{\gamma x}{\delta^2} ,$$

$$\frac{\partial^2 \ell(\delta,\gamma)}{\partial \delta^2} = \frac{\gamma}{\delta^2} - \frac{2x}{\delta^3} ,$$

and

$$\frac{\partial^2 \ell(\delta,\gamma)}{\partial \delta \partial \gamma} = \frac{\partial^2 \ell(\delta,\gamma)}{\partial \gamma \partial \delta} = - \frac{1}{\delta} + \frac{x}{\delta^2} .$$

Since $E(\tilde{x}) = \delta$, we immediately obtain the information matrix

$$I(\delta,\gamma) = \begin{bmatrix} -\gamma^{-1} + \psi'(\gamma) & 0 \\ 0 & \gamma\delta^{-2} \end{bmatrix} .$$

It follows from the discussion on pp. 216-218 of DeGroot (1970) that <u>a posteriori</u>, when n is large, $\tilde{\delta}$ and $\tilde{\gamma}$ are approximately independently and normally distributed.

Discussion by Dale Lamps of Insurance Credibility Theory and Bayesian Estimates

Introduction

In their paper on Bayesian Credibility, Hickman and Miller discuss cases where the exposure, T, is large. My interest, and the primary area of group marketing activity in my company, is group health cases with a small number of lives. I am primarily concerned with the development of a credibility process for a group with T employees (some with single coverage and some with family coverage) based on their claim experience over the most recent twelve months. In the credibility process, I am not concerned about environmental factors, such as inflation, which will be handled by other techniques.

In this paper, I shall present some exploratory work aimed at using Bayesian methods to develop a credibility process. My discussion will touch on alternative prior distributions, the design of parameters, and some numerical examples together with the computer program used to generate the numerical examples.

Basics of Bayesian Statistics

In the problem I am addressing, there are two random variables. One deals with the premium level and the other with claims. I will use the following definitions:

$\tilde{X}$ Total twelve months claims for the group

$\tilde{P}$ True pure premium per employee for the group

$\tilde{X}$ and $\tilde{P}$ are both random variables on the interval $[0,\infty\rangle$. There are four frequency distributions with respect to these random variables which are of interest in Bayesian analysis.

They are the distributions of $\tilde{X}$, $\tilde{P}$, $(\tilde{P}|\tilde{X} = X)$, and $(\tilde{X}|\tilde{P} = P)$. According to Bayes' theorem,

$$f(\tilde{X}) \cdot f(\tilde{P}|\tilde{X} = X) = f(\tilde{P}) \cdot f(\tilde{X}|\tilde{P} = P)$$

In the application of Bayes' theorem to credibility, we want to determine

$$E(\tilde{P}|\tilde{X} = X_0) \; ,$$

where X_0 is the most recently observed value of $\tilde{X}$. In this case, where an observed value of $\tilde{X}$ is known, Bayes theorem becomes

$$f(\tilde{P}|\tilde{X} = X_0) \; \alpha \; f(\tilde{P}) \cdot f(\tilde{X}|\tilde{P} = P) \; ,$$

where α is to be read "is proportional to." This means that the credibility process depends on a prior determination of two things: the distribution of $\tilde{P}$ and the distribution of $(\tilde{X}|\tilde{P} = P)$. In every case where these two distributions are defined, a credibility process is defined. Unfortunately the resulting process, although defined, is not always manageable; practical application of the process may be beyond reach. An example of such a situation is described below.

Use of Gamma Distributions

What distributions are likely candidates for $\tilde{P}$ and $(\tilde{X}|\tilde{P} = P)$? Since we are interested in small T, we would expect a distribution with some fairly strong capacity for skewness, so the normal distribution can be eliminated. The most likely candidates seem to be the Log-Normal and Gamma distributions.

Since the Gamma distribution shows up as an intermediate result in the work by Hickman and Miller, it seems to be a likely starting place.

Unfortunately, the Gamma distribution, while yielding a well defined result, proved to be an example of a distribution which yields an unmanageable result. The posterior distribution proved to be of the form

$$f(\tilde{P}|\tilde{X} = X_0) = k_{X_0}\left(\frac{1}{P}\right)^{c_1} e^{-\left[c_2(P-P_0)^2 + \frac{c_3}{P}\right]}$$

I have not yet been able to find an algorithm to determine $E(\tilde{P}|\tilde{X} = X_0)$ based on this distribution.

Use of Log-Normal Distributions

Attempts to use the Gamma distribution for one variable and the Log-Normal distribution for the other ended in a similar way.

However, when both random variables are assumed to be Log-Normal the result is easily managed by "completing the squares" in the exponential portion of the resulting posterior frequency function. The posterior frequency function is also Log-Normal.

The problem of defining the parameters of the frequency functions was approached by starting with the obvious value for the mean of each distribution and a fairly flexible expression for each variance. These are given below.

Random Variable	$\tilde{P}$	$(\tilde{X}\|\tilde{P} = P)$
Mean	P_0	PT
Variance	$\frac{k_1 P_0^2}{f_1(T)}$	$\frac{k_2 P^2 T^2}{f_2(T)}$

P_0 is the pure premium reflected in the existing rate being charged to the case. The random variable $\tilde{P}$, the true (but unknown) pure premium, has mean P_0. P is any particular value of $\tilde{P}$. $(\tilde{X}|\tilde{P} = P)$ will have different distribution for each different value of the random variable $\tilde{P}$.

An outline of the algebraic development of $f(\tilde{P}|\tilde{X} = X_0)$

follows. In this development, let $a_i = \frac{k_i}{f_i(T)} + 1$ for $i = 1,2$.

$f(\tilde{P})$ has the parameters

$$\mu_1 = \ln \frac{P_0}{\sqrt{\frac{k_1}{f_1(T)} + 1}} = \ln P_0 - \sigma_1$$

$$\sigma_1^2 = \ln\left(\frac{k_1}{f_1(T)} + 1\right) = \ln a_1$$

$f(\tilde{X}|\tilde{P} = P)$ has the parameters

$$\mu_2 = \ln \frac{PT}{\sqrt{\frac{k_2}{f_2(T)} + 1}} = \ln PT - \sigma_2$$

$$\sigma_2^2 = \ln\left(\frac{k_2}{f_2(T)} + 1\right) = \ln a_2$$

$$\therefore f(\tilde{P}|\tilde{X} = X_0) \; \alpha \; f(\tilde{P}) \cdot f(\tilde{X} = X_0|\tilde{P} = P)$$

$$\alpha \; \frac{1}{P} \, e^{\frac{-(\ln P-\mu_1)^2}{2\sigma_1^2}} \, e^{-\frac{(\ln X_0-\mu_2)^2}{2\sigma_2^2}}$$

The remainder of the development consists of adding exponents and completing the squares.

$$\frac{(\ln P - \mu_1)^2}{2\sigma_1^2} + \frac{(\ln X_0 - \mu_2)^2}{2\sigma_2^2}$$

$$= \frac{1}{2\sigma_1^2\sigma_2^2}\left[(\sigma_2 \ln P-\mu_1\sigma_2)^2 + \left(\sigma_1 \ln P-\sigma_1\left(\ln X_0-\ln T + \frac{\sigma_2^2}{2}\right)\right)^2\right]$$

$$= \frac{1}{2\sigma_1^2\sigma_2^2}\left[(\sigma_1^2+\sigma_2^2)(\ln P)^2 - 2 \ln P\left(\sigma_2^2\left(\mu_1 + \frac{\sigma_1^2}{2}\right)+\sigma_1^2 \ln \frac{X_0}{T}\right)+c\right]$$

$$= \frac{\left[\ln P - \dfrac{\sigma_2^2\left(\mu_1 + \dfrac{\sigma_1^2}{2}\right) + \sigma_1^2 \ln \dfrac{X_0}{T}}{\sigma_1^2 + \sigma_2^2}\right]^2}{2\,\dfrac{\sigma_1^2\sigma_2^2}{\sigma_1^2 + \sigma_2^2}} + c$$

Therefore $f(\tilde{P}|\tilde{X} = X_0)$ is Log-Normal with parameters

$$\mu = \frac{\sigma_2^2 \ln P_0 + \sigma_1^2 \ln \dfrac{X_0}{T}}{\sigma_1^2 + \sigma_2^2}$$

$$\sigma^2 = \frac{\sigma_1^2\sigma_2^2}{\sigma_1^2 + \sigma_2^2}$$

The mean of $(\tilde{P}|\tilde{X} = X_0)$ is:

$$e^{\mu + \frac{\sigma^2}{2}} = e^{\dfrac{\ln a_1 \ln \frac{X_0}{T} + \ln a_2 \ln P_0 + \frac{1}{2}(\ln a_1)(\ln a_2)}{\ln a_1 + \ln a_2}}$$

$$= P_0 \cdot L_0^{\left(\dfrac{\ln a_1}{\ln a_1 \cdot a_2}\right)} \cdot e^{\left(\dfrac{\ln a_1 \cdot \ln a_2}{2 \ln a_1 \cdot a_2}\right)} \quad \left(\text{for } L_0 = \frac{X_0}{P_0 T}\right)$$

Credibility

The usual credibility process involves the use of a credibility factor. The Log-Normal credibility process does not. However, it is interesting and useful to analyze the lveel of credibility associated with a marginal claim dollar. This marginal credibility is the first derivative of $[T \cdot E(\tilde{P}|\tilde{X} = X_0)]$ with respect to X_0.

$$C_T(X_0) = \frac{\partial}{\partial X_0}[T \cdot E(\tilde{P}|\tilde{X} = X_0)] = \frac{\ln a_1}{\frac{X_0}{T} \ln a_1 a_2} \cdot E(\tilde{P}|\tilde{X} = X_0)$$

Note that $f_1(T)$ and $f_2(T)$ will normally be increasing functions on T, with

$$\lim_{T\to\infty} f_1(T) = \lim_{T\to\infty} f_2(T) = \infty .$$

Therefore, for large T, $C_T(X_0)$ will tend to

$$\frac{f_2'(T)/f_1'(T)}{f_2(T)/f_1(T) + \frac{X_0}{P_0T} \cdot \frac{k_2}{k_1}}$$

If $\frac{f_2(T)}{f_1(T)} \to T$ as $T \to \infty$, then

$$C_T(X_0) \to \frac{T}{T + k_2/k_1}$$

This conforms with the result of Hickman and Miller where, for any δ

$$\mathrm{pr}\left[\left|\frac{X_0}{P_0T} \cdot \frac{k_2}{k_1} - T\right| < \delta\right] \to 1 \qquad T \to \infty$$

In the light of this result, the variance of $(\tilde{X}|\tilde{P} = P)$ can be described as

$$\frac{k_2P^2T}{f_1(T) \cdot f_2'(T)}, \qquad \text{where} \quad \lim_{T\to\infty} f_2'(T) = 1 ,$$

without loss of flexibility; the result is in conformity with that of Hickman and Miller.

Numerical Examples

Appendix I shows examples for various values of T and $\frac{X_0}{P_0T}$ (the loss ratio). These examples were calculated with

$$k_1 = .6$$

$$k_2 = 70$$

$$f_1(T) = T^7$$

$$f_2(T) = T^{1.7}$$

They have the following noteworthy characteristics:

- Marginal credibility exceeds one for low T and low

loss ratios.

- Marginal credibility decreases with increasing loss ratio. This corresponds with increasing pooling of large losses.
- $E(\tilde{P}|\tilde{X} = X_0) > P_0$ for small T, with the difference decreasing with increasing T.

Appendix I

Numerical Examples. The following numerical examples are based on:

$$P = 300$$

$$k = .6$$

$$k = 70$$

$$f_1(T) = T^{.7}$$

$$f_2(T) = T^{1.7}$$

For each combination of T and $\frac{X_0}{P_0T}$, two values are shown. The first is $E(\tilde{P}|\tilde{X} = X_0)$. The second, in parentheses, is $C_T(X_0)$.

Table 1

General Patterns of $E(\tilde{P}|\tilde{X} = X_0)$ and $C_T(X_0)$

T	Loss Ratio .01	.50	1.00	1.50	10.00
10	186 (7.11)	291 (.22)	315 (.12)	330 (.084)	411 (.016)
100	36 (5.54)	219 (.68)	302 (.46)	364 (.37)	875 (.13)
1,000	5 (1.45)	161 (.96)	300 (.90)	431 (.86)	2,358 (.70)
10,000	3 (1.04)		300 (.99)		

Table 2

Pattern of Values for T = 15

Loss Ratio	$E(\tilde{P}\|\tilde{X} = X_0)$	$C_T(X_0)$
.01	164	7.62
.1	226	1.05
.2	249	.58
.3	263	.41
.4	274	.32
.5	283	.26
.6	290	.225
.7	296	.197
.8	302	.176
.9	307	.159
1.0	311	.145
1.2	319	.124
1.4	326	.109
1.6	332	.097
1.8	338	.087
2.	343	.080
3.	363	.056
5.	390	.036
10.	430	.020
30.	501	.008
100.	593	.003
1,000	817	.0004
10,000	1,128	.00005
100,000	1,556	.000007
1,000,000	2,147	.0000010

Table 3

Pattern of Values for Loss Ratio of 1.00

T	$E(\tilde{P} \mid \tilde{X} = X_0)$	$C_T(X_0)$
3	335	.101
5	325	.102
7	320	.108
10	315	.120
15	311	.145
25	308	.196
35	306	.24
50	304	.31
70	303	.38
100	302	.46
200	301	.63
500	300	.81
1,000	300	.90
3,000	300	.96
10,000	300	.988
30,000	300	.995

Are the Classical and Bayesian Approaches to Credibility Empirically Valid?

Myron H. Margolin
The Prudential Insurance Company of America

Proposing a mathematical model for credibility is one thing. Showing that the model is empirically valid or relevant is quite another.

Several years ago I was given the assignment of reviewing Prudential's rerate procedures (i.e., prospective experience-rating formulas) for group life and health insurance. My superiors doubted that the credibility formulas then in use were proper. No one recalled how they had been derived--perhaps they were more or less pulled out of the air.

The first step was to study the accessible actuarial literature on credibility. The various articles contained a number of mathematical models, both "classical" and "Bayesian." For months I struggled unsuccessfully to apply them to the problem at hand. Why I failed, and why I believe failure is usually inevitable, are the subject of this paper.

All of the mathematical models, whether classical or Bayesian, seemed essentially identical. In all instances, the actual claims X, for a particular group in a particular year, are supposedly distributed about a parameter θ in accordance with a function $g(X|\theta)$. Furthermore, all the models presupposed another distribution $p(\theta)$. They applied Bayes theorem to obtain $f(\theta|X) = Z \cdot X + (1 - Z) \cdot \overline{\theta}$, a new estimate for θ, given X. Of course, Z was the credibility factor.

The classical and Bayesian approaches seemed to differ mainly in interpretation. The classical view treated θ as a true or underlying claims rate, $g(X|\theta)$ as a conditional probability, $p(\theta)$ as the frequency distribution of the θ's for the various members of a set of risks (in this instance, a set of group policies), and Bayes Theorem as the method of inverse probability.

The Bayesian interpretation seemed less clear. θ is some kind of subjective quantity--a hypothesis or opinion, $g(X|\theta)$ is called a likelihood function, $p(\theta)$ is an initial estimate or prior distribution of θ, and $f(X|\theta)$ is a posterior distribution. Yet the mathematics of the two approaches were indistinguishable.

But it was clear from the start that θ is not an observable, measurable quantity. It is either a hidden parameter or a subjective quantity. Thus, no empirical data could tell me unequivocally what were the "right" assumptions, in order to choose specific functions for p and for g. Furthermore, none of the published papers offered much guidance. They expressed Z in terms of the variance of p and the variance of g, but gave no clues as to how to measure these variances.

Next I noticed that the models are mathematically tractable only for certain pairs ("conjugates") of simple functions. I have never understood why we should expect something as complex as group insurance to obey such restrictions--why the functions should be simple and conjugate when the benefit plans can be so complicated.

Finally, I realized that the models lead to an absurd conclusion--that equal quantities of claim experience deserve equal credibility, regardless how old. For example,

50 years of experience on a group of 20 lives allegedly deserves as much credibility as the latest year of experience on a 1,000-life group. This is impossible. No one can realistically maintain that group major medical experience more than a few years old is of much value; and even for group life the value must diminish with age. Only one of the papers even alluded to this problem. I call it the problem of "non-uniform conditions," that paper called it "heterogeneity in time." The only aspect of heterogeneity it tried to account for was uniform inflation, but this does not really get at the problem.

To a limited extent, our rerate procedures did already cope with this problem. For groups large enough to get full credibility, we did not assume that the dollar amount of next year's claims would equal last year's. Instead we projected the same percentage of "manual premium," a standardized premium which is a function of several items such as the number of lives or amount of insurance, age, sex, plan of benefits, et al. Likewise, for very small groups (zero credibility), our estimates were based on a company average percentage of manual premium. Thus, our rerate procedures were responsive to changes in those items on which manual premium is based.

But the use of manual premiums poses new problems for the classical and Bayesian models. Different companies use different manual premium rating schemes. No one scheme is the "right" one, although some schemes are undoubtedly better than others. Don't Z, $p(\cdot)$, $g(\cdot)$ and θ each depend on which particular scheme you're using? (Intuitively, actual experience should get more credibility the worse the scheme.) Relative to selecting p and g, it's bad enough that θ is unobservable--but you've also got somehow to take into account the particular characteristics of your own manual premium scheme. Also, won't the degree of non-uniformity or heterogeneity in time, as well as the form of the functions, depend on the units in which X and θ are expressed?

I gave up--or rather I took a different approach (Margolin, 1971). I won't argue its merits here, except to state that it works, while the classical and Bayesian methods seem generally not to. The distinguishing characteristic of my approach is that it measures the relationships among observables only--no θ's, no hidden parameters.

But there is another perspective from which to consider these models. Aside from the practical difficulties, there is the more basic question of whether they are logically meaningful. When is it meaningful to assert that actual claims X are distributed about a parameter θ? Following is a resumé of my views (Margolin, 1974).

Consider the three possibilities:

1. θ is objective and constant in time. ("Objective" means that the statement "$\theta = k$ at time t" is either true for all persons or false for all persons, given any quantity k and time t. "Objective and constant" means that the statement "$\theta = k$" is either true for all persons or false for all.)
   This is logically meaningful. θ is operationally definable (in principle) as the average value of X over infinite time.
   This possibility corresponds to "uniform conditions," which, as we shall see, does not obtain for group insurance.
2. θ is objective but not constant in time.
   This is not logically meaningful. One cannot

distinguish even <u>in principle</u> random changes in X from the non-random changes in θ. I.e., given measurements X_1 and X_2 at times t_1 and t_2, there is no unique way to divide the difference $X_2 - X_1$ into a non-random component $\theta_2 - \theta_1$ and a random component $(X_2 - \theta_2) - (X_1 - \theta_1)$. Any definition or description of how the components might be distinguished is arbitrary or tautological. Thus, the mathematical symbol θ has no objective counterpart in the real world.

3. θ is subjective.

This, as I understand it, is the Bayesian interpretation. θ represents an estimate, a hypothesis, or an opinion. (However, some Bayesians seem inconsistent or ambiguous on this point, sometimes calling θ an estimate but sometimes a quantity whose value we wish to estimate.)

I cannot make logical sense of this interpretation. I agree that it is meaningful to use probability subjectively--e.g., to bet on a horse race.

I also agree that one may offer a subjective prior estimate $p(\theta)$ for the value of an objective quantity θ. (E.g., we can accept the meaningfulness of "I'll bet you 2 to 1 that Wilt Chamberlain is between 7'2" and 7'4" tall," or "I'll bet 5 to 1 that next year's actual claims on ABC Co. will not exceed $53,000." These statements are logically of the same type as $p(\theta)$, where θ is measurable.)

But it does not seem meaningful to use a subjective $p(\cdot)$ to estimate a subjective θ. Consider the example, "I'll bet you 5 to 1 that my θ (or my estimate or opinion) for next year's claims does not exceed \$53,000"?! Subjective p's and θ's cannot be meaningfully conjoined.

Where conditions are uniform, the mean of the X's goes to a limit. For this special case, $p(\cdot)$ may be taken as a subjective prior estimate of this limit. If this limit is denoted by θ, then $p(\theta)$ is meaningful but now θ is objective and constant.

The logical difficulties are not remedied by supposing that $p(\cdot)$ is an estimate of the "expected value" of X. This evidentally refers to $E(X) = \int Xf(X)dX$. Hence, the supposition presupposes that the distribution $f(\cdot)$ is meaningful, and in particular its first moment. But by the same tests of meaningfulness, this distribution and its moments are meaningful only if they are objective and constant--requiring once again uniform conditions.

We should not fail to notice that the foremost exponent of the Bayesian attitude, Bruno de Finetti, bases his position on the concept of "exchangeability." It seems to me that non-uniformity or heterogeneity in time imply non-exchangeability. Thus by its own terms the Bayesian approach is inapplicable.

Yet perhaps the most serious charge against the Bayesian models (and the classical ones too) is that they violate the elementary scientific canons of testability and verifiability. If someone asserts, on the basis of such a model plus whatever data he chooses to use, that a certain credibility formula furnishes the best least-squares estimate of some quantity θ, and if θ is not observable, then it is not possible to test his assertion; conversely, credibility models and formulas are testable only if they are used to estimate future claims or if the special case of uniform conditions obtains.

Thus, only the first possibility is logically meaningful. But is a model presupposing objective, constant θ's realistic for group insurance? Most actuaries would probably concede that it is not <u>precisely</u> correct for any group coverage and not even approximately valid for health coverages; but many seem to believe that it's a reasonable approximation for group life.

Given the scanty evidence to support this belief, it may be little more than wishful thinking. One piece of evidence to the contrary was shown at TSA XXIII, p. 270. Following is an even more striking counterexample, based on experience under the Servicemen's Group Life Insurance Program.

NON-VIETNAM SGLI MORTALITY EXPERIENCE

Group Covered: Servicemen on Active Duty other than in Vietnam

Exposure Period

1966-1968

Age Group	Deaths	Annual Rate Per M
17-19	1310	1.04
20-24	6288	1.47
25-29	1696	1.47
30-34	1129	1.37
35-39	1340	1.86
40-44	762	2.55
45-49	646	3.49
50 & over	559	7.30

1970-1972		
Deaths	Annual Rate Per M	Change in Rate over 1966-68 as Number of Standard Deviations
1706	1.73	+19.8
5153	1.45	- 1.0
1391	1.30	- 4.8
946	1.29	- 1.9
1113	1.56	- 6.1
747	2.08	- 5.6
420	3.13	- 2.4
353	4.56	- 9.9

(Source: Fourth and Eighth Annual Reports, Servicemen's Group Life Insurance Program, Veterans Administration)

Obviously, many of these changes are much too large to be due to chance alone, and seem also to be a good deal greater than corresponding changes in population mortality or group mortality generally. The non-random character of changes of this magnitude becomes evident only for jumbo groups; for groups of lesser size, similar changes in mortality rates would erroneously be attributed solely to "random fluctuation."

Non-random change is real and undoubtedly impacts on groups of all sizes. It is not a question simply of abrupt but infrequent dislocations, like the discovery of a cure for cancer. Group insurance risks are not isolated from our rapidly changing society. Every day we read of changes in the economy, in the environment, or in health care which must effect group insurance experience, and not all risks in the same way; and we can scarcely imagine the myriad of smaller changes which are not reported. Our credibility procedures should not ignore the effects of change.

What has Statutory Valuation in the United States to do with Credibility and Risk Theory?

John O. Montgomery
California Department of Insurance

1. The answer to the title question at the present time is absolutely nothing! There is really no aspect of the present statutory valuation system in the United States that in any way involves the use of credibility or risk theory as has been developed over the past few decades. So what am I, as Chief Actuary for the California Insurance Department and the working Chairman of the National Association of Insurance Commissioners' Task Force to review the status of Valuation and Nonforfeiture legislation and regulation, doing here? Frankly, this is going to be an appeal for assistance.

2. First for those of you who have not been attending meetings of the NAIC (National Association of Insurance Commissioners), that body designated a Task Force in December 1973:

a. To review valuation and nonforfeiture value legislation;

b. To determine the nature of problems currently encountered and recommend practical solutions which can be implemented now; and finally

c. To consider the fundamental purposes of statutory regulation, to make studies of systems alternative to the present one by using theories and techniques not previously available, and eventually to recommend some course of long range development of statutory regulation.

3. Nearly a year previous to the naming of the NAIC Task Force the Society of Actuaries had appointed a "Special Committee on Valuation and Nonforfeiture Laws" to study somewhat the same area. After considerable discussion and investigation that committee decided first to concentrate on the nonforfeiture value problems and is soon to come forth with recommendations.

4. It is intended that there be a close liaison between the NAIC Task Force and the Society of Actuaries Committee to avoid duplication of effort and to exchange findings and ideas. The NAIC Task Force will, however, retain its own advisory committes, some members of which may also be members of the Society Committee. This will enable the Society Committee to function as a truly independent body whose members are serving as individual professional actuaries and not as representative of their employers or clients.

5. As presently organized the Advisory Committee to the NAIC Task Force consists of five members representing various actuarial spheres of influence:

Robert Houser, for the Society of Actuaries (also a member of the Society Committee)

Gary Corbett, for the American Academy of Actuaries

Richard Minck, for the Americal Life Insurance Association (the ALIA is represented on the Society Committee by John Booth)

Michael Jordan, for the National Association of Life Insurance Companies

James Hickman, for the academic community

6. Currently the Task Force, comprised of representatives from California, New Jersey, New York, Texas and Wisconsin is tn the process of naming some advisory subcommittees to handle the more immediate problems. By December we hope to have the ground work laid also for the more extensive long range studies to be made and to be able to ask for

advisory subcommittee help.

7. Since we are very much in the formative stages, anything said here about possible future plans will be subjected to many hours of discussion and much revision before any report or recommendations can be made. This paper includes some of the material presented to the NAIC in June and some observations gleaned from subsequent discussions and readings.

8. I mentioned earlier that this was an appeal for assistance. This help is needed in handling some of the long range problems that continue to disturb the solvency and equity aspects of statutory valuation regulation of life and health insurance companies in the United States. Indeed, some of these problems may also be evident in statutory valuation regulation for other lines of business, but for this presentation only life and health insurance are to be considered.

9. The statutory reserve valuation system for life and health insurance companies in the United States has been designed with the intent of providing a conservative estimate of funds needed to provide for all possible future claims, expenses, taxes and adverse contingencies. In the recent experience it has been observed that companies are still becoming insolvent, primarily from improper evaluation and matching of assets which are necessary to support the reserve required by the statutory system. In some other situations the reserves required have been such that in the light of either present experience or possible future adverse contingencies, the premium charges the policyholder are artificially inflated.

10. Other problems with the current valuation legislative, and regulatory system, and its limitation to policy reserves, which the Task Force has identified are summarized below.

a. The present system ignores the variation of the credibility of experience with respect to the number and relative magnitude of the separate risks assumed with respect to investment, mortality and morbidity.

b. The present system ignores the effect of reinsurance in spreading risk.

c. It is difficult under the present system to reflect adequately changes in mortality, morbidity, expenses, interest rates or other factors involved in the operations of an insurance company.

d. To obtain earnings comparable to those reported for companies in other industries requires adjustment to the present system.

e. The present system is not readily adaptable to products of an index related nature.

11. Turning to the other side, the relative simplicity of the present system dominates all other considerations, and the excellent solvency record of companies using this system with appropriate and conservative premium rates and dividend scales has given the system a reputation for providing a strong basis for solvency. The current system recognizes only three parameters:

a. Interest

b. Mortality and/or morbidity and

c. The various modified reserve systems which make some provision for expenses.

12. The simplicity of the present system is in:

a. Its relative ease of examination and regulation.

b. The facility for the passage of legislation for changing the dimensions of various parameters provided by such simplicity.

c. The generally well established mathematics for

calculating statutory reserves required by this system for traditional insurance products.

d. The well defined parameters used which depend as little as possible upon individual judgment of those making such valuations.

e. The individually identifiable status of the reserves developed by the system.

13. What then should be considered for any alternative policy reserve valuation system to be used for regulatory purposes?

a. The system must be readily susceptible to adequate regulation. Reserve formulas, theories or developments must be carefully explicit and understandable to the regulatory technicians who will be using them.

b. The variation of credibility of experience with the number and relative magnitude of the separate risks assumed should be recognized. These separate risks are not only those involving mortality, morbidity or other claim losses, but also those involving investments and possibly even expense, tax and persistency fluctuation. Reinsurance is a vital part of this recognition.

c. The assumptions for the various parameters of valuation must fall within certain well defined limits which may be broader or include more parameters than those now permitted by the present valuation statutes and may vary with the credibility of experience for each company.

d. The assumptions used for the various parameters required by the system should be based on the most reasonably expected values of those parameters whth an adjustment or additional value to take into account the chances of deviation from those expected values.

e. For companies with credibility falling below

established limits, industry average assumptions for the various parameters should be required.

f. The present statutory valuation reserve system should be continued until any alternate valuation system has been carried along on a parallel operation for a sufficient length of time to develop a reservoir of reliable and intimate knowledge of the operation of the new system and until it is possible to develop a reliable set of industry wide assumptions which could be used by companies not meeting the credibility tests.

g. When the assumptions used in a valuation vary, or when the form of the valuation itself varies, from one year to the next the effect of such changes must be determined and shown separately (as part of Exhibit 8A, and in the Surplus Account for Life Insurance, and as a separate reported item in the Surplus Account for Health Insurance in the NAIC Annual Statement).

14. What types of alternative regulatory valuation systems appear possible? Two approaches to this question are, first, through a gross premium valuation system with appropriate recognition of the chance of deviation from expected values for the various assumptions, and, second, through the development of statistical models by which the various assumptions for each company may be tested to develop the probabilities of ruin and to determine what reserves are needed to keep these probabilities within a defined tolerance level.

a. Under the gross premium valuation method the recognition of the chance of deviation from expected assumption values may either be developed as a set of contingency reserves separate from the gross premium valuation reserves based on expected assumptions, or the expected assumptions may include such recognition thus requiring the presentation of only one set of reserves. The gross premium valuation would be defined as the present value of all future guaranteed benefits including nonforfeiture benefits and expense and tax assumptions less the present value of all future gross premiums to be received using assumptions within the credibility limits established for investment yields, mortality and/or morbidity, persistency, expenses and taxes. In any event the adjustment for the chance of fluctuation of experience greater than an established tolerance level will depend upon the definition of those tolerance levels through the use of appropriate risk theory.

b. The statistical model approach will probably require considerably more research and testing to make it a regulatory tool than would the use of the gross premium valuation approach. The statistical model approach to regulatory valuation cannot be defined specifically at present since much more research is needed to make it a practical tool.

15. The Society of Actuaries and the Casualty Actuarial Society Joint Committee on Theory of Risk has had as its primary objectives:

a. To explore alternative reserving methods which accomplish the matching of revenue and costs;

b. To demonstrate relative patterns of earnings generated by these reserving methods for selected plans and ages, and for a model company; and

c. To demonstrate the sensitivity of earnings generated by selected reserving methods for a model company to changes in certain underlying assumptions.

16. That Committee's major focus has been on the earnings aspect, rather than the solvency aspect, although it is possible for solvency to be considered in some ways as a special, and perhaps limiting, condition of the earnings aspect.

17. The Society of Actuaries Committee on Research has among its various objectives those to foster research and maintain contact with current thinking in the theory of risks and in new methods of statistical analysis.

18. The NAIC Task Force intends that a close liaison should be maintained with all such committees as those mentioned in this paper.

19. In conclusion, whatever is developed must be simple enough for the non-mathematician to understand. This is probably the most demanding condition that will be imposed on any alternative valuation system. The use of expressions like "gamma function" or "asymptotic probability" will mean nothing unless they are explicitly and simply defined. If needed they possibly could be defined without even resorting to such frightening labels to the layman.

20. Specifically some areas where we need help are:

   a. For those areas where theory is now adequate to accomplish some of the tasks set forth, that theory should be re-expressed or developed in as simple a form as possible taking care not to use expressions, common to the mathematical world, which are unknown to the layman, without properly defining them.

   b. The development of statistical models for insurance companies.

   c. The development of theory adequate to derive expressions for the chances of fluctuation of experience from that reasonably expected for the various assumptions required in a gross premium valuation.

d. Further develomment of sampling techniques needed to build models from which gross premium valuations may be constructed.

21. I realize that considerable and significant research has already been accomplished in some of these areas but nothing has been developed yet of truly practical value in insurance company regulation. Part of the difficulty has been such overwhelming confidence in the present statutory system that the idea of an alternate system has not been really seriously considered in the last century. However with increasing numbers of life insurance company insolvencies and with the growing consumer concern over the cost of insurance products, a serious investigation of statutory solvency regulation seems more needed now than any time since Elizur Wright.

Discussion by Russell M. Collins, Jr. of What has Statutory Valuation in the United States to do with Credibility and Risk Theory?

Mr. Montgomery is to be complimented on his excellent approach to a very important and controversial task. The Task Force is approaching the problem with open-mindedness, a desire to use all of the currently available knowledge which might bear on the subject, and is involving and coordinating closely with other groups working on related problems. The Society of Actuaries recognized the need for a thorough review of valuation and nonforfeiture standards and established the special Committee on Valuation and Nonforfeiture Laws in order to assure that the subject received the concentrated actuarial thinking which it deserves. The Joint Committee on Theory of Risk has been engaged in related work on which I will comment later. The Committee on Research of the Society of Actuaries - 10 years old this year - while not directly addressing itself to this particular subject, has promoted increased knowledge, understanding and application of the theory of risk and other related topics in this country. It is quite appropriate that Mr. Montgomery has chosen to make this presentation at this particular research conference, as the announced purpose of the Committee is to - and I quote from the Society of Actuaries Yearbook - "foster research and maintain contact with current thinking in, (a) the theory of risks, (b) the application of various operations research techniques, (c) new methods of statistical analysis, and (d) such other scientific disciplines as may lead to new and better methods of performing the work of the actuary." Certainly, Mr. Montgomery's presentation and appeal is in the spirit of that charge.

In his paper today, Mr. Montgomery has specifically concentrated his attention on valuation, noting that the Society of Actuaries Committee has chosen to concentrate on the nonforfeiture value problems. A recent study which addresses itself to very nearly the same questions, but with respect to another environment, is Financial Guarantees Required From Life Assurance Concerns, published in 1971 by the Organization for Economic Cooperation and Development. The report was prepared by a Working Party under the chairmanship of Mr. Buol, who at the time was a member of the Swiss Insurance Supervisory Service, assisted by an international sub-group of very prominent actuaries, and is commonly referred to as the "Buol Report." The objectives of this Working Party were very nearly the same as those of Mr. Montgomery's Task Force (with respect to valuation) and I commend it to all those involved in the Task Force study or otherwise interested in this subject.

As Mr. Montgomery points out, the current statutory valuation system has, in the main, operated quite successfully and has the important advantages of simplicity, relative ease of understanding, and uniformity of application. It is certainly timely, however, to examine the fundamentals of the valuation of life insurance obligations from basic principles, and to critically examine the current system. The approach suggested by Mr. Montgomery's group, utilizing concepts of risk analysis and credibility, can scarcely be improved upon.

In any discussion of valuation requirements for life insurance, it seems appropriate to distinguish between permanent and term insurance.

In the case of permanent insurance the dominant factor is the interest factor; this has been demonstrated in both the Buol Report and the work of the Joint Committee on Theory of Risk. The selection of an appropriately conservative interest assumption nearly assures adequacy of the reserves. The interest factors used in current statutory valuation are quite conservative and, together with the conservative mortality bases prescribed, produce a conservative policy liability. Thc only question can be whether or not the results are overly conservative. The selection of an "appropriately conservative" interest rate is an interesting problem but need not be overly difficult. The Buol report suggests the average effective rate of interest earned on the company's assets, observed over a sufficiently long period of time, for example 20 years, reduced approximately 30%, subject to certain limiting conditions.

A more difficult question, and probably the source of most insurance company solvencies in recent years, is the quality of the assets supporting a company's liabilities. Also, in testing the adequacy of reserves, appropriate account must be taken of inflation and its effect on future expenses, as well as its relation to investment return. This is a difficult problem and part of a larger problem of economic forecasting. We all recognize the current chaotic state of economic forecasting. The models which gave reasonably accurate results in the sixties and early seventies have proven inadequate for the current period, and economists and model builders face perplexing problems in constructing new forecasting methods which will deal adequately with conditions such as the simultaneous inflation and recession which we are experiencing today. This subject deserves more attention from actuaries in this country.

The case of term insurance is much different. Here mortality and other factors, including persistency and expenses, play a more prominent role in the valuation result. This case is also more susceptible to risk theoretical analysis. This is recognized in the Buol Report. In those cases where term insurance constitutes a significant portion of the company's portfolio, or where the portfolio is either too small or has not been in existence long enough to contain a sufficient savings element, the Working Party has recommended the prescription of an absolute minimum reserve, this fixed minimum reserve subsequently counting towards the mathematical reserve once it exceeds the fixed minimum. A formula developed by the Working Party using risk theoretical methods, is

$$\text{Reserve} = \frac{K_1}{\lambda} \sum P' + \frac{K_2}{\lambda} \overline{S}$$

where

λ = safety loading in premium

$\sum P'$ = total net premium for the portfolio

$\overline{S}$ = probable average amount of all claims

The second term represents the fixed minimum reserve and is eclipsed by the first term for very large portfolios.

In discussing the criteria for acceptable valuation systems, Mr. Montgomery has suggested the use of parameters based on "the most reasonably expected values of those parameters with an adjustment or an additional value to take into account the chances of deviation of those expected values." This has a ring of familiarity! It is, of course, the same basic principle as adopted for the AICPA Audit Guide for Stock Life Insurance Companies - so-called "GAAP accounting." Indeed, the only differences in the application of this principle to valuation regulation on the one hand, and GAAP accounting on the other, would seem to be the selection of the "expected values" and the degree of certainty required in the element of protection against adverse deviations. This suggests that the ideas and techniques developed by the Joint Committee on Theory of Risk are pertinent to the work of the Task Force. John Beekman's excellent paper (Beekman, 1973) presents an analytic approach to the problem of the selection of appropriate margins in the parameters for adverse fluctuations. The Joint Committee has also developed a computerized life insurance company model for the purpose of examining the problem using simulation. It would appear that there is a good probability that the model could be useful in the work of the Task Force.

I certainly agree with Mr. Montgomery that a thorough examination of our valuation standards is very appropriate at this time. The results of any proposed alternate valuation system should be compared with those of our current system in order to determine the degree to which they produce essentially equivalent results. It is conceivable that the current system, with possibly some modification for term insurance and other similar high risk coverages, can be "revalidated," so to speak. It is my hope that those of our profession who can contribute to the important work of the Task Force will respond to Mr. Montgomery's appeal for assistance. It is encouraging that the Task Force already numbers among its contributors a number of highly qualified actuaries, including many at this meeting.

Reinsurance - A Practical Application of Credibility Theory

Richard S. Robertson
The Lincoln National Life Insurance Company

Many reinsurance arrangements provide for experience refunds. Under such arrangements, if the financial experience under the reinsurance ceded by a particular company to a reinsurer has been sufficiently favorable, the reinsurer agrees to share part of the gain resulting from that reinsurance with the original company. The portion of the profits to be shared is determined by a formula which would be part of the reinsurance agreement between the companies. This paper considers a particular type of experience refunding arrangement--that applicable to Risk Premium Reinsurance and more specifically the formula used by my company, The Lincoln National Life Insurance Company. The paper identifies certain problems which relate to credibility theory and which have arisen on account of the experience refunding arrangement. It then discusses the approach used by The Lincoln to analyze these problems.

The Lincoln's Risk Premium Reinsurance agreements provide for an annual experience refund (ER) to the reinsured company according to the following formula.

$$ER = \tfrac{1}{2}(P + A - C - E)$$

P is the earned premimm in the refund account for the year, calculated as the mean of the annual premiums received in the current and previous calendar years.

A is an adjustment for increasing volume equal to 50% of the excess of premiums received in the current year over premiums received in the previous year. If premium volumes are decreasing, 50% of the decrease will be a charge to the refund base.

C is the amount of claims incurred in the year.

E is an "expense charge" computed as a percentage of the earned premium, eP, where e varies between 6% and 10% depending on the size of the account.

If P + A - C - E is negative, that negative amount is carried forward as a charge against the following year's experience. However, any such loss not absorbed by gains of a specified number of future years--typically three or four--is forgiven and not further charged against gains of subsequent years.

This is obviously a relatively simple formula and fails in many respects to accurately measure the true profit contribution of a given reinsurance account. Each company's claims are given full credibility regardless of the size of the reinsurance account. The expense charge is strictly nominal and in no way reflects the actual expenses attributable to an account. No recognition is given to interest earned on reserves and other funds; neither is interest charges against losses carried forward against future years' experience. The "production adjustment," A, has no relation to any element contributing to the profitability of an account but simply is a feature to improve the attractiveness of the reinsurance product by producing experience refunds earlier than otherwise.

One might ask why the formula does not more accurately measure the true contribution of a given reinsurance account to profits. Surely the actuarial tools are available to do so. The answer is largely a matter of customer preference. In the past, we have experimented with refund formulas which more accurately measure the contribution made by a given account. The response to these experiments was that companies purchasing reinsurance much prefer to share in their own full claim experience, regardless of whether that experience could be considered fully credible. It has also been our experienee that persons who have not been deeply involved in credibility theory tend to assign much greater credibility to specific experience than statistical theory indicates would be appropriate.

The cost of experience refunds

The actuarial techniques for pricing Risk Premium Reinsurance are similar to the techniques for pricing other forms of non-participating life insurance. As part of the process, it is necessary to measure the expected profitability of one or more proposed rate schedules. The profitability test would typically involve a formula such as the following:

$$PVP_n = \sum_{x=1}^{n} v^{x-1}(G_x - Q_x - E_x - R_x) - v^{n-1}M_n$$

where:

PVP_n is the present value of profits for the first n years following issue

v is the interest discount factor $\frac{1}{1+i}$

G_x is the expected reinsurance premium from policies in force in year x

Q_x is the expected claim cost for year x

E_x is the expected premium taxes and other expenses in year x

R_x is the expected experience refunds in year x, and

M_n is the reserve at the end of year n, based on the expected in force at that time.

If this expression is written as,

$$PVP_n = \sum_{x=1}^{n} v^{x-1}(G_x - Q_x - E_x) - v^{n-1}M_n - \sum_{x=1}^{n} v^{x-1}R_x$$

the first two terms can be evaluated by normal actuarial techniques, using expected interest, mortality, lapses, etc. The last term, representing the present value of expected experience refunds, requires special handling.

R_x can be expressed as

$$\tfrac{1}{2}\left[H_x - C_x - \sum_{t=1}^{a} {}_tL_{x-t}\right] \quad \text{if} \quad C_x \leq H_x$$

$$\text{or} \quad 0 \quad \text{if} \quad C_x \geq H_x$$

where:

H_x is the expected earned premium plus production adjustment less expense charge in the refund formula--P + A - E.

C_x is a random variable representing the amount of claims in the year. The mean of C_x is the amount of expected claims in the year.

${}_tL_{x-t}$ is the amount of loss represented by excess of C_{x-t} over H_{x-t} in the tth preceding year which is offset in year x.

a is the number of years for which losses may be carried forward.

Algebraically, ${}_tL_{x-t}$ is the smaller of

$$C_{x-t} - H_{x-t} - \sum_{k=1}^{t-1} {}_kL_{x-t} \quad \text{and}$$

$$H_x - C_x - \sum_{k=1}^{t-1} {}_kL_{x-k}$$

but in no event less than zero.

The cost of experience refunds,

$$\sum_{x=1}^{n} V^{x-1} R_x ,$$

can be expressed as

$$\tfrac{1}{2} \sum_{x=1}^{n*} V^{x-1}(H_x - C_x) - \tfrac{1}{2} \sum_{x=1}^{n} \left(V^{x-1} \sum_{t=1}^{a} {}_tL_{x-t} \right)$$

where the asterisk* indicates that only positive terms are to be included in the summation.

$\sum_{x=1}^{n} V^{x-1} \sum_{t=1}^{a} {}_tL_{x-t}$ is equivalent to $\sum_{x=1}^{n} V^{x-1} \sum_{t=1}^{a} V^t \, {}_tL_x$,

as long as ${}_tL_x$ is considered to be zero whenever $x < 1$ or $x + t > n$. Thus,

$$\sum_{x=1}^{n} V^{x-1} R_x = \tfrac{1}{2} \sum_{x=1}^{n*} V^{x-1}(H_x - C_x) - \tfrac{1}{2} \sum_{x=1}^{n} V^{x-1} \sum_{t=1}^{a} V^t \, {}_tL_x$$

$$= \tfrac{1}{2} \sum_{x=1}^{n} V^{x-1} A_x$$

where $A_x = H_x - C_x$ whenever $C_x \leq H_x$

$A_x = \sum_{t=1}^{a} V^t \, {}_tL_x$ whenever $C_x \geq H_x$

(recognizing that ${}_tL_x = 0$ whenever $C_x \leq H_x$).

If $f(y)$ is the frequency distribution function of the random variable, C_x, the expected value of A_x is:

$$\text{Exp}(A_x) = \int_0^{H_x} (H_x - y)f(y)dy - \text{Exp}\left(\sum_{t=1}^{a} V^t \, {}_tL_x \right)$$

$$= \int_0^{\infty} (H_x - y)f(y)dy - \int_{H_x}^{\infty} (H_x - y)f(y)dy - \text{Exp}\left(\sum_{t=1}^{a} V^t \, {}_tL_x \right)$$

$$= H_x - \int_0^{\infty} yf(y)dy + \int_{H_x}^{\infty} (y - H_x)f(y)dy - \text{Exp}\left(\sum_{t=1}^{a} V^t \, {}_tL_x \right) .$$

These expected values can be discounted and summed to give the expected cost of experience refunds.

The first two terms of the above expression represent the cost of the experience refund if experience follows expected mortality. The third term is the expected cost of claims in excess of the portion of the premium which is available to fund those claims. The last term represents the expected amount of such excess which can be recovered out of future profitable years, discounted for interest.

We have not yet been able to develop an analytical method for evaluating the last term. Lacking such a procedure, we have two other methods which we have used for estimating the cost of the experience refund in excess of what the cost would be if expected mortality is realized: a historical method and a simulation method.

Historical cost

Historically, our records tell us each year how much of the year's claims are charged against the current year's premiums and how much are carried forward against future years' experience. Those records also indicate the aggregate amount of losses of each previous year which are effectively offset in the current year. Hence, we have a good record of the historical cost of our experience refund formula.

There are a number of limitations on the degree to which historical cost is a reasonable measure of future cost. First, the historical cost varies from year to year as a result of statistical fluctuation. Hence, there is a limitation on the degree of accuracy with which it measures expected cost. Second, the cost depends on the gross premium structure. The lower the reinsurance premium, the less margin available to absorb loss fluctuations and therefore the greater the cost. If the historical method is to be used to estimate the change in cost of experience refunds after a change in premiums, it is necessary to recalculate, on an account by account basis, what the experience refunds would have been had a different premium structure been in effect. The third limitation of the historical method is that it measures costs in aggregate and does not indicate the extent to which those costs vary by size and character of the account. Although historical cost measures can be made of various classes of accounts, statistical fluctuations become significant enough that information gained from such studies is limited.

Simulation

We have had considerable success in measuring the cost of the experience refund formula through simulating the experience of individual accounts. By constructing a model reinsurance account, determining claims according to a random process, applying the experience refund formula using those claims, and repeating the process a large number of times, we determine the portion of claims which are charged against experience in the current year, the portion charged against the experience of each of the next a years, and the amount which represents losses which are forgiven without being charged against the experience of any year. This, then, enables us to determine the cost of the experience refund formula for accounts which are similar in characteristics to the model.

By varying the characteristics of the model, it is possible to develop a formula which measures the cost of a function of the size of the account, the average size policy exposed, and other characteristics of the distribution of the account. That formula can then be applied to each account to determine the cost of its experience refunds and the results combined to determine the total cost of the refund formula for all accounts.

We have used both the historical method and the simulation method to calculate the cost. Because we realized approximately the same result both ways, we are confident that our procedures are correct.

Other uses of the simulation method

The simulation method makes it possible to evaluate the cost of various changes in the experience refund formula. For example, our procedures provide that no more than a specified amount per life can be included in the experience refunding experience. Larger amounts of reinsurance on one life are accepted on the basis of lower, non-refunding rates. By varying the maximum amount exposed in an account, we have been able to determine the effect of changing the rules which define how much can be exposed on one life. It turns out that this maximum amount is a very critical item in determining the cost of the refund formula.

As another example, we have been able to evaluate the effect of changing a, the number of years losses can be carried forward.

Occasionally, a customer wishes to have modifications made in his experience refund formula. We are willing to do so provided that the net cost is not significantly changed. We might be willing, for example, to increase the maximum amount which can be included on one life in return for lengthening the carryforward period or increasing the expense charge. The simulation method allows us to determine what a fair trade-off would be.

We also determined that for certain classes of accounts, typically the smaller accounts, the cost of the experience refund formula was substantially out of line with the cost of other accounts. As a result of such studies, we now require that, for accounts of less than a certain minimum size, the experience refunds will be calculated on the pooled experience rather than for each company individually. At the same time, we initiated a program of varying the expense charge by size of account to recognize the variation in cost for different size accounts.

GAAP accounting

The procedures and formulas we use for establishing GAAP reserves on Risk Premium Reinsurance are designed so that, if mortality and other experience follows the actuarial assumptions, the profit will be released uniformly over the life of the reinsurance. However, those reserves do not recognize that a claim occurring in one accounting period may have the effect of reducing the experience refund in a subsequent accounting period. If no adjustment is made, adverse experience in one accounting period could have the effect of actually increasing profits in a subsequent period. This did not seem reasonable. Accordingly, we took steps to recognize that losses being carried forward into subsequent years have value and that value should be attributed to the accounting period in which the losses arose.

The historical method proved to be the most effective way of determining how these losses should be recognized. Working with our historical records as to the portion of loss carryforwards which will be charged against the experience of each of the a subsequent years, we developed factors representing "expected recoveries." These expected recoveries were then discounted with interest to develop factors which can be applied to the amount of the loss to determine its value for accounting purposes. That accounting value was then deducted from the aggregate reserves to produce the net reserve which we carry.

In actual experience, the amount of losses which are recovered in a given year may be greater or less than the expected amounts. If the losses recovered are greater, the experience refunds which are paid will be less than expected, and there will be additional profit in such subsequent years. Similarly, if the recoveries are less than anticipated, this would be a source of loss in the subsequent year.

Discussion by John C. Wooddy of Reinsurance - A Practical Application of Credibility Theory

The first thing I noted in the experience refund formula in Dick Robertson's paper is that the quantity $P + A$ is the premiums received during the year, which my company refers to as "cash premiums."

I concur with the comment that this type of formula, which is general in the life reinsurance business in the United States, does lack theoretical justification.

Also, it is true that a reinsurer's expenses on a given account are not generally covered by the expense charge in the refund formula even if every account had low enough claims so that E were collectible.

The question may be raised as to whether Reinsurance experience refunds do, in fact, constitute an example of an application of credibility theory. As I understand the underlying condition which leads to use of credibility concepts, there is uncertainty as to what the "true" premium should be, but it is possible to develop an acceptable "manual" premium, with the final, actual premium to be determined partly by the actual experience on the case. In theory this should allow for actual premiums to be either higher or lower than manual premiums. Reinsurance experience refunds are never negative, however.

With some heavy-handed manipulation, it might be said that the refund formula in the paper implies 50% credibility of the ceding company's reinsurance claim experience, rather than 100% as stated (in the paper). A more fruitful approach, and one which is implied by the development of the cost of refunds, is to regard reinsurance experience refunds as reinsurance benefits, amounts of money which are paid on the occurrence of specified contingencies. This view acquires even more plausibility when a particular reinsurance account is followed over a period of years. In any case, the concepts of participating individual insurance should not be applied to reinsurance experience refunds.

Dick notes that the prevalence of the present formula for calculating refunds is a matter of customer preference; it is also a matter of reinsurance salesman preference. This may have something to do with sticking to what is easy to explain. As a sidelight, it is curious that Group business, presumably sold by less sophisticated salesmen to less sophisticated buyers, is characterized by more complex refund formulae. Perhaps in the Group field both parties are more resigned to not understanding insurance - or actuaries. Another explanation may be that the ceding company executive recognizes the chance to "stick" the reinsurer with a string of no-claim years followed by a string of heavy-claim years. I have toyed with the idea of offering our clients a lottery ticket each year in lieu of experience refunds.

As Dick points out, the historical approach to costing Experience Refunds has limitations. A particular reinsurance account will typically have premiums based on several different scales. Also, the in force will be subject to several different standards of expected mortality, which will not vary in step with the variation in premium rate scales.

The simulation approach is interesting and more details would be welcome. In particular, are simulations run only to determine expected values or also to learn something regarding variation around expected values?

DISCUSSION

As a reinsurance practitioner, I found Dick's paper most interesting. I think that actuaries who work for ceding insurers also will gain some understanding of the reinsurer's point of view on the matter of refunds. Finally, it is useful to have in written form a "state of the art" description of YRT experience refunds in the 70's.

Credibility in Workmen's Compensation Ratemaking*

David Skurnick
California Inspection Rating Bureau

1. The ratemaking method

In recent years great progress has been made in credibility theory and exciting new discoveries continue to appear. The process of advancing the state of the art will not be complete until these improved theoretical concepts lead to the development of improved practical rating and ratemaking plans, and to their implementation. It is appropriate then to present to the Berkeley Actuarial Conference a description of a particular plan or method in current use along with suggestions of aspects wherein modern credibility theory might be applied to improve it.

Across the Bay lies the California Inspection Rating Bureau, which makes rates for a billion dollars of workmen's compensation business. Under its ratemaking procedure, an overall rate level change is calculated on the basis of total statewide experience, then this change is distributed to the individual classifications based upon class experience. The class experience is given a credibility reflecting its volume. This paper will present a description of the class credibility procedure and a discussion of areas of possible improvement.

It should be noted that only class credibility will be

*Any opinions expressed herein are those of the writer and should not be taken to reflect the position of the California Inspection Rating Bureau, its members, or its Committees.

discussed, not risk credibility, as used in experience rating. These appear quite different from a theoretical viewpoint, although by pretending that an individual classification is one large risk, one can see that the two types of credibility are closely related.

In the C.I.R.B.'s annual rate review, the overall rate change is allocated to classification based upon pure premiums by policy year. (For the benefit of the life actuaries present, a pure premium is the ratio of losses to exposure, measured in hundreds of dollars of payroll.) Credibility is applied separately to serious, non-serious and medical pure premiums for each classification, with the amount of credibility depending upon the amount of expected losses. A serious case is one involving either death, permanent total disability, or major permanent partial disability. A non-serious case is one involving either minor permanent partial or temporary total disability. Medical losses include medical incurred on compensable cases and also medical only cases.

The criteria for assigning 100% credibility to the pure premium indications for any classification have been set at:

(1) Serious expected losses equal to 50 times the state average cost of a serious case.

(2) Non-serious expected losses equal to 300 times the state average cost of a non-serious case.

(3) Medical expected losses equal to 80% of the non-serious expected losses required for 100% credibility.

Partial credibility is assigned by the formula

$$\begin{pmatrix}\text{partial}\\\text{credibility}\end{pmatrix} = \left(\frac{\text{actual expected losses}}{\text{expected losses required for 100\% credibility}}\right)^{2/3}$$

The credibility table used for the 1974 rate filing is shown in Figure 1. This table is recalculated each year. Its values have tended to increase with inflation and benefit increases.

A second aspect of credibility is the varying number of years. Between two and five years of experience are used for each classification, in each case using the minimum number of years necessary to achieve 100% credibility in all three loss categories. Figure 2, which shows the pure premium review sheets for several classes, illustrates this principle.

Classes 0016 and 0017 exemplify the case where two years of experience provide 100% credibility. Even five years of experience failed to provide 100% credibility for classes 0013, 0034, and 0035, while four years were enough for class 0005.

The pure premium review sheets are used to determine the proper relative level among classifications. First the payrolls and losses for up to five policy years are listed. These losses have been adjusted to current benefit and loss level and developed to a third report basis. The policy year totals produce the pure premiums indicated by policy year experience. The pure premiums underlying on indicated level represent the actual dollar provisions for losses in the current rates, adjusted to be on a comparable basis with the indicated pure premiums. The formula pure premiums are the weighted averages of the indicated and underlying pure premiums, where the weights applied to the indicated pure premiums are the credibilities, shown in the lower left-hand corner of the sheet.

A third aspect of credibility is that classes are limited to a 25% increase or decrease in underlying pure premium in

Credibility Table

Cred.	Expected Serious Losses	Expected Non-Serious Losses	Expected Medical Losses
1.00	980,500	459,200	367,400
.95	907,900	425,300	340,200
.90	837,300	392,200	313,800
.85	768,700	360,000	288,000
.80	702,000	328,800	263,100
.75	637,300	298,500	238,800
.70	574,600	269,100	215,300
.65	513,800	240,600	192,500
.60	455,900	213,500	170,800
.55	400,000	187,400	149,900
.50	347,100	162,600	130,100
.45	296,100	138,700	111,000
.40	248,100	116,200	93,000
.35	203,000	95,100	76,100
.30	160,800	75,300	60,300
.25	122,600	57,400	45,900
.20	87,300	40,900	32,700
.15	56,900	26,600	21,300
.10	31,400	14,700	11,800
.05	10,800	5,100	4,000

Figure 1

a single year. Code 0035 illustrates this situation. In this year's rate filing, out of 418 classes, 14 were affected by this rule. They are shown in Figure 3.

It is noteworthy that beyond providing separate crediblity criteria for each of the three claim categories, no further action is taken to smooth out the effects of large losses. By comparison, in property insurance ratemaking catastrophes are excluded, and in California workmen's compensation experience rating there is a separation of individual claims into primary and excess portions with different credibilities for each as well as a per accident limit and a special treatment of accidents involving two or more persons.

2. Effect of the limitation rule

The selected pure premium is limited to a maximum departure of 25% from the pure premium underlying the present Manual rate. In order to study the effect of this rule, the number of classes affected were tabulated on Figure 4.

Number of Classes Limited to a 25% Increase or Decrease

Year	Inc.	Dec.	Total
1964	7	6	13
1965	5	2	7
1966	4	1	5
1967	7	4	11
1968	9	3	12
1969	5	5	10
1970	12	3	15
(Began use of 5 years of classification experience rather than 2.)			
1971 (4/1/72)	10	3	13
1972	8	6	14
1973	4	0	4
1974	10	4	14
	81	37	118

Figure 4

Codes Affected by Limitation Rule

Code	Page #	Deviation from Underlying P.P. Prior to Limit	After Limit
Limited to 25% Decrease:			
5507	78	.745	.750
5606	79	.717	.750
5651	80	.701	.750
7410	97	.605	.750
Limited to 25% Increase:			
0035	2	1.257	1.250
0251	5	1.400	1.250
1122	7	1.267	1.250
1624	7	1.267	1.250
7424	98	1.463	1.250
7429	99	1.270	1.250
7722	104	1.519	1.250
8838	124	1.257	1.250
9410	134	1.395	1.250
9610	139	1.302	1.250

Figure 3

(C.I.R.B. - October, 1974 Revision)

It is apparent that relatively few classes are affected, an average of about 10 per year out of over 400. The number of classes affected has not changed during the period 1964-1974 despite inflation and a change in ratemaking methodology, to include up to five years of class experience rather than just two. Increases were limited more than twice as often as decreases, which is not surprising.

It is my opinion that the limitation rule has been a useful part of the ratemaking process. It would be interesting to see a theoretical justification for this type of limitation.

3. Relative equality of the three credibilities

An important feature of the ratemaking system is that the three types of loss have separate credibility standards, the amount of expected losses for 100% credibility being 50 average serious claims for serious, 300 average non-serious claims for non-serious and 80% of the non-serious amount for medical. In the 1974 filing the dollar amounts corresponding to this rule were $980,500 for serious, $459,200 for non-serious and $367,400 for medical. Thus the medical pure premiums, which fluctuate less, can be given a higher credibility, while the serious pure premiums, which fluctuate more, are given a lower credibility. The standards are defined in terms of expected loss rather than actual loss to avoid the bias of giving poor experience higher credibility than good experience. Also, since the standards are defined in terms of average claims, they are not affected by inflation and do not need frequent revision. In fact, these standards are unchanged from the ones long utilized by the National Council as described in Marshall's 1954 article.*

---

*Marshall, R. M., Workmen's Compensation Insurance Ratemaking, P.C.A.S. XLI (1954).

The long use of these particular standards raises the question of whether they are still in balance, whether 300 expected non-serious claims still merit the same credibility as 50 expected serious claim and so forth. But what does this balance consist of? How can it be measured statistically? Unfortunately, it has not been possible to locate a description of the type of equivalence that the standards were designed to achieve. It was necessary to consider the question afresh.

Clearly, the standards do not reflect the variation in the pure premium from year to year, but rather the variation in incurred loss. Two classes with the same expected loss and, presumably, the same variability in incurred loss will receive the same credibility, even though the one with the larger payroll will have less variation in pure premium. More precisely, the standards reflect variation in incurred loss, but not the portion of this variation resulting from changes in exposure from year to year.

In order to test the equivalence of the three credibility standards, samples were taken from the 1974 pure premium review sheets consisting of the serious losses for all classes with serious credibility between .45 and .55, the non-serious losses for all classes with non-serious credibility between .45 and .55 and the medical losses for all classes with medical credibility between .45 and .55. Each sample consists of five years of experience, adjusted to current benefit level, for between 25 and 30 classes. It was initially suspected that the amount of variance would serve as a measure of fluctuation, but the serious losses had by far the largest variance because they had the largest dollars of expected loss corresponding to 50% credibility. If the standard for 100% credibility were increased, then there would be an increase, not a decrease, in the variance of the losses of those classes with credibility between .45 and .55.

The coefficient of variation appeared to be a more appropriate measure, so it was estimated from the samples.

Incurred Loss - Classes with Credibility between .45 and .55

		Serious	Non-Serious	Medical
1.	Mean	67,377	34,887	27,600
2.	Variance	1,622,331,760	375,440,001	145,544,777
3.	Standard Deviation	40,278	19,376	12,064
4.	Coefficient of Variation (3) ÷ (1)	.598	.555	.437

The coefficients of variation indicate that the three credibility standards are fairly well in balance. The figures also suggest that there is more variation in severity among non-serious claims than among serious claims, relative to the average claim size in the category.

Of course, this reasoning does not prove that the coefficient of variation of incurred loss is the best indicator of balanced credibility standards. The coefficient of variation of the pure premiums may well be better. This portion of the article ends with a request to the theoreticians present to study this problem and either justify the use of the coefficient of variation of incurred loss or of pure premium for determining equality of credibility standards or discover a superior measure.

4. The time series viewpoint

When credibility is applied in experience rating, the selected value is the weighted average of an indicated value, based upon the individual risk's experience, and an underlying value, based upon the experience of all risks in the class. By comparison, in the application of credibility to class ratemaking, the selected value is the weighted average of an indicated value, based upon the individual classification's experience, and an underlying value, based upon the current rate of the same individual classification. The current rate was based upon the individual classification's prior experience and prior rate, and so forth. In effect, the class credibility mechanism produces a function which forecasts a time series from its past values.

There is an overlap between the experience contributing to the indicated value and the experience contributing to the current rate. As a result, it will be shown that the forecast function which is derived from the credibility formula does not appear to be the best one available.

For example, consider a class for which the full five years of experience produces 50% credibility for each of serious, non-serious and medical. For the sake of the example, assume that the use of five years of class experience has been part of the ratemaking for a long time and that in all past rate revisions this class has developed precisely 50% credibility. The 1974 rate is a weighted average of the 1973 rate and the experience of policy years 1971, 1970, 1969, 1968 and 1967, with weights:

1971	experience	10%
1970	"	10%
1969	"	10%
1968	"	10%
1967	"	10%
1973	rate	50%

The 1973 rate is itself a weighted average of the 1966-1970 experience and the 1972 rate, with weights corresponding to those above, so the 1974 rate may be expressed as a weighted average of the 1966-1971 experience and the 1972 rate, with weights:

1971	experience	10%
1970	"	15%
1969	"	15%
1968	"	15%
1967	"	15%
1966	"	5%
1972	rate	25%

It is easy to see that if this process is continued the sequence of weights will converge, so that the 1974 rate can be expressed as a weighted average of the experience of policy years 1971, 1970, 1969, 1968, 1967, 1966, 1965,..., with weights .10, .15, .175, .1875, .19375, .19375 × 1/2, .19375 × 1/4,..., respectively. Of course, all these years are adjusted to current level, so there is no bias, but responsiveness could only be improved by giving the greatest weight to the most recent possible year.

5. A serious claim is a serious claim is a serious claim

In assigning a credibility to a classification's serious pure premium based upon expected serious losses, one in effect assumes that the severity distribution of serious losses is the same from class to class. The same assumption is made for non-serious and medical losses.

To test this assumption, ten classes of varying types and degrees of hazard were selected and their average serious and non-serious losses were calculated.

In fact, the average claim sizes do not very too much from class to class. High average serious claims do not necessarily correlate with high average non-serious claims. Average serious claim size varies less from class to class than average non-serious claim size.

Average Claim Size by Classification*

	Serious	Non-Serious
0017 - Truck Farms and Vineyards	18,860	967
2081 - Butchering	16,699	1048
3085 - Foundries--non-ferrious N.O.C.	14,800	1456
7219 - Truckmen N.O.C.	20,582	1709
7405 - Aircraft Operation--Scheduled--Flying Crew	22,635	584
8350 - Gasoline or Oil Dealers--wholesale	20,758	1555
8803 - Auditors, Accountants	13,204	1398
8810 - Clerical Office	16,717	1705
8875 - Public Colleges or Schools	21,395	1202
9050 - Hotels and Motels	14,183	1165

Even though the variation in average size from class to class is not too great, it would be desirable to adjust the credibility standards in some appropriate way to take into account the differences in average claim size. Perhaps there is some simple adjustment formula that uses the average claim size to increase the accuracy of the credibility assigned. This would be a useful result for someone to obtain.

6. Stability and responsiveness

Credibility serves the purpose of striking a balance between stability and responsiveness. The higher the volume required for 100% credibility, the more stable the rates will be. The lower the volume required for 100% credibility, the more responsive the rates will be to current conditions. In this sense it is possible to measure the effectiveness of a particular credibility scale by checking the premium rates it produces over time for stability and responsiveness.

*At current benefit level developed to a third report basis.

Of course, it would not do to simply compare actual rates, since a portion of the rate change results from items to which the credibility is unrelated. In the case of the C.I.R.B.'s ratemaking, these items include the overall rate level change due to experience, changes in benefits and merit rating off-balance changes. Seven classes were chosen and their rates were adjusted to indicate only the effect of the credibility related portion; the adjusted rates were then expressed as a multiple of the 1955 rate and twenty years of rates were graphed. These graphs are shown on Figure 5.

The first two classes, Code 7219 - Truckmen N.O.C. and Code 8810 - Clerical Office Employees, are so large that their rates can be considered to be perfectly responsive and without any excess instability. Both codes had gradual rate increases of about 10% during the 20 year period.

Code 8106 - Iron or Steel Merchants is barely 100% credible. Its rate has fluctuated above and below the 1955 level, although it is currently very close to it. A higher standard for 100% credibility would have reduced the rate fluctuation for this class.

Code 7601 - Telephone Line Construction has only moderate crediblity. It has been slightly more stable than Iron or Steel Merchants. Incidentally, prior to 1972, only two years of experience were used in ratemaking for all classes and so the credibility for Code 7601 was even lower than indicated on Figure 5.

Code 9078 - Commissary Work is a low credibility class. Its rate has been quite stable. Apparently the low credibility damped out the fluctuations in indicated pure premium.

Code 8215 - Hay, Grain or Feed Dealers was chosen because it had a single large loss during policy year 1960, which first entered the ratemaking process in 1963. The loss amount was $186,000, as compared with $171,788 for the total of all losses the year before. This one loss had an ephemeral effect on the rate level, which suggests that rates could be more accurate if very large losses were spread over a greater number of years. Use of five years of experience has improved the situation, but the problem is apt to become more serious due to advances in health care that make it possible for severely injured people to survive but at enormous medical cost. Large losses could also become more common under the increased benefits recommended by the National Commission on State Workmen's Compensation Laws and included in the proposed Williams-Javits Bill.

Code 5606 - Contractors--Executive Supervisors has probably had the most unstable rate of any class in the Manual. Perhaps it should not have been included in this article, since there is no reason to believe that the instability results from any credibility problems. Rather, the shifting rate is probably due to revisions in the application of the class and misassignment of losses. Nevertheless, it is useful to observe the effect of the credibility criteria on this erratic class. Without the 25% limitation, its rate would have been even more unstable.

An analysis of six classes cannot be conclusive, but Figure 5 illustrates one technique that can be used for evaluating a particular credibility system. In addition, it suggssts that the current system generally produces reasonably stable rates, although the system might be improved by introducing a new technique to handle large losses.

In order to measure responsiveness to current conditions it is necessary to somehow measure current conditions. This is not easy. One possible approach would be to take the actual experience for a year as reflecting the current conditions. In order to take this approach a number of problems would first have to be solved, including the following:

(1) Rates are effective for the year beginning October 1; experience is kept for the policy year beginning January 1.

(2) There have been frequent mid-year rate changes.

(3) Adjustments should be made for benefit changes and for those aspects of the rate level not related to credibility.

(4) The actual class experience for a year is subject to random fluctuation.

Nevertheless, it is possible that responsiveness of a ratemaking scheme could be tested by designing an objective function or loss function that represents the sum of the differences between the expected losses and the actual losses for each class. (See, for example, Peters (1941), wherein he measured the deviation of actual from expected losses as $\log_{10}$ (actual losses/expected losses).) Then a particular credibility scheme could be given a responsiveness rating based upon the value assumed by this objective function when applied to the expected losses, at the rates generated by this credibility scheme and the actual losses.

C.I.R.B. PURE PREMIUM REVIEW SHEET – 1974 PAGE 1

CODE: 0005 0 CLASS: Nurseryman

POLICY YEAR	PAYROLL	SERIOUS NO.	SERIOUS AMOUNT	NON-SERIOUS NO.	NON-SERIOUS AMOUNT	MEDICAL AMOUNT	TOTAL AMOUNT	TOTAL P.P.
1967								
1968	45,728,112	14	304842	266	236346	257685	798873	1.747
1969	50,984,345	8	122879	286	289251	251411	663541	1.301
1970	54,550,789	24	378967	271	294015	342906	1015888	1.862
1971	60,725,192	16	212761	297	331009	348445	892215	1.469
TOTAL	211,988,438	62	1019449	1120	1150621	1200447	3370517	XXXX
P.P. INDIC. BY POL. YR. EXP.			.481		.543	.566		1.590
P.P. UND. ON INDIC. LEVEL			.553		.512	.574		1.639
P.P. FORMULA	SER 1.00 NS 1.00	MED 1.00	.481		.543	.566		1.590

CODE: 0013 M CLASS: Salt Production

POLICY YEAR	PAYROLL	SERIOUS NO.	SERIOUS AMOUNT	NON-SERIOUS NO.	NON-SERIOUS AMOUNT	MEDICAL AMOUNT	TOTAL AMOUNT	TOTAL P.P.
1967	881,940	1	14233	7	9003	6925	30161	3.420
1968	860,228					914	914	.106
1969	384,235			2	671	2590	3261	.849
1970	902,545	2	51972	4	7449	9701	69122	7.659
1971	1,215,414	1	11268	8	3675	5833	20776	1.709
TOTAL	4,244,362	4	77473	21	20798	25963	124234	XXXX
P.P. INDIC. BY POL. YR. EXP.			1.825		.490	.612		2.927
P.P. UND. ON INDIC. LEVEL			2.002		.780	.748		3.530
P.P. FORMULA	SER .20 NS .15	MED .20	1.967		.737	.720		3.424

CODE: 0016 0 CLASS: Orchards

POLICY YEAR	PAYROLL	SERIOUS NO.	SERIOUS AMOUNT	NON-SERIOUS NO.	NON-SERIOUS AMOUNT	MEDICAL AMOUNT	TOTAL AMOUNT	TOTAL P.P.
1967								
1968								
1969								
1970	181,448,123	103	1812956	1673	1602052	1799946	5214954	2.874
1971	185,218,054	125	1782695	1610	1668698	1725305	5176698	2.795
TOTAL	366,666,177	228	3595651	3283	3270750	3525251	10391652	XXXX
P.P. INDIC. BY POL. YR. EXP.			.981		.892	.961		2.834
P.P. UND. ON INDIC. LEVEL			1.037		.971	1.122		3.130
P.P. FORMULA	SER 1.00 NS 1.00	MED 1.00	.981		.892	.961		2.834

C.I.R.B. PURE PREMIUM REVIEW SHEET – 1974 PAGE 2

Exhibit 2

CODE: 0017 0 CLASS: Truck Farms and Vineyards

POLICY YEAR	PAYROLL	SERIOUS NO.	SERIOUS AMOUNT	NON-SERIOUS NO.	NON-SERIOUS AMOUNT	MEDICAL AMOUNT	TOTAL AMOUNT	TOTAL P.P.
1967								
1968								
1969								
1970	422,563,526	144	3047834	2283	1947341	2117491	7112666	1.683
1971	475,870,983	193	3308014	2382	2565476	3078381	8951871	1.881
TOTAL	898,434,509	337	6355848	4665	4512817	5195872	16064537	XXXX
P.P. INDIC. BY POL. YR. EXP.			.707		.502	.578		1.787
P.P. UND. ON INDIC. LEVEL			.612		.507	.542		1.661
P.P. FORMULA	SER 1.00 NS 1.00	MED 1.00	.707		.502	.578		1.787

CODE: 0034 0 CLASS: Poultry Raising

POLICY YEAR	PAYROLL	SERIOUS NO.	SERIOUS AMOUNT	NON-SERIOUS NO.	NON-SERIOUS AMOUNT	MEDICAL AMOUNT	TOTAL AMOUNT	TOTAL P.P.
1967	30,660,635	21	326886	322	263335	302965	893186	2.913
1968	30,091,407	15	200129	241	255116	214774	670019	2.227
1969	34,210,308	18	242243	281	273442	279766	795451	2.325
1970	37,232,308	16	370028	277	308855	288481	967364	2.598
1971	37,223,433	16	253450	242	296774	278505	828729	2.226
TOTAL	169,418,091	86	1392736	1363	1397522	1364491	4154749	XXXX
P.P. INDIC. BY POL. YR. EXP.			.822		.825	.805		2.452
P.P. UND. ON INDIC. LEVEL			.685		.887	.797		2.369
P.P. FORMULA	SER 1.00 NS 1.00	MED 1.00	.822		.825	.805		2.452

CODE: 0035 0 CLASS: Florists - cultivating

POLICY YEAR	PAYROLL	SERIOUS NO.	SERIOUS AMOUNT	NON-SERIOUS NO.	NON-SERIOUS AMOUNT	MEDICAL AMOUNT	TOTAL AMOUNT	TOTAL P.P.
1967	32,964,999	6	124892	154	142548	140975	408415	1.239
1968	37,723,002	8	185838	162	140030	173350	499218	1.323
1969	42,387,170	8	153999	143	125860	133930	413789	.976
1970	45,156,566	5	79734	176	160428	169241	409403	.907
1971	47,388,115	14	350150	161	201833	312683	864666	1.825
TOTAL	205,619,852	41	894613	796	770699	930179	2595491	XXXX
P.P. INDIC. BY POL. YR. EXP.			.435		.375	.452		1.262
P.P. UND. ON INDIC. LEVEL			.294		.329	.374		.997
P.P. FORMULA	SER .70 NS 1.00	MED 1.00	.393		.375	.452		1.220
P.P. Selected (Ltd.)			.390		.373	.449		1.212

Exhibit 5
Sheet 1

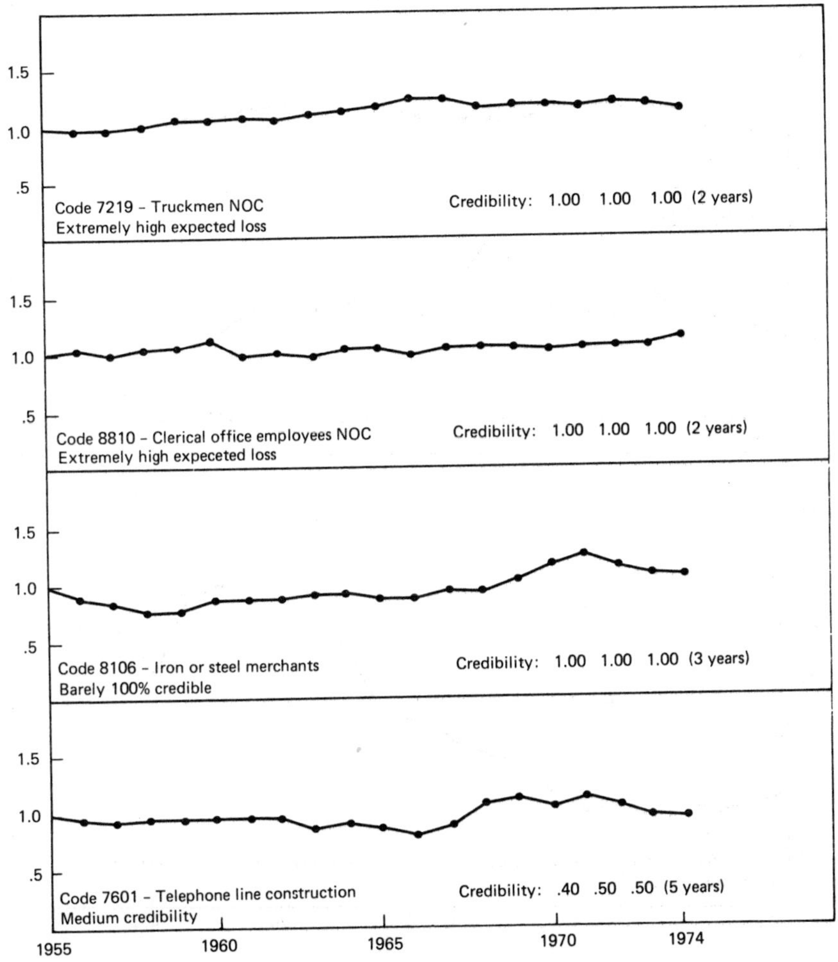

Classification Rates Indexed to 1955

Adjusted to remove effects of overall rate level change due to experience, benefit changes, and experience rating off-balance changes

Exhibit 5
Sheet 2

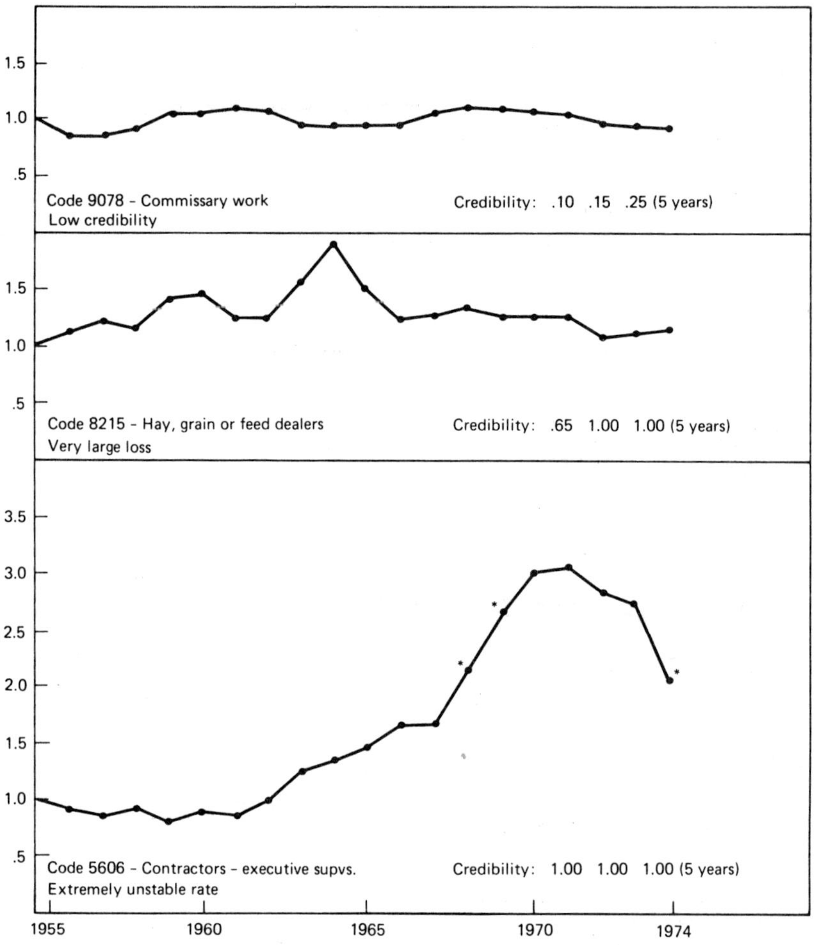

* Subject to 25% limitation

Classification Rates Indexed to 1955

Adjusted to remove effects of overall rate level change due to experience, benefit changes, and experience rating off-balance changes

Discussion by Clarence R. Atwood of Credibility in Workmen's Compensation Ratemaking

David Skurnick's paper describes the credibility procedures used in California for Workmen's Compensation rates by class. These procedures are set forth in detail together with a discussion of their ramifications. His paper describes the problems that arise in evaluating the appropriateness and consistency of the credibility procedures used in this particular application.

Two unique features of credibility as applied in Workmen's Compensation Classification Ratemaking are:

1. There are separate credibility requirements for the three Categories of "serious" and "nonserious" and "medical" claims.
2. Credibility varies with the total dollar amount of expected claims when applied. Other lines of insurance often use credibility keyed solely to number of claims.

The standards for full credibility are 50 "serious" claims, 300 "nonserious" claims and 80% of the "nonserious" claims for "medical." Skurnick sampled those classes with credibility between .45 and .55 to analyze the relative credibility of "serious," "nonserious" and "medical" claims. He then compared the coefficient of variation for these three categories of claims by calculating the variances and means of the incurred losses from the five policy years of data which he analyzed. Using these five observations of the random variable T to calculate the variance and mean of the total losses has its limitations. Skurnick mentioned one of the limitations when he discussed the distortions caused by changes in exposure by policy year. Another limitation is the use of only five values for estimating the moments of T. By use of the Mayerson, Jones and Bowers formula he could have calculated the moments of the total losses from the moments of the frequency and claim amount distributions separately. For example, on page 180 of the Mayerson, Jones and Bowers' paper, P.C.A.S., Vol. LV (1968), the expected number of claims for full credibility is:

$$\lambda = \frac{Z_e^2}{k^2}\left(\frac{\lambda_2}{\lambda} + \frac{\mu_2}{\mu^2}\right) \tag{1}$$

where,

μ = mean of claim amount distribution

μ_2 = variance of claim amount distribution

λ = mean of claims distribution

λ_2 = variance of claims distribution

$Z_e = 100\left(\frac{1+P}{2}\right)$ percentile of standard normal distribution with P and k equal assumed values, usually $P = .90$ and $k = .05$

If one assumes a Poisson distribution for the number of claims then:

$$\lambda_2 = \lambda$$

and,

$$\lambda = \frac{Z_e^2}{k^2}\left(1 + \frac{\mu_2}{\mu^2}\right) \tag{2}$$

A more accurate calculation of the coefficient of variation for the total loss can be derived from large bodies of data by analyzing the frequency and claim amount distributions separately. On page 183 of the paper by Mayerson, Jones and Bowers an example of Perryman's credibility techniques as applied to California Workmen's Compensation losses is illustrated. From these calculations it would appear that the moments of the claim amount distribution were ignored in establishing the standards of 50 "serious" claims and 300 "nonserious" claims for full credibility. Secondly, the Mayerson, Jones and Bowers" calculations indicate that there should be two and a half times as many "nonserious" claims for full credibility as for "serious." The present California procedures require six times as many "nonserious" claims as "serious." The Mayerson, Jones and Bowers calculations were based upon data by Dropkin in his paper, "Size of Loss Distributions in Workmen's Compensation Insurance," published in 1964 in The Proceedings of the Casualty Actuarial Society. They calculated that 1610 claims were needed for full credibility after analyzing 4721 major permanent partial cases which were included in the Dropkin study. They further concluded that 4,016 claims were needed for full credibility after analyzing 60,398 temporary total disability claims also included in the Dropkin study. Both of these calculations were based upon values of $k = .05$ and $P = .90$. However, there are probably practical reasons why standards for credibility can not be set at the higher values derived by Mayerson, Jones and Bowers.

Skurnick wrote, "Credibility serves the purpose of striking a balance between stability and responsiveness. The higher the volume required for 100% credibility, the more stable the rates will be. The lower the volume required for 100% credibility, the more responsive the rates will be to current conditions." Since the overall rate level is calculated separately, and it does not depend upon the credibility standards imposed by class, his statements apply to the relationship between the classes. It would be appropriate to view credibility as a formulization by which we consistently respond to new information using as much of the new information as possible without discarding what we already know. The claim amount distribution and to a lesser extent the frequency distribution are changing with time and we must respond to these changes subject to practical limitations. Credibility standards should not be used to keep the rates stable but used to stabilize fluctuations caused by sparseness of data.

In California the number of policy years used for each classification's experience varies between 2 and 5 years using the minimum number of years necessary to achieve 100% credibility in all three loss categories for that particular class. This variation in number of policy years to achieve full credibility illustrates another function of credibility often de-emphasized in the ratemaking process. Through standards of credibility we are merging the new experience with the old experience subject to the constraints that we give maximum response to new experience and the time interval for the experience be as short as possible. Too often we use credibility to give proportional weights to the pure premium underlying the current rate and new experience and assume the current rate represents the optimum estimate derived from all prior knowledge. Loss costs and frequencies change over time and when the time span varies from class to class, as in ratemaking for California Workmen's Compensation, it is difficult to establish equitable rates unless a base classification is used. The base classification could be one for which we are confident of the pure premium and one for which we can relate the pure premiums of each of the other classes. The time period could then vary considerably by class provided the base pure premium was re-calculated to correspond. In other words, if the initial objective was to calculate a relativity factor for each class rather than the pure premium one could vary the time period used for each class to obtain full credibility. However, the small variation in time period without a base class as used in California should not cause a serious problem.

Skurnick said, "Even though the variation in average claim size from class to class is not too great, it would be desirable to adjust the credibility standards in some appropriate way to take into account the differences in average claim size. Perhaps there is some simple adjustment formula that uses the average claim size to increase the accuracy of the credibility assigned. This would be a useful result for someone to obtain." He notes that there is little variation in the average size of claim from class to class for each of the three categories of "serious," "non-serious" and "medical" claims. It is customary to combine "death," "permanent total," and "major permanent partial" cases under the category "serious." Perhaps the variation in the average size of claim would be reduced further if he compared the average "death" claim from class to class and the average "permanent total" claim from class to class etc., rather than the average "serious" claim. This separation would also apply to "nonserious" claims which are composed of "minor permanent partial," and "temporary total." In other words, it would be appropriate to investigate the credibility standards for each of the subcategories that comprise "serious" and "nonserious" claims in any attempt to derive separate credibility standards for each class.

Skurnick notes, "It is noteworthy that beyond providing separate credibility criteria for each of the three claim categories, no further action has taken to smooth out the effects of large losses"...A third aspect of credibility is that classes are limited to a 25% increase or decrease in underlying pure premiums in a single year." To some extent the limitation rule does smooth out the effects of large losses but it would appear more manageable to limit the size of loss to be included in the pure premlum calculations. A limit on the size of the loss would change the moments of the loss amount distribution and reduce the number of claims required for full credibility.

Mr. Skurnick has made a major contribution to credibility discussion by highlighting several practical problems that need to be solved and asking for help in resolving these problems.

Discussion by Oakley E. Van Slyke of Credibility in Workmen's Compensation Ratemaking

Mr. Skurnick has attempted to present a description of the current method of ratemaking used by the California Inspection Rating Bureau and to provide "suggestions of aspects wherein modern credibility theory might be applied" to provide an improved system. He has presented a good summary of those aspects of class ratemaking where credibility plays a part. Regretfully, his suggestions for applications of credibility theory are no more than an index of the current uses of credibility, stopping at each to say to the theoreticians, "can't you do better?" I think we can.

There is one major element in the use of credibility which Skurnick has not questioned explicitly; the calculation of partial credibility using

$$z = \left(\min \frac{p \cdot lr}{k}, 1\right)^{2/3}$$

where z is partial credibility, $p \cdot lr$ is "actual expected losses," and k is a constant across all classifications, but differing for serious, nonserious and medical losses. For this formula no reasoning is given. Hans Bühlmann has told us that no mathematical model can be given to justify a formula of this type. As we shall see, the formulas of the form $z = n/(n + k)$ seem to fit Skurnick's data better.

Skurnick's "second aspect of credibility" is that another calculation of credibility is used to determine the pure premium indicated by policy year experience. In this method each year's pure premium is given a weight

$$z_i = \frac{\text{payroll in year i}}{\text{total payroll in n years}}$$

where total payroll is that of the n years being used and n is sufficient to make total payroll times expected pure premium greater than k, the constant defined above, but n is not more than 5. Expressing the pure premium indicated by policy year experience in terms of new and past data, we have

$$\hat{\mu} = z \cdot X + (1 - zk)\bar{X}.$$

However, formulas based on models are

$$\hat{\mu} = z \cdot X + (1 - z)\tilde{X} \text{ and}$$

$$\mu = z \cdot X + (1 - z)m ,$$

where $\tilde{X}$ is the past estimate of $\hat{\mu}$, and m is the expected value of μ. The formula utilizing z_i = (payroll in year i)/(total payroll in n years) clearly lacks a model.

The result of using two credibility formulas is that time series are used which are not desirable. New data is brought in discounted by two credibility factors, and one result is that older data may get more weight. This time series problem pointed out by Skurnick can be corrected by using just one credibility formula to create a weighted average of the indicated value based on data not previously incorporated, and the indicated value based on past data (and possibly judgment). For example, if

$$z_i \cdot (\text{pure premium of year i}) + (1 - z_i) \cdot (\text{past pure premium})$$

were used, then the series would be z_i, $z_{i-1} \cdot (1 - z_i)$, $z_{i-2} \cdot (1 - z_{i-1})(1 - z_i)\ldots$ If all $z_i = z$, then greater weight is assured to more recent data. If $z_i \neq z$, then years of much greater credibility continue to exert greater weight. This is as it should be. Our suggestion to the CIRB then, is: use only new data and old rates. Of course, modify old rates by judgment and data as you are now.

Skurnick's "third aspect of credibility" is that rate changes are limited to 25% per year. That is,

$$.75 \leq \frac{z\cdot(\text{pure premium of year i})+(1-z)\cdot(\text{past pure premium})}{\text{past pure premium}}$$

$$\leq 1.25 \quad \text{or}$$

$$z_i \leq .25/(|1 - \text{pure premium of year i/past pure premium}|)$$

although z should certainly decrease if the data is quite different from that expected, the use of a 25% rule with its implications on z are not justified. Whitney (1918) pointed out that, "if the standard deviation is large, that is if the risks are diverse, it is inherently likely that [experience] that departs from the average is to be accounted for by a real difference in the hazard." In other words, z should decline less slowly if there is large variation in pure premium from year to year, more quickly if there is small variation in pure premium from year to year. Our suggestion here is: divide the exposure by the variance observed in the new data to determine a weight for the new data. Further, allow for the uncertainty in the past pure premium (the rate) by dividing by the observed variance in the rate. Oh--this pair of weights won't add to 1, so we must divide our weighted sum by the sum of the weights to get a weighted average.

Our suggestion is obviously Bühlmann's 1967 formulation, slightly relaxed, and with a simple choice of estimators.

Skurnick has asked us to give standards measuring the relative equality of the credibility standards--the k for each type of loss--as they have been used for over 20 years. An equivalent problem is to generate a formula for the k's based upon experience. But that is what we have just done above. Skurnick has also asked for an adjustment formula that uses average claims size and variability in the determination of credibility, and for a technique to handle large losses. These are all features of the method given above. So we can look forward to a real contribution from the theoretical field to the ratemaking field.

An additional extension of theory that would be of great benefit to the workmen's compensation field would be the formulation of the credibility to be assigned to the various subtotals of the data.

Let us see if we can draw some conclusions from the data given. Skurnick gave no experimental justification for the use of

$$z = \left(\min \frac{p \cdot lr}{k}, 1\right)^{2/3}$$

I desired to test it as best I could with Skurnick's illustrative data.

Hypothesis: $z = \left(\frac{p \cdot lr}{k}\right)^{2/3}$ or 1 is better than

$$z' = \frac{p \cdot lr}{p \cdot lr + k'}$$

Predictions based on hypothesis:

- When $z = 1$ the classification rates indexed to 1955 (Exhibit 5) will be smooth even if z' gets to be significantly less than 1.
- For sufficiently low amounts of exposure, z' must assign lower credibility than z. If z is a better value, then there is no group of low-z classes for which charts such as Exhibit 5 show too much instability.

Results:

- Hypothesis rejected. For Code 8106, $z = 1$, $z' < 1$, and rate is not smooth. (Exhibit 5)
- Hypothesis not rejected. However, with a greater study of low exposure classes, we may find the

evidence we are seeking.

The CIRB system has worked fairly well. How well? In a talk with Mr. Skurnick on September 19, 1974, he mentioned the possibility of testing the existing and the proposed methods using the CIRB's wealth of data. Certainly the small time it would take to draft the tests would be worthwhile if it could cause an improvement in the methods.

In summary, the credibility of the pure premium of year i, z_i, should increase, as Skurnick says,

- with an increase in the volume of experience in the year i,
- with a decrease in the spread between the pure premium of year i and its expected value,
- with an increase in the variation from year to year of the pure premium.

A simple formula for z which would have these three attributes would solve the problems of fit of the data, time series generation, the arbitrariness and force of the 25% limitation, and the effect of large losses. The formulas we see today and an extension of them to include the random variation of payroll all meet these criteria.

Credibility in Practice

Erwin Straub
Swiss Reinsurance Company, Zurich

1. Homogeneous against inhomogeneous formulae (see Appendix 1)

Theoretically, credibility formulae are - as we know from Bühlmann's work (see, e.g., Bühlmann 1970) - least square linear estimators for the unknown posterior mean of the loss ratio of a given risk category within a heterogeneous portfolio.

Depending on whether or not allowance of inhomogeneous estimators is made we get

$$\hat{\mu}_k = \gamma_k X._k + (1 - \gamma_k)m \qquad \text{(IC)}$$

or

$$\hat{\mu}_k = \gamma_k X._k + (1 - \gamma_k)\tilde{X} \qquad \text{(HC)}$$

which may be translated into a verbal rule:

"As a pure risk premium rate for class no. k take $100\gamma_k\%$ of the individual loss ratio $X._k$ plus $100(1 - \gamma_k)\%$ of the collective loss ratio m or $\tilde{X}$" depending on whether the inhomogeneous (IC) or homogeneous credibility formula (HC) is used.

According to (HC) the pure risk premium is zero if all loss ratios observed in the past are zero. This is why (HC) is called homogeneous in opposition to the inhomogeneous formula (IC) where, (as least for $m > 0$), the pure risk premium turns out to be different from zero even if there has never been a claim.

Here $X._j$ = average observed loss ratio of class j $(j = 1,2,\ldots,N)$

$$\gamma_j = \frac{wP._j}{v + wP._j} = \text{credibility factor,}$$

$$P._j = \text{volume of class } j$$

and v and w measure the fluctuations of loss ratios <u>in time</u> and <u>within the portfolio</u> respectively since (if υ_j = risk parameter characterizing class j)

$$\frac{v}{P._j} = E[Var[X._j|\upsilon_j]] \quad \text{and} \quad w = Var[E[X._j|\upsilon_j]]$$

Finally $m = E[E[X._j|\upsilon_j]]$ is the theoretically exact collective mean assumed to be known within formula (IC) whereas $\tilde{X} = \sum_{j=1}^{N} \frac{\gamma_j}{\gamma} X._j$ (with $\gamma = \sum_{j=1}^{N} \gamma_j$) in (HC) is the best linear estimator for the actually unkownn value of m. Note that $\tilde{X}$ is not the usual average because the $X._j$ are weighted here with the credibility factors.

From a practical point of view (HC) is of much greater importance than (IC) because it contains an "automatically built in" estimator for the unknown m.

Formula (HC) also tells us that $\tilde{X}$ is the right overall loss ratio to be taken <u>and not</u> $\bar{X} = \sum_{j=1}^{N} \frac{P._j}{P} X._j$ as everybody would expect at first sight.

As a consequence it may occasionally happen e.g. that $X._k < \bar{X}$ (individual loss ratios below the "natural" average loss ratio) but at the same time $\hat{\mu}_k > \bar{X}$ (pure risk premium above average) - a situation which is not easy to explain to non-statisticians in practice!

As a numerical example to illustrate this, consider a portfolio consisting of 3 classes,

with volumes $P._1 = 1$, $P._2 = 4$, $P._3 = 20$,

and loss ratios $X._1 = 0$, $X._2 = 2.5$, $X._3 = 0.05$.

$\bar{X}$ is 0.44 and with $v/w = 10$ we find $\tilde{X} = 0.717$ and consequently by applying (HC), we find that for the pure risk premium rates, $\hat{\mu}_1 = 0.65$, $\hat{\mu}_2 = 1.23$, $\hat{\mu}_3 = 0.27$. That is to say, $X._1 < \overline{X}$ and $\hat{\mu}_1 > \overline{X}$.

2. Assessing the degree of heterogeneity (see Appendix 2)

In

$$\gamma_k = \frac{wP._k}{wP._k + v} = \frac{w}{w + \frac{w}{P._k}}$$

the quantity $w = \mathrm{Var}[E[X._j|\upsilon_j]]$ being the variance of the mean loss ratios within the collective, measures the heterogeneity of the collective. The greater w is, the higher the credibility factors are, i.e. the more weight is put on the individual experience $X._k$.

The other component of the total variance $w + \frac{v}{P._k}$ namely $\frac{v}{P._k}$ is the variance of the loss ratio in time.

Estimating v from claims statistics is usually no problem in opposition to w which (apart from an unknown positive factor) must be estimated by the difference $W - V$ where

$$W = \frac{1}{N-1} \sum_{j=1}^{N} \frac{P._j}{P} (X._j - \overline{X})^2$$

and

$$V = \frac{1}{N} \sum_{j=1}^{N} \frac{1}{n-1} \sum_{h=1}^{n} \frac{P_{hj}}{P} (X_{hj} - X._j)^2$$

(the subscript h denotes the statistical year) because unexpectedly W is not an unbiased estimator for w. (See Bühlmann and Straub, 1972).

So one may occasionally get a negative estimator for a nonnegative variance component (namely if $V > W$). The best thing to do in such a situation is probably to set $w = 0$, i.e. to assume the collective to be completely homogeneous since - at least statistically - no heterogeneity could be detected.

However, there is another, perhaps more serious, uncertainty in evaluating v and w, in that the practical partition of the collective into tariff groups may not be identical with the true underlying structure. That brings us to questions like:

Which horsepower classes should be distinguished within a Motor portfolio?

How many age groups?

Is it - statistically - worthwhile to break up the tariff geographically?

or more generally

What is a good tariff structure?

Pereira Cabral and Afonso Garcia (1974) have dealt with this question quite extensively.

A shorter but less refined statistical solution to the problem is based on the following argument (see Schmitter and Straub (1974)).

A good tariff structure is one which reflects efficiently the heterogeneity of the collective. Consequently, if we can choose from different partitions of the collective, we calculate $(N - 1)(W - V)$ for each partition where N is the number of risk classes within the partition and pick out the one with the highest value.

We may illustrate this by a very simple example of a 3-risk collective. Call the risks A, B and C, and assume $E[X_A] = E[X_B] = 1$, $E[X_C] = 2$.

Theoretically, there are 5 different tariff structures possible here, namely

Tariff No.	classes 1 2 3	N = number of tariff positions	E[(N-1)(W-V)]	E[W]
1	A B C	3	$\frac{4}{9}$ w	$\frac{2}{9}$ w + $\frac{v}{3}$
2	AB C	2	$\frac{4}{9}$ w	$\frac{4}{9}$ w + $\frac{v}{3}$
3	AC B	2	$\frac{1}{9}$ w	$\frac{1}{9}$ w + $\frac{v}{3}$
4	BC A	2	$\frac{1}{9}$ w	$\frac{1}{9}$ w + $\frac{v}{3}$
5	ABC	1	0	0 + $\frac{v}{3}$

Of course, tariff no. 2 is the "right" one as it puts the risks A and B which are of the same type into one group and defines a second tariff position consisting of the different risk C only. And as can be seen from the right hand column, the proposed test statistic $(N - 1)(W - V)$ is a good criterion since it is - at least in terms of mathematical expectations - maximum for the right partition and decreases with decreasing quality of the partition. However, also tariff no. 1 which is a refinement of the "right natural" tariff no. 2 shows the same maximum value of $\frac{4}{9}$ w.

3. Credibility Excess of loss rating (see Appendix 3)

In rating excess of loss covers, we would expect the credibility factors to decrease with increasing priority since the higher the priority the smaller the number of excess claims, i.e. the less reliable the individual burning costs (= excess of loss ratios). Very often in practical cases, however, credibility factors do not decrease with increasing priority. We therefore need either some parametric model or some sort of isotonic regression procedure, see Jewell (1974b).

Another difficulty in this field is the fact that the collective usually changes with changing priority because, for example if statistics in excess of say \$200,000 all treaties with priority \$200,000 or less can be taken into account in opposition to e.g. statistics above \$100,000, where only data of treaties with a priority of \$100,000 or less can be used.

4. The classical model is sometimes too narrow (see Appendix 4)

Here we have a problem which I personally struggled with for a long time without success, until I finally gave up.

If the collective is structured not only by one but by two criteria simultaneously (e.g. horsepower and driver's age), we would also like to have a nice and explicit rule for the calculation of the pure risk premium according to which one should take say

γ% of the individual loss ratio
plus δ% of the loss ratio of all risk with the same horsepower class (1st criterion)
plus ε% of the loss ratio of all risks with the same age (2nd criterion)
plus ϕ% of some overall loss ratio.

But apparently, so far, nobody has given concrete formulae for γ, δ, ε and ϕ.

The extension of the classical one dimensional model onto two or more dimensions in the above sense is formally very simple. Take two or more risk parameters instead of only one. The general system of linear equations can still be easily written down. The crucial covariance matrix, however, can no longer be inverted explicitly. Therefore, we have no explicit solution and things are difficult to interpret and to explain to nonmathematicians.

Another problem of practical importance which is more likely to have a neat solution is the following.

For collectives with relatively few but large risks (like e.g. Industrial Fire, Aviation, Engineering or Reinsurance Portfolios) the assessment of the indivudal pure risk premium is only of minor importance. Here we are much more concerned about the fluctuation loading part of the premium or perhaps we even would like to calculate iterative premiums of the form $v^{-1} \circ E[v(X)]$ as proposed recently by Gerber.

This means that the classical model based on inferences of X_{hj} on expectations has to be extended to some other kind of inferences, for example X_{hj}^2 on variances.

It seems that some generalized explicitly invertible covariance matrix recently found by Bill Jewell will provide the key for the solution of these problems.

5. Multidimensional credibility

The generalizations to multidimensional observables can readily be written down as indicated in Appendices 5, 6 and 7. It is very much my belief that these generalizations and their proofs should be formulated in a wider, non-insurance context.

Appendix 1. Homogeneous against inhomogeneous formulae

Homogeneous	Inhomogeneous
(HC) $\hat{\mu}_k = \gamma_k X_{\cdot k} + (1-\gamma_k)\tilde{X}$	(IC) $\hat{\mu}_k = \gamma_k X_{\cdot k} + (1-\gamma_k)m$

Interpretation: As risk premium rate for class k take $100\gamma_k\%$ of the individual loss ratio $X_{\cdot k}$ plus $100(1-\gamma_k)\%$ of

the collective loss ratio $\tilde{X}$	the collective loss ratio m

Properties

m unknown, estimated by $\tilde{X}$	m assumed to be known

If there are no claims at all

prpr. = 0	prpr. > 0 (at least if $m > 0$)

Consequently, we use

(HC) where we have some claims statistics. m is estimated "automatically."	(IC) if there are no (or almost no) observed claims and fix m in a nonstatistical way.

Model

N homogeneous risk classes. Explain $X_{\cdot j}$, $P_{\cdot j}$ and $\gamma_j = \frac{wP_{\cdot j}}{wP_{\cdot j} + V}$ as well as v and w. For details see the paper.

<u>Not easy to explain to non-statistician:</u>

$\tilde{X}$ is the right overall loss ratio <u>and not</u>

$$\bar{X} = \sum_{j=1}^{N} \frac{P_{\cdot j}}{P} X_j$$

It can therefore happen e.g. that

$$X_{\cdot j} < \bar{X} \text{ and } \hat{\mu}_k > \bar{X}$$

<u>Appendix 2. Assessing the degree of heterogeneity</u>

The credibility factor for class no. k is

$$\gamma_k = \frac{wP_{\cdot k}}{wP_{\cdot k} + v} = \frac{w}{w + \frac{v}{P_{\cdot k}}}$$

The <u>total variance</u> of the loss ratio $X_{\cdot k}$ is $w + \frac{v}{P_{\cdot k}}$

thereof w is the <u>variance</u> of the mean loss ratio <u>within the collective</u> and $\frac{v}{P_{\cdot k}}$ the mean <u>variance</u> of loss ratios <u>in time</u>

(for a volume $P._k$) v and w are estimated from claims statistics by V and $(N - 1)(W - V)$ respectively, where

$$W = \frac{1}{N-1} \sum_{j=1}^{N} \frac{P._j}{P} (X._j - \overline{X})^2 \quad \text{and} \quad V = \frac{1}{N} \sum_{j=1}^{N} \frac{1}{n-1} \sum_{h=1}^{n} \frac{P_{hj}}{P} \cdot (X_{hj} - X._j)^2$$

(P_{hj} and X_{hj} are <u>yearly</u> figures)

<u>Remarks</u>: - w measures the heterogeneity; $\gamma_j \uparrow w$, $j = 1,2,\ldots,N$

- W is not unbiased for w but $T = (N - 1)(W - V)$ is and we therefore take it as <u>statistical yardstick for heterogeneity</u>, however
- <u>1st problem</u>: T may be negative: (⇒ assume homogeneity)
- <u>2nd problem</u>: if tariff is not identical with true underlying structure, then w is underestimated and v is overestimated
- <u>3rd problem</u>: how to choose a good partition of the collective into a number of risk classes (⇒ take the one which maximizes $T = (N - 1)(W - V)$ and consider also W if there is more than one)

<u>Appendix 4. Two desirable extensions of the model</u>

1. Breaking up the portfolio <u>by two</u> instead of only one criterion (e.g. motor into horsepower and age groups simultaneously) we would like to have a rule of the following kind:

"pure risk premium rate for a given tariff position =

γ% of the individual loss ratio

plus δ% of the loss ratio of the horsepower-class

plus ε% of the loss ratio of the age group

plus ϕ% of some overall loss ratio

As it seems, nobody has given concrete formulae for the calculation of γ, δ, ε and ϕ so far.

2. For unbalanced collectives, i.e. collectives with relatively few but large risks (e.g. Industrial Fire, Aviation, Engineering or Reinsurance Portfolios), a reliable assessment of the fluctuation loading is much more important than the calculation of pure risk premiums.

<u>Appendix 3</u>

<u>Credibility Rating, Switzerland, Motor Liability</u>

		Company Code									
		1261	1308	220	439	28	632	364	302	1191	
	BP in Mio. s.Fr.	23	25	22	77	169	171	368	481	185	
	ind. BC in %	1.78	0.00	0.00	0.06	0.53	0.02	0.77	1.09	1.25	$\tilde{X} = 0.65\%$
688' × 688'	Cred. BC in %	0.95	0.47	0.49	0.33	0.57	0.19	0.75	1.04	1.09	$\tilde{X} = 0.77\%$
	Credibility in %	26.4	27.7	25.1	54.4	72.3	72.5	85.1	88.1	74.1	
	ind. BC in %	3.62	8.30	6.91	4.82	5.37	2.97	$\tilde{X} = 4.80\%$			
1100' × 275'	Cred. BC in %	4.61	5.40	5.12	4.81	5.13	3.73	$\tilde{X} = 4.58\%$			
	Credibility in %	16.2	17.1	15.2	39.1	58.4	58.7				
	ind. BC in %	1.57	5.19	3.78	2.07	3.30	$\tilde{X} = 3.05\%$				
800' × 200'	Cred. BC in %	3.05	3.05	3.05	3.05	3.05	$\tilde{X} = 3.05\%$				
	Credibility in %	0.0	0.0	0.0	0.0	0.0					

This table illustrates the two difficulties, namely

- collective shrinks with decreasing priority
- credibilities may not decrease with increasing priority

BP = Bureau Premium

BC = Burning Cost

Appendix 5. First Remark on Multidimensional Credibility

One Dimensional	Multidimensional
$\hat{\mu}_k = \sum_{j=1}^{N} \alpha_j X_{\cdot j} = \gamma_k X_{\cdot k} + (1 - \gamma_k)\tilde{X}$	$\hat{\underline{\mu}}_k = \sum_{j=1}^{N} A_j \underline{X}_{\cdot j} = \Gamma_k \underline{X}_{\cdot k} + (1 - \Gamma_k)\tilde{\underline{X}}$
$\gamma_k = \frac{P_{\cdot k} w}{v + P_{\cdot k} w}, \quad \tilde{X} = \sum_{j=1}^{w} \frac{\gamma_j}{\gamma} X_{\cdot j}$	$\Gamma_k = P_{\cdot k} W (V + P_{\cdot k} W)^{-1}, \quad \tilde{\underline{X}} = \Gamma^{-1} \sum_{j=1} \Gamma_j \underline{X}_{\cdot j}$
$\frac{v}{P_{\cdot j}} = E[Var[X_{\cdot j} \mid \upsilon_j]],$	$\frac{1}{P_{\cdot j}} V = E[Cov[\underline{X}_{\cdot j} \mid \upsilon_j]],$
$w = Var[E[X_{\cdot j} \mid \upsilon_j]]$	$W = Cov[E[\underline{X}_{\cdot j} \mid \upsilon_j]]$

A_j, Γ_k, Γ, V and W are $m \times m$-matrices

Appendix 6. Second remark on multidimensional credibility

Multidimensional

$$\hat{W}^{(g)} = \frac{1}{Ng - 1} \sum_{r=1}^{Ng} \frac{P_{\cdot r}^{(g)}}{P} (\underline{X}_{\cdot r}^{(g)} - \underline{X}_{\cdot\cdot}) \circ (\underline{X}_{\cdot r} - \underline{X}_{\cdot\cdot})$$

$$\hat{V}^{(g)} = \frac{1}{Ng} \sum_{r=1}^{N} \frac{1}{n - 1} \sum_{t=1}^{n} \frac{P_{hr}^{(g)}}{P} (\underline{X}_{hr}^{(g)} - \underline{X}_{\cdot r}) \circ (\underline{X}_{hr}^{(g)} - \underline{X}_{\cdot r}^{(g)})$$

$T^{(g)} = (Ng - 1)(\hat{W}^{(g)} - \hat{V}^{(g)}) \overset{E}{=}$ maximum componentwise if and only if g is natural or a refinement.

Formally the same as in one dimension but squares replaced by tensor products.

Appendix 7. Third remark on multidimensional credibility

The last two Appendixes summarize and generalize results by Bühlmann, Jewell, Schmitter and myself. Also note that formulae remain essentially same if assumption of independency between risks is dropped. Only changes: V and W replaced by linear combinations of V, U, Q and W, V, Q respectively

where U = covariances between two different individuals within the same class

and Q = same, but for two individuals from different classes of the natural subdivision.

Discussion by Craig F. Ansley of Credibility in Practice

I have a number of comments to make on this paper, and I shall deal with them in the order they arise in the paper.

1. Homogeneous and Inhomogeneous Formulae

Straub points out that the best linear estimator for overall loss ratio is:

$$\tilde{X} = \sum \frac{\gamma_j}{\gamma} X._j$$

and not:

$$\bar{X} = \sum \frac{p_j}{p} X._j$$

as one would expect. The problem in practice is to explain to the non-statistician why it may happen that $X._k$ is less than $\bar{X}$ while $\hat{\mu}_k$ is greater than $\bar{X}$.

A problem indeed. My comment is that one can look forward to the possibility that $X._k$ is above $\bar{X}$ (individual loss ratio above the natural average) while $\hat{\mu}_k$ is below $\bar{X}$!

2. Assessing the Degree of Heterogeneity

Straub discusses the estimation of

$$w = \mathrm{Var}(E(X._j \mid \nu_j))$$

and

$$v = P._j E(\mathrm{Var}(X._j \mid \nu_j))$$

in the formula for the credibility factor

$$\gamma_k = \frac{w}{w + \frac{v}{P._k}} .$$

He considers the estimators for w and v:

$$W = \frac{1}{N-1} \sum \frac{P._j}{P} (X._j - \bar{X})^2$$

and

$$V = \frac{1}{N} \sum_{n=1}^{N} \frac{1}{n-1} \sum_{j=1}^{n} \frac{P_{nj}}{P} (X_{nj} - X_{\cdot j})^2$$

and points out that while V is unbiased, W is not. However, the estimator $W - V$ is unbiased for w and is therefore adopted in practice, but unfortunately it can lead to a negative estimate for w.

Straub suggests that in this situation one adopt the rule:

$$\begin{aligned} w &= W - V \qquad && W - V > 0 \\ &= 0 && W - V \leq 0 \end{aligned}$$

There are three criticisms that can be made of this approach.

(1) The new estimator is no longer unbiased.

(2) In a Bayesian context, with mean squared error loss, unbiasedness is by no means an optimal criterion for an estimator. (See Fergusson, 1967).

(3) The whole approach bothers me somewhat. It seems to depart from the Bayesian framework on which credibility theory is founded. The prior is not assumed to be known, and we revert to "classical" inference on its parameters.

I do not know the answers to these problems, but suggest that the "middle course" of the empirical Bayes approach could be a fruitful area for research.

3. A Two-Criteria Model

The problem of a two-criteria model

$$\hat{\mu}_{jk} = \gamma_{jk} X_{\cdot jk} + \delta_{jk} X_{\cdot j \cdot} + \varepsilon_{jk} X_{\cdot\cdot k} + \phi_{jk} X_{\cdot\cdot\cdot}$$

is brought up but not resolved. Jewell has looked at some aspects of the general problem in his paper in this collection.

Whilst I cannot see the solution either, I point out that its existence can be established by considering projections on to appropriate subspaces of the Hilbert space of random variables X_{ijk}.

Finally, I would like to comment on the nature of this paper - it presents problems, not solutions. One of the most difficult aspects of research is identifying the problem. Erwin Straub has identified several problems, and it remains for other actuarial researchers to join in solving them.

Credibility for Time-Heterogeneous Loss Ratios

G. C. Taylor
School of Economic and Financial Studies
Macquarie University
Sydney, Australia

Abstract

The paper surveys a number of existing credibility models and observes that few attempts have been made to deal with time-heterogeneity in loss-ratios. A new model is then set up which allows for variation in expected loss-ratios in the following way:

expected loss-ratio

in year i and risk-class $j = a_j + b_j\, c(i)$,

where a_j and b_j are taken to be unknown but $c(.)$ is known. The paper then develops a credibility formula for predicting loss-ratios for year $n + 1$ given the loss-ratios of each risk-class in years $1,2,\ldots,n$. It is noted that negative credibility coefficients inevitably occur. The credibility coefficients are complicated but, in view of the importance of the problem, may nevertheless be useful. A numerical example is given to illustrate the use of the credibility formula. This example suggests a few qualitative properties of the credibility formula which are then investigated.

1. Introduction

Heterogeneity of a claims process over time poses a serious problem for the actuary. The majority of the models which comprise his tools of trade assume homogeneity, and, consequently, any appearance to the contrary in past claims data will undermine his confidence in his prognostications of future experience.

It is of course sometimes possible to remove this problem by using "as-if statistics." This could be done if, for example, the changes in the claims process are due to changes in the conditions of reinsurance treaties, the action of a given level of inflation of claims costs, etc.-in short, any factors whose effects are predictable. However, in the case of, say, intrinsically changing claim frequencies or the drift in the courts towards higher (in real terms) damages awards - things for which we have no gauges for measurement - "as-if" statistics cannot be constructed readily.

Despite the importance of this problem, very little work on it has appeared in actuarial literature concerned with credibility theory. An isolated and brief treatment of the topic is given by Bühlmann (1969), where he considers the case of a collective of different risks in which the expected claims experience of each risk changes linearly over time. Bühlmann comments (op. cit., p. 165):

> "This last specialization which tackles the heterogeneity in time appears to me to be very promising. As we live in a constantly changing world, we ought to adapt our models to this reality of change."

The aim of the present paper is to elaborate somewhat on Bühlmann's model. We shall use credibility techniques to do so, i.e. the claims experience for the next time period will be predicted by means of a linear combination of past experiences. Before embarking on this project, we shall describe the conventional credibility model, Bühlmann's time-heterogeneous modification of it, and the extended time-heterogeneous model to be analysed in this paper. This will serve to bring into focus the similarities and dissimilarities of the different models.

2. Notation and Assumptions

Since the present analysis will, in part, follow almost identically that of a time-homogeneous analysis presented by Bühlmann and Straub (1970), it will be of considerable advantage to follow their notation wherever possible. In common with them, we express all of our reasoning in terms of reinsurance, being concerned with estimating the expected reinsurance claims under a given reinsurance treaty per unit of direct insurance premium. This setting is, however, chosen merely to fix ideas, and the methods do have much wider application, of course.

In this spirit we consider a portfolio consisting of N risk-classes, each of which has its experience recorded separately over time-periods $1,2,\ldots,n$. Let

S_{ij} = total reinsurance claims in risk-class j in time-period i;

P_{ij} = direct insurance risk premium income in risk-class j in time-period i;

$X_{ij} = S_{ij}/P_{ij}$ = loss ratio in risk-class j in time-period i.

υ_{ij} = a quantity (unknown) which, together with P_{ij}, characterizes the distribution of X_{ij}, thus:

$$\text{Prob}\{X_{ij} < x | \upsilon_{ij} = \upsilon,\ P_{ij} = P\} = F_{\upsilon}(x|P)\ .$$

$$\mathcal{P} = \{P_{ij} | i = 1,2,\ldots,n;\ j = 1,2,\ldots,N\}$$

$$\mathcal{X} = \{X_{ij} | i = 1,2,\ldots,n;\ j = 1,2,\ldots,N\}.$$

Assumptions 1. $E[X_{ij} | \upsilon_{ij} = \upsilon, P_{ij} = P] = \mu(\upsilon)$ independently of P;

2. Independence of Loss Ratios. For fixed values of the υ_{ij} ($i = 1,2,\ldots,n$; $j = 1,2,\ldots,N$) the variables X_{ij} are stochastically independent.

The Problem. To estimate $\mu(\upsilon_{n+1:j})$, $j = 1,2,\ldots,N$ from the available information, viz. $\mathcal{P}$, $\mathcal{X}$ (recall that $\upsilon_{n+1:j}$ is unknown). Call the estimator

$$\hat{\mu}_{n+1:j} = \hat{\mu}_{n+1:j}(\mathcal{P},\mathcal{X}) .$$

3. The Credibility Models

3.1 The Conventional Credibility Model

The ideas of credibility theory were developed basically by Whitney (1918) and were treated in rather piecemeal fashion by various writers until Bühlmann (1967) gave a proper formulation of the credibility problem. In this formulation the following assumptions are made in addition to those stated in Section 2.

Assumptions 3. Time-homogeneity. The loss ratios in each risk-class are i.i.d. over time, i.e. $\upsilon_{ij} = \upsilon_j$ independently of i for $j = 1,2,\ldots,N$.

4. Independence of Characterization Parameters. The parameter values υ_j ($j = 1,2,\ldots,N$) are i.i.d. random variables with d.f. $U(\upsilon)$.

5. Admissible Estimators. The estimator $\hat{\mu}_{n+1:k} = \hat{\mu}_k$ is to be chosen from the set of functions of the form

$$\hat{\mu}_k = \alpha_{o,k} + \sum_{j=1}^{N} \sum_{i=1}^{n} \alpha_{ij,k} X_{ij} ,$$

where $\alpha_{o,k}$ and the $\alpha_{ij,k}$ are all real

constants.

6. Optimal Estimation Criterion. This is the least squares criterion, i.e. the optimal estimator $\hat{\mu}_k^*$ is that which minimizes the expression:

$$E[\{\hat{\mu}_k^*(\mathcal{P},\mathfrak{X}) - \mu(\upsilon_k)\}^2]$$

where the expectation is taken with respect to the "ddnsity function":

$$\prod_{j=1}^{N} dU(\upsilon_j) \prod_{i=1}^{n} dF_{\upsilon_j}(x_{ij}|P_{ij})$$

The complete form of the optimal estimator in this case is not especially important for the present purposes. However, it should be noted that, in the optimal estimator,

$$\alpha_{o,k} = \alpha_o^* = E_U[\mu(\upsilon_k)] \times \text{const.}$$

This feature of the optimal estimator is sometimes regarded as unsatisfactory since $U(.)$, and hence $E_U[\mu(\upsilon_k)]$, will usually be unknown. A solution to this difficulty is provided by Bühlmann and Straub (1970) who replace Assumptions 5 and 6 by

Assumptions 5'. Admissible Estimators.

$$\hat{\mu}_{n+1:k} = \hat{\mu}_k = \sum_{j=1}^{N} \sum_{i=1}^{n} \alpha_{ij,k} X_{ij} .$$

6'. Optimal Estimation Criterion. As for Assumption 6 except that the minimization is performed subject to the unbiasedness constraint:

$$E[\mu_k^*] = E[\mu(\upsilon_k)] .$$

Assumptions 1, 2, 3 and 4 are retained, and Assumption 7 given below is added.

Assumption 7. $\text{Var}[X_{ij}|\upsilon_{ij} = \upsilon, P_{ij} = P] = \sigma^2(\upsilon)/P$; Bühlmann and Straub quote Bühlmann (1964) as the justification for this assumption.

3.2 Bühlmann's Time-Heterogeneous Model

Bühlmann suggested a model which incorporated Assumptions 1, 2, 4, 5 and 6, but dropped Assumption 3 concerning time-homogeneity. In its stead, he suggested

Assumption 3". There exist numbers υ_j, $j = 1,2,\ldots,N$ such that

$$\upsilon_{ij} = (i + c)\upsilon_j,\ i = 1,2,\ldots,n;\ j = 1,2,\ldots,N;$$

where c is a constant. Moreover,

$$\mu(\upsilon) = \upsilon .$$

Bühlmann showed that, under the assumption that $U(.)$ is a gamma d.f., the optimal estimator $\hat{\mu}_k^*$ is exactly equal to the posterior mean,

$$E[\mu(\upsilon_k)|\mathcal{P},\mathcal{X}]$$

This result meant that, for the time-heterogeneous model considered by Bühlmann, the set of admissible estimators chosen (see Assumption 5) was a reasonable one.

There is a major difficulty in the use of Bühlmann's model - one must know in advance the value of c, i.e. one must know the rate at which each $\mu(\upsilon_{ij})$ is changing over time. In practice, of course, the estimation of this rate will very often present a problem of equal proportions with the problem of experience rating within a single unit of time. It is this difficulty which the model described in Section 3.3 will attempt to deal with.

3.3 The Model of the Present Analysis

The simplest elaboration Bühlmann's model would arise by altering Assumption 3" so that c is no longer a constant, but instead a random variable with a prior distribution. The experience rating problem then consists of estimating c - which measures the time rate of change of the collective claims experience - as well as carrying out the experience rating of each risk class for each separate value of i.

An alternative to the form of υ_{ij} given in Assumption 3" which one might wish to consider is:

$$\upsilon_{ij} = \upsilon_j + ic, \ i = 1,2,\ldots,n; \ j = 1,2,\ldots,N;$$

where c (for the purposes of the present paper) would be a random variable. In order to cover this case and the one of the previous paragraph, the function form of υ_{ij} has been chosen as generally as is possible without increasing the complexity of the analysis. The form is:

$$\upsilon_{ij} = a(\upsilon_j) + b(\upsilon_j)c(i) ,$$

where any parameters occurring in the functions a(.) and b(.) have prior d.f.'s and c(.) is predetermined.

With these brief explanations, let us describe our model precisely.

We make Assumptions 1, 2, 4, 5' and 7. In addition, we make the following.

Assumptions 3'''. There exist numbers υ_j, j = 1,2,...,N such that

$$\upsilon_{ij} = a(\upsilon_j) + b(\upsilon_j)c(i)$$

where c(.) is a known function, and any parameters occurring in the functions a(.) and b(.) have a joint prior d.f. G. Moreover,

$$\mu(\upsilon) = \upsilon .$$

6'''. The optimal estimator $\hat{\mu}_k^*$ is that which minimizes the expression:

$$E[\{\hat{\mu}_k^*(\mathcal{P},\mathcal{X}) - \mu(\upsilon_{n+1:k})\}^2] ,$$

where the expectation is taken with respect to the "density function":

$$dG(\gamma_1,\ldots,\gamma_p) \prod_{j=1}^{N} dU(\upsilon_j) \prod_{i=1}^{n} dF_{\upsilon_j}(x_{ij}|P_{ij}) ,$$

and where the minimization is subject to the unbiasedness constraints (see remark below):

$$\left.\begin{aligned}\sum_{i=1}^{n}\sum_{j=1}^{N} \alpha_{ij,k} &= 1; \\ \sum_{i=1}^{n}\sum_{j=1}^{N} c(i)\alpha_{ij,k} &= c(n+1) .\end{aligned}\right\} \quad (k = 1,2,\ldots,N) .$$

<u>Remark on Assumption 5'.</u> The choice of Assumption 5' rather than Assumption 5 means that our admissible estimators do not contain a constant term. The reason for this is essentially the same as in the time-homogeneous case. If the constant term were allowed, then the optimal estimator $\hat{\mu}_k^*$ would involve the terms $E[a(\upsilon_j)]$ and $E[b(\upsilon_j)]$ of which our knowledge is very restricted.

<u>Remark on Assumption 6'''.</u> The natural unbiasedness constraint to consider initially is:

$$E[\hat{\mu}_k^*] = E[\mu(\upsilon_{n+1:k})] .$$

$$\text{i.e.} \quad \sum_i\sum_j \alpha^*_{ij,k} E[X_{ij}] = E[\mu(\upsilon_{n+1:k})] .$$

$$\text{i.e.} \quad \sum_i\sum_j \alpha^*_{ij,k}\{E[a(\upsilon_j)] + c(i)E[b(\upsilon_j)]\}$$

$$= E[a(\upsilon_k) + c(n+1)E[b(\upsilon_k)]$$

However, once again, as our knowledge of $E[a(\upsilon_j)]$ and $E[b(\upsilon_j)]$ is restricted, it is desirable to make our unbiasedness constraint independent of these quantities. The simplest way of achieving this is to replace the last equation by the pair of equations:

$$\sum_i \sum_j \alpha^*_{ij,k} E[a(\upsilon_j)] = E[a(\upsilon_k)];$$

$$\sum_i \sum_j c(i)\alpha^*_{ij,k} E[b(\upsilon_j)] = c(n+1)E[b(\upsilon_k)];$$

which yield the equations exhibited in Assumption 6'''.

4. The Suitability of the Credibility Approximation

In Section 3.3 we made Assumption 5', i.e. we chose to estimate $\mu(\upsilon_{n+1:k})$ by means of a linear combination of the X_{ij}. Is there any reason to regard such an estimator as reasonable? It will be shown in this section that there is.

It is easy to verify that the optimization problem posed in Section 3.3 is equivalent to the one which arises if $\mu(\upsilon_{n+1:k})$ in Assumption 6''' is replaced by the posterior mean conditional upon $\mathcal{P}$ and $\mathfrak{X}$:

$$E[\mu(\upsilon_{n+1:k})|\mathcal{P},\mathfrak{X}] .$$

Hence our question in the previous paragraph is equivalent to the question of whether our estimator provides a reasonable approximation to $E[\mu(\upsilon_{n+1:k})|\mathcal{P},\mathfrak{X}]$.

Now what is the criterion of "reasonableness"? Probably, an approximation to $E[\mu(\upsilon_{n+1:k})|\mathcal{P},\mathfrak{X}]$ would be fairly generally accepted as reasonable, if it produced exactly the correct answer for some particular realistic choice of $G(.)$, $U(.)$ and $F_\upsilon(.|.)$. This was certainly the approach of Whitney (1918). The classical credibility formula received a further vindication along these lines when Jewell (1973) showed that, if the d.f.'s $F_\upsilon(.|.)$ of Section 3.1 are identical and chosen from the Pitman-Koopman-Darmois family, and if $U(.)$ is the conjugate prior d.f. of F_υ, then the credibility approximation is exact.

In testing the reasonableness of our choice of estimators in Section 3.3, we take our cue from Jewell, and consider the case in which $G(.)$, $U(.)$ and $F_\upsilon(.|.)$ are all normal d.f.'s. In this case the density function of Assumption 6''' becomes:

$$\text{const.} \times \exp\left\{-\tfrac{1}{2}\left[\sum_{\ell=1}^{p} \gamma_\ell^2/2\sigma_{\gamma_\ell}^2 + \sum_{j=1}^{N}\left[\upsilon_j^2/2\sigma_\upsilon^2 + \sum_{i=1}^{n} [X_{ij} - (a(\upsilon_j) + b(\upsilon_j)c(i))]^2 P_{ij}/2\sigma^2(\upsilon_{ij})\right]\right]\right\}, \quad (1)$$

where $\sigma_{\gamma_\ell}^2$ and σ_υ^2 are constants, and where, without real loss of generality, we have taken G and U to each have zero mean. By Bayes' theorem, this expression is proportional to the posterior density of $\gamma_1,\ldots,\gamma_p$, $\upsilon_1,\ldots,\upsilon_N$ conditional upon $\mathcal{P}$ and $\mathfrak{X}$. If we now specialize to the case in which $a(.)$ and $b(.)$ are each polynomials in $\gamma_1,\ldots,\gamma_N$, υ_j of degree not greater than 1, and $\sigma^2(\upsilon) = \sigma^2$ independent of υ, then it is easily seen that

$$E[\mu(\upsilon_{n+1:k})|\mathcal{P},\mathfrak{X}] = \int [a(\upsilon_k) + b(\upsilon_k)c(n+1)] \times \text{expression (1)} \; d\upsilon_1 \ldots d\upsilon_N \, d\gamma_1 \ldots d\gamma_p$$

$$= \text{a linear combination of the } X_{ij},$$

just by direct integration with respect to the successive variables.

The restriction of the functional forms of a and b is quite realistic - in fact, the two cases of greatest interest mentioned early in Section 3.3 are both still covered when a and b are so restricted.

The requirement that $\sigma^2(\upsilon) = \sigma^2$ is not so realistic. A more likely possibility is that $\sigma^2(\upsilon)$ is proportional to $\mu(\upsilon)$. Nevertheless, with the two above restrictions we see that the linearlized approximation to $E[\mu(\upsilon_{n+1:k})|\mathcal{P},\mathfrak{X}]$ is exact, and so it is not unreasonable to accept the same approximation for cases where the distributions involved are moderately non-normal and there is moderate variation of $\sigma^2(\upsilon)$ over υ. At least this is so when a and b are polynomial in $\gamma_1,\ldots,\gamma_p$, υ_j of degree not greater than 1 - the case of greatest interest. In case of other functional forms for a and b, the linearized approximation may be less appropriate. If this justification of the use of the credibility (i.e. linearized) approximation in the model of Section 3.3 seems insubstantial, it may be recalled that it is no more so than in the case of conventional credibility formulas.

5. The Credibility Formula

In the following, expectation operators are taken with respect to the "density function" of Assumption 6''' unless the contrary is indicated.

The solution of the minimization problem posed in Assumption 6''', is very similar to the solution of the Bühlmann-Straub problem described in the latter part of Section 3.1. In fact, a large part of the following analysis is a direct and simple adaptation of their work to the model of Section 3.3. The author wishes to acknowledge his debt to them.

In order to determine the optimal coefficients $\alpha^*_{ij,k}$, let us consider the Lagrange function:

$$\phi_k(\alpha_{11,k},\ldots,\alpha_{nN,k}) = E\left[\left\{\sum_{i,j} \alpha^*_{ij,k}X_{ij} - \mu(\upsilon_{n+1:k})\right\}^2\right] - 2\alpha\sum_{i,j}\alpha^*_{ij,k} - 2\beta\sum_{i,j} c(i)\alpha^*_{ij,k},$$

where 2α, 2β are Lagrange multipliers.

The system of equations:

$$\partial\phi_k/\partial\alpha^*_{gh,k} = 0,\ g = 1,2,\ldots,n;\ h = 1,2,\ldots,N;$$

for the best weights, $\alpha_{gh,k} = \alpha^*_{gh,k}$ gives us then

$$\partial\phi_k/\partial\alpha^*_{gh,k} = 2E\left[\left\{\sum_{i,j} \alpha^*_{ij,k}X_{ij} - \mu(\upsilon_{n+1:k})\right\}X_{gh}\right] - 2\alpha - 2\beta c(g) = 0 \qquad (2)$$

$$\text{i.e.} \quad E\left[\mu(\upsilon_{gh}) \sum_{i,j} \alpha^*_{ij,k}\mu(\upsilon_{ij}) + \alpha^*_{gh,k}\sigma^2(\upsilon_{gh})/P_{gh} - \mu(\upsilon_{n+1:k})\mu(\upsilon_{gh})\right] = \alpha + \beta c(g), \qquad (3)$$

where the square-bracketed term in (3) has been obtained by taking the expectation of the square-bracketed term in (2) with respect to

$$\prod_{i=1}^{n} dF_{\upsilon_j}(x_{ij}|P_{ij}) .$$

If we now define the d.f. V by:

$$dV(\gamma_1,\ldots,\gamma_p,\upsilon_1,\ldots,\upsilon_N) = dG(\gamma_1,\ldots,\gamma_p) \prod_{j=1}^{N} dU(\upsilon_j) ,$$

then (3) can be expanded to give:

$$E_V[\mu(\upsilon_{gh}) \sum_{i,j} \alpha^*_{ij,k}E[X_{ij}] + \sum_{i=1}^{n} \alpha^*_{ih,k} \operatorname{Cov}_V[\mu(\upsilon_{gh}),\mu(\upsilon_{ih})] + \alpha^*_{gh,k}E_V[\sigma^2(\upsilon_{gh})/P_{gh}] - E_V[\mu(\upsilon_{n+1:k})]E_V[\mu(\upsilon_{gh})] - \delta_{hk} \operatorname{Cov}_V[\mu(\upsilon_{n+1:k}),\mu(\upsilon_{gk})] = \alpha + \beta c(g) , \qquad (4)$$

where δ_{hk} is the Kronecker delta symbol.

But we know that (see the Remark on Assumption 6'''):

$$\sum_{i,j} \alpha^*_{ij,k}E[X_{ij}] = E_V[\mu(\upsilon_{n+1:k})] ,$$

so that the first and fourth terms on the left of equation (4) cancel, giving

$$\sum_{i=1}^{n} \alpha^*_{ih,k} \operatorname{Cov}_V[\mu(\upsilon_{gh}),\mu(\upsilon_{ih})] + \alpha^*_{gh,k}E_V[\sigma^2(\upsilon_{gh})/P_{gh}] - \delta_{hk} \operatorname{Cov}_V[\mu(\upsilon_{n+1:k}),\mu(\upsilon_{gk})] = \alpha + \beta c(g) . \qquad (5)$$

If we now introduce the notation:

$$v_{gh} = E_V[\sigma^2(\upsilon_{gh})], \quad C_i^g = \mathrm{Cov}_V[\mu(\upsilon_{gh}),\mu(\upsilon_{ih})] ,$$

then (5) becomes:

$$\sum_{i=1}^{n} \alpha^*_{ih,k} C_i^g + \alpha^*_{gh,k} v_{gh}/P_{gh} = \delta_{hk} C^g_{n+1} + \alpha + \beta c(g) ,$$

$$g = 1,2,\ldots,n; \; h = 1,2,\ldots,N . \tag{6}$$

It is clear that this system of equations breaks up into N independent systems of n equations, each of these systems corresponding to a constant h. For a given h, (6) gives the vector equation:

$$A_h \underset{\sim}{\alpha}^*_{h,k} = \underset{\sim}{\beta}_{h,k} , \tag{7}$$

where

$$\underset{\sim}{\alpha}^*_{h,k} = (\alpha^*_{1h,k}, \alpha^*_{2h,k}, \ldots, \alpha^*_{nh,k})' ;$$

$$\underset{\sim}{\beta}_{h,k} = \delta_{hk}(C^1_{n+1}, C^2_{n+1}, \ldots, C^n_{n+1})' + \alpha(1,1,\ldots,1)' + \beta(c(1),c(2),\ldots,c(n))' ;$$

and A_h is the matrix:

$$A_h = \begin{pmatrix} C_1^1 + v_{1h}/P_{1h} & C_2^1 & \cdots & C_n^1 \\ C_1^2 & C_2^2 + v_{2h}/P_{2h} & \cdots & C_n^2 \\ \vdots & \vdots & & \vdots \\ C_1^n & C_2^n & \cdots & C_n^n + v_{nh}/P_{nh} \end{pmatrix} . \tag{8}$$

The solution of (7) is, of course,

$$\underset{\sim}{\alpha}^*_{h,k} = A_h^{-1} \underset{\sim}{\beta}_{h,k} ,$$

and so the problem consists of inverting the matrix (8).

This can be done explicitly when the form of C_i^g is recalled, although some effort is required and details are banished to an appendix. The solution of (6) turns out to be

$$\alpha^*_{gh,k} = (P_{gh}/v_{gh}) \times \Big\{\delta_{hk} C^g_{n+1} + \alpha\Big\{1 + \sum_{i=1}^{n} \frac{P_{ih}}{v_{ih}} \cdot [c(i) - c(g)][w_{ab} + c(i)w_{bb}]\Big\}$$
$$+ \beta\Big\{c(g) - \sum_{i=1}^{n} \frac{P_{ih}}{v_{ih}} [c(i) - c(g)][w_{aa} + w_{ab}c(i)]\Big\}\Big\}\Big/\Big\{1 + \sum_{i=1}^{n} C^i_i P_{ih}/v_{ih}\Big\}; \quad (9)$$

where

$$w_{aa} = \mathrm{Var}_V[a(\upsilon_h)], \quad w_{ab} = \mathrm{Cov}_V[a(\upsilon_h), b(\upsilon_h)], \quad w_{bb} = \mathrm{Var}_V[b(\upsilon_h)]$$

and where α, β are given by the constraints:

$$\sum_{g=1}^{n} \sum_{h=1}^{N} \alpha^*_{gh,k} = 1; \quad (10)$$

$$(k = 1,2,\ldots,N)$$

$$\sum_{g=1}^{n} \sum_{h=1}^{N} c(g)\alpha^*_{gh,k} = c(n + 1); \quad (11)$$

as written in Assumption 6''' of Section 3.3.

It is possible to use equations (10) and (11) to eliminate the multipliers α and β from (9), but the resulting formula for $\alpha^*_{gh,k}$ then becomes very complicated, suggesting that in practical calculation one would be better advised to evaluate the $\alpha^*_{gh,k}$ by means of (9) with α, β undertermined and <u>then</u> apply (10) and (11).

Once the $\alpha^*_{gh,k}$ have been found by the above means we have

$$\hat{\mu}^*_k(\mathcal{P}, \mathcal{X}) = \sum_{g,h} \alpha^*_{gh,k} X_{gh} \quad (12)$$

as our best linearized estimate of $\mu(\upsilon_{n+1:k})$. Formula (12) can legitimately be referred to as a <u>credibility formula</u> if one accepts this term in the wide sense in which any formula (12) obeying constraint (10) is a credibility formula with $\alpha^*_{gh,k}$ <u>the credibility of</u> X_{gh} <u>in the estimation of</u> $\mu(\upsilon_{n+1:k})$.

6. Some Special Cases

6.1 Linear Change over Time in Expected Loss Ratios

The most important special case of the form of υ_{ij} prescribed in Assumption 3''' of Section 3.3 is that in which υ_{ij} changes linearly with i, i.e.

$$c(i) = i \,.$$

In this case, equations (9), (10) and (11) simplify somewhat giving:

$$\alpha^*_{gh,k} = (P_{gh}/v_{gh}) \times \Big\{\delta_{hk}C^g_{n+1} + \alpha\Big\{1 + \sum_{i=1}^{n} \frac{P_{ih}}{v_{ih}}(i-g)(w_{ab}+iw_{bb})\Big\} + \beta\Big\{g - \sum_{i=1}^{n}\frac{P_{ih}}{v_{ih}}(i-g)(w_{aa}+iw_{ab})\Big\}\Big\} \Big/ \Big\{1 + \sum_{i=1}^{n} C^i_i P_{ih}/v_{ih}\Big\}; \tag{13}$$

with

$$\sum_{g=1}^{n}\sum_{h=1}^{N} \alpha^*_{gh,k} = 1\,, \tag{14}$$

and

$$\sum_{g=1}^{n}\sum_{h=1}^{N} g\alpha^*_{gh,k} = n + 1 \tag{15}$$

One interesting fact which may be deduced from (14) and (15) is that inevitably, for each k, some of the $\alpha^*_{gh,k}$ will be strictly negative. For, if this were not so, then we would have

$$\sum_{g,h} (n+1)\alpha^*_{gh,k} = n + 1, \quad \text{by (14)}\,,$$

whereas

$$\sum_{g,h} (n+1)\alpha^*_{gh,k} > \sum_{g,h} g\alpha^*_{gh,k} = n + 1, \quad \text{by (15)}$$

In view of these negative coefficients, the reader may pause to reconsider whether he wishes to regard (12) as a credibility formula.

If $w_{ab} = 0$, e.g. if $a(\upsilon_j) = a\upsilon_j$ and $b(\upsilon_j) = b$, with a, b now (independent) constants; then (13) simplifies further:

$$\alpha^*_{gh,k} = (P_{gh}/v_{gh}) \times \left\{\delta_{hk}C^g_{n+1} + \alpha\left\{1 + w_{bb}\sum_{i=1}^{n}\frac{P_{ih}}{v_{ih}}i(i-g)\right\}\right.$$
$$\left.\left. + \beta\left\{g - w_{aa}\sum_{i=1}^{n}\frac{P_{ih}}{v_{ih}}(i-g)\right\}\right\}\bigg/\left\{1 + \sum_{i=1}^{n} C^i_i P_{ih}/v_{ih}\right\}. \quad (16)$$

6.2 Zero Change over Time in Expected Loss Ratios

In the case $b(\upsilon_j) \equiv 0$, we are back to the model of Bühlmann and Straub (Section 3.1). We shall show that this is indeed a special case of the model which the present paper deals with.

If $b(\upsilon_j) \equiv 0$, then it will do no harm to assume that $c(i) \equiv 0$ also. Moreover, we have $w_{ab} = w_{bb} = 0$. With these observations, we can reduce equation (9) as follows:

$$\alpha^*_{gh,k} = (P_{gh}/v_{gh}) \times \{\delta_{hk}w_{aa} + \alpha\}\bigg/\left\{1 + w_{aa}\sum_{i=1}^{n} P_{ih}/v_{ih}\right\}, \quad (17)$$

where α is determined by the constraint (10). Note that (11) becomes trivial on the substitution of $c(i) \equiv 0$.

Now in the Bühlmann and Straub case of "uniform as-if statistics," $v_{ih} = v$, constant. Using this fact, and supressing the subscript on w, we can write

$$\alpha^*_{gh,k} = P_{gh}(\delta_{hk}w + \alpha)/(v + wP_{.h}), \quad (18)$$

where

$$P_{.h} = \sum_{i=1}^{n} P_{ih}.$$

It is now simple to apply (10) to (18), hence obtain α, substitute back in (18) and so obtain:

$$\alpha^*_{gh,k} = \frac{v}{v + P_{.k}w} \times \frac{P_{gh}/(v+P_{.h}w)}{\sum_{j=1}^{N} P_{.j}/(v + P_{.j}w)}$$
$$+ \delta_{hk}\frac{P_{.k}w}{v + P_{.k}w} \times \frac{P_{gk}}{P_{.k}},$$

as Bühlmann and Straub do in special case (b) of their paper.

7. Numerical Methods and an Example

Although formula (9) is perhaps the most informative expression of $\alpha^*_{gh,k}$ from a theoretical viewpoint, it can be rendered in a form more convenient for calculations. Multiplying out the square-bracketed terms in (9), applying the summations term by term, and writing

$$\kappa_h^r = \sum_{i=1}^{n} [c(i)]^r \frac{P_{ih}}{v_{ih}}, \quad r = 0,1,2;$$

we obtain

$$\alpha^*_{gh,k} = (P_{gh}/v_{gh}) \times \{\delta_{hk}C^g_{n+1}+\alpha\{1-w_{ab}c(g)\kappa_h^o+(w_{ab}-w_{bb}c(g))\kappa_h^1 + w_{bb}\kappa_h^2\}+\beta\{c(g)+w_{aa}c(g)\kappa_h^o+(w_{ab}c(g)-w_{aa})\kappa_h^1 - w_{ab}\kappa_h^2\}\}/\{1+w_{aa}\kappa_h^o+2w_{ab}\kappa_h^1+w_{bb}\kappa_h^2\} . \tag{19}$$

In the case in which $w_{ab} = 0$, equation (19) becomes:

$$\alpha^*_{gh,k} = (P_{gh}/v_{gh}) \times \{\delta_{hk}C^g_{n+1}+\alpha\{1-w_{bb}c(g)\kappa_h^1+w_{bb}\kappa_h^2\}+\beta\{c(g) + w_{aa}c(g)\kappa_h^o-w_{aa}\kappa_h^1\}\}/\{1+w_{aa}\kappa_h^o+w_{bb}\kappa_h^2\} . \tag{20}$$

We now give an example which illustrates the application of our credibility formula. The data for the example is that used by Bühlmann and Straub (1970) in their numerical example (see Table 1).

These loss ratios show a distinct tendency to increase with time. For example, in five of the seven treaties $X_{5h} > X_{1h}$, and in six of the seven $X_{4h} + X_{5h} > X_{1h} + X_{2h}$. The aim of the present section will be to apply our time-heterogeneous model in order to determine the difference in predictions about year 6 between it and the time-homogeneous model of Bühlmann and Straub. This is the reason for the use of the same data as Bühlmann and Straub.

TABLE 1

Treaty h	1		2		3		4		5		6		7	
Year *g	P_{gh}**	X_{gh}***	P_{gh}	X_{gh}	P_{gh}	X_{gh}	P_{gh}	X_{gh}	P_{gh}	X_{gh}	P_{gh}	X_{gh}	P_{gh}	X_{gh}
1	5	0.0	14	11.3	18	8.0	20	5.4	21	9.7	43	9.7	70	9.0
2	6	0.0	14	25.0	20	1.9	22	5.9	24	8.9	47	14.5	77	9.6
3	8	4.2	13	18.5	23	7.0	25	7.1	28	6.7	53	10.8	85	8.7
4	10	0.0	11	14.3	25	3.1	29	7.2	34	10.3	61	12.0	92	11.7
5	12	7.7	10	30.0	27	5.2	35	8.3	42	11.1	7C	13.1	100	7.0

*Our numbering of years is in an order opposite to that of Bühlmann and Straub.

**Premiums in millions

***Loss Ratios as percentages

We shall assume, for illustrative purposes, that equation (16) is appropriate with $c(i) = i$. The credibility premiums to which this and the above data then lead have been computed for a number of different selections of the parameters w_{aa}, w_{bb} (all the v_{gh} being set equal to 209.0×10^{-4} as in Bühlmann and Straub).

The results of the calculations are summarized in the following table. (A sample print-out including all the $\alpha^*_{gh,k}$ is given in Appendix 2).

Table 2 indicates several things:

(i) As regards treaties 4 to 7, where the bulk of premium income is to be found, and where the values of X_{gh} progress fairly regularly as g changes, the credibility premiums are to a large extent independent of the values of w_{aa} and w_{ab}.

(ii) In only two treaties (viz. 1 and 3) are the time-heterogeneous credibility premiums ever found to be less than the time-homogeneous ones, confirming our original suspicion that loss ratios were tending to increase with time. The two exceptional treaties include one in which the premium volume is very small (treaty 1) and one in which the progression of loss ratios is quite irregular (treaty 3).

(iii) In Group II, w_{aa} and w_{bb} are varied in such a way as to keep the function,

$$w_{aa} + 3^2 \cdot w_{bb} \,,$$

approximately constant. The significance of this function is that it is a rough average of

$$C_i^i = \mathrm{Var}_V[\mu(\upsilon_{ih})] = w_{aa} + [c(i)]^2 w_{bb}$$

over the values of i $(= 1,2,\ldots,5)$ with which we are concerned. We see that the credibility premiums can vary quite widely as w_{aa} and w_{bb} vary in this way.

			CREDIBILITY PREMIUMS* (year 6)						
			Treaty						
Group	$w_{aa}\times 10^4$	$w_{bb}\times 10^4$	1	2	3	4	5	6	7
I	Bühlmann-Straub**		5.0	17.3	5.6	7.3	9.5	11.9	9.2
II	0.1	1.25	5.1	27.7	4.8	8.5	11.8	15.6	10.7
	1.0	1.20	5.3	27.4	5.1	8.6	11.9	15.7	10.8
	6.0	0.7	5.8	24.2	6.1	8.9	11.8	15.1	11.1
	11.0	0.1	10.2	24.3	11.0	12.7	15.0	17.7	14.9
III	0.1	0.1	9.8	16.4	8.5	10.0	11.7	14.1	10.8
	1.0	1.0	5.6	26.8	5.3	8.7	12.0	15.6	10.9
	10.0	10.0	3.4	30.5	4.3	8.3	11.9	15.7	10.8
	100.0	100.0	3.1	31.1	4.3	8.3	11.9	15.8	10.8
IV	10.0	0.1	10.5	24.4	11.2	12.9	15.1	17.8	15.0
	10.0	1.0	5.5	25.0	6.1	9.0	12.0	15.3	11.3
	10.0	10.0	3.4	30.5	4.3	8.3	11.9	15.7	10.8
	10.0	100.0	3.0	31.8	4.0	8.1	11.8	15.8	10.7
V	0.1	1.0	5.5	26.9	5.0	8.5	11.8	15.6	10.7
	1.0	1.0	5.6	26.8	5.3	8.7	12.0	15.6	10.9
	10.0	1.0	5.5	25.0	6.1	9.0	12.0	15.3	11.3
	15.0	1.0	5.6	24.7	6.5	9.2	12.1	15.3	11.5
	200.0	1.0	5.9	23.2	7.9	9.9	12.4	15.2	12.2
VI	0.1	10.0	3.3	31.3	4.1	8.2	11.9	15.8	10.7
	1.0	10.0	3.3	31.3	4.1	8.2	11.9	15.8	10.7
	15.0	10.0	3.5	30.2	4.5	8.3	11.9	15.7	10.8
	200.0	10.0	4.7	25.6	6.4	9.2	12.1	15.3	11.6
VII	0.1	50.0	3.0	31.8	4.0	8.1	11.9	15.9	10.7
	1.0	50.0	3.0	31.8	4.0	8.2	11.9	15.9	10.7
	15.0	50.0	3.0	31.5	4.1	8.2	11.8	15.8	10.7
	200.0	50.0	3.6	29.2	5.0	8.6	12.0	15.7	11.1

TABLE 2

*Premiums as percentages

**The parameters w_{aa}, w_{bb} have no place in the Bühlmann-Straub model. Instead Bühlmann and Straub use a different parameter which they call w.

(iv) The Group III calculations show that wide variations in the credibility premiums can also occur as w_{aa} and w_{bb}, both equal, are allowed to vary. There is however some tendency for the premiums to stabilize as w_{aa} and w_{bb} become large together.

(v) The Group IV calculations show that this variation also occurs if w_{bb} is allowed to vary with w_{aa} held constant.

(vi) The Group V calculations indicate a much smaller sensitivity of the premiums to variations in w_{aa} with w_{bb} held constant. This point was examined further in Groups VI and VII in each of which a different (constant) value of w_{bb} was chosen. The result of Group V was still found to hold.

8. Some Qualitative Properties of the Time-Heterogeneous Credibility Premium

The observations listed at the end of Section 7 prompt some further analytic investigation of the credibility premium.

As regards observation (iv) that the credibility premiums tend to stabilize as w_{aa} and w_{bb}, both equal, are increased, it soon becomes clear that we can obtain some fairly simple limiting results for large and small values respectively of these parameters. More precisely, in the case where $w_{ab} = 0$, if both

$$w_{bb}|c(g)\kappa_h^1 - \kappa_h^2| \tag{21}$$

and

$$w_{aa}|c(g)\kappa_h^o - \kappa_h^1| \tag{22}$$

are large in relation to 1 and $c(g)$, then, from equation (20)

$$\alpha^*_{gh,k} \approx (P_{gh}/V_{gh}) \times \{\delta_{hk}(1 + \rho c(g)c(n+1)) + \alpha\rho(\kappa_h^2 - c(g)\kappa_h^1) + \beta(c(g)\kappa_h^o - \kappa_h^1)\}/\{\kappa_h^o + \rho\kappa_h^2\}, \tag{23}$$

where $\rho = w_{bb}/w_{aa}$. It is thus clear that when expressions (21) and (22) become large, the credibility premiums are dependent upon the ratio $\rho = w_{aa}/w_{bb}$ rather than upon the parameters w_{aa} and w_{bb} independently.

Similarly, as the ratios

$$w_{aa}P_{ih}/v_{ih}$$

and

$$w_{bb}P_{ih}/v_{ih}$$

all approach zero, equation (20) yields

$$\alpha^*_{gh,k} \approx (P_{gh}/v_{gh}) \times \{\alpha + \beta c(g)\} \; , \qquad (24)$$

with α and β determined by (10) and (11). It will be seen that $\alpha^*_{gh,k}$ is independent of k, and therefore so is $\hat{\mu}^*_k(\rho,\chi)$, the credibility premium for risk-class k. Formula (23) corresponds to the process of amalgamating the data of all risk-classes (with adjustment for differing variances) and then determining a uniform $\hat{\mu}^*_k$ by simple linear regression.

Although relations (23) and (24) are comparatively simple, it is an unfortunate fact that the conditions which lead to them will seldom be found to hold in practice. These results do serve as a guide to intuition, however. We see that most practical situations lie somewhere between these two extremes.

Of some practical interest is the phenomenon noted in observation of (vi) of Section 7, i.e. that credibility premiums seem to be comparatively insensitive to variations in w_{aa} if w_{bb} is held fixed. This result could also have been predicted from analytic considerations. This can be seen as follows.

If equation (20) is substituted in constraints (10) and (11), expressed in matrix form, and the matrix equation then solved, we obtain:

$$\begin{pmatrix}\alpha\\ \beta\end{pmatrix} = \begin{pmatrix} \sum_{h=1}^{N} \frac{\kappa_h^2+w_{aa}[\kappa_h^2\kappa_h^o-(\kappa_h^1)^2]}{1+w_{aa}\kappa_h^o+w_{bb}\kappa_h^2} & -\sum_{h=1}^{N} \frac{\kappa_h^1}{1+w_{aa}\kappa_h^o+w_{bb}\kappa_h^2} \\ -\sum_{h=1}^{N} \frac{\kappa_h^1}{1+w_{aa}\kappa_h^o+w_{bb}\kappa_h^2} & \sum_{h=1}^{N} \frac{\kappa_h^o+w_{bb}[\kappa_h^o\kappa_h^2-(\kappa_h^1)^2]}{1+w_{aa}\kappa_h^o+w_{bb}\kappa_h^2} \end{pmatrix}$$

$$\cdot \begin{pmatrix} * \\ * \end{pmatrix} \times \text{const.}$$

In each denominator, w_{bb} occurs in conjunction with a higher order term than w_{aa} does. The numerator of the top left sum will usually be dominated by the terms κ_h^2, the terms involving w_{aa} being relatively small, whereas the influence of the terms involving w_{bb} in the numerators of the bottom right sum will be relatively larger. Thus α and β will normally be more sensitive to w_{bb} than to w_{aa}.

Furthermore, α will usually be of higher order than β. Referring back to (20), we see that α occurs in conjunction with w_{bb} and β in conjunction with w_{aa}. Thus, in most circumstances, the $\alpha^*_{gh,k}$ will be more sensitive to variations in w_{bb} than in w_{aa}.

9. Conclusions

(i) If mean loss ratios are varying over time, it may be possible to apply time-homogeneous credibility procedures to them through the medium of as-if statistics, but there are cases where this cannot be done and a time-heterogeneous credibility model is required (Section 1).

(ii) If it is assumed that the mean loss ratio in risk-class j in time-period i is

$$a_j + b_j c(i) ,$$

where a_j, b_j are unknown constants and $c(.)$ is some

known function, then a time-heterogeneous model can be developed (Section 3.3).

(iii) The model leads to the estimation of the mean loss ratio is risk-class k in the next time-period by means of the formula

$$\sum_{j=1}^{n} \sum_{h=1}^{N} \alpha^{*}_{gh,k} X_{gh} ,$$

where the $\alpha^{*}_{ij,k}$ are given by equations (9) to (11) (Section 5).

(iv) The time-homogeneous model of Bühlmann-Straub (1970) is a special case of our time-heterogeneous model (Section 6.2).

(v) An alternative expression for $\alpha^{*}_{gh,k}$ is given in (20) which is more adapted to numerical calculation (Section 7).

(vi) Both expressions given for $\alpha^{*}_{gh,k}$ are complicated even when $c(.)$ is simple. On the other hand, time-heterogeneity poses a serious problem, and relatively complicated methods of dealing with it may well be warranted.

(vii) The time-heterogeneous model has the apparent disadvantage that prior variances and covariance of a_j, b_j (for a precise statement of the meaning of the parameters w_{aa}, w_{ab} and w_{bb}, see Section 5, between equations (9) and (10)), though in practice one may well take one of these parameters (viz. w_{ab}) to be zero and, of the remaining two, one (viz. w_{bb}) is of significantly greater importance in determining credibility premiums (Section 8).

(viii) Some limiting cases of the credibility formula are examined, since, although they rarely arise in practice, they serve as a guide to intuition (Section 8).

<u>Appendix I</u>

As pointed out just before equation (9) it is possible to obtain an explicit solution to (7) if the form of

C_i^g is recalled. Now

$$C_i^g = \text{Cov}_V[\mu(\upsilon_{gh}),\mu(\upsilon_{ih})]$$
$$= \text{Cov}_V[a(\upsilon_h) + b(\upsilon_h)c(g), a(\upsilon_h) + b(\upsilon_h)c(i)]$$
$$= w_{aa} + [c(g) + c(i)]w_{ab} + c(g)c(i)w_{bb} \ , \qquad (A.1)$$

where

$$w_{aa} = \text{Var}_V[a(\upsilon_h)], \quad w_{ab} = \text{Cov}_V[a(\upsilon_h),b(\upsilon_h)],$$
$$w_{bb} = \text{Var}_V[b(\upsilon_h)] \ .$$

From (8) and (A.1),

$$A_h = w_{aa}\underset{\sim}{e}\underset{\sim}{e}' + w_{ab}[\underset{\sim}{c}\underset{\sim}{e}' + \underset{\sim}{e}\underset{\sim}{c}'] + w_{bb}\underset{\sim}{c}\underset{\sim}{c}' + D_h \qquad (A.2)$$

where

$$\underset{\sim}{e}' = (1,1,\ldots,1), \quad \underset{\sim}{c}' = (c(1),\ldots,c(n)), \quad \text{and}$$
$$D_h = \text{diag}(v_{1h}/P_{1h},\ldots,v_{nh}/P_{nh}) \ .$$

Now multiply equation (7) on the left by the matrix LM, where

$$L = \begin{pmatrix} 1 & 0 & 0 & 0 & \cdot\ \cdot & 0 \\ 0 & 1 & 0 & 0 & \cdot\ \cdot & 0 \\ 0 & c(1)-c(3) & c(2)-c(1) & 0 & \cdot\ \cdot & 0 \\ 0 & c(1)-c(4) & 0 & c(2)-c(1) & \cdot\ \cdot & 0 \\ \vdots & \vdots & & & & \vdots \\ 0 & c(1)-c(n) & 0 & 0 & \cdot\ \cdot & c(2)-c(1) \end{pmatrix},$$

and

$$M = \begin{pmatrix} 1 & 0 & 0 & 0 & \cdot\ \cdot\ \cdot & 0 \\ 1 & -1 & 0 & 0 & \cdot\ \cdot\ \cdot & 0 \\ 1 & 0 & -1 & 0 & \cdot\ \cdot\ \cdot & 0 \\ 1 & 0 & 0 & -1 & \cdot\ \cdot\ \cdot & 0 \\ \vdots & & & & & \vdots \\ 1 & 0 & 0 & 0 & \cdot\ \cdot\ \cdot & -1 \end{pmatrix}.$$

Then we obtain:

$$\{w_{aa}LM\underset{\sim\sim}{ee'} + w_{ab}[LM\underset{\sim\sim}{ce'} + LM\underset{\sim\sim}{ec'}] + w_{bb}LM\underset{\sim\sim}{cc'} + LMD_h\}\underset{\sim}{\alpha}^*_{h,k}$$
$$= \delta_{hk}\{w_{aa}LM\underset{\sim}{e} + w_{ab}[LM\underset{\sim}{c} + c(n+1)LM\underset{\sim}{e}] + w_{bb}c(n+1)LM\underset{\sim}{c}\}$$
$$+ \alpha LM\underset{\sim}{e} + \beta LM\underset{\sim}{c} \ . \qquad (A.3)$$

It is routine to verify that

$$LM\underset{\sim}{e} = (1,0,0,\ldots,0)' \ , \qquad (A.4)$$

and

$$LM\underset{\sim}{c} = (c(1),c(1)-c(2),0,0,\ldots,0)' \ . \qquad (A.5)$$

Therefore, if $g > 2$, the g-th equation of system (A.3) has all terms zero except those arising from LMD_h, i.e. the g-th equation is $(g > 2)$

$$[c(2)-c(g)](v_{1h}/P_{1h})\alpha^*_{1h,k}+[c(g)-c(1)](v_{2h}/P_{2h})\alpha^*_{2h,k}$$
$$+[c(1)-c(2)](v_{gh}/P_{gh})\alpha^*_{gh,k} = 0 \ .$$

i.e.

$$\alpha^*_{gh,k} = \frac{[c(2)-c(g)](v_{1h}/P_{1h})\alpha^*_{1h,k}+[c(g)-c(1)](v_{2h}/P_{2h})\alpha^*_{2h,k}}{[c(2)-c(1)](v_{gh}/P_{gh})}$$
$$g = 1,2,\ldots,n \ . \qquad (A.6)$$

Now, by (A.4) and (A.5), the first two equations of system are:

$$\sum_{i=1}^{n} C_i^1\alpha^*_{ih,k} + (v_{1h}/P_{1h})\alpha^*_{1h,k} = \delta_{hk}C^1_{n+1} + \alpha + \beta c(1); \qquad (A.7)$$

$$\sum_{i=1}^{n} (C_i^1 - C_i^2)\alpha^*_{ih,k} + (v_{1h}/P_{1h})\alpha^*_{1h,k} - (v_{2h}/P_{2h})\alpha^*_{2h,k}$$
$$= \delta_{hk}(C^1_{n+1} - C^2_{n+1}) + \beta[c(1) - c(2)] \qquad (A.8)$$

Substituting (A.6) into (A.7) and (A.8):

$$\alpha^*_{1h,k}(v_{1h}/P_{1h})\left[1 + \sum_{i=1}^{n} \frac{c(i)-c(2)}{c(1)-c(2)} \ \frac{C_i^1P_{ih}}{v_{ih}}\right] + \alpha^*_{2h,k}(v_{2h}/P_{2h})$$
$$\cdot \left[\sum_{i=1}^{n} \frac{c(i)-c(1)}{c(2)-c(1)} \ \frac{C_i^1P_{ih}}{v_{ih}}\right]$$
$$= \delta_{hk}C^1_{n+1} + \alpha + \beta c(1) \qquad (A.9)$$

and

$$\alpha^*_{1h,k}(v_{1h}/P_{1h})\left[1 + \sum_{i=1}^{n} \frac{c(i)-c(2)}{c(1)-c(2)} \frac{(C^1_i-C^2_i)P_{ih}}{v_{ih}}\right]$$

$$+ \alpha^*_{2h,k}(v_{2h}/P_{2h})\left[-1 + \sum_{i=1}^{n} \frac{c(i)-c(1)}{c(2)-c(1)} \frac{(C^1_i-C^2_i)P_{ih}}{v_{ih}}\right]$$

$$= \delta_{hk}(C^1_{n+1} - C^2_{n+1}) + \beta[c(1) - c(2)] \qquad (A.10)$$

The solution of (A.9) and (A.10) for $\alpha^*_{1h,k}$ is, after a little algebraic manipulation, found to be:

$$\alpha^*_{1h,k} = (P_{1h}/v_{1h}) \times \left\{\delta_{hk}C^1_{n+1} + \alpha\left\{1 + \sum_{i=1}^{n} \frac{P_{ih}}{v_{ih}} \cdot [c(i)-c(1)][w_{ab}+c(i)w_{bb}]\right\}\right.$$

$$\left.+ \beta\left\{c(1) - \sum_{i=1}^{n} \frac{P_{ih}}{v_{ih}} [c(i)-c(1)][w_{aa}+w_{ab}c(i)]\right\}\right\}\bigg/\left\{1 + \sum_{i=1}^{n} C^i_i P_{ih}/v_{ih}\right\} \qquad (A.11)$$

By the symmetry with which the argument g appears in (6), we see immediately that (A.11) implies the general solution (9) which is written in the body of the paper.

Credibility Under Conditions of Imperfect Persistency

G. C. Taylor
School of Economic and Financial Studies
Macquarie University
Sydney, Australia

Abstract

The situation in which the decision of an individual insured to effect, continue or cancel an insurance is influenced by the level of premium chargeable is considered. In this context the mean square deviation criterion commonly used in Credibility Theory for optimizing premium rates is reexamined and found to be deficient.

A more reasonable loss function is used for developing linearized experience rating formulas. These formulas are dependent upon elasticity, the extent to which the size of a risk-class alters for a given change in premium rate. Two possibilities are analysed:

(i) the case where insureds are perfectly capable of assessing themselves as risks;

(ii) the case where insureds are overly influenced by their recent claims experiences in assessing themselves.

It is found that a linearized experience rating formula can always be devised which will lead to an expected profit (over the whole collective) to the insurer in case (ii), but not always in case (i). Whether or not the case (i) collective can be insured profitably depends upon whether

uncertainty of claims process $\geq$ elasticity,

in a sense defined precisely in the body of the paper.

In those cases where the collective can be insured profitably, the optimal experience rating formula is:

$(1 - Z^*) \times$ expected claims $+ Z^* \times$ actual claims
+ loading independent of risk-class,

where Z^* is the normal credibility factor in case (i) but a higher credibility factor in case (ii), and the "loading" mentioned in the formula varies inversely with elasticity.

1. Existing Credibility Theory

One of the fundamental ideas of Credibility Theory has recently been challenged. In order to understand the theory as it now exists and the criticism which has been made, let us formulate the following standard

Credibility Problem. Consider an insurance portfolio which consists of N risk-classes, and let X_j be a random variable representing the risk performance in risk-class j over a given time-period and having a distribution which is characterized by some quantity θ_j. Let the d.f. involved here be $F_{\theta_j}(.)$.

Assume that

1. The quantities θ_j $(j = 1,2,\ldots,N)$ are i.i.d. random variables with d.f. (called the structure function) $U(\theta)$;

2. For fixed values of the θ_j $(j = 1,2,\ldots,N)$, the variables X_j are stochastically independent.

The problem is to estimate $E[X_j|\theta = \theta_j]$, denoted by $\mu(\theta_j)$.

The credibility solution of this problem is now well-known. As far back as 1918 Whitney assumed that the estimator $\hat{\mu}_j$ of $\mu(\theta_j)$ should be the posterior mean $E[\mu(\theta_j)|X_j]$. He showed that this statistic could be approximated by

$$\hat{\mu}_j \sim (1 - Z)m + ZX_j \; , \qquad (1)$$

where

$$m = E_\theta[\mu(\theta)] \; , \qquad (2)$$

and

$$Z = 1/(1 + N) \ . \tag{3}$$

Here N is some constant.

The coefficient Z is called the credibility of the experience.

During the 50 years or so succeeding Whitney's paper, Credibility Theory developed in a somewhat different direction from this, mainly through the agency of Perryman (1932, 1937), but still the notion of the posterior mean exhibited above was important.

With the later work of Bailey (1945) and Mayerson (1964), this notion once again became explicit, and finally the Credibility Problem was rigorously formulated by Bühlmann (1967) in terms of this posterior mean. He gave this Rigorous Formulation. The estimator $\hat{\mu}_j$ is the member of the family of functions $a + bX_j$ which minimizes the quantity

$$E[\{E[\mu(\theta_j)|X_j] - (a + bX_j)\}^2] \ . \tag{4}$$

The result was the same as equations (1) - (3) with

$$N = E_\theta[\sigma^2(\theta)]/Var_\theta[\mu(\theta)] \tag{5}$$

where

$$\sigma^2(\theta) = Var[X_j|\theta_j = \theta] \ . \tag{6}$$

In the same paper and again in 1969, Bühlmann went to some trouble to justify the use of the posterior mean. Subsequent papers (see, e.g., Bühlmann and Straub (1970), Jewell (1973a, 1973b), and the papers by Hachemeister and Taylor in this collection) have taken the use of this statistic for granted.

2. The Decision-Theoretic Criticism of the Existing Theory

The papers quoted above have taken for granted the minimization of expression (4) because of the power of the arguments in its favor. Not only does this procedure have strong intuitive appeal, but also Bühlmann (1967, 1969), in an argument attributed to Thyrion, points out that this method of experience rating ensures that the expected premium income from an arbitrary subset of the risks of the portfolio will exactly equal the sum of correct premiums over this subset.

In putting forward these arguments, Bühlmann tacitly makes one assumption which is of crucial importance to the manager of a risk portfolio. The assumption is effectively that risks will be indifferent to whatever rerating they suffer. If, however, in practice risks which are rerated upward tend to cancel while risks rerated downward do not, it is no longer clear that this equality of expected premium income and correct premium income still holds.

This is part of the argument of Bolnick and Falk in their paper to this conference, although it seems to confuse a couple of ideas, viz.

1. The idea outlined in the previous paragraph;

2. The fact that the assumption of an incorrect value of m can lead to profits or losses.

There is, however, a suggestion in the paper that, if the persistency of the insurance contracts undertaken by the insurer is imperfect, then any experience-rating procedure should recognize the impact of this imperfection on the company's operations. Equally, it is not necessarily sufficient to use a credibility formula which gives a good estimate of $E[\mu(\theta_j)|X_j]$ in the statistical sense.

We can represent these ideas in decision-theoretic terms as follows. If $\hat{\mu}_j$ is the premium rate which the insurer decides to charge risk-class j in the next time-period, then we assume that the insurer has some <u>loss function</u> $L(\mu(\theta_j),X_j,\hat{\mu}_j)$ for risk class j, and that the insurer will wish to minimize the expected value of its loss function over all risk-classes, i.e. to minimize the function

$$\mathcal{L} = \int L(\mu(\theta_j),X_j,\hat{\hat{\mu}}_j) \prod_{j=1}^{N} dF_{\theta_j}(X_j)dU(\theta_j) \, . \tag{7}$$

It is possible to choose

$$L(\mu(\theta_j),X_j,\hat{\hat{\mu}}_j) = \{E[\mu(\theta_j)|X_j] - \hat{\hat{\mu}}_j\}^2 \, , \tag{8}$$

and, if $\hat{\hat{\mu}}_j$ is of the form $a + bX_j$, then (8) will lead to the same result as the minimization of (4). That is to say, the loss function (8) is the one implied by the standard credibility formula.

However, in terms of risk management, the appropriateness of (8) is much more debatable. It might, for example, be considered more reasonable to set $L(\mu(\theta_j),X_j,\hat{\hat{\mu}}_j)$ equal to the financial loss suffered by the insurer in connection with the triple $(\mu(\theta_j),X_j,\hat{\hat{\mu}}_j)$. Thus, we could set

$$L(\mu(\theta_j),X_j,\hat{\hat{\mu}}_j) = p(\mu(\theta_j),X_j,\hat{\hat{\mu}}_j)\cdot(\mu(\theta_j) - \hat{\hat{\mu}}_j) \, , \tag{9}$$

where $p(.)$ is a <u>persistency function</u> giving the ratio of exposure in risk class j (with mean risk performance $\mu(\theta_j)$) in the next time-period to the exposure in risk-class j in the previous time period, when the risk performance in the previous period was X_j and the premium rate in the next period is $\hat{\hat{\mu}}_j$.

If we restrict $\hat{\hat{\mu}}_j$ to the family $a + bX_j$, then we can combine (7) and (9) to give

$$\mathcal{L} = \int p(\mu(\theta_j),X_j,\hat{\hat{\mu}}_j)\cdot(\mu(\theta_j) - (a + bX_j))dV \, , \tag{10}$$

where dV represents the "differential" in (7). The function $\mathcal{L}$ is to be minimized.

3. The Case of Unbiased Insureds

Let us consider now the case in which the insured individuals are capable of assessing their own expected risk performance in an unbiased manner. It is then reasonable to suppose that p(.) is a function only of the excess of the charged premium over the correct premium, i.e. of

$$(\hat{\hat{\mu}}_j - \mu(\theta_j)) = (a + bX_j - \mu(\theta_j))$$

One possibility is

$$p(\mu(\theta_j), X_j, \hat{\hat{\mu}}_j) = 1 - e(a + bX_j - \mu(\theta_j)) \ , \tag{11}$$

where e is a constant which can reasonably be called the <u>price-elasticity of exposure</u>. Equation (11) implies that the greater the premium charged a particular risk, the less business will the insurer retain (assuming $e > 0$).

The shortcomings of this function as a persistency factor are fairly obvious. Firstly, it implies that if premiums are set high enough, the amount of business on the insurer's books will actually become negative, which is of course impossible. Secondly, it would be rather surprising if the supposed linearity relation held over any but the smallest range of the variables involved, and indeed if the left side of (11) even included all of the independent variables.

On the other hand, however, (11) represents a first approximation to reality which leads to the simple and transparent results of later sections, these then serving as a guide to our intuition as applied to the complexities of reality.

Combining (10) and (11):

$$\begin{aligned} \mathcal{L} &= \int [1 - e(a + bX_j - \mu(\theta_j))][\mu(\theta_j) - (a + bX_j)]dV \\ &= \int \{\mu(\theta_j) - (a + bX_j) + e[\mu(\theta_j) - (a + bX_j)]^2\}dV \ . \end{aligned} \tag{12}$$

Differentiating with respect to a, b:

$$\frac{\partial \mathcal{L}}{\partial a} = -1 - 2e[m - (a + bm)] \tag{13}$$

$$\frac{\partial \mathcal{L}}{\partial b} = -m - 2e\{E_V[X_j\mu(\theta_j)] - am - bE_V[X_j^2]\}$$

$$= -m - 2e\{(1 - b)(\text{Var}[\mu(\theta)] + m^2) - am - bE[\sigma^2(\theta)]\} \tag{14}$$

Setting $\partial\mathcal{L}/\partial a$, $\partial\mathcal{L}/\partial b$ equal to zero and solving for a and b, we obtain

$$a = (1 - b)m + 1/2e \ , \tag{15}$$

and

$$b = 1/\{1 + E_\theta[\sigma^2(\theta)]/\text{Var}_\theta[\mu(\theta)]\} \ . \tag{16}$$

Thus, in terms of the credibility problem dealt with in Section 1, we now have

$$b = Z \ ,$$

and hence

$$\hat{\hat{\mu}}_j = (1 - Z)m + ZX_j + 1/2e \ . \tag{17}$$

This means that the unbiased insured with imperfect persistency should be charged the normal credibility premium plus a flat loading which is dependent upon the price-elasticity of exposure but not upon the risk-class.

4. The Case of Biased Insureds

Insureds are notoriously poor assessors of their own risk levels. Thus, in some lines, an insured's decision as to whether or not to cancel a policy may be based upon a comparison of his rerated premium with his recent claims experience rather than with a realistic assessment of his expected claims experience. In this case, (11) might be replaced by

$$p(\mu(\theta_j), X_j, \hat{\hat{\mu}}_j) = 1 - e(a + bX_j - X_j) \ . \tag{18}$$

Then (12) is replaced by:

$$\mathcal{L} = \int \{\mu(\theta_j) - (a + bX_j) - e[\mu(\theta_j) - (a + bX_j)] \cdot [a - (1 - b)X_j]\}dV \tag{19}$$

Equations (13) and (14) are replaced by:

$$\frac{\partial \mathcal{L}}{\partial a} = -1-e[2(1-b)m-2a];$$

$$\frac{\partial \mathcal{L}}{\partial b} = -m-e\{2(1-b)(m^2+\mathrm{Var}_\theta[\mu(\theta)]-2am+(1-2b)E_\theta[\sigma^2(\theta)]\};$$

and (15) and (16) by:

$$a = (1 - b)m + 1/2e; \tag{20}$$

$$b = \tfrac{1}{2} + \tfrac{1}{2}/\{1 + E_\theta[\sigma^2(\theta)]/\mathrm{Var}_\theta[\mu(\theta)]\} . \tag{21}$$

Thus, $b = \frac{1}{2}(1 + Z) = Z^*$, so that

$$\hat{\hat{\mu}}_j = (1 - Z^*)m + Z^*X_j + 1/2e . \tag{22}$$

This means that the biased insured represented by (18) should be charged a <u>credibility premium based upon a credibility factor of $Z^* = \frac{1}{2}$(1 + normal credibility factor) plus a flat premium loading which is dependent upon the price-elasticity of exposure but not upon the risk-class.</u>

5. The Case of Somewhat Biased Insureds

In practice, an insured could probably be expected to lie somewhere between the extremes represented by equations (11) and (18). That is to say, they have some ability to assess themselves as risks, but perhaps give too much weight to recent claims experience in determining the maximum premiums that they are prepared to pay.

In this case, the most profitable premium to charge is somewhere between those given by (17) and (22), i.e. we use a somewhat greater credibility factor than the standard one and also add a flat loading over all risk-classes.

6. Insurability of a Risk

Hitherto we have followed the standard credibility approach of setting premiums in such a way as to minimize our loss function. This procedure is acceptable in the standard credibility context because, as pointed out in the first paragraph of Section 2, it ensures neither expected gain nor expected loss to the collective.

However, with the changes made to the credibility model in the present paper, the question naturally arises as to whether a collective is insurable at all under experience rating formulas such as (17) and (22). The point here is that it is not sufficient to minimize $\mathcal{L}$ - we must ensure that it is ≤ 0, i.e. that the insurer does not expect a net loss from the business he underwrites.

6.1 Unbiased Insureds

The requirement that $\mathcal{L} \leq 0$ can be transformed by means of (12), (15) and (16) to:

$$-\frac{1}{2e} + e\left\{\frac{E_\theta[\sigma^2(\theta)] \cdot Var_\theta[\mu(\theta)]}{E_\theta[\sigma^2(\theta)] + Var_\theta[\mu(\theta)]} + \frac{1}{4e^2}\right\} \leq 0$$

i.e. $$e \leq \tfrac{1}{2}\{1/E_\theta[\sigma^2(\theta)] + 1/Var_\theta[\mu(\theta)]\}^{-\frac{1}{2}} . \qquad (23)$$

Now $E_\theta[\sigma^2(\theta)]$ and $Var_\theta[\mu(\theta)]$ each represent an element of uncertainty in the claims process, and hence it is reasonable to regard the right side of (23) as a measure of the uncertainty of the process. Thus (23) says that a collective can be experience rated profitably by means of a credibility formula if and only if

$$\text{uncertainty} \geq \text{elasticity} . \qquad (24)$$

6.2 Biased Insureds

The requirement that $\mathcal{L} \leq 0$ can be transformed by means of (19), (20) and (21) to:

$$-\frac{1}{2e} + e\left\{\frac{1}{4e^2}\right\} \leq 0 ,$$

which is always true.

We see therefore that a collective of insureds biased in the way described by equation (18) can always be rated by a credibility formula to produce an expected net profit for the insurer.

Comparing this result with that of Section 6.1 we observe the unsurprising phenomenon that the more capable are insureds of assessing themselves as risks, the more difficult is it for the insurer to insure them at a profit.

To the extent that insureds differ from the type of biasedness described by (18) it will be necessary to scrutinize the relation between the certainty and elasticity of the claims process as is done in (24).

In Search of a General Parameter-Free Credibility Formula

G. C. Taylor
School of Economic and Financial Studies
Macquarie University
Sydney, Australia

Abstract

The paper traces the line of development of Credibility Theory over the years. Particular attention is given to the growing tendency to seek greater independence of credibility formulas from the properties of the distributions involved. It is shown that the ultimate extension of these developments, a credibility formula which is entirely independent of the distributions, cannot be achieved since such a formula does not exist.

1. Background to the problem

This paper is of a negative nature in that it points out the impossibility of extending Credibility Theory in a very attractive direction. The logical extreme of recent development in the theory is a blind alley.

In order to clarify these statements it is necessary to review briefly the history of Credibility Theory. We begin by formulating the problem.

Consider an insurance portfolio consisting of N risk-classes, each of which has its experience recorded separately over time-periods $1,2,\ldots,n$. Let X_{ij} denote some statistic from risk class j in time-period i. Let υ_{ij} be some (unknown) quantity which characterizes the distribution of X_{ij} thus:

$$\text{Prob.}\{X_{ij} \leq x | \upsilon_{ij} = \upsilon\} = F_{\upsilon}(x) .$$

Let

$$\mathcal{X} = \{X_{ij} | i = 1,2,\ldots,n;\ j = 1,2,\ldots,N\} ,$$

and

$$\mu(\upsilon) = E[X_{ij} | \upsilon_{ij} = \upsilon] .$$

We make the

<u>Assumptions.</u> 1. For fixed values of the υ_{ij} $(i = 1,2,\ldots,n;\ j = 1,2,\ldots,N)$, the variables X_{ij} are stochastically independent.

2. The statistics X_{ij} in each risk-class are i.i.d. over time, i.e. $\upsilon_{ij} = \upsilon_j$ independently of i for $i = 1,2,\ldots,N$.

3. The parameter values υ_j $(j = 1,2,\ldots,N)$ are i.i.d. random variables with d.f. $U(\upsilon)$.

<u>The Problem.</u> To estimate $\mu(\upsilon_j)$, $j = 1,2,\ldots,N$ from the available information, viz. $\mathcal{X}$. Call the estimator $\hat{\mu}_j = \hat{\mu}_j(\mathcal{X})$.

Credibility Theory began in 1918 when a problem of a type similar to this was solved by Whitney. He dealt with a rather special case, but his end result was:

$$\hat{\mu}_j = (1 - Z)\overline{X} + Z\overline{X}_j , \tag{1}$$

where

$$\overline{X}_j = \frac{1}{n} \sum_{i=1}^{n} X_{ij} , \tag{2}$$

$\overline{X}$ is some weighted average of the $\overline{X}_j$

and

$$Z = \frac{n}{n + K} , \quad \text{for some constant } K . \tag{3}$$

As we shall see, this is almost the same as the classical credibility formula that we know today.

During the half-century following Whitney's paper considerable confusion developed in Credibility Theory, mainly because the credibility problem was not rigorously formulated. A rather brief review of the methods of this period is given by Longley-Cook (1962).

A huge step forward was taken in 1967 when Bühlmann posed the problem properly and solved it. The problem, as then stated, was to choose μ_j from the set of estimators of the form

$$\hat{\mu}_j(\mathfrak{X}) = a + b\overline{X}_j \quad (a,\ b \text{ constants}) , \tag{4}$$

according to the least squares criterion

$$E[\{\hat{\mu}_j(\mathfrak{X}) - \mu(\upsilon_j)\}^2] \text{ is minimized} , \tag{5}$$

where the expectation operator is taken with respect to the "density function":

$$dU(\upsilon_j) \prod_{i=1}^{n} dF_{\upsilon_j}(x_{ij}) .$$

The result was:

$$\hat{\mu}_j = (1 - Z)m + Z\overline{X}_j , \tag{6}$$

where

$$m = E[X_{ij}] \tag{7}$$

and equation (3) holds with

$$K = E_U[\mathrm{Var}[X_{ij}|\upsilon_j = \upsilon]]/\mathrm{Var}_U[E[X_{ij}|\upsilon_j = \upsilon]] .$$

The similarity of equations (1) and (6) is obvious.

Bühlmann's approach to the problem had a great advantage over previous ones in that it was distribution-free. The credibility formula depended, as can be seen from (6) and the expression for K, only upon first- and second-order moments of the distributions involved.

However, the fundamental role played by m, which was usually unknown, now caused dissatisfaction, and Bühlmann himself, together with Straub (1970), succeeded in eliminating this term by choosing $\hat{\mu}_k$ from the set of estimators of the

$$\hat{\mu}_k(\mathfrak{X}) = \sum_{i=1}^{n} \sum_{j=1}^{N} \alpha_{ij,k} X_{ij} , \tag{8}$$

again according to criterion (5) and the requirement that the $\hat{\mu}_k$ be unbiased, but with the expectation operator taken with respect to:

$$\prod_{j=1}^{N} dU(\upsilon_j) \prod_{i=1}^{n} dF_{\upsilon_j}(x_{ij}) \,. \qquad (9)$$

This approach produced a result in which $\hat{\mu}_k$ was again distribution-free, depending only upon second-order moments of the distributions involved.

There was still room for dissatisfaction, however, since these second-order moments were usually not known either. With this in mind, Bühlmann and Straub attempted to rectify the situation further by replacing these moments with unbiased estimates. This produces the extreme of the line of development of credibility formulas which has been traced in this section, for the emerging formula in this case is not only distribution-free, but also parameter-free. It is a function of $\mathfrak{X}$ which is entirely independent of distributions.

2. Commentary on the existing parameter-free approach

The first observation that one can make on the Bühlmann-Straub parameter-free formula is that, as a function of the X_{ij}, it is nonlinear, whereas all of the preceding formulas were linear. It is, however, homogeneous of degree one which is a property that we would expect intuitively of it, i.e. if each X_{ij} is changed by some particular factor, then each $\hat{\mu}_k$ also changes by this factor.

This nonlinearity has serious consequences. As long as our admissible estimators were of the form (4) or (8) (where the $\alpha_{ij,k}$ are independent of $\mathfrak{X}$), we knew that $\hat{\mu}_k$ was unbiased if and only if the credibility coefficients appearing in it summed to unity. However, once we admit nonlinear credibility formulas, the question of biasedness becomes very much more obscure. In particular, although Bühlmann and Straub prove that their second-order moment estimators are unbiased, it does not follow that their $\hat{\mu}_k$ are unbiased, since the estimators do not enter into the $\hat{\mu}_k$ in a linear fashion.

One can object further to the Bühlmann-Straub procedure in that it lacks the methodology which the other formulas possess. Let us review the structure of the problems solved by Bühlmann (1967) and Bühlmann and Straub (1970) (with reference to (8)). It was:

(i) Define a set of admissible estimators from which the $\hat{\mu}_k$ are to be chosen;

(ii) Define a criterion for selecting the optimal $\hat{\mu}_k$ from this set;

(iii) Perform the optimization.

Now let us consider the structure of the problem solved by Bühlmann and Straub (1970) leading to their parameter-free formula. It was:

(i), (ii), (iii) } As above but temporarily disregarding the requirement of parameter-freeness in the final formula;

(iv) Estimate the parameters produced in phase (iii).

(v) Replace these parameters by their estimates.

While I do not for a moment question the practical value of this formula, I would claim that the method used for its production contains some artificiality. The set of admissible estimators is not prescribed in advance, and nor is the criterion by which the optimal estimator is chosen.

Therefore, accepting the desirability of having a parameter-free credibility formula at our disposal, but noting the objections to the existing formula of this type, let us see if we can rationalize the method of selecting one.

3. Concerning the existence of a general parameter-free credibility formula

We need to select an estimator $\hat{\mu}_k(\mathcal{X})$ of $\mu(\upsilon_j)$ which is not dependent in any way on the distributions involved. Let us reformulate our problem in this way.

Reformulation of the problem.

Find, if there exists, the function $\hat{\mu}_k(\mathcal{X})$ of the X_{ij} which is optimal with respect to criterion (5) and the requirement that $\hat{\mu}_k$ be an unbiased estimator of $\mu(\upsilon_k)$, where the expectation operator in (5) is taken with respect to the "density" (9), and where the function $\hat{\mu}_k$ is independent of the d.f.'s U and F_υ (for all υ).

Clearly, the existence of such an estimator as described here would be a desirable state of affairs, and therefore considerable effort could be expended in quest of it. The purpose of this paper is to show that such effort would be futile, since the desired estimator does not exist.

The proof of this is effected fairly simply by showing, for a particular choice of the structure function U and the d.f.'s F_υ, that the optimal $\hat{\mu}_k$ must be a linear function of the X_{ij}. Since the $\hat{\mu}_k$ which we seek has to be independent of U and the F_υ, the same formula will have to hold generally, whereas it will be clear that in fact it does not hold.

The structure function which we choose is the following:

$$U(\upsilon) = 0, \quad \upsilon < c;$$
$$= 1, \quad \upsilon \geq c;$$

where c is same constant. In this case, the "density" (9) becomes simply:

$$\prod_{j=1}^{N} \prod_{i=1}^{n} dF_c(x_{ij});$$

and the problem is to find an estimator $\hat{\mu}_k(\mathcal{X})$ of $\mu(c)$. Now suppose that F_c is a normal d.f. Then it is well known that the minimum-variance unbiased estimator of $\mu(c)$ is

$$\frac{1}{nN} \sum_{i=1}^{n} \sum_{j=1}^{N} X_{ij} . \qquad (10)$$

But the minimum-variance unbiased linear estimator of $\mu(c)$ is what is required by criterion (5) plus the unbiasedness condition. Thus, (10) is the required credibility formula in the case of the above particular choice of U and the F.

Now, repeating the argument given at the beginning of the previous paragraph, since the general credibility formula which we seek has to be entirely independent of U and the F_υ, it must, if it exists, remain as (10) however U and the F_υ are varied. This, however, is contrary to known fact, since it is quite simple, within existing Credibility Theory, to construct examples in which (10) is <u>not</u> the correct credibility formula. Our conclusion can be stated as a

<u>Theorem.</u> There does not exist a general parameter-free credibility formula in the sense required by the "Reformulation of the Problem" at the beginning of this section.

4. What next?

The author has no wish at all to decry the value of Bühlmann's and Straub's work. Its pragmatic value is undoubted, and, in fact, the author himself would probably make use of it if faced with a practical experience rating problem. Nevertheless, it is claimed that the Bühlmann-Straub parameter-free credibility formula constitutes a dislocation in the logical development of Credibility Theory.

The question which this naturally provokes is: In what alternative direction should Credibility Theory develop. If one wishes to develop it at all in the general direction of eliminating parameters from credibility formulas, then one apparently has two possible areas in which to modify existing procedures:

(i) the choice of admissible estimators;

(ii) the criterion for selecting the optimal estimator from the admissible set.

It is clearly insufficient to modify (i) alone, by exactly the same arguments as used in Section 3. Beyond this observation, however, the author is at a loss!

BIBLIOGRAPHY

Anderson, T. W. (1953). An Introduction to Multivariate Statistical Analysis. New York: John Wiley & Sons.

Bailey, A. L. (1950). Credibility Procedures in Proceedings of the Casualty Actuarial Society, 37.

Bailey, A. L. (1955). A Generalized Theory of Credibility, in Proceedings of the Casualty Actuarial Society, 32.

Bickerstaff, D. R. (1972). Automobile Collision Deductibles and Repair Cost Groups: The Lognormal Model, in Proceedings of the Casualty Actuarial Society, 59.

Blackwell, David and M. A. Girshick (1954). Theory of Games and Statistical Decisions. New York: John Wiley & Sons.

Bohman, Harald and Frederik Esscher (1963). Studies in Risk Theory with Numerical Illustrations Concerning Distribution Functions and Stop Loss Premiums, Part I., in Skandinavisk Aktuarietidskrift, 46.

Bolnick, Howard J. (1974). Experience Rating Group Life Insurance, in Transactions of the Society of Actuaries, 26.

Box, G. E. P. (1953). Non-normality and tests on variances, in Biometrika, 40.

Braakman, T. C. (1968). Experience Rating and Credibility, in The ASTIN Bulletin, 5.

Bühlmann, Hans (1964). A Distribution Free Method for General Risk Problems in The ASTIN Bulletin, 3.

Bühlmann, Hans (1967). Experience Rating and Credibility in The ASTIN Bulletin, 4.

Bühlmann, Hans (1969). Experience Rating and Credibility in The ASTIN Bulletin, 5.

Bühlmann, Hans (1970). Mathematical Methods in Risk Theory. New York: Springer Verlag.

Bühlmann, Hans and Erwin Straub (1970). Glaubwuerdigkeit fuer Schadensaetze, in Bulletin de l'Association des Actuaires suisses, 70. (Translation by C. E. Brooks in ARCH, 1972.)

Bühlmann, Hans (1971). Credibility Procedures, in Sixth Berkeley Symposium in Probability and Statistics. Berkeley: University of California Press.

Bühlmann, Hans (1974). A Comparison of Three Credibility Formulae using Multidimensional Techniques, in The ASTIN Bulletin, 7.

Chow, Y. S. and Harold Robbins (1961). On Sums of Independent Random Variables with Infinite Moments and "Fair" Games, in Proceedings of the National Academy of Sciences of the United States of America, 47.

Cramér, Harald (1930). On the Mathematical Theory of Risk in Skandia Jubilee Volume. Stockholm: Almqvist and Wiksells.

Cramér, Harald (1946). Mathematical Methods of Statistics. Princeton: Princeton University Press.

Cramér, Harald (1955). Collective Risk Theory: A Survey of the Theory form the Viewpoint of the Theory of Stochastic Processes, in Skandia Jubilee Volume. Stockholm: Almqvist and Wiksells.

De Finetti, Bruno (1964). Sulla Teoria della Credibilità in Giornale dell'Istituto Italiano degli Attuari, 27.

De Groot, M. (1970). Optimal Statistical Decisions. New York: McGraw-Hill.

Doob, J. L. (1953). Stochastic Processes. New York: John Wiley & Sons.

Dropkin, Lester (1959). Some Considerations on Automobile Rating Systems Utilizing Individual Driving Records, in Proceedings of the Casualty Actuarial Society, 46.

Dropkin, Lester (1964). Size of Loss Distributions in Workmen's Compensation Insurance, in Proceedings of the Casualty Actuarial Society, 51.

DuMouchel, W. H. (1974a). Stable Distributions in Statistical Inference: 2. Information from Stably Distributed Samples. Technical Report No. 46. Ann Arbor: The University of Michigan Department of Statistics.

DuMouchel, W. H. (1974b). Stable Distributions in Statistical Inference: 3. Estimation of the Parameter of a Stable Distribution by the Method of Maximum Likelihood. Technical Report No. 47. Ann Arbor: The University of Michigan Department of Statistics.

Ericson, W. A. (1970). On the Posterior Mean and Variance of a Population Mean, in Journal of the American Statistical Association, 65.

Fama, Eugene (1970). Efficient Capital Markets: A Review of Theory and Empirical Work in Journal of Finance, 25.

Feller, William (1966). An Introduction to Probability Theory and Its Applications, v. II. New York: John Wiley & Sons.

Feller, William (1968). An Introduction to Probability Theory and Its Applications, v. I, third edition. New York: John Wiley & Sons.

Ferguson, T. S. (1967). Mathematical Statistics: A Decision Theoretic Approach. New York: Academic Press.

Franckx, Edouard (1968). La théorie du comportement et la Credibility Theory américaine, in The ASTIN Bulletin, 5.

Freifelder, Leonard (1974). A Statistical Decision Theory Model for Ratemaking on Individual Insurance Contracts, Ph.D. Dissertation, University of Pennsylvania.

Gerber, Hans U. and Donald A. Jones (1975). Credibility Formulae with Geometric Weights, in Transactions of the Society of Actuaries, 27.

Gerber, Hans-Ulrich (1972). Iterative Premium Principles, in Bulletin de l'Association des Actuaires suisses, 72.

Hachemeister, Charles A. (1970). Discussion of C. C. Hewitt's Credibility for Severity, q.v.

Hanoch, G. and Haim Levy (1969). The Efficiency Analysis of Choices Involving Risk in Review of Economic Studies, 5.

Hewitt, Charles C. (1970). Credibility for Severity in Proceedings of the Casualty Actuarial Society, 57.

Heyde, C. C. (1963). On a Property of the Lognormal Distribution, in Journal of the Royal Statistical Society, Series B, 25.

Hill, B. M. (1974). A Simple General Approach to Inference about the Tail of a Distribution. Technical Report No. 34. Ann Arbor: The University of Michigan Department of Statistics.

Jackson, Paul H. (1953). Experience Rating, in Transactions of the Society of Actuaries, 5.

Jackson, Paul H. and James A. Hamilton (1968). The Valuation of Pension Fund Assets, in Transactions of the Society of Actuaries, 20.

Jewell, William S. (1973a). Multi-dimensional Credibility, Operations Research Center Report No. 73-7. Berkeley: Operations Research Center, University of California. (Also, in ARCH, 1973.)

Jewell, William S. (1973b). Credible Means are Exact Bayesian for Exponential Families. Technical Report. Berkeley: Operations Research Center, University of California.

Jewell, William S. (1974a). The Credible Distribution, in The ASTIN Bulletin, 7.

Jewell, William S. (1974b). Isotonic Optimization in Tariff Construction, a paper read before the 11th ASTIN Colloquium.

Jewell, William S. (1974c). Regularity Conditions for Exact Credibility, Operations Research Center Report No. 74-22. Berkeley: Operations Research Center, University of California.

Jewell, William S. (1974d). Exact Multi-dimensional Credibility, in Bulletin de l'Associatin des Actuaires suisses, 74.

Jones, Donald A. (1965). Bayesian Statistics, in Transactions of the Society of Actuaries, 17.

Johnson, N. L. and S. Kooz (1970). Continuous Univariate Distributions, v. 2. New York: Houghton-Mifflin Co.

Kahn, P. M. (1967). An Overview of Credibility, a paper read before the Actuarial Research Conference at Yale University.

Kahn, P. M. (1968). A Survey of Some Recent Developments in Credibility Theory and Experience Rating from the Bayesian Viewpoint, in Transactions of the XVIII-th International Congress of Actuaries.

Kamreiter, H. and Erwin Straub (1974). On the Calculation of IBNR Reserves II, in Bulletin de l'Association des Actuaires suisses, 73.

Kimeldorf, George S. and Donald A. Jones (1965). Bayesian Graduation, in Transactions of the Society of Actuaries, 17.

Kormes, Mark (1968). A Practical Application of Credibility to Experience Rating Plans for Hospitalization and Medical-Surgical Insurance, in The ASTIN Bulletin, 5.

Longley-Cook, L. H. (1962). An Introduction to Credibility Theory in Proceedings of the Casualty Actuarial Society, 49.

Lundberg, Filip (1909). Ueber die Theorie der Rueckversicherung, in Transactions of the VI-th International Congress of Actuaries.

Mandelbrot, B. (1963). The Variation of Certain Speculative Prices, in Journal of Business of the University of Chicago, 26.

Maguire, R. D. (1971). An Empirical Approach to the Determination of Credibility Factors, in Transactions of the Society of Actuaries, 21.

Margolin, Myron H. (1971). On the Credibility of Group Insurance Claim Experience, in Transactions of the Society of Actuaries, 1971.

Margolin, Meyer H. (1974). A Critical Look at the Foundations of Credibility Theory, in ARCH.

Mayerson, Allen L. (1964a). A Bayesian View of Credibility, in Proceedings of the Casualty Actuarial Society, 51.

Mayerson, Allen L. (1964b). The Uses of Credibility in Property Insurance Ratemaking, in Giornale dell'Istituto Italiano degli Attuari, 27.

Mayerson, Allen L., Donald A. Jones and Newton L. Bowers, Jr. (1968). On the Credibility of the Pure Premium, in Proceedings of the Casualty Actuarial Society, 55.

Miller, Robert B. and James C. Hickman. Insurance Credibility and Bayesian Estimation, to be published in Proceedings of the Casualty Actuarial Society.

Mowbray, A. H. (1914). How Extensive a Payroll Exposure is Necessary to Give a Dependable Pure Premium? in Proceedings of the Casualty Actuarial Society, 1.

Neyman, J. (1959). Optimal Asymptotic Tests of Composite Statistical Hypotheses, in The Harald Cramér Volume. New York: John Wiley & Sons.

Pereira Cabral, M. A. and J. M. Afonso Garcia (1974a). Calculation of Provisions Using Credibility Theory, in The ASTIN Bulletin, 7.

Pereira Cabral, M. A. and J. M. Afonso Garcia (1974b). Study of the Risk Influent Factors and Its Relation with Credibility Theory, a paper presented to the 11th ASTIN Colloquium.

Perryman, F. A. (1932). Some Notes on Credibility Theory, in Proceedings of the Casualty Actuarial Society, 19.

Perryman, F. A. (1937). Experience Rating Plan Credibilities, in Proceedings of the Casualty Actuarial Society, 24.

Peters, Stefan (1941). Ratemaking Procedure in Workmen's Compensation Insurance, in Proceedings of the Casualty Actuarial Society, 28.

Raiffa, Howard and Robert Schlaifer (1961). Applied Statistical Decision Theory. Cambridge, Mass.: MIT Press.

Rao, C. R. (1965). Linear Statistical Inference and Its Applications. New York: John Wiley & Sons.

Scheffe, Harold (1959). The Analysis of Variance. New York: John Wiley & Sons.

Seal, Hilary L. (1969). Stochastic Theory of a Risk Business. New York: John Wiley & Sons.

Schmitter, H. and Erwin Straub (1974). How to Find the Right Subdivision in to Tariff Classes, a paper presented to the 11th ASTIN Colloquium.

Simon, Leroy (1965). The 1965 Table M, in Proceedings of the Casualty Actuarial Society, 52.

Society of Actuaries, Committee on Cost Comparison Methods and Related Issues. (1974). Preliminary Report. Chicago: Society of Actuaries.

Stone, M. (1963). Robustness of Non-ideal Decision Procedures, in Journal of the American Statistical Association, 58.

Straub, Erwin (1972). On the Calculation of IBNR - Reserves, in IBNR - The Prize-Winning Papers in the Boleslaw Monic Fund Competition Held in 1971. Amsterdam: Nederlandse Reassurantie Groep, N.V.

Taylor, G. C. (1974). Experience Rating with Credibility Adjustment of the Manual Premium, in The ASTIN Bulletin, 7.

Whitney, A. W. (1918). The Theory of Experience Rating, in Proceedings of the Casualty Actuarial Society, 4.

A 5
B 6
C 7
D 8
E 9
F 0
G 1
H 2
I 3
J 4